THE YOUTH WORKER'S ENCYCLOPEDIA OF BIBLE-TEACHING IDEAS:

Old Testament

Loveland, Colorado

**The Youth Worker's Encyclopedia of Bible-Teaching Ideas:
Old Testament**
Copyright © 1994 Group Publishing, Inc.

Scripture quoted from The Youth Bible, New Century Version, copyright © 1991
by Word Publishing, Dallas, Texas 75039. Used by permission.

Credits
Compiled by Mike Nappa and Michael Warden
Edited by Mike Nappa, Stephen Parolini, Michael Warden, Rick Lawrence, and
Jody Wakefield Brolsma
Cover designed by Liz Howe
Interior designed by Lisa Smith
Illustrations by Amy Bryant and Joel Armstrong
Copy edited by Cheryl Adams Eisel and Stephanie G'Schwind
Typesetting by Joyce Douglas and Rosalie Lawrence

Library of Congress Cataloging-in-Publication Data

The youth worker's encyclopedia of Bible teaching ideas.

       Includes indexes.
       Contents: [1] Old Testament -- [2] New Testament.
       1. Bible--Indexes. 2. Church work with teenagers.
I. Group Publishing.
BS432.Y685 1994   268'.433   94-12166
ISBN 1-55945-184-X : (O.T.)
ISBN 1-55945-183-1 : (N.T.)

10 9 8 7 6 5 4 3 2   03 02 01 00 99 98 97 96 95

Printed in the United States of America.

CONTENTS

CONTRIBUTORS

Many thanks to the following people, who loaned us their creative expertise to help bring together this volume of ideas:

Alan Scott
Amy L. W. Nappa
Annie Wamberg
Berry Richardson
Beth Snowden
Bob Easton
Bob Latchaw
Bryan Dykes
Chip Borgstadt
Christina Medina
David Cassady
David Mahnke
Deena Borchers
Donald Hinchey
Edwin Lee Hill
James D. Walton
Jamie Snodgrass
Jane Vogel
Janet R. Balmforth
Janice Thatcher
Jody Wakefield Brolsma
Karen Dockrey
Kathy J. Smith
Katrina Johnson

Lane Black
Linda Joyce Heaner
Linda Robinson
Lisa Lauffer
Lynn Potter
Margaret Hinchey
Mark Oestreicher
Michael Capps
Michael Warden
Michelle Anthony
Mike Bradley
Norman H. Coleman III
Norman Stolpe
Paul Peavy
Paul Woods
Rex Stepp
Rick Bundschuh
Rick Chromey
Rick Lawrence
Roger J. Rome
Ron Jensen
Stephen Parolini
Steve Wamberg
Tommy Baker

INTRODUCTION

Once upon a time, a little publishing company in Colorado had a dream.

"What if," the people there said, "instead of simply *teaching* teenagers about the Old Testament, we had a way to help them *learn* about it—a way to help them experience and apply the truths found in Scripture?"

So they went right to work. They contacted the most inventive minds in youth ministry and asked them to create innovative, Old Testament-based learning experiences for teenagers. Then they compiled those ideas into this volume: *The Youth Worker's Encyclopedia of Bible-Teaching Ideas: Old Testament.*

Suddenly, it wasn't just a dream anymore. It was reality. And it was ready to be shared with youth workers around the world—with youth workers like you.

In the following pages, you'll find hundreds of active, guided experiences that take scriptural truths from the Old Testament and bring them to life for kids. Your teenagers will gain a deeper understanding of the Bible through a variety of experiential activities such as:

learning games,

skits,

affirmation activities,

creative readings,

retreats and overnighters,

creative prayers,

adventures,

devotions,

music ideas,

object lessons,

projects,

and parties!

With such a wide variety of carefully planned, scripturally focused activities, your kids will never think of the Bible as "boring" again. Instead, they'll discover how to embrace Old Testament truths for themselves and then apply those truths effectively to their lives.

The Youth Worker's Encyclopedia of Bible-Teaching Ideas: Old Testament is an essential tool for any youth worker interested in helping kids explore and understand the Bible. You can use it with your group in several ways—for Sunday school, midweek meetings, Bible study groups, camp and retreat meetings, or any other time you gather your youth group together. Try it today! You—and your teenagers—will be glad you did.

GENESIS

"In the beginning God created..."

Genesis 1:1a

GENESIS 1:1-31

THEME:
Creation

SUMMARY:
On this overnight RETREAT, kids will learn to appreciate the beauty of God's creation by linking what they see around them to the Creation story.

PREPARATION: Plan an overnight camping trip in the woods, preferably near a lake or river. Be sure to pack Bibles.

Arrive at your camping site in the morning or early afternoon. Give kids time to hike, swim, climb, and generally enjoy God's creation. Around a campfire at night, have someone read aloud the Creation story (Genesis 1:1-31). Then have that person read it through again, pausing after each different "day." At each pause, ask kids to think about what God created on that day, then tell how they saw, appreciated, or enjoyed those creations. For example, after verses 14-19, in which God creates the sun, moon, and stars, someone may tell how good it felt to just lie in the sun that afternoon.

Then stir your kids' creativity by asking them to speculate how they might have created things differently. For example, someone might say, "I would have made the deer roar" or "What if fish had hands?"

Close by singing songs about God's creation such as "Awesome God" by Rich Mullins.

GENESIS 1:1-31

THEME:
Creation

SUMMARY:
In this OBJECT LESSON, make the Creation story in Genesis come to life by staging your own real-life creation activity.

PREPARATION: You'll need an aquarium, de-chlorinized water, aquarium gravel, plastic plants, an aquarium hood and lamp, a few goldfish, some dolls and toy farm animals, fish food, and Bibles.

Gather kids together and do the following steps:
• First Day: Light (Genesis 1:1-5). Turn out the lights. Place the empty aquarium in the middle of the room. Read the Scripture, then have a group member turn on the room light.
• Second Day: Division of the water with the sky (Genesis 1:6-8). Read the Scripture, then have kids fill the aquarium three-quarters full with the de-chlorinized water.
• Third Day: Land (Genesis 1:9-13). Read the Scripture, then have kids gently pour well-cleaned aquarium gravel into the bottom to create a mountain or two. Have kids place plants around the bottom.
• Fourth Day: Outer space (Genesis 1:14-19). Read the Scripture, then have kids place the aquarium hood and light on the aquarium. Turn off the room light.

• Fifth Day: Birds and fish (Genesis 1:20-23). Read the Scripture, then have kids place goldfish in the aquarium.

• Sixth Day: Animals and humans (Genesis 1:24-31). Read the Scripture, then have kids surround the aquarium with dolls and toy animals.

For the closing, sprinkle fish food on the water and talk about God's continuing commitment to take care of us and provide for us.

have kids each pick a cookie, spread icing on it, then decorate it especially for the person whose name they drew. Encourage teenagers to be creative, original, outrageous, positive, and personal.

To close the activity, form a circle and have kids exchange cookies, telling why they decorated their cookie the way they did.

GENESIS
1:27-31

THEME:
Created in God's image

SUMMARY:
In this AFFIRMATION, kids encourage each other by decorating a cookie in honor of another person.

PREPARATION: On a table, set out large, plain sugar cookies; icing (various colors); plastic knives; and decorating items, such as cake sprinkles, M&M's, red hots, colored sugar, and chocolate chips. Write each person's name on a slip of paper and put the slips in a hat or bowl. You'll also need Bibles.

Have someone read aloud Genesis 1:27-31. Then have group members each draw names out of the hat or bowl. Tell them to keep the names a secret. Then

GENESIS
2:1-3

THEME:
Rest

SUMMARY:
On this RETREAT, kids learn to appreciate rest by working hard for the first part of the retreat, then resting for the remainder of the time.

PREPARATION: Call around to find a Christian campground or retreat center that needs cleaning and/or simple repair work done. You might even ask if your kids can stay two nights for free in exchange for their hard work, and ask the campground or retreat center to provide the necessary tools and supplies. Plan a working retreat where kids can spend a few hours working in groups or pairs, sprucing the place up. Tell kids to be sure to bring Bibles along with work clothes to wear while cleaning.

Go to the campground or retreat center on a Friday night. Before kids go to bed, post a list of the jobs that must be done and assign groups or pairs to do them.

Start early Saturday and work until just after lunch. Devote the rest of the time to rest. Plan Saturday-evening and Sunday-morning sessions on Genesis 2:1-3 and why God chose to rest after creating the world. Intersperse your sessions with quiet walks around the campground or retreat center, and "silent times" gathered around a cross inside or in a secluded spot outside.

It's difficult for many teenagers to really understand the necessity of rest, so this is a good time to focus on the importance of rest—physically, emotionally, and spiritually.

group members volunteer for the following parts: God, the Man, the Woman, the Serpent, and the Narrator. Have groups sit in a circle and read aloud Genesis 3:1-19, each person reading his or her part with much expression.

The narrator takes the apple first when he or she reads the beginning of the passage, then must pass it to whoever speaks next. The apple continues to be passed as each character speaks. Try it a few times, with kids switching characters each time. Then serve apples (apple slices) or apple snacks and ask groups to discuss:

∎ **Is it possible to avoid temptation? Why or why not?**

∎ **What's the best way to battle temptation? Explain.**

∎ **What's the best thing to do when we give in to temptation?**

∎ **How can Jesus help us in the midst of temptation?**

GENESIS 3:1-19

THEME:
Temptation

SUMMARY:
Kids use a CREATIVE READING to bring to life Satan's temptation of Adam and Eve.

PREPARATION: You'll need Bibles, an apple for every five kids, and some kind of apple snack.

Form groups of five and give each group an apple. Have

GENESIS 6:1-7

THEME:
Taking our relationship with God for granted

SUMMARY:
Use this SKIT to help kids see that their actions affect their relationships.

DON'T COUNT YOUR CHICKENS

SCENE: Three girls meet in a common area at school and gripe about unfairness.

PROPS: A piece of sheet music and a couple of chairs. You'll also need Bibles for the discussion after the skit.

CHARACTERS:
Crissy
Bess
Karen

SCRIPT

(Crissy is sitting, looking at a sheet of music and humming through it. Bess enters, upset.)

Bess: Oh, there you are! Did you hear?

Crissy: Hear what?

Bess: About the select choir!

Crissy: *(Smugly)* Sure, I saw the list of people chosen. Don't worry, we both made it.

Bess: *(Shaking her head)* No, no, that's not the latest. Karen said she saw Mr. Todd take the first list down and say he was gonna start all over again with auditions.

Crissy: *(All ears)* What? How can he do that?

Bess: I don't know, but he did it.

Crissy: Why? I mean...we were chosen, we were in!

Bess: WERE in is right. Now we have to prove ourselves all over again.

Crissy: That's not fair! I sweated over that audition for a month! *(Karen enters.)*

Karen: *(Glumly)* Hi.

Bess: Hi. I was just telling Crissy.

Karen: *(To Crissy)* Can you believe it?

Crissy: *(Worked up)* What exactly did he say?

Karen: Well, he was with Ms. Smith when he went to the bulletin board and took the list down. I heard him complain that since he had selected some of the students for choir, they had been rude and quit paying attention at rehearsals. He said he wasn't going to reward that kind of behavior by allowing them to be in a select group.

Bess: How stupid!

Karen: He was even complaining about how some of us are late to class sometimes!

Crissy: Big deal!

Karen: Well, it must be to him. He said he was going to start over from scratch.

Bess: This really stinks! We earned a spot in select choir!

Crissy: *(Angrily)* That's right. Let's go tell him what we think of this whole thing!
(They walk off, full of purpose. Karen follows after them by a few feet.)

Karen: *(Lost in thought)* I know what I think. I think I'm going to apologize. *(She exits.)*

If you use this skit as a discussion starter, here are possible questions:

■ **Why is it so difficult for us to see our own sin and how it affects our relationship with God?**

∎ **What sins might be harder to spot in our lives? Why?**
Read Genesis 6:1-7. Ask:

∎ **How do you think God felt about destroying his creation?**

∎ **How might that feeling affect the way you act on a day-to-day basis?**

GENESIS
7

THEME:
   The Story of Noah

SUMMARY:
   Teenagers will enjoy a PARTY based on the story of Noah and the ark.

PREPARATION: You'll need to find a small place for the party. Ask kids to each bring two packages or containers of an assigned refreshment or snack, such as animal crackers, goldfish crackers, pigs in a blanket, Otter Pops ice treats, or whatever you can think of that's connected to animals. Make punch and have a toy boat floating in the punch bowl. Bring cups or glasses and put little umbrellas in each one. Write animal names on slips of paper—two paper slips for each animal—and put them in a hat or bowl. You'll also need Bibles.

The ark must have been a crowded place, so plan this party for a small house, apartment, or room in your church. As kids arrive, have them draw the name of an animal out of a hat or bowl but keep the name a secret. Later have them find their "partners" by making their animals' noises or actions. Then have partners imitate their animals for the group.

Have the group simulate a rainstorm by following what you do. First, snap your fingers for 20 or 30 seconds. Then pat your legs for 20 or 30 seconds. Then pat your legs and stomp your feet for 20 or 30 seconds. Then go back to patting your legs. Finally, go back to snapping your fingers.

Ask kids to tell their partners how rainstorms make them feel. Have volunteers read aloud Genesis 7. Then ask teenagers to imagine they were part of Noah's family—how would they feel before, during, and after the storm?

For fun, play music such as "Sit Down, You're Rocking the Boat," "Singing in the Rain," and "The Rainbow Connection."

GENESIS
11:1-9

THEME:
   Worshiping God in any language

SUMMARY:
   In this creative MUSIC IDEA, kids learn to worship God in sign language.

PREPARATION: Contact a local American Sign Language group, or a member of your church who knows ASL, and ask the signer to take part in a youth group worship service. You'll also need Bibles.

Have someone read aloud Genesis 11:1-9 (in a foreign language if possible). Then say: **We can worship God in any language. Today we'll learn how to worship God in sign.**

Have the signer perform a song without music and see if anyone can guess which song it is. If the signer is a Christian, invite him or her to tell his or her faith story in sign language, using an interpreter if necessary. Then have kids each communicate what they love most about God by using their own sign or body language.

Close by asking the signer to teach a worship song to the group in sign language. Then have everyone perform the song.

GENESIS
12:1-8

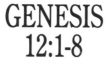

THEME:
Chosen by God

SUMMARY:
In this AFFIRMATION activity, kids experience choosing one object over others and discover what it feels like to be chosen by God.

PREPARATION: Collect an assortment of odd objects such as a can opener, squirt bottle, empty box, can of soda, Popsicle sticks, or a light bulb. Bring more items than group members. You'll also need Bibles. Larger groups may want to

do this activity in pairs, with one item per pair.

Place the items you collected on a table. Have each teenager choose one item then sit down. After all kids have chosen, ask the following questions:

■ **Why did you choose your item?**

■ **What are two things that set your object apart from everyone else's?**

■ **How is your object useful?**

Have the last speaker read aloud Genesis 12:1-8. Ask:

■ **How do you think Abram felt, knowing that God had chosen him for something special?**

■ **How are we like Abram?**

■ **What might God want to use you for?**

Have each person tell two unique, positive things about the person to his or her left.

Close in prayer, thanking God for choosing us and making us so special.

GENESIS
16

THEME:
Our sin affects others.

SUMMARY:
In this LEARNING GAME, kids will experience the effects of sin as they play volleyball (volleyballoon) with a shaving cream-filled balloon.

PREPARATION: You'll need several balloons, shaving cream, and snacks. This is a messy game, so you may want to play it outside and when your teenagers aren't dressed up. (Have paper towels for cleanup handy.) Before beginning, pull a couple of group members aside and tell them that you want them to hit the balloon really hard when it comes to them. You'll also need Bibles.

Fill a balloon with shaving cream. Form two teams and have them face one another, as if playing volleyball. Put a barrier between the teams to serve as a net (you could simply make a line of chairs).

Say: **Let's play volleyballoon! But be careful. This balloon is very fragile! We'll toss it back and forth, just like in volleyball, except you need to catch it rather than hit it. Go!**

When someone pops the balloon, shaving cream will probably spray onto everyone. Give kids a few minutes to wipe the shaving cream off. Then play as many rounds as kids want to play. Afterward, ask:

■ **Why did the balloon pop?**

■ **How did you feel when the balloon broke?**

■ **How did you feel toward the person who hit the balloon?**

Tell the group about your instructions to your "confederates." Then have the person who popped the balloon read Genesis 16. Ask:

■ **How was Sarai's sin like the balloon popping?**

■ **Who did Sarai's sin affect, and how did it make them feel?**

■ **Why did Sarai sin in the first place?**

■ **How does our sin affect others?**

■ **How should we handle it when we sin?**

GENESIS 17:1-16

THEME:
  Being called Christians

SUMMARY:
  In this DEVOTION, kids will learn the meaning of their own names and discuss what it means to be called Christian.

PREPARATION: You'll need two books that give definitions of names, and Bibles.

EXPERIENCE
  Form two groups and give each group a book of names. Have kids look up their names and share the meanings with the group. Then have kids give each other new names based on the meanings listed in the name books. Encourage kids to be positive but to choose names for each other that reflect something about that person's personality or interests.

RESPONSE
  When everyone has had a chance to tell about his or her name, ask:

■ **How are some of the meanings appropriate for certain people?**

■ **How does it feel to know**

that your name has a meaning?
■ Why don't many of us fit the meanings of our names?

Have a volunteer read Genesis 17:1-16 aloud. Then ask:

■ Why did God give Abram and Sarai new names?

■ If God chose to change your name to reflect who you are and what he thinks of you, what do you think it would be? Explain.

■ How does it feel to be named by God?

■ What does the name "Christian" mean to you? Why is it important that we follow that meaning?

CLOSING
Have the two groups discuss ways that they can be true to their name "Christian." Then have two or three people from each group close in prayer, asking for God's guidance and strength to live like Christians.

GENESIS
18:20-33

THEME:
Praying for our cities

SUMMARY:
In this CREATIVE READING, kids survey their city from a high place as they ask God to respond to its needs.

PREPARATION: Get permission to take the group to the top of the tallest building in your city. You'll need Bibles.

Meet at the church in the evening and car pool to the tallest building in your area. (If a tall building isn't available, get flashlights and hike up a hill just outside the city.) Take the elevator to the highest floor and gather near a window overlooking the city.

Read aloud Genesis 18:20-33 and ask kids to read aloud God's answers to Abraham's plea, in unison. Then have kids tell about prayer concerns regarding the community (gangs, local violence, prejudice, poor leadership, and so on). Break into groups of three and have kids pray for those concerns.

GENESIS
19:1-26

THEME:
Sin

SUMMARY:
Through this OBJECT LESSON, kids learn that some things "soak up" sin and others don't.

PREPARATION: For every two people you'll need a sheet of wax paper, a glass of water, and a sheet of newspaper. You'll also need Bibles.

Form pairs and give each pair a sheet of wax paper, a glass of water, and a sheet of newspaper. Have several volunteers read aloud Genesis 19:1-26. Then have one partner in each pair pour a few drops of water onto the wax paper. Ask partners to discuss:

■ **How do the wax paper and water react together?**

■ **How is this like God and sin?**

■ **How did God react to the sin in Sodom and Gomorrah?**

Have the other partner in each pair pour a few drops of water onto the newspaper. Then ask:

■ **How does the newspaper react to the water?**

■ **What effect does the water have on the newspaper?**

■ **How is this like us and sin?**

■ **How did Lot's wife react to the sin in Sodom and Gomorrah?**

Say: **Like the wax paper and water, God can't have anything to do with sin. Unfortunately we're sometimes more like the newspaper. We let sin into our lives where it can destroy and weaken us. With your partner brainstorm one way you can let God make you more resistant to sin and its harmful effects. Then commit to trying your idea starting this week.**

GENESIS
21:1-7

THEME:
Joy

SUMMARY:
In this MUSIC IDEA, kids will choose and sing songs that focus on joy.

PREPARATION: You'll need a hymnal, a worship songbook, and a children's songbook. You'll also need paper, pencils, and Bibles.

Form three groups and have one person in each group read aloud Genesis 21:1-7. Give group 1 a hymnal, group 2 a worship songbook, and group 3 a children's songbook. Each group should have a sheet of paper and a pencil. Allow three minutes for groups to write the titles of songs from their hymnal or songbook that focus on joy.

After the time is up, have groups read aloud their lists. Have each group choose two songs for the entire group to sing. After singing each song, have kids tell about great things God has done in their lives.

GENESIS
22:1-12

THEME:
Sacrifice

SUMMARY:
Use this SKIT to help kids see that a great sacrifice may sometimes be necessary.

CURFEW

SCENE: Two teenagers contemplate how to get home after a party.

PROPS: Two jackets for the skit and Bibles for the discussion afterward.

CHARACTERS:
Mark
Sarah

SCRIPT

(Sarah is standing, waiting, when Mark enters with both jackets.)

Mark: Here they are. Boy, you should've seen some of the ugly jackets I had to dig through to find yours and mine. Where's Marshall?

Sarah: He left.

Mark: He what? How does he think I'm gonna get home?

Sarah: I don't know. He just said he had to get home before midnight or his parents would ground him, so he left.

Mark: *(Wide-eyed)* He left! Oh, great. What about me? The grounding potential of this situation is starting to rise dramatically!

Sarah: Maybe you can catch a ride with someone else. There are still a few people here at the party.

Mark: Oh, sure, I could always get a ride with Boots McClann. I hear his Harley holds two. I can smell his sweaty leather jacket now. Or maybe Sherry would give me a ride. She's feelin' real good about me since I told Boots I saw her at Tuna King with Joel! No, I don't think the prospects look too good, considering those are the only two people I know who are left here. Except... you!

Sarah: Me? I can't give you a ride. You live all the way across town. By the time I got home, I'd be late for my OWN curfew!

Mark: Come on. Please? I'm sure your parents would understand, you being such a great student and all. Sarah, when's the last time you've even been in trouble? They'll go easy on you if you just tell 'em you helped a friend. What are they gonna do to you, take away your word processor?

Sarah: I don't know, and I don't want to find out. I've never been late, and I really don't want to start now.

Mark: PLEASE? I'm gonna be dead meat if my old man sees me coming in late. I might as well not go home at all.

Sarah: Mark, it'll take me 45 minutes to get you home and then get home myself. My parents will have a fit!

Mark: Come on, Sarah, I need your help! You'd be a lifesaver.

Sarah: Well... *(sizes up the situation)* I guess you ARE stuck. Let me call my parents and let them know I'll be late.

(Freeze.)

If you use this skit as a discussion starter, here are possible questions:

■ **Why do you think Sarah was willing to sacrifice her time and effort, and risk possible punishment for Mark?**

■ **What would you be willing to sacrifice for a friend?**

Read Genesis 22:1-12. Ask:

■ **Why was Abraham so willing to sacrifice his son for the Lord?**

■ **Why was God pleased with Abraham's willingness?**

■ **What would you be willing to sacrifice for God?**

GENESIS
22:1-18

THEME:
Trusting in God

SUMMARY:
In this CREATIVE READING, kids will hear the story of Abraham's sacrifice of Isaac, interspersed by a chorus reciting psalms and proverbs that apply to each aspect of the story.

PREPARATION: Recruit readers to read the script and make a photocopy of the "Creative Reading for Genesis 22:1-8" handout (p. 18) for each reader. You'll also need Bibles.

Choose readers for the roles below and have them read the script on page 18.
God
Abraham
Chorus
Narrator
Isaac
Angel of the Lord

GENESIS
25:27-34

THEME:
Priorities

SUMMARY:
In this DEVOTION, kids must choose whether or not to give up a valuable raffle ticket in exchange for dinner.

PREPARATION: Make up raffle tickets for a nice prize, such as free summer-camp registration, or free admission to an amusement park or water park. Ask kids to bring food for a potluck dinner. You'll also need Bibles and enough small prizes (such as discount coupons for the next youth event, or candy bars) for everyone.

EXPERIENCE
Have kids each bring a food item for a potluck dinner. As kids arrive, give each person a raffle ticket for a great prize (free admission to an amusement park or water park, or free summer-camp registration, for example). Spend time getting good and hungry by singing songs, playing volleyball, running wacky relays, or playing water games or crazy softball.

After an hour or so, gather everyone and ask who would be willing to trade their raffle tickets for dinner. Allow those who trade in their tickets to go to the head of the line. Those who don't trade their tickets must wait until everyone else finishes eating. Then they may eat.

Afterward, hold a drawing with the tickets from the people who refused to trade their tickets in order to eat first. Give the winning person the big prize and give small prizes (such as discount coupons for the next youth event, or candy bars) to everyone else who didn't trade away their tickets.

RESPONSE
Read aloud Genesis 25:27-34 and discuss:
■ **What are precious things in our life that we give up too easily?**

(continued on p. 19)

CREATIVE READING FOR GENESIS 22:1-18

God: Abraham!

Abraham: Here I am.

God: Take your son, your only son, Isaac, whom you love, and go to the region of Moriah. Sacrifice him there as a burnt offering on one of the mountains I will tell you about.

Chorus: Offer right sacrifices and trust in the Lord. *(Psalm 4:5)*

Narrator: Early the next morning, Abraham got up and saddled his donkey. He took with him two of his servants and his son, Isaac. When he had cut enough wood for the burnt offering, he set out for the place God had told him about. On the third day, Abraham looked up and saw the place in the distance. He said to his servants...

Abraham: Stay here with the donkey, while my son and I go over there. We will worship, and then we will come back to you.

Chorus: Those who know your name will trust in you, for you, Lord, have never forsaken those who seek you. *(Psalm 9:10)*

Narrator: Abraham took the wood for the burnt offering and gave it to his son, Isaac, while Abraham himself carried the fire and the knife. As the two of them went on together, Isaac spoke up and said to his father...

Isaac: Father?

Abraham: Yes, my son?

Isaac: The fire and the wood are here, but where is the lamb for the burnt offering?

Abraham: God himself will provide the lamb for the burnt offering, my son.

Chorus: The Lord is my strength and my shield; my heart trusts in him, and I am helped. *(Psalm 28:7)*

Narrator: When they reached the place God had told him about, Abraham built an altar there and arranged the wood on it.

Chorus: Trust in the Lord with all your heart and lean not on your own understanding. *(Proverbs 3:5)*

Narrator: He bound his son, Isaac, and laid him on the altar, on top of the wood.

Chorus: I trust in you, O Lord. *(Psalm 31:14)*

Narrator: Then he reached out his hand and took the knife to slay his son.

Chorus: I will trust and not be afraid. *(Isaiah 12:2)*

Angel of the Lord: *(Loudly)* Abraham! Abraham!

Abraham: Here I am.

Angel of the Lord: Do not lay a hand on the boy. Do not do anything to him. Now I know that you fear God, because you have not withheld from me your son, your only son.

Narrator: Abraham looked up and, there in a thicket, he saw a ram caught by its horns. He went over, took the ram, and sacrificed it as a burnt offering instead of his son. So Abraham called that place, "The Lord Provides."

All: But as for me, I trust in you. *(Psalm 55:23)*

■ **Why do we give them up?**

CLOSING
Form pairs and have partners answer the question:
■ **How can we keep from foolishly trading away our "valuables"?**
Then ask partners to pray for each other to guard what is valuable in their lives.

GENESIS
28:10-22

THEME:
Worries

SUMMARY:
In this OBJECT LESSON, teenagers will build an altar.

PREPARATION: Have kids each bring a fist-sized rock with them to the meeting. Have them each write their names on their rocks with markers. You'll also need Bibles.

Lead the group in a study of Jacob's encounter with God at Bethel (Genesis 28:10-22).

Have kids use their rocks to build an altar in a corner of the youth room. Have kids make an agreement together to turn the youth room into a "Bethel" or "House of God," where they can leave their worries at the door and share their hearts openly. Have kids set up rules of behavior, such as "No put-downs" or "Everything said in the Bethel will be held in confidence."

Keep the altar in the corner of the room as a reminder of the Bethel covenant.

GENESIS
29:15-30

THEME:
Love vs. infatuation

SUMMARY:
On this RETREAT, kids work hard for a reward and learn that real love requires sacrifice.

PREPARATION: Plan a weekend retreat with the theme of true love vs. infatuation, based on the story of Jacob working seven years so he could marry Rachel. Be sure to include ice cream in your supplies and bring plenty of Bibles.

Form two teams and give each team a list of seven chores or activities to complete by Saturday at lunch time. These may include sweeping out the leaders' cabins or rooms, doing dishes, preparing a meal, setting up the chairs for a group time, preparing a skit, or picking weeds. Announce that when everything on the list has been completed, the team will get an ice-cream party (or a swimming party or some other great reward).

When teams complete their chores and come to lunch for their rewards, tell them that the rules have been changed and they must complete another list of activities. You may want to make these activities sillier—walking backward to lunch, doing a scavenger hunt, filling up water balloons for a game, or making up a song to the tune of "Yankee Doodle." This list must be completed by Saturday at dinner.

After dinner, give both teams the promised reward. Congratulate them on their hard work, then focus your discussion and activities on the sacrifice that love often requires. Contrast that sacrifice with the feelings that usually drive infatuation. Have small groups read and study Jacob and Rachel's story in Genesis 29:15-30.

GENESIS
32:22-32

THEME:
Struggling with God

SUMMARY:
In this ADVENTURE hike, kids will compare a physical challenge to the challenge of following God.

PREPARATION: Plan a challenging hike in a forest or city park. Have kids bring lots of water, sunscreen, and oranges (good for quick energy). Be sure to bring Bibles and carry a first aid kit for added safety.

The hike should be difficult enough to be a challenge but not so difficult that some teenagers don't finish. When you reach your destination (the top of the mountain, a certain place in the woods, or the end of the trail), have kids

relax and enjoy the view. While everyone is resting, ask:

■ **How was this hike like other challenges you face in life?**

■ **How have you seen God help you through the challenges in your life?**

■ **Why don't we always like the path that God chooses for us?**

Have a volunteer read aloud Genesis 32:22-32. Then ask:

■ **How do we wrestle with God?**

■ **Jacob got a new name after wrestling with God. How are we changed after wrestling with God?**

■ **How is wrestling with God like making it to the end of our hike?**

GENESIS
33:1-14

THEME:
Serving one another

SUMMARY:
Through this blood-drive PROJECT, kids learn how to humbly serve others.

PREPARATION: Contact a blood bank and arrange to hold a blood drive at your church. Make sure youth group members get parental permission before allowing them to give blood. You'll also need to bring Bibles.

Help your young people experience servanthood by sponsoring a blood drive at your church.

This provides two opportunities for your kids to give: by donating life-giving blood as well as providing the time, place, and support for others to do the same.

Most local blood banks are willing to come to your church if they're guaranteed a sizable turnout. That's where your teenagers can help out. Have them make posters and fliers, print a creative announcement in the church bulletin, and even perform a skit to promote the blood drive.

During the drive they can play music (taped or live), show a funny movie, or come up with their own entertainment ideas. Assign a group of teenagers to coordinate refreshments for people to enjoy after they've donated blood. (Check with the workers at the blood bank for recommendations on what kinds of refreshments to provide.)

After the blood drive, gather kids together and ask:

■ **What was it like to run this blood drive?**

■ **Why did you work on the blood drive?**

■ **What have we accomplished?**

Have someone read aloud Genesis 33:1-14. Ask:

■ **How is our work on the blood drive like the way Jacob pictured himself as a servant in this passage?**

■ **Why do you think Jacob presented himself as a humble servant to his brother, Esau?**

■ **What can we learn from Jacob's example to help us humbly serve others this week?**

GENESIS 37:1-35

THEME:
Family joys and struggles

SUMMARY:
In this barbecue PARTY, families learn to appreciate the joys and struggles God has brought them through.

PREPARATION: Plan a barbecue by asking each of your group members' families to bring meat to grill and a side dish to share. Find an outdoor location, perhaps in a park, that has one or more grills. You'll need Bibles.

After you've finished eating, ask a volunteer to read aloud Genesis 37:1-35. Then say: **At one time or another, many of us have probably considered selling a younger sister or brother. Well, Joseph's brothers actually did it. Like our own families, Joseph's family had its ups and downs. Today we're going to celebrate the family God has given us.**

Have families each gather together, then complete the following sentences:

•**One fact I was surprised to learn about my dad . . .**

•**When Mom was a little girl, she wanted to be a . . .**

•**I'll never forget the time that my little brother/sister ate . . .**

•**Our best vacation was . . .**

•**Our worst vacation was . . .**

•**The toughest time our family ever faced was...**
•**The greatest time of joy our family ever had was...**
•**Our family is unique because...**

Have families share their best answers. Then host a mock auction in which each family chooses one member to "sell." The rest of the family must give a sales pitch, telling all prospective "buyers" about that family member's strengths. Other families may bid with M&M's. The highest-bidding family keeps their "purchase" for the rest of the afternoon as an honorary family member.

Have teenagers think of blessings that begin with the letters in their names and write the blessings next to the letters. For example, Chad might write that he's blessed with Christian friends, Health, Athletic ability, and his Dad.

Give your young people plenty of time to think of the many blessings they might normally overlook or take for granted. It's OK if some kids aren't able to fill in all of their letters. Then form pairs and have partners tell each other about their blessings lists. Next ask partners to pray for each other, thanking God for each of the ways they've been blessed.

In closing, encourage your teenagers to keep their lists in a visible place at home where they can be reminded of God's constant love.

GENESIS
39:1-6

THEME:
Blessings

SUMMARY:
In this CREATIVE PRAYER activity, kids each think of blessings they can tie into their names as an acrostic.

PREPARATION: You'll need paper, markers, and Bibles.

Give your kids paper and markers and ask them to write their full names vertically down the left side of the paper.

Then read aloud Genesis 39:1-6. Say: **God blessed Joseph greatly. And God has also blessed each of us.**

GENESIS
40:1-23

THEME:
How God talks to us

SUMMARY:
In this LEARNING GAME, kids form two groups and try to communicate a message despite obstacles they must overcome.

PREPARATION: You'll need blindfolds for half of the kids in your group, a blackboard and chalk (or newsprint and a marker), and Bibles.

Form two groups. Blindfold the kids in group 1 and have them stand at one end of the room. Inform the kids in group 2 that they have five minutes to convey a specific message to group 1, but they may not speak or make any noise.

Write the message on a blackboard or on newsprint. The message could be some activity that you'll be doing later in the week ("We're going bowling next Wednesday night") or instructions for what to do now ("Sit in a circle and open your Bibles to Genesis 40:1-23").

Members of group 1 who figure out the message may join group 2 in assisting others—but they can't speak or make noise when they join team 2. After five minutes, ask members of group 1:

■ **How did you feel when you were blindfolded?**

Ask members of group 2:

■ **What was it like not being able to speak to people in group 1?**

Ask everyone:

■ **What made it easier to communicate?**

■ **How was this activity like communicating with God?**

Have a volunteer read aloud Genesis 40:1-23. Then ask:

■ **Why do you think Joseph could interpret the dreams?**

■ **How does God speak to us today?**

■ **How can we learn to listen for God?**

GENESIS 41:41-43

THEME:
Treating others with respect

SUMMARY:
In this LEARNING GAME, kids must race to blow a bubble across the room without breaking it.

PREPARATION: You'll need two bottles of bubble solution used for blowing bubbles and Bibles.

Form two teams. Have each team form a line at one end of the room, opposite a chair. Give the first person in each line a bottle of bubble solution. Have each person blow a bubble, release it from the wand, then gently blow it to the chair at the other end of the room. They then pop it, race back to the line, and hand the bottle of bubbles to the next person. If the bubble pops before the racer reaches the chair, that person must return to the starting line and try again.

The first team to have each member successfully finish, wins. Afterward, have teams sit down, then ask:

■ **What was difficult about this race?**

■ **What seemed to be the key to working with the bubbles?**

■ **How is this like the way we should treat each other?**

Have the girls read aloud Genesis 37:1-5. Then have the guys read aloud Genesis 41:41-43. Ask:

■ **What do you find in these passages that's like what we learned in the bubble race?**

■ **What happens when we don't treat people with respect?**

■ **What happens when we treat people with respect?**

■ **Why does God want us to treat others gently, like the bubbles?**

Pass a bottle of bubbles around and have each person blow a bubble and release it, telling one way that he or she can treat someone with respect this week.

GENESIS
45:1-8

THEME:
God works things out in the end.

SUMMARY:
In this CREATIVE PRAYER activity, kids write prayer requests on the back of puzzle pieces, then put the puzzle together. Then each person chooses a puzzle piece to focus his or her prayer on for the week.

PREPARATION: Obtain a 25-piece puzzle or two 10-piece puzzles. The pieces should be fairly large. You'll also need felt-tip markers and Bibles.

Have someone read aloud Genesis 45:1-8. Ask:

■ **How did God work out Joseph's situation with his brothers?**

■ **How is that like the way God works things out when we pray about them?**

Give your young people each a puzzle piece and have them write their names and prayer requests on the back. Put all of the pieces back in a pile and have kids work to put the puzzle together.

Next, have kids each randomly pick a piece, making sure it isn't their own. Have each person keep the puzzle piece during the week and pray for the person whose name is on the back. The following week, put the puzzle back together and have kids tell what God has done to answer each prayer.

GENESIS
46:28-34

THEME:
Forgiveness

SUMMARY:
In this DEVOTION, kids will experience what total forgiveness means.

PREPARATION: You'll need two deflated, "fat" balloons and a marker for each person. You'll also need Bibles.

EXPERIENCE
Give each person two deflated balloons and a marker. Say: **On one of your balloons, write something someone has done to you that's been hard for you to forgive. However, to maintain confiden-**

tiality, don't write a person's name on your balloon.

After everyone is done writing, have kids blow up their balloons. On the count of three, have everyone think about the situation written on his or her balloon—then pop the balloon.

RESPONSE

■ **How did it feel to pop your balloon?**

■ **As you popped it, what were you feeling about the incident you'd written on the balloon?**

■ **How is that like forgiveness?**

■ **Why is it important for us to forgive others?**

■ **What happens when we don't forgive?**

■ **What happens when we do forgive?**

Have a volunteer read aloud Genesis 46:28-34. Then ask:

■ **Do you think it was hard for Joseph to forgive his brothers? Why or why not?**

■ **How did he show that he'd forgiven them?**

■ **What was his attitude toward his brothers?**

■ **What might have happened if he'd held a grudge against them?**

CLOSING

Have kids pair up and tell one way that they can show forgiveness to someone who's hurt them. Ask partners to pray for each other to have the strength to forgive. Then have them blow up, tie off, and keep the second balloon as a reminder of what forgiveness means.

GENESIS 47:13-25

THEME:
Feeding the hungry

SUMMARY:
In this PROJECT, kids will plant and harvest food in their own garden to help needy people.

PREPARATION: Find a plot of ground at your church or in a church member's yard where your teenagers can plant a vegetable garden. Each climate differs, so consult a local nursery for the best way to prepare the soil and what kinds of produce to grow. You'll need seeds (let kids select what kind) and gardening tools. Also bring along Bibles.

Have your kids plant a "hunger garden" to help needy people. They'll need to prepare the soil for planting, choose what they want to grow, plant the seeds, and set up a weeding and watering schedule that they're responsible to keep. When the vegetables are ripe, donate them to a local food bank, a homeless shelter, or to your church for a special meal for needy people.

After you finish the project, have someone read aloud Genesis 47:13-25. Ask:

■ **How is our garden project like what Joseph did? How is it unlike what Joseph did?**

■ **What did you enjoy most about the garden? What did you** least enjoy?

■ **How does it feel to have provided food for someone?**

■ **What's one way you can help hungry people get the food they need?**

GENESIS 49:1-28

THEME:
We're all unique and special.

SUMMARY:
In this DEVOTION, kids will decorate blank cards to show how they are unique individuals.

PREPARATION: For each person you'll need a 3×5 card and colored markers. You'll also need Bibles.

EXPERIENCE

Pass out a 3×5 card and colored markers to each young person. Have kids spend a few minutes decorating one side. Collect the cards, then redistribute them randomly, face down.

Say: **From the back, these cards all look alike. There's nothing special or unique about any of them.**

Then have everyone turn over the cards and inspect the front side. Ask kids to tell what's unique about their cards.

RESPONSE

■ **What was it like to share something special about your card?**

■ **How are these cards like us?**

■ **Why do we like to feel special?**

Have the oldest teenager read aloud Genesis 49:1-28. Ask:

■ **What do you notice about Jacob's blessings to his sons?**

■ **How do you think they each felt?**

■ **How might the blessings have helped them in their future?**

■ **How can we help others feel special?**

■ **Why is it important to help others see their uniqueness?**

CLOSING

Form a circle. One at a time, have kids pass their cards to the right and tell something unique and special about the person on their right. The last person can place all the cards in the middle of the circle and pray, thanking God for creating us each in a special way.

EXODUS

"I am the God of your ancestors—the God of Abraham, the God of Isaac, and the God of Jacob."

Exodus 3:6a

EXODUS
1:8-21

THEME:

Obeying God in the face of danger

SUMMARY:
In this CREATIVE READING, kids will explore the advantages of obeying God in the face of specific dangers.

PREPARATION: You'll need Bibles for each person. Before class, make large name tags for the following characters:

King
King's People (two)
Slave Masters/Egyptians (two)
Israelites (any number)
Hebrew Midwives (two) with imaginary babies

Assign each person a role from this passage and have him or her wear the appropriate name tag. If you have fewer than eight group members, kids may play more than one role.

Have kids use Exodus 1:8-21 as the script for an interactive drama. Encourage teenagers to read their words and perform their actions as they think the events really happened. Have everyone participate, standing off-center when they're not in the action. Kids will need the same translation of the Bible to make this run more smoothly.

Use the following ideas to direct the action:

Verses 8-10: The King and the King's People are in this scene.

Verses 11-14: Slave Masters/ Egyptians and a few Israelites begin the scene. More Israelites enter in verse 12.

Verses 15-16: The King and the Hebrew Midwives are in the scene.

Verse 17: The Hebrew Midwives and the Israelites (with imaginary babies) are in the scene.

Verse 18: The King and the Hebrew Midwives are in this scene.

Verses 19-21: The King and Midwives are in the scene for verse 19, the Israelites for verse 20, and imaginary babies for verse 21.

After the interactive reading, ask the following questions. Have kids answer the questions from the viewpoint of the characters they played:

■ **King and King's People, you were in power, so why did you fear the Israelites?**

■ **Israelites, how did you feel about the treatment you received from the King and his People? from the Midwives? How did God guide you to act toward both?**

■ **Midwives, why did you go against a direct order and let the babies live?**

Have kids answer the following questions from today's perspective:

■ **How might this same experience happen today?**

■ **What role would you play (or have you played)?**

■ **How would you obey God in this role?**

After discussion, invite kids to replay the drama, but this time using a modern threat and a reward for obedience (let kids choose these). Then invite teenagers to ask you questions about the drama.

EXODUS
3:1-8a

THEME:

God appears in unexpected but true ways.

SUMMARY:
This CREATIVE READING helps teenagers focus on the details of God's appearance to Moses.

PREPARATION: You'll need NIV Bibles and hard candy.

Say: **Find the mistakes in my reading of Exodus 3:1-8a. Read along with me, and each time I make a mistake, stand and yell "Stop!" The first person standing may correct my mistake. Each time someone corrects a mistake and gives the right name or word, he or she will get a piece of candy.**

Read the following version of Exodus 3:1-8a aloud. The mistakes are followed by the actual name or word. Each time someone stands and corrects you, toss that person a candy. Then reread the phrase with the right name or word.

Now Jethro (Moses) **was tending the flock of Moses,** (Jethro) **his brother-in-law** (father-in-law), **the priest of Midian, and he led the sheepdog** (flock) **to the far side of the desert and came to Nazareth** (Sinai), **the mountain of God. There the song** (angel) **of the Lord appeared to him in flames of fire from within a bush.**

Jethro (Moses) **saw that even though the match** (bush) **was on fire, it burned up** (did not burn up). **So Moses thought, "I will go home** (go over and see this strange sight)—**and find out why the bush does not burn up."**

When the Lord saw that he had gone home (over to look), **God called to him from within the bush, "Jethro, Jethro!"** (Moses, Moses!)

And Noah (Moses) **said, "I'm outta here."** (Here I am.)

"Come closer," (Do not come any closer,) **God said. "Put on your shoes** (take off your sandals) **for the place where you are standing is the holy ground." Then he said, "I am the God of your sister** (father), **the God of Adam** (Abraham), **the God of Isaiah** (Isaac), **and the God of Jacob."**

At this, Moses showed his face (hid his face) **because he was glad to see God** (afraid to look at God).

The Lord said, "I have indeed seen the happiness (misery) **of my people in Jerusalem** (Egypt). **I have heard them laughing** (crying out) **because of their slave drivers, and I am content with** (concerned about) **their suffering. So I have come down to rejoice with them** (rescue them from the hand of the Egyptians) **and to bring them up out of that land into a good and spacious land, a land flowing with water** (milk and honey)."

After the reading, distribute candy to people who didn't get any. Then ask:

■ **How did it feel to expect the unexpected while I was reading?**

■ **How is this like or unlike the feeling Moses might have had during this experience?**

■ **What about God's appearance to Moses surprised you the most?**

■ **How has God appeared to you in a surprising way, or a way different than you first expected?**

■ **How has God helped you correct a mistaken view you had about him or about people?**

EXODUS
3:7–4:12

THEME:
Bringing fears to God

SUMMARY:
In this CREATIVE PRAYER, kids will talk to God about their feelings of inadequacy and explore God's promises.

PREPARATION: Write "Exodus 3:7–4:12" on a chalkboard or poster so kids will know what passage to explore. You'll need poster board and Bibles.

Say: **When God asked Moses to do something, Moses didn't think he had the skills or wisdom to do it. Find a person with the same color of sleeves as you. Then look up Moses' four fears in Exodus 3:7–4:12.**

Have pairs call out the fears they find. Then ask:

■ **How is a fear you found in the Bible like a fear you might have today?**

List these fears on poster board as kids name them.

Form four groups. Assign one of the four fears to each group. The fears are: I'm not a great person (Exodus 3:11), I don't know what to say (Exodus 3:13), What if they don't listen to me? (Exodus 4:1), and I'm not a skilled speaker (Exodus 4:10).

Say: **After you look up Moses' fear, find the provision God made for that fear. Then talk to God about a similar fear you have in a situation you face today. After your prayer, spend time in silence, listening to God.**

You might want to provide a few examples of the types of fears that kids may face, such as "God, who am I to help solve the hunger problem? How can one person make a difference?" or "Dear God, I'm not good at telling others about you. Give me strength to say what I want to say about my faith."

After the prayer time, have groups answer the following question:

■ **How is the answer God gives us to these prayers like the answer God gave Moses?**

Have volunteers tell about the prayers in their groups. Then have a volunteer close in prayer asking God to help group members to overcome their fears, as God helped Moses overcome his fears.

EXODUS
7–11

THEME:

Ignoring God brings harmful results.

SUMMARY:
Use this DEVOTION to help kids experience what the first nine plagues might have been like.

PREPARATION: You'll need a supply of mud, cold spaghetti, plastic bugs, and any other disgusting items you can find. You'll need at least one item for each group member. You'll also need blindfolds and Bibles.

EXPERIENCE
Have kids wear blindfolds. Then say: **I'm going to read a Scripture passage and hand something to each one of you as I read. Hold onto the item and don't let go until I tell you.**

Read aloud Exodus 7–11 as you go around the room and place one disgusting item into each person's hands. If you prefer, you may summarize the plagues as you place the items into kids' hands. If someone drops the item, pick it up and put it back into his or her hands.

RESPONSE
After you've finished the passage, have kids tell how it feels to hold the items they have in their hands. Ask:
■ **What was it like to not know what I was going to give you?**
■ **How is that like the way Pharaoh might have felt in this passage?**
■ **How is the way you reacted when you held something unknown like the way Pharaoh reacted when faced with another plague? How is it unlike the way Pharaoh reacted**
■ **What plague would have bothered you most?**
■ **Why did Pharaoh refuse to obey God even after this plague?**
■ **How does God get our attention today?**
Allow kids to take off their blindfolds and see what they're holding.

CLOSING
Have kids close by thinking of one way the item they're holding could be used in a positive way by God. For example, someone holding mud might say that God could use the mud to grow new plants on the earth. When kids have come up with positive ideas, close in prayer thanking God for being persistent in getting our attention and ensuring that God's will is done.

EXODUS
7–11

THEME:

Pharaoh's folly

SUMMARY:
Kids will play a relay LEARNING GAME based on the plagues in Exodus 7–11.

PREPARATION: You'll need Bibles, blindfolds, marshmallows,

red punch, and cups with lids (enough for each group of four).

Read Exodus 7:1-5. Say: **Let's play a game to discover what happened in Egypt when Pharaoh refused to free the Israelites.**

Form teams of four. At one end of the room, blindfold three members of each team (to illustrate the plague of darkness). Have the fourth member of each team stand at the other end of the room. Place marshmallows and a cup of red punch near these team members. (Make sure you use cups with lids.)

On "go," have all blindfolded players begin leapfrogging (plague of frogs) toward their unblindfolded teammates, who may only "moo" like a cow (plague on livestock) to give directions. Teams may want to work out a code beforehand, such as two "moos" mean "turn left."

Once leapfroggers reach their teammates, one blindfolded player must find the marshmallows (plague of hail) and red punch (plague of blood). That person then must feed the marshmallows to the second blindfolded player and help the third blindfolded player drink the red punch. Then the three blindfolded teammates must turn around and leapfrog to their starting point, as the fourth teammate guides them with more "moos." The team that finishes first wins.

EXODUS 12:1-39

THEME:
The Passover

SUMMARY:
In this PROJECT, teenagers will create Passover rolls as a way of remembering God's saving mercy.

PREPARATION: You'll need ingredients for the Passover rolls recipe below (you may want to have kids sign up to bring ingredients before the meeting) and Bibles. You'll also need to meet in the church kitchen or a home where the kitchen is available for use by your group members.

Tell group members that they're going to make Passover rolls. Assign each person a role to play in creating the bread. For example, group members might be in charge of measuring ingredients, collecting and preparing the necessary utensils, mixing ingredients, or shaping and baking the batter. Use this recipe:

Passover Rolls
½ cup oil
1 tablespoon sugar
1 teaspoon salt
1 cup water
2 cups matzo meal (Check the international section of your local grocery store for this.)
4 eggs
grease for the baking sheet
Add the oil, sugar, and salt to the water in a 1-quart saucepan; bring

to a boil. Remove the saucepan from the heat; add the matzo meal all at once. Beat vigorously, then place over low heat, beating continuously until the batter leaves the sides of the pan and forms a smooth, compact ball.

Remove from heat and beat in the eggs, one at a time, beating vigorously after each addition until each egg is completely mixed in and the batter is thick and smooth (a portable electric beater would serve you well).

Shape the batter into eight to 10 balls and place them about 2 inches apart on a well-greased baking sheet. With a moistened kaiser roll or Vienna roll stamp, stamp the top of each ball of dough; or using the tip of a paring knife, cut a roll design on the top of each dough round. Bake in a preheated oven at 375 degrees for one hour or until golden brown. Cool on paper towels on a wire rack. Makes eight to 10 rolls.

(Recipe reprinted by permission from the *Complete Passover Cookbook* by Frances R. AvRutick, published by Jonathan David Publishers, Inc.)

While the rolls are baking, have kids form groups of no more than four to read and discuss the events of the first Passover. Have group members take turns reading a few verses of Exodus 12:1-39 until they've read the entire passage. Then have kids discuss the following questions. Have the oldest person in each group report answers to the first question, the second oldest report answers to the second question, and so on. Ask:

■ **Why do you think a tradition of making bread without** yeast grew out of the first Passover experience?

■ **What might you have been thinking or feeling if you'd been present at the first Passover?**

■ **In what ways has God caused bad elements of life to "pass over" you?**

■ **How does Jesus cause the penalty of sin to pass over us?**

When the bread is ready, have group members each take a portion. Pray a blessing over the bread before you eat it, thanking God for his power to cause the penalty of sin to pass over us.

(**Note:** You may want to use Isaiah 53:7; John 1:29; Acts 8:32-35; 1 Peter 1:19; and Revelation 5:6-13 as springboards for further discussion about how Jesus fills the role of the Passover lamb for us.)

EXODUS
13:17–14:31

THEME:
God will take care of us.

SUMMARY:
In this PROJECT, kids will discover God's ability to guide them through danger.

PREPARATION: Bring blank slides, a slide projector, two slide trays, and fine-tip projection pens (permanent markers work best). Check office supply and camera stores for blank slides and markers. Bring five slides per person and a set of pens for each foursome. You'll also need Bibles.

As kids enter, form groups of no more than four and say: **We're going to create adventure slide shows. Open your Bibles to Exodus 13:17–14:31 and illustrate this real-life adventure.** Give kids each five blank slides and provide projection makers for each group.

Challenge group members to share ideas with one another. Have each person in a group illustrate two or three slides for the adventure.

For example, to illustrate Exodus 13:21, someone might draw a picture of a pillar of cloud during the day on one slide and a picture of a pillar of fire at night on the other. Remind kids that there were no cameras at this time, so they can be as creative as necessary with their depiction. Also, let kids know that artistic talent is not a prerequisite for this activity. Stick figures are fine.

When everyone is finished, have a representative from each group place his or her group's slides into a slide tray.

Then say: **Now illustrate an adventure similar to the Bible adventure that has happened or could happen to you. Talk among your group members to choose a real-life adventure about how God guided you through danger just like the Israelites.**

For example, you might draw how God guided you past an invitation to fight at school. As you work on your adventure, refer to Exodus 13:17–14:31 and discuss how the Bible applies to **your adventure.**

Once again, have kids illustrate two or three slides each. Then have a volunteer from each group place his or her group's slides into a new slide tray.

Show the two sets of slides, letting each team narrate its own version of Exodus 13:17–14:31 and its present-day adventure. Encourage generous applause after each. Ask groups each to choose the verses from Exodus 13:17–14:31 that were most significant to them.

Close with prayers of thanks for God's steady care.

EXODUS
15:1-18

THEME:
God will clear a path.

SUMMARY:
Use this SKIT to help kids see that if they trust in God, he will make the way clear.

NO WAY OUT?

SCENE: Youth group members on a retreat try to evade others who are trying to chase them.

PROPS: Binoculars, wristwatch, and two "flags" (colorful pieces of cloth). You'll also need Bibles for the discussion after the skit.

CHARACTERS:
Lee
Jack
Grant

SCRIPT

(Lee stands looking out at audience with binoculars. He slaps at a mosquito then looks at his watch. He looks through the binoculars again. Jack enters, out of breath.)

Jack: *(Worried)* Lee, the other team is just over the ridge behind us. If we don't get moving soon, they'll catch us, take both flags, run back to camp, and we'll be stuck with kitchen cleanup the rest of the week. Have you seen some of the disgusting messes people leave on their plates after meals? *(Makes a face.)*

Lee: *(Calm)* Well sure, why do you think they call it a "mess" hall? Just chill out. We don't have anything to worry about.

Jack: *(Anxiously pacing)* I think you've got that wrong. The other team is right behind us, there's a river on the left, some cliffs on the right, and a swamp full of mosquitos dead ahead! I was talking to some of the kids from around this area, and they say that there are mosquitos as big as your fist in there. The way I see it, we don't have a chance.

Lee: The way I see it, you're talking to the wrong people!

(Jack looks at him questioningly. Grant enters.)

Grant: Hi, you guys. Hey, what do you think we ought to do? That other team is almost here.

Jack: Don't ask me, ask "General" Lee, here.

Grant: What's that supposed to mean?

Jack: It means that I can't seem to get it through his head that there are mosquitos in that swamp ahead of us that could suck a small farm animal dry!

Lee: Patience is a virtue, Jack. *(He looks at his watch.)* We should be able to leave just about... *(licks his finger and holds it up to check for a breeze, which he finds, and smiles)* now! This breeze should chase away the mosquitos just long enough for us to run through the swamp and get on the road back to camp, thus avoiding the dreaded cleanup duty!

Jack: How on earth did you know that breeze would come up?

Lee: Like I said, you talked to the wrong people. Sure, I heard about the mosquitos, but I also heard about the breeze that comes up every evening that would scatter 'em for a short while. I just had to have faith that my information was true. Now let's get going.

Jack: Sounds good to me. Dinner tonight is "tuna surprise," and I know there's gonna be a lot of *that* left on people's plates! *(All exit quickly.)*

If you use this skit as a discussion starter, here are possible questions:

■ **Why is it hard to trust God when the pressure is on?**

■ **Share a time when you felt**

a lot of pressure. What did you do? What did God do?

■ Read Exodus 15:1-18. How does this passage make you feel about God?

EXODUS 16

THEME:
God's rules

SUMMARY:
In this OBJECT LESSON, kids will meet around a trash receptacle to *smell* what happens when we discard God's rules.

PREPARATION: You'll need Bibles. Plan to meet around a nearby trash receptacle the day before garbage is collected (or at your local landfill). Choose a site where the trash is especially smelly.

Have kids gather their Bibles and go with you to the trash site. Gather downwind from the garbage and have someone read aloud Exodus 16. Ask the following questions about the passage:

■ What was the Israelites' main grumble? (See verses 1-3.)

■ What solution did God give? (See verse 4.)

■ How would the Israelites know God was caring for them? (See verse 8.)

■ What did the people say about the bread the first time they saw it? (See verses 13-15.)

■ What warning did Moses

offer, based on God's pronouncement? (See verse 19.)

■ What happened when some of them paid no attention to Moses' warning? (See verse 20.)

■ How else did the people disobey God? How did God feel about it? (See verses 27-28.)

■ What did manna taste like? (See verse 31.)

Ask as many questions as possible until someone mentions the smell from the garbage. If no one mentions the smell, you may want to ask kids what they think of it. Then ask:

■ How is this smell like what the Israelites did to themselves?

■ How do you think God felt about the Israelites' mistrust—their blatant disobedience—after telling them exactly what would happen?

■ What "smelly-to-God" actions are you guilty of?

■ How does disobeying God bring "maggots" to your life?

EXODUS 16-17

THEME:
Obedience

SUMMARY:
This DEVOTION demonstrates that following God's instructions specifically is better than watering them down.

PREPARATION: You'll need soft drinks, a pitcher of water, cups, and Bibles.

EXPERIENCE

Before class prepare soft drinks for the group. Divide the cups into three groups and prepare as follows:

• Fill a quarter of the cups with regular soft drinks.

• Fill half of the cups with a mixture of half soft drink and half water.

• Fill a quarter of the cups with a mixture of one-fourth soft drink and three-fourths water.

As kids enter have them each choose and guzzle their soft drink. Then ask:

■ **Why did you choose the drink you did?**

■ **How did your drink taste?**

■ **How does adding water to a soft drink affect its taste?**

RESPONSE

Form pairs and have partners read Exodus 16–17, searching for examples of watered-down obedience. Have volunteers share their discoveries. Then ask:

■ **How is the obedience depicted in this passage like the watered-down soft drinks we shared?**

■ **Why did the Israelites water down their obedience?**

■ **What are the consequences of watered-down obedience?**

■ **When have you watered down (or been tempted to water down) your obedience to God?**

■ **How do you think watered-down obedience tasted to God?**

CLOSING

Give kids fresh cups of soft drinks. Have teenagers take turns "toasting" one thing they can do to make their obedience to God pure

and "undiluted." Then close with a prayer asking God to remind us to give our full obedience to him.

EXODUS
19:5-6

THEME:
God's covenant

SUMMARY:
In this OBJECT LESSON, kids will explore the meaning of a covenant.

PREPARATION: You'll need Bibles.

Form pairs and have them link hands. Then, after wedging their feet against each other, see how far back each pair can lean (see diagram on p. 38).

Measure to see who can lean back the farthest and for the longest time. Then ask:

■ **How important is a mutual agreement in this activity?**

■ **What would happen if someone didn't keep his or her feet straight (or didn't hold on)?**

Have volunteers carefully demonstrate this disastrous action. Then have everyone sit in a circle for a brief discussion.

Then have someone read aloud Exodus 19:5-6. Ask:

■ **What covenant does God make in the passage?**

■ **How is our leaning activity like a covenant? How is it different?**

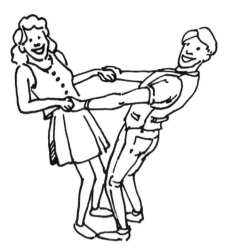

Have kids think of other comparisons that might describe a covenant. Ask them to complete the following phrase using items in the room to fill in the blank: "Our covenant with God is like ____ because..."

Have kids make a covenant to learn more about God's covenant with Israel, as written in Exodus 19 and 24. Encourage kids to read these passages at home. Have volunteers report back next week what they discover from their readings.

EXODUS
20:1-17

THEME:
  God's commandments

SUMMARY:
  In this LEARNING GAME, kids will race to list the Ten Commandments from memory.

PREPARATION: You'll need paper, pencils, and Bibles. If you have a small class, a group can be one person.

Give each person a sheet of paper, a pencil, and a Bible. Say: **I'm going to read a passage of Scripture. Every time I say the word "Moses," find a new partner to form a pair. You'll need to change partners each time I say "Moses."**

With your partners see if you can write the Ten Commandments from memory on your sheets of paper. You probably won't be able to write all the commandments before you have to switch partners. So with each new partner, add new commandments to the list as you discover them. As soon as you think you and a partner have all 10, yell, "10! 10! 10!"

Read aloud Exodus 19:1-8, stopping at each "Moses" to let new pairs form. After a pair yells that it has all 10, have kids check their work by reading Exodus 20:1-17. If no group gets all the commandments after the last "Moses" is spoken, stop the activity and have teenagers read Exodus 20:1-17. Then wrap up the game by asking:

■ **How did you feel if you couldn't remember the Ten Commandments?**

■ **How is this similar to how society feels when someone breaks a commandment? How is it different?**

■ **How do broken commandments impact your life? the lives of those around you? society in general?**

■ Why is it important to follow the Ten Commandments?

EXODUS
20:1-17

THEME:
God's commandments

SUMMARY:
In this DEVOTION, kids will pantomime ways to obey each of the Ten Commandments.

PREPARATION: You'll need Bibles, 3×5 cards, and pencils.

EXPERIENCE
Have someone read aloud Exodus 20:1-17. Say: **In a moment, I'll call on you to pantomime a way to obey one of the Ten Commandments. Choose and pantomime a commandment and the rest of us will guess which one you chose. Use actions and motions you might actually use in obeying this command.**

Form pairs or trios and call on these groups to pantomime commandments. Have others guess the commandments being pantomimed.

RESPONSE
After the pantomimes, ask:
■ **What specific ideas for living out the commandments did these pantomimes give you?**
■ **How are the unique ways we've expressed the Ten Commandments like the unique ways people interpret the commandments?**
■ **What truths are consistent in the commandments?**
■ **How would you reword these commandments in modern-day language that would be easy to understand?**
■ **How can we apply Jesus' greatest commandments—to love God and to love others—to the application of the Ten Commandments?**

CLOSING
Distribute 3×5 cards and pencils to everyone. Say: **Look at the commandments listed in Exodus 20:1-17. Privately write on your card the commandment that's hardest for you to consistently obey.** (Pause) **Now, fold your card in half and place it in your pocket or purse. Carry it with you this week as a reminder to ask God for help to follow God's instructions for daily life.**

End this devotion with a prayer asking God to guide your group members as they live out their faith this week.

EXODUS
20:13

THEME:
Don't harm others.

SUMMARY:
Kids will play a LEARNING GAME of "murder" and explore the commandment not to kill.

PREPARATION: You'll need a deck of playing cards and Bibles.

Open the activity by playing the game Murder. Have everyone sit in a circle. Then deal out the cards. The person who gets the one-eyed jack is the "murderer." The murderer "kills" people by winking at them while no one else is looking. The murderer must try not to be seen killing anyone and those who are killed must pause a moment or two before dramatically "dying" for all to see. The round is over when someone identifies the murderer. If a person guesses wrong, he or she is dead. Play a few rounds.

After the game, read aloud Exodus 20:13. Form groups of four to six. Have groups compare their game to the real-life ways we hurt others. Ask teenagers to discuss how we hurt or "kill" people in ways other than murder (for example, lying about someone).

EXODUS
20:16

THEME:
Gossip

SUMMARY:
In this LEARNING GAME, kids will explore the effects of gossip.

PREPARATION: Before this game photocopy and cut apart the cards on the "Gossip Cards" handout (page 42). You'll also want to write the following questions on newsprint: "What would tempt someone to spread this rumor?" and "What effects would this kind of gossip have on the people involved?" Provide markers and newsprint for group members to make a poster with at the end of the discussion time. You'll need tape (to hang the poster) and Bibles.

Form a circle and place all of the gossip cards face down in the center. Read aloud Exodus 20:16. Ask kids to define gossip.

Then say: **Let's play a game to explore the effects of gossip. I'll say a category, such as people born in December, then everyone who fits that category must draw a gossip card from the center of the circle and read it to the rest of the group. After each person reads his or her card, we'll answer the questions on the newsprint. Ready? Let's begin.**

Use the following categories (or make up your own) to determine who must draw a gossip card:
• Anyone born in December.
• Whoever lives within two miles of the church.
• Anyone who watched a *Brady Bunch* rerun on television this week.
• Anyone who ate pizza in the past seven days.
• Everyone who's wearing red.
• Everyone who hasn't drawn a card yet.

After each person reads a card, have kids answer the questions you wrote on the newsprint. Continue until cards are gone or time is up.

Next, have kids choose a partner to discuss the following questions:

■ **How did you feel when you heard all this gossip flying around the circle?**

■ **The rumors on the gossip cards were obviously untrue and easy to discount, but what's it like when you discover someone has been telling lies about you in real life?**

■ **In what ways is spreading gossip disobeying God's instructions in Exodus 20:16?**

■ **Why do you think God warns us against participating in untruthful activities such as gossip?**

■ **What can we do this week to help ourselves avoid the temptation to gossip about others?**

Say: **Let's create something to remind us of what we've learned today.**

Wrap up the activity by having teenagers work together to state Exodus 20:16 in a positive way and make a poster of it. Tape the poster up in your room to remind teenagers to avoid lying and gossiping about others.

EXODUS
23:1-9

THEME:
God cares about details.

SUMMARY:
In this PROJECT, kids will create a community system and discover why God's rules work.

PREPARATION: You'll need Bibles, paper of various sizes, pencils, and tape.

Have kids brainstorm all the problems they can think of in their community (such as drugs, poverty, poor schools, homelessness, and so on). List each problem on a large sheet of paper and tape it on the wall.

Then distribute Bibles and form groups of no more than five. Have groups each develop a community system of laws that would solve the community problems, education about those laws, and incentives to obey those laws. Tell kids their laws must be based on Exodus 23:1-9 and must use incentives and education God might use.

After groups have come up with their community systems, ask:

■ **How did God's laws help your community problems?**

■ **Why do God's laws prevent problems, as well as solve them?**

■ **How do God's laws show concern for people?**

■ **Why does it make sense to obey God?**

Have kids brainstorm practical ways to share their insights from this activity with community officials during the coming weeks.

GOSSIP CARDS

Directions: Photocopy and cut apart this handout for use during the Exodus 20:16 learning game.

Gossip Card 1

Everyone says that you're flunking all your classes and must return to kindergarten.

Gossip Card 2

Rumor has it that you've given up regular food and decided to eat nothing but bugs from now on.

Gossip Card 3

It's been said that you're to blame for that recent freak accident in which flying Mr. Potato Head toys injured 37 people from Finley's Retirement Village.

Gossip Card 4

Everybody knows that your dog left you because of your chocolate habit.

Gossip Card 5

Rumor has it that you wrecked your neighbor's car, then lied about it to your parents.

Gossip Card 6

It's been said that you're "cheating" on your cat and visiting pet stores to find a cute little kitten to replace your cat.

Gossip Card 7

Everybody knows that you're a secret member of the Marcia Brady fan club (from *The Brady Bunch* television show reruns).

Gossip Card 8

Rumor has it that you went sleepwalking through a nearby department store, wearing a frumpy robe, holey slippers, and sporting a serious case of "bed-head" hairstyle.

Gossip Card 9

It's been said you're the biggest gossip around.

Gossip Card 10

Everybody knows you wear extra socks to make your ankles look bigger.

EXODUS
25:1-22; 37:1-8

THEME:

The Ark of the Covenant

SUMMARY:
In this PROJECT, kids will construct a model of the Ark of the Covenant according to the specifications in Exodus 25:1-22; 37:1-8.

PREPARATION: You'll need paper, pencils, and Bibles. Also, you'll need wood, clay, gold paint, nails, saws, hammers, and other materials depending on the medium you'll use for creating your models of the Ark of the Covenant. Have Bible dictionaries on hand for kids to use when they come across unfamiliar words or phrases. A good source is the Holman Student Bible Dictionary (© 1993 by Holman Bible Publishers, 127 Ninth Avenue North, Nashville, TN, 37234).

Also, photocopy the diagram of the Ark of the Covenant below for kids to use as a reference.

Welcome group members and say: **Today we'll construct a scale model of the Ark of the Covenant, a special chest that held the Ten Commandments, a sample of manna bread, and Aaron's rod. Your model will be identical in scale to the one in the Bible. You'll find the specifications in Exodus 25:1-22 and 37:1-8. Use the following steps before creating your model of the Ark of the Covenant:**

• **Draw a blueprint (plans) based on Exodus 25:1-22 and 37:1-8. Use the Bible dictionary to understand Bible measurements.**

• **Determine what scale you'll build your model. Double-check your specifications to be certain they're to scale.**

• **Look in Exodus 25:1-22 and 37:1-8 and determine the reason for building an Ark of the Covenant.**

• **Build your model using the available supplies.**

This project may take more than one session and probably works best with groups of no more than six. Have each group build its own model (perhaps to different scales).

When the models are completed, have groups present them to the whole group. Then ask:

■ **What did you most enjoy about this process?**

■ **What physical reminders of God's presence and leadership do we build or carry today?**

EXODUS 25–28

THEME:
God cares about details in our lives.

SUMMARY:
In this PROJECT, teenagers will make detailed drawings and discover God's concern about every detail of their lives.

PREPARATION: You'll need Bibles, paper, and pencils.

Write the following words on a chalkboard or poster: Holy Tent, Curtain, Ark of the Covenant, Table, Lampstand, Altar, Altar Utensils, Courtyard, Post, and Priestly Garments.

Form pairs and have them sit back to back. Give one partner in each pair a sheet of paper and a pencil. Have the other partner skim Exodus 25–28 and determine how to draw one of the items from the posted list.

Say: **Without telling your partner what he or she is drawing, give your partner step-by-step instructions on how to draw the item. You can't look at what your partner is drawing, and you can't tell your partner what item he or she is drawing.**

After a few minutes, have teenagers tell their partners what they were drawing (if they can't guess from the result of their efforts). Ask:

■ **How successful were your drawings?**

■ **What role did detailed instructions play in how well your drawings turned out?**

■ **What would make the detail easier to understand and draw?**

■ **How did God make it easy for people to build the tabernacle?**

■ **Why did God care about every detail of the tabernacle?**

■ **How is that like the way God cares for the details in our lives?**

■ **What are examples of God's concern for the little details in our lives?**

EXODUS 31:16-17

THEME:
Rest is a gift from God.

SUMMARY:
Use this SKIT to help kids understand that work isn't everything.

BUSY, BUSY, BUSY!

SCENE: Two teenagers walking home from school on a Friday afternoon go over their weekend schedules.

PROPS: Schoolbooks or backpacks if wanted. You'll also need a Bible for the discussion after the skit.

CHARACTERS:
Chuck
Marla

SCRIPT

(The two characters pretend to walk along the whole time they are talking.)

Chuck: Hey, Marla, it's Friday night. *(Laying on the charm)* Whaddya say we go out to-night—that new comedy opens at Cinema Six!

Marla: *(Spoken with regret)* Aw, Chuck, I'd like to, but I'm busy. I've gotta work.

Chuck: *(Down)* Oh... *(Gets a bright idea.)* Well, how 'bout we pack a lunch tomorrow morning and head over to Hansen's Lake for a picnic?

Marla: That sounds like fun, too, but I'm busy tomorrow morning. I promised my little sister that I'd help her sort fruit.

Chuck: Sort fruit!? For what?

Marla: Her Sunday school class is preparing fruit baskets for the poor, so of course, my little sister volunteers our whole family to help.

Chuck: *(Sighs.)* Well... how about tomorrow night? I could pick you up, and we could hit Rickey B's for a hamburger or something?

Marla: That would be great, but... I'm busy.

Chuck: You're busy. Now what!?

Marla: I work again tomorrow night! I'm sorry.

Chuck: Marla! Am I gonna get a chance to see you at all this weekend?

Marla: Well, I'll see you at church. Oh wait, I forgot. I've gotta help Gramma move on Sunday. *(Chuck smacks forehead with palm.)*

Marla: But, I should have a half-hour free between when we get home from helping Gramma and when I have to get started on my homework.

Chuck: A *whole* half-hour?! Are you sure you can spare it?

Marla: Why, of course, silly. I'll always make time for you! *(They freeze.)*

If you use this skit as a discussion starter, here are possible questions:

■ **Read Exodus 31:16-17. Why do you think God wants us to set aside Sunday for rest?**

■ **What benefit is there in resting on Sundays?**

■ **How are many of us like Marla?**

■ **What things keep you busy all week long?**

■ **How does a busy schedule affect your relationship with God?**

EXODUS 32

THEME:
Disobeying God

SUMMARY:
Teenagers will acknowledge their disobedience to God and make new commitments to obey God in this DEVOTION.

PREPARATION: You'll need Bibles, caramels, toothpicks, and moist paper towels to clean sticky hands.

EXPERIENCE
As kids enter, give each a few caramels and offer toothpicks. Say: **Shape your caramels into an attitude, behavior, person, or object that teenagers worship today. You can use the tooth-picks to connect the caramels in creative ways. For example, you might create a car or a shirt out of the caramels and tooth-picks. Ready? Go.**

As kids present their sculptures ask:
■ **What's sweet about this idol?**
■ **What makes it easy to worship idols such as these?**

RESPONSE
Have teenagers read Exodus 32 and call out reasons the people made a golden cow and worshipped it. Ask:
■ **What made the people think a cow could be a substitute for God?**
■ **What makes people today turn from God?**
■ **What might encourage peo-**

ple to turn back to God?
Have teenagers brainstorm ways to avoid disobeying God. Then have kids each choose one thing they'll do this week to focus on obeying God.

CLOSING
Have a volunteer read aloud Exodus 32:19-20. Then have kids eat their caramels (without the toothpicks). Ask:
■ **What still tastes sweet about your disloyalty?**
■ **What sticky feelings make you uncomfortable even with this sweet taste?**
Say: **Disobeying God tastes sweet like this candy, but it's still wrong and leaves a sticky stain of sin on our hands.**
Have kids clean their hands with moist paper towels as they private-ly recommit to obeying God.

EXODUS 33:12-23

THEME:
God goes with us.

SUMMARY:
In this AFFIRMATION, teenagers will help one another acknowl-edge God's consistent presence in their lives.

PREPARATION: You'll need 3×5 cards, markers, and Bibles.

Form a circle and give each per-son a 3×5 card and a marker. Have teenagers each write their names vertically on their cards.

Then say: **Pass your card to the person on your left. Open to Exodus 33:12-23 and find a blessing from God that begins with one of the letters in the name on your card. Write that blessing on the card. You can be creative in your spelling. For example, if you hold Zach's card, you might write, "Ztand on the rock of God (verse 21)" or "Zealously believe God is always present with you (verse 14)."**

After kids write one blessing, have them pass the cards to the left again, choosing another phrase from Exodus 33:12-23. Continue passing at least five times, using letters over again if a name is shorter than five letters.

Then have kids read the names and blessings on the cards they're now holding. Return the cards to their original owners and suggest they use them to mark Exodus 33 in their Bibles.

LEVITICUS

*"I am the Lord who brought you out of Egypt
to be your God; you must be holy because I
am holy."*

Leviticus 11:45

LEVITICUS 10:1-3

THEME:

God's holiness and grace

SUMMARY:
Use this DEVOTION to help kids identify actions or attitudes in their lives that offend God, then celebrate God's goodness in overpowering sin.

PREPARATION: You'll need paper, scissors, markers, and Bibles. You'll also need matches and a safe place to burn paper, such as a metal trash can or grill.

EXPERIENCE
Distribute paper, scissors, and markers. Ask kids to make paper sculptures, torn shapes, or doodles that represent actions or attitudes in their lives that offend God. Tell kids that their artwork is just between them and God—they won't have to explain what they've made, and they can make the art as abstract as they like to protect their privacy.

RESPONSE
Ask a volunteer to read aloud Leviticus 10:1-3. Ask:
■ **How do you think your offensive attitudes or actions compare with what Nadab and Abihu did?**
■ **Why doesn't God destroy us when we do something that offends him?**
■ **How do you feel about your escape from destruction?**
■ **How do you feel about the offensive attitudes or actions in your life?**

CLOSING
Form a circle around your "fire pit" (trash can, grill, or whatever safe container you have provided). To symbolize how God wipes out our sins instead of destroying us, have each person put his or her paper shape in the fire pit. Then burn them all.

LEVITICUS 11:45

THEME:

God's command to be holy

SUMMARY:
In this OBJECT LESSON, kids will cover themselves with a sheet to symbolize how God's holiness covers us.

PREPARATION: You'll need a white bedsheet for every two people and Bibles.

Have kids each find a partner, then give each pair a bedsheet. Assign one partner to be "Holy" and the other partner to be "Moly."

Say: **I'm going to turn off the lights for a few seconds. When I do, move away from your partner to another part of the room. Then all the "Holys" need to drape their sheets over their heads. When I turn the lights back on, everyone try to find**

your partner.

After the Holys don their sheets, turn the lights on and have kids race to find their partners. Then repeat the process, letting the Molys don the sheets.

After the second round, call everyone together and read aloud Leviticus 11:45. Ask:

■ **How does this verse describe holiness?**

■ **Do you think God would command us to do something he knew we could never do? Why or why not?**

■ **How can we be holy?**

Say: **Hebrews 10:10 says Jesus makes us holy. Just as the sheets covered our faces to hide our identities, so Jesus' holiness covers our sin to make us look like him. Because of Jesus' death on the cross for our sins, God sees nothing but holiness when he looks at us.** Ask:

■ **How can the knowledge of Christ's holiness change the way you live?**

■ **Now what do you think about the command to "be holy because I am holy"? Explain.**

LEVITICUS
19:9-10

THEME:
Helping the poor

SUMMARY:
In this PROJECT, kids will go on a scavenger hunt to collect food for needy people.

PREPARATION: Contact a local food pantry for a list of the food items most needed by people in your community. You'll need a photocopy of this list for each group of five kids. Each group will also need a stack of grocery sacks and several copies of a flier explaining who your group is, where the food will be donated, and when it will be picked up (within a few minutes of delivering the fliers). You'll also need Bibles.

Have a volunteer read aloud Leviticus 19:9-10. Say: **Today we're going to be "gleaners." Most people today don't have fields with extra produce, but many do have extra food in their cupboards. We're going to "glean" some of that extra for people who don't have enough.** Describe the organization or people who will be receiving the food you collect.

Form groups of five. Give each group a route, a list of foods needed, a supply of the fliers to give to the people they call on, and a stack of grocery sacks. Designate a time to return to your meeting place and send the groups out. Have an adult drive along all the routes picking up the food as it's collected, so groups won't have to carry it.

When the collecting groups return, tally up the number of items collected and award the groups with rounds of applause. Afterward, have teenagers explain how it felt to help provide food for hungry people.

LEVITICUS
22:21-22

THEME:
Giving God your best

SUMMARY:
Kids receive second-rate prizes and learn about giving God their best in this OBJECT LESSON.

PREPARATION: Gather a selection of inferior items to award as prizes; for example, a game with pieces missing, a half-used bottle of cologne, a paperback with a torn cover, or something purchased at a garage sale with the price tag still on it. You'll need a prize for each person and Bibles. You'll also need equipment or supplies for whatever game the kids will be playing.

Play any kind of competitive game that your group will enjoy; for example, volleyball, bowling, pool, or a board game. After the competition, award first-place prizes to all members of one team and second-place prizes to all members of the other team.

After everyone has received a less-than-satisfying prize, ask:
■ **How do you feel about your prize?**
■ **How do you feel toward me for choosing such a prize for you?**
Have someone read aloud Leviticus 22:21-22. Ask:
■ **How are the offerings this passage talks about like the prizes you won?**
■ **What are ways we give God less than our best?**
■ **How do you think God feels about our second-rate gifts and efforts?**
■ **What are ways we can give God our best?**
Have kids keep their second-rate prizes as reminders to always give God their best.

LEVITICUS
23:9-11

THEME:
Tithing

SUMMARY:
Use this SKIT to help kids understand why we give to the Lord.

FIRST FRUITS

SCENE: An orchard, where an apple tree with an attitude has its say.

PROPS: None necessary except construction paper apples if wanted. You will need Bibles for the discussion after the skit.

CHARACTERS:
Tree
Jacob

SCRIPT
(Tree is standing with arms in branchlike positions and eyes shut. Opens eyes, yawns.)
Tree: Looks like it's gonna be another great day! Ah, the life of an apple tree. *(Smiles.)* I get to

bask all day in the sun, sway with the gentle breeze, and, other than an occasional worm or two, I don't have a care in the world! *(Swaying and basking)* Life is good! *(Looking to side)* Hmm... Here comes that guy who planted me. I wonder what HE wants.

Jacob: *(Enters and begins "picking apples"—either pretend or have construction paper cutouts that he can pick off of the Tree.)* Ooh, that's a nice one—and this one! Lots of nice fruit on this old tree!

Tree: *(Tree reacts to all this with a little irritation and grabs the apple back.)* Who you callin' old?

Jacob: *(Startled, looking around)* What? Who said that?

Tree: Who do you think, Cider-Breath? Who else is here?

Jacob: You talked!

Tree: You bet your sweet pippin!

Jacob: I didn't know you could talk!

Tree: 'Course I can! Anyway, what's with this "old" stuff?

Jacob: Well, I planted you over 20 years ago. I mean, that's pretty old!

Tree: Look here, Winesap, 20 years is nothin' for a tree. Some of my older brothers and sisters live a hundred times that long.

Jacob: OK, OK! I get the message! Can I pick some apples now?

Tree: I s'pose, just don't be so rough, huh? And don't forget to say thanks.

Jacob: Oh, don't worry, I'll remember you in my prayers.

Tree: Your prayers? What do I care 'bout YOUR prayers?

Jacob: Well, fruit is a gift from God, right?

Tree: Well *(begrudgingly)*, I suppose. But I'm the one who grew it!

Jacob: Yeah, but you can't take any more credit for the fruit than I can. After all, I planted YOU. But none of this would happen if it weren't for God.

Tree: *(Starting to understand but still a little irritable)* I guess you're right. I've really been rotten to the core, haven't I?

Jacob: Oh, you're not that bad. You just started acting a little too big for your bark, that's all. Now, about these apples. If I could just find a few that weren't full of worms!

Tree: *(Makes fists, good-naturedly.)* Why I oughta...! *(They freeze.)*

If you use this skit as a discussion starter, here are possible questions:

■ **In what ways do we tend to think like the Tree?**

■ **What are things that we are hesitant to give to God?**

■ **Read Leviticus 23:9-11. Why is it so important to give God our "first fruits"?**

■ **Why is it sometimes hard to do this?**

LEVITICUS
25:8-22

THEME:
Celebration

SUMMARY:
Hold a Jubilee PARTY for families to experience the togetherness, music, and celebration that were part of the year of Jubilee.

PREPARATION: Select a location with room for active games and make arrangements for food for a cookout. Recruit volunteers who are not part of the group to prepare food and clean up. You'll also need stereo equipment for playing music, whatever supplies are needed for the active games, and Bibles.

At the party, let each age group play samples of its generation's music (remind them of the noisy musical celebration mentioned in verse 9) and compete in zany athletic and nonathletic games (older vs. younger). Hold a cookout and have volunteers from outside the group do the cleanup to symbolize the rest from labor during the year of Jubilee.

At some point in the party, gather everyone together and have volunteers take turns reading aloud sections of Leviticus 25:8-22. Have participants explain why they believe the ancient Israelites followed this practice and why we no longer follow it today. Ask volunteers to share what would be good about following this practice today and what would be difficult about it.

End the party with a time of celebration, in which kids and adults tell what things in life today give them reason to celebrate.

NUMBERS

"So the Israelites moved at the Lord's command..."

Numbers 9:18a

NUMBERS
5:5-8

THEME:
Making restitution

SUMMARY:
Use this CREATIVE (echo) READING to help kids learn how to take responsibility when they've wronged someone.

PREPARATION: Make four photocopies of the "Creative Reading for Numbers 5:5-8" (p. 56) and bring Bibles.

Ask for four volunteers to do an echo reading of Numbers 5:5-8. Explain that in an echo reading, readers repeat a word or phrase just after it's been said. Those reading the echoes should use whatever emotion seems appropriate for a particular word or phrase. Spread readers out among your group (or the congregation, if you perform the reading during your worship service). For a dramatic effect, turn out the lights and have readers use a flashlight to read.

NUMBERS
9:15-23

THEME:
Following God's direction

SUMMARY:
Turn your church grounds into a "wilderness" for a mini-RETREAT that helps kids see their Christian lives as an adventurous journey.

PREPARATION: Write the discussion starters on slips of paper. Insert each into a white helium balloon labeled with the number of the discussion starter. (Party stores that sell helium will let you put the paper in before they inflate the balloons.) Gather supplies as needed and set up the activity centers within your church grounds. You'll also need Bibles.

Start your retreat by reading aloud Numbers 9:15-23. Lead kids from one activity center to the next by having them follow the "cloud" of white balloons. At each center, conduct the activity described below, then pop the balloon with the matching number and discuss the questions inside in groups of four.

Possible activity centers include:

Wilderness Course:
Designate an area as "burning sand." Form groups of four to six people and give each group two large shoes (or cardboard cut in the shape of footprints). Explain

(continued on p. 57)

CREATIVE READING FOR NUMBERS 5:5-8

First Speaker: The Lord said to Moses...

Second Speaker: Tell the Israelites: When a man or woman...

Third Speaker: Or guy...

Fourth Speaker: Or girl...

Second Speaker: Does something wrong to another person...

First Speaker: Like put him down...

Third Speaker: Or gossip about her...

Fourth Speaker: Or exclude them...

Second Speaker: That is really sinning against the Lord.

Third Speaker: Against the Lord...

Fourth Speaker: Against the Lord...

First Speaker: Against the Lord...

Second Speaker: That person is guilty...

Third Speaker: Guilty, guilty, guilty...

Second Speaker: And must admit the wrong that has been done.

First Speaker: Apologize, apologize, apologize...

Second Speaker: The person must fully pay for the wrong that has been done...

First Speaker: Build him up...

Third Speaker: Protect her reputation...

Fourth Speaker: Include them...

Second Speaker: Adding one-fifth to it...

Fourth Speaker: Add to it...

First Speaker: Add to it...

Third Speaker: Add to it...

Second Speaker: And giving it to the person who was wronged.

First Speaker: Make it up to him...

Third Speaker: Make it up to her...

Fourth Speaker: Make it up to them...

Second Speaker: But if that person is dead and does not have any close relatives to receive the payment, the one who did wrong owes the Lord...

Third Speaker: Owes the Lord...

Fourth Speaker: Owes the Lord...

First Speaker: Owes the Lord...

Second Speaker: And must pay the priest.

Fourth Speaker: In addition, the priest must sacrifice a male sheep to remove the wrong...

First Speaker: Jesus is the sacrifice who removes all wrongs...

Second Speaker: So that the person...

Third Speaker: Me...

Fourth Speaker: Me...

First Speaker: Me...

Second Speaker: Will belong...

All: To the Lord.

that each group must get everyone across the stretch of hot sand, but they have only the shoes provided to protect their feet from scorching. They may share the shoes and help each other in any way, but nobody part unprotected by the shoes may touch the ground.

Afterward, use these discussion starters:

■ **How did you feel about facing the challenge with only two shoes and your teammates?**

■ **How do you suppose the Israelites felt about facing a wilderness journey with nothing but faith in God's leading to get them safely through it?**

■ **What challenges do we face today that seem almost impossible to get through?**

Manna Hunt:

Have kids hunt for food hidden in an area. If possible, hide food that can be cooked over an open fire. A meal could include hot dogs with buns and condiments; a snack could include marshmallows, graham crackers, and chocolate for S'mores. Wrap items in plastic to keep them clean and have kids carry them along to the next center.

Afterward, use these discussion starters:

■ **How would you feel if you had to find your food every day?**

■ **How do you suppose the Israelites felt?**

■ **In what ways do you depend on God for your everyday needs?**

Fireside Chat:

Have kids build a fire (use a fireplace if your facility has one, or several large grills or a metal trash can) and cook their food from the Manna Hunt. Then enjoy the campfire as a setting for deeper sharing.

Afterward, use these discussion starters:

■ **How do you think the Israelites felt when they saw the cloud of fire?**

■ **When did you first experience the warmth of God's love?**

■ **How does God's love warm you or light your life now?**

Tenting Tonight:

Lead kids to the area where they'll sleep and have them set up tents or roll out their sleeping bags. If possible, sleep outside.

Afterward, use these discussion starters:

■ **How do you think the Israelites felt about sleeping on the ground night after night?**

■ **If you'd been with the Israelites, how do you think you would have felt about your life in the wilderness compared with your life back in Egypt?**

■ **As you move forward in your Christian life, what things are hard to leave behind?**

■ **In what ways is moving forward in your Christian life like an exciting adventure?**

Promised Land:

Provide a wonderful breakfast in comfortable surroundings.

Afterward, use these discussion starters:

■ **If you had been an Israelite, how would the promise of a wonderful new homeland have made you feel?**

■ **What are some of the promises that motivate you in your Christian journey?**

NUMBERS 10:1-10

THEME:
Showing your faith

SUMMARY:
Use this SKIT to help kids see that they can influence others by showing and sharing their belief in the Bible.

A BEST SELLER

SCENE: A teenager decides that it's not such a bad thing to let others know about your faith.

PROPS: Two benches (perhaps made of chairs) and a Bible for use in the skit and for the discussion afterward.

CHARACTERS:
Lydia
Janet

SCRIPT

(Janet is sitting on a bench, reading the Bible. Lydia enters, sits down at another bench.)

Lydia: Uh, hi...

Janet: *(Looking up from her reading)* Oh, hi. You're...Linda, right?

Lydia: Actually, Lydia. Aren't you new? I thought I saw you in French this morning.

Janet: Yeah, we just moved here. My name's Janet.

Lydia: Oh, that's right. *(With a French accent)* Jah-net! Oui!

Janet: *(Laughing)* Hey, that's pretty good!

Lydia: It should be. My parents have forced me to take three years of that torture so far! So, how do you like it here?

Janet: It's OK. I had a few people give me some looks when they saw me carrying this, though. *(She holds Bible up.)*

Lydia: *(Thinks.)* I guess I kind of gave you one myself. Do you really...read it? I mean, talk about a chore!

Janet: It's not so hard once you get used to it. As a matter of fact, it's got everything. Drama, murder, humor, romance, something for everyone. *(Pauses.)* And, it's all true.

Lydia: I suppose.

Janet: Don't you believe it?

Lydia: Well, yeah, I guess. I just never met anybody who felt so strongly about it. I mean, I go to church and all, but outside of there, I never hear anyone talk about God or anything, except when they're cussing.

Janet: I know, isn't it the truth? That's too bad because God hears all of that. I figure as long as he's listening, why not say something worth saying? Anyway, you ought to try reading this best seller!

Lydia: *(Hesitates.)* Yeah... You may have something there. *(Janet hands her the Bible.)*

If you use this skit as a discussion starter, here are possible questions:

■ **How else could you show your faith to someone like Lydia?**

■ **Read Numbers 10:1-10. In what ways is showing our faith like blowing the silver trumpets?**

■ **How is the effect similar?**

NUMBERS
11:25-30

THEME:
Speaking out for God

SUMMARY:
In this PROJECT, kids will speak out among God's people just as the people in the passage spoke out in their camp.

PREPARATION: You'll need Bibles.

Arrange for kids to participate in worship service by reading Scripture, praying, leading singing, and sharing their testimonies or faith stories. Help your kids gain confidence for this project by giving clear guidelines about when each person will speak, how long they're expected to talk, where microphones are if they'll be needed, and so on.

After the service, ask:

■ **How did you feel speaking out for God in this worship service?**

■ **If you were a pastor, how would you feel about having teenagers participate in the service the way you did?**

Have a volunteer read aloud Numbers 11:25-30. Ask:

■ **How was what you did**

today like what Eldad and Medad did in this passage?

■ **How did God's Spirit help you speak out today?**

■ **Where else do we need to speak out for God?**

■ **How can God's Spirit help us do that?**

■ **What's one way you can speak out for God this week?**

NUMBERS
13:1-33

THEME:
Risks

SUMMARY:
Kids will face physical risks to learn about taking risks for God in this ADVENTURE.

PREPARATION: Set up a risk-taking course in a park with various physical challenges. (Some communities or college campuses have rope courses or team courses that you can use with the assistance of a professional facilitator.) You'll need supplies and equipment for the course activities and Bibles.

Form teams of no more than eight and have each team work together to meet each challenge on the course you've chosen. The activities should have some element of perceived risk so that kids have to overcome apprehension, but none should be truly dangerous. At each challenge, stress safety. Insist on having at least two spotters whenever a team member is off the ground (determine the size of your teams accordingly). Possible challenges could include

• The team must place an inflated swim ring over a vertical pole (look for volleyball-net standards or a tetherball post, or provide a 10-foot pole that some team members can hold upright) without any member of the team touching the pole and without the ring touching the pole. After they have lowered the ring from the top to the ground, they must lift it off again, still without touching the pole.

• The team must get every member over a playground barrel, but only two members of the team are allowed to touch the barrel. (For a variation of this, have everyone take turns going up and sliding down a slide, with only two team members allowed to touch any part of the slide.)

• Lay out bricks on which 2×4s can be set to form balance beams. Set up a balance beam "course," which will involve four lengths of board, but provide only two boards. The team must pick up and pass each board ahead after everyone has crossed it, all while standing on the bricks or the other board.

After you've done all the activities, ask:

■ How did you feel about taking these risks?

■ What things did we do to make sure these risks weren't unreasonably dangerous?

■ Where do you draw the line between a risk that's worth taking and a risk that is simply foolish?

Have a volunteer read aloud Numbers 13:1-33. Ask:

■ If you'd been with the group of Israelites who explored the land, do you think you would've wanted to risk fighting those giants, or would you have sided with the spies who said the risk was too great? Explain.

■ What risks have you taken for God?

■ What risk do you want to take in your Christian life?

■ What do you need from God and your Christian friends to give you the courage to take that risk for God?

NUMBERS 20:1-13

THEME:
God provides.

SUMMARY:
In this OBJECT LESSON, kids will get thirsty during a church picnic and learn how God provides the things we really need.

PREPARATION: Prepare a meal or snack of salty and spicy foods—potato chips, salted nuts, taco salad, nachos, or fried chicken would be good choices. Take along picnic supplies, such as colorful plates and tablecloths to spread on the ground. Have soft drinks and Bibles available.

Set up a festive picnic in your church building or on church grounds. Enjoy the food but don't provide any drinks. If kids complain, empathize with their feelings but don't offer drinks. After kids have had time to eat most of the food, have a volunteer read aloud Numbers 20:1-5.

Form pairs and have partners discuss the following questions:

■ **How do you feel about our drinkless picnic?**

■ **How is our picnic like what the Israelites experienced?**

■ **If you'd been with the Israelites, how would you have reacted to your leaders?**

Bring out the soft drinks and let everyone drink as much as they want. Have another volunteer read aloud Numbers 20:6-13. Ask:

■ **How is your reaction to these soft drinks different from what it would be if you'd had them before you got so thirsty?**

■ **What do you suppose the Israelites learned about themselves from their experience?**

■ **What did they learn about God?**

■ **What tough times have you experienced that made you "thirsty" for God's help?**

■ **How did God provide what you needed?**

NUMBERS
22:21-34

THEME:
Following God

SUMMARY:
Use this SKIT to help kids see that God wants us to go in a particular direction.

BALAAM-BING,
BALAAM-BOOM

SCENE: Balaam finds that where he wants to go and where his transportation will take him are two different things.

PROPS: A pair of paper donkey ears for the donkey, a toy sword, and a stick. You'll also need a Bible for the discussion after the skit.

CHARACTERS:
Balaam
Donkey
Angel

SCRIPT

(Donkey is down on all fours, looking around in a bored fashion and chewing hay. Donkey yawns. Balaam enters.)

Balaam: Aha! There you are! Come on, we need to go with the Moabites.

(He straddles the back of the Donkey, and they pretend to walk. The Donkey talks to audience.)

Donkey: What on earth is a Moabite? If it ain't one thing, it's another. Ya start hangin' around with the wrong crowd, goin' wherever they go, and the first thing you know, badabing-badaboom, youse are starin' straight into some trouble.

(Angel enters and stands in front of Balaam and Donkey, waving sword. Balaam doesn't see the Angel, but the Donkey does.)

Donkey: Whad I tell ya? I'm history!

(Donkey turns away from Angel, takes off in different direction. Angel exits.)

Balaam: Whoa! Whoa, you stupid

animal!! What are you doing? *(Balaam pretends to hit Donkey's head.)* Get back on the road!!

(Donkey looks back at where Angel was, sees that Angel is gone, shakes head in a bewildered fashion, and goes back to the road.)

Donkey: Well whaddya know. If dat ain't da strangest thing! I could swear I saw a angel wavin' a sword right in front of me and the next thing ya know, badabing-badaboom, it's gone! *(To audience)* It just goes to show ya'.

(Angel enters.)

Donkey: The mind can play all sorts of funny tri... *(Notices Angel.)* Whoops. Hooves, don't fail me now!

(Donkey heads off in another direction with a mad Balaam on his or her back. Angel exits.)

Balaam: Whoa! Whoooaa! You rotten donkey! You behave, or I'll sell you to the glue factory!

(Balaam pretends to hit Donkey again, a little harder. Donkey stops.)

Balaam: Now, get back to that road!

Donkey: *(Sees that the Angel is gone once again. Goes back to road and continues walking.)* Dere's somethin' fishy goin' on here! All I know is I'm gettin' a LITTLE bit tired of Mr. Slaphappy on my back!

(Angel enters, Donkey sees him.)

Donkey: I give up!

(Donkey collapses flat on the floor. Balaam gets off and pretends to hit Donkey with his stick. Angel exits.)

Balaam: You rotten, no good, fleabitten, mangy pile of fur! When I tell you to go somewhere, you go there! Do you hear me?

Donkey: *(Stands up and puts one hand on hip while waving the other index finger at Balaam, who is shocked to hear the Donkey talk.)* Now youse just wait one Old Testament minute! I've always been a good donkey, ain't I? *(Puts on a goofy expression.)* Yup, yup, sure, I'll take you there, sure I'll take you here! *(Balaam is still shocked.)*

Donkey: So, just this once, this one time, mind youse, I don't zactly go where you tell me and badabing, ya hit me, and badaboom, ya hit me again, and badabing-badaboom, you even hit me with a stick! Where do youse get off actin' like that, anyways? Did ya ever think I might have a reason for not going where youse wanted me to?

(Angel re-enters. Donkey points at Angel.)

Donkey: Ha! Whad I tell ya! That ain't no palm leaf he's holdin'! *(Balaam looks at Angel, noticing him for the first time. He kneels down and bows his head close to the ground.)*

Angel: *(To Balaam)* You've got an itchy stick-finger, did you know that? If your donkey hadn't noticed me and turned away each time she did, you wouldn't be here now. You'd be here... *(pointing at ground)* and here... *(pointing at a different place)* and here... *(pointing at yet another place)* and here...

Balaam: I get the picture! *(To Donkey)* I am sorry, noble friend.

Donkey: Hey, don't go getting all mushy on me now. Just trust me from now on!

If you use this skit as a discussion starter, here are possible questions:

■ **How does God speak to you?**

■ **How does God grab your attention?**

■ **The Donkey directed Balaam's attention to the Lord. Who are some "donkeys" in your life?**

■ **What have they done to help you see God?**

NUMBERS
35:9-15, 26-28

THEME:
Safety in God

SUMMARY:
Kids enjoy a "safety PARTY" and learn how God provides safe places for them.

PREPARATION: Plan activities on the theme of safety. Consider activities such as these:

• Set up a mini drivers' racetrack with cardboard traffic signs and roads marked off by chalk or masking tape. Borrow tricycles and children's ride-on toys to use as cars.

• Play any of your group's favorite games that involve "safe zones" (for example, Capture the Flag, Tag, or Bombardment).

• If your group is athletically inclined, play softball or Wiffle ball, with much emphasis by the umpire whenever anyone is "safe" on base.

You'll need appropriate supplies and Bibles.

After you've enjoyed the games and activities, ask:

■ **How did you feel when you were "safe" in our games?**

■ **How did you feel when you were out of the safety zone? When other drivers ignored the safety laws? When you were caught off base?**

Have a volunteer read aloud Numbers 35:9-15, 26-28. Ask:

■ **How were the cities of safety in this passage like the safe zones in our games?**

■ **If you were being hunted down for something you did accidentally, how would you feel about the cities of safety? Explain.**

■ **When have you felt like you were "on the run" and needed a safe place to go?**

■ **When have you felt God make a "safe place" for you— either physically, emotionally, or spiritually?**

■ **How can we be like "cities of safety" for each other?**

DEUTERONOMY

*"I am the Lord your God; I brought you out
of the land of Egypt where you were
slaves. You must not have any
other gods except me."*

Deuteronomy 5:6-7

DEUTERONOMY
1:9-18

THEME:
Leadership

SUMMARY:
In this AFFIRMATION, kids will make military-type patches identifying leadership characteristics they see in each other.

PREPARATION: You'll need construction paper, markers, masking tape, and a chalkboard and chalk (or a large sheet of newsprint posted on the wall). You'll also need Bibles.

Have a volunteer read aloud Deuteronomy 1:9-18. Ask:
■ **What were the qualities of the leaders Moses appointed?**

List kids' responses on the chalkboard or newsprint. Qualities suggested by the passage include wisdom, understanding, experience, fairness, willingness to listen, good judgment, not "playing favorites," courage, and dependence on God in making decisions.

Form trios. Have each trio team up with another trio and work together to identify three leadership qualities of each person in the partner trio. The qualities may be from the list just created or other characteristics they see in the partner trio's members. Have kids use construction paper and markers to create military-type patches (playing off the idea of "commanders" in verse 15) with three stripes, writing one quality on each stripe. Kids should make one patch for each member of the partner trio.

When kids are ready, have each trio give examples of how they've seen these qualities lived out in the people they've written about, then have members of both trios stick the patches on each other's arms (using the masking tape) in a whole-group "commissioning" ceremony.

Afterward, have kids discuss the following questions:
■ **How do you feel about being a "commissioned officer" for God?**
■ **How can you use one of your leadership qualities this week?**

DEUTERONOMY
3:23-29

THEME:
When God says no

SUMMARY:
In this DEVOTION, kids will discuss their reactions to various prayer requests to learn that God isn't rejecting group members when he doesn't give them what they ask for.

PREPARATION: Have a list of sample prayer requests handy that you will read. You'll also need Bibles.

EXPERIENCE
Have kids line up in single file. Say: **I'm going to read some prayer requests. After each one,**

take one step to the right if you think God would certainly give the person praying what he or she asked for. Take one step left if you think it's not a sure thing.

Read the following sample requests, pausing after each request for kids to step left or right. Also, use this time to let volunteers explain why they stepped the direction they did.

•Please give me a red convertible.

•Please let my little brother get laryngitis for the next five years.

•Please help me pass my test tomorrow, though I know I didn't study enough.

•Please help me ace my test tomorrow, since I studied so much for it.

•Please let my grandmother get better.

•Please help my friend become a Christian.

•Please forgive my sins and save me.

RESPONSE

Ask:

■ How do you feel when God says no?

Have someone read aloud Deuteronomy 3:23-29. Ask:

■ How do you think Moses might have felt when God told him no?

■ How do you feel realizing that even God's chosen leader got turned down?

■ What are ways we can cope with our disappointment when God doesn't give us what we want?

CLOSING

Say: **Moses climbed to the top of the mountain to get God's perspective. Sometimes we need help getting above our own concerns so we can accept God's answers, too.**

As a whole group, pray for each member one at a time, saying in unison: **God, please give** (name) **the courage to cope when you tell** (him or her) **no.**

DEUTERONOMY 5:6-21

THEME:
Rules

SUMMARY:
Use this SKIT to help kids understand that the Ten Commandments are intended to be taken seriously.

CALL TO ORDER

SCENE: The first meeting of a school service club (like a key club). The whole skit is performed by just one person who has to look like he is really listening to and responding to an obnoxious person in the audience.

PROPS: Desk or podium and a gavel. You'll also need a Bible for the discussion after the skit.

CHARACTERS:
Mo

SCRIPT
Mo: Hear ye, hear ye! The first meeting of the (*insert name of*

church or local school) chapter of the Carefree Order of Wandering Samaritans or "C.O.W.S." Club is now called to order! *(Bangs gavel.)*

The first order of business is to review the club rules so that we may vote on agreement to follow them. *(Notices an imaginary hand in the audience.)* The chair recognizes Harry Lewya. *(Nods head as if listening for a moment.)* In response to your question, Harry, the rules were prepared by the national office of C.O.W.S. They expect every new chapter to formally review the rules—actually they call them "commandments," which sounds a little more authoritative. Anyway, they want each new chapter and new member to understand what's expected. OK? *(Pauses.)* OK.

Now I know you all have heard from C.O.W.S. about joining, so you already know a little bit about the club. As you can see from the pamphlets in front of you, rule—I mean—commandment number one is... *(Notices a hand.)* Uh, yes, Harry? *(Listens.)*

Oh, you're not happy with the word "commandments"? Well, just think of them as rules. *(Listens.)* You don't like that either, hmm? Well, what would you call them? *(Listens. Acts a little embarrassed and upset.)* No, no, I don't think the national C.O.W.S. would be too happy if we called them the ten "suggestions"!

Now, if I could continue, you'll see in your pamphlets that the first sugges...ru...commandment... refers to... *(Seeing Harry's hand again, gets exasperated.)* What now, Harry?! *(Listens, growing increasingly impatient.)* No, we can't just dispense with the rules! *(Listens, then answers.)* Because the head of the C.O.W.S. says they're important! C.O.W.S NEED RULES, OK?! *(Starts getting really upset, but tries to keep control.)* If you don't want to follow the commandments, don't join the C.O.W.S.! *(Pauses to listen, then starts calming down.)*

I'm sorry, I just don't think you should start trying to change things. I mean, after all, we aren't really even C.O.W.S. yet. Let's just follow instructions or we'll be "udder" failures. *(Laughs nervously.)*

(Calmer) Now, let's look again at this first commandment. As you can see, it says, "Members shall not..." *(Notices Harry again and starts to get angry.)* Now what? *(Listens, blows top.)* No, it's not time for refreshments! *(Collapses in exaggerated sobs on podium, while hitting it with the gavel.)*

If you use this skit as a discussion starter, here are possible questions:

■ **Read Deuteronomy 5:6-21. Why did God call them commandments?**

■ **Why should we take each commandment seriously?**

■ **Which commandments does**

our society tell us to treat as mere suggestions?

■ What is the difference between a commandment and a suggestion?

■ How does that difference affect your life?

DEUTERONOMY 6:4-9

THEME:
Putting God first

SUMMARY:
Kids will design hats to remind them of ways to show their love for God in this DEVOTION.

PREPARATION: You'll need markers in a variety of colors and plain, white painters' caps (available at most discount department stores, such as Wal-Mart or Target). If your budget is tight or caps are unavailable, you can use plain white bandannas or strips of white cloth as headbands instead. You'll also need Bibles.

EXPERIENCE
Have someone read aloud Deuteronomy 6:4-9.

Say: **This passage tells us to love God with all our heart, soul, and strength. Then it tells us to wear that commandment on our heads. Design a hat that will remind you of specific ways you can show your love for God. You can use symbols, words, pictures, or whatever you want.**

Give each person a hat and markers and let creativity take over.

RESPONSE
Invite volunteers to display their hats and explain their designs. Then ask:

■ **How would our lives be different if we were reminded every minute of every day to love God?**

■ **What things can we do to keep God's command to love on our minds all the time?**

CLOSING
Form a circle. Give a countdown saying: **"Heart, soul, strength..."** instead of "Three, two, one," and have everyone toss his or her hat in the air and yell, "Live it!"

DEUTERONOMY 8:10-18

THEME:
Remembering God's goodness

SUMMARY:
Kids will create a video focusing on God's goodness in this PROJECT.

PREPARATION: You'll need a video camera for every four kids. (Note: Parents are usually willing to lend cameras if their kids are using them. You may want to recruit responsible adults to handle the cameras if you borrow them from outside the group.) You'll also need a cassette tape or compact disc player, a videocassette recorder, a television, and Bibles.

Read Deuteronomy 8:10-18, then have foursomes put together video segments focusing on God's goodness. Suggest these ideas:

•Interview congregation members of different ages about what God has done for them.

•Videotape scenes from nature or family life to accompany a hymn or contemporary song about God's goodness. (When you view this segment, turn down the volume on the video and play the song on a separate player.)

•Create a video montage showing scenes of God's goodness (children's smiles, friends talking, and so on).

To keep everyone involved, have each foursome assign these roles: scriptwriter (responsible for writing down the group's ideas, drafting the final list of interview questions, and putting video shots in order), director (responsible for arranging the interviews and location shots, and getting music), camera operator (responsible for doing the actual filming), and interviewer/narrator (responsible for any on-camera talking or cueing of music).

If appropriate to the end product and your church's worship style, consider showing the video to the whole church.

(**Note:** For a more in-depth video project, check out the Project With a Purpose™ for Youth Ministry curriculum titled *Videotaping Your Church Members' Faith Stories*. It's available through Group Publishing, Inc.)

DEUTERONOMY 14:22-29

THEME:
Tithing

SUMMARY:
Kids will experience tithing by giving 10 percent of everything they receive in this "top-10" OVERNIGHTER.

PREPARATION: Publicize the overnighter with fliers that look like top-10 music lists. Include the top-10 reasons to attend and the top-10 things to pack. Plan activities for one full day and one night. Be sure kids bring their Bibles.

Structure as many activities as you can in which kids can give away 10 percent of what they receive. Activities could include

•Holding a fund-raiser for your group (carwash, soup supper, whatever your group can do in a few hours) and giving 10 percent of the profits to a designated charity.

•Taking kids to an event that charges admission and challenge them to give 10 percent of the amount they spend on themselves to the same charity.

•Preparing meals together using nonperishables, such as boxed cereal and pasta, and set aside 10 percent of the groceries for a food pantry.

Include plenty of fun events but spend at least 10 percent of the total time in a service project. If you really want to get serious, cut out 10 percent of the normal sleep time and spend that time in worship or Bible study!

Allow time to discuss Deuteronomy 14:22-29, emphasizing tithing as a heart gesture of gratitude, not a legalistic requirement. Talk about whether we tend to give God our "top-10" percent or just whatever is left over when we've taken what we want. Discuss how calculating 10 percent of everything over the weekend has raised their awareness of how much (money, time, and other resources) they have to give. You might also suggest that the class tithe 10 percent of their allowances or wages to go toward a special youth group project in the coming year.

DEUTERONOMY 20:1-4

THEME:
Confidence in
God's power

SUMMARY:
Kids will provide up-to-date examples to personalize this CREATIVE READING about God's power.

PREPARATION: Make a photocopy of the "Creative Reading for Deuteronomy 20:1-4" handout (p. 71) for yourself and have a pencil handy to write in kids' contributions. Without telling kids anything about the script, ask them for words or phrases that fit each category listed after the blanks (like a

"Mad Lib"). Jot down their suggestions in the blanks. (If you want kids to be able to respond anonymously, provide paper and pencils, collect their suggestions, and use them to fill in the blanks.) Then read the personalized paraphrase while kids follow along with the original in their Bibles.

DEUTERONOMY 28:1-14

THEME:
God's blessings

SUMMARY:
Kids will encourage each other by writing positive qualities on candy wrappers in this AFFIRMATION.

PREPARATION: You'll need paper, colored pens or markers, tape, Bibles, and a variety of candy that can represent abilities or characteristics kids have been blessed with. Use the ideas here and any others that come to mind in a trip down the candy aisle:

• Almond Joy for a cheerful, joyful personality.

• Snickers or Chuckles for a good sense of humor.

• Baby Ruth for athletic ability.

• Jolly Rancher for a good-natured personality.

• Smarties for someone with good ideas.

• 3 Musketeers for someone who is a faithful friend.

(continued on p. 72)

CREATIVE READING FOR
DEUTERONOMY 20:1-4

When you come face to face with your problems and you

see _____ and _____
      (a problem you might face)   *(another problem you might face)*

and _____ that seem bigger than you,
     (another problem you might face)

don't be afraid of them. The Lord your God, who _____
                                                (something good

_____, will be with you. God will send _____
God has done for you)   *(someone or some*

_____ to speak to you before you face your
way God uses to speak to you)

problem. He will say, "Listen,_____
                              (name of each person in the group)

_____.

Today you're going into battle against your enemies. Don't

lose your courage or be afraid. Don't panic or be frightened,

because the Lord your God goes with you to _____
                                           (places where you

_____
need God's help)

to fight for you against your enemies and to save you."

• M&M's for anything with two M's—musical and merry, muscular and mighty, marvelously mathematical.

Have a volunteer read aloud Deuteronomy 28:1-14.

Say: **God promised to bless his people with the things they needed, but he also promised to bless them by making them special people. God has blessed everyone here with qualities that make them special, too.**

Show kids the candies and suggest qualities each might represent. Urge kids to be creative in their meanings for the candies—as long as they're positive.

Next, have kids draw names and then select a candy for the person whose name they've drawn. Tell kids to make new wrappers, label them with the characteristics and the person's name, then tape the new wrapper over the existing one. Have kids give the candies to each other saying, "God has blessed you with _____ (for example, a joyful smile)."

DEUTERONOMY 30:11-20

THEME:
Following God

SUMMARY:
In this PROJECT, kids will decorate youth-room walls with handprints and footprints in which they write ways to follow God.

PREPARATION: You'll need a variety of wall paints, dish pans or trays to pour paint into, dropcloths to protect the floor, a ladder or two, appropriate materials for cleanup, markers, and Bibles. You'll also want to get permission to decorate the walls in this way! (If painting directly on the walls isn't possible, you can adapt this project by painting on huge sheets of paper and posting them on the walls.) Warn kids to wear old clothes.

Protect the floor with a dropcloth. Pour small amounts of the paint into the dish pans or trays. Let kids dip their hands and feet into the paint and press them on the wall to make handprints and footprints.

Try these tips for controlling the mess:

• Pair up to make footprints first. Have one person dip his or her left foot in one color, then have the partner help the painter up a ladder to reach various points on the wall. Clean up that foot and repeat with the right foot in a different color. Then have the partners switch roles.

• Make all footprints before doing handprints—you'll want clean hands when you boost the "foot painters."

• Use paint sparingly. It doesn't take much paint to make an effective footprint or handprint. And too much paint will make the prints run (no pun intended).

• Have kids make several handprints of one color before cleaning up and switching colors. Suggest holding a paper towel in the clean hand to catch any drips.

When the painting is done and

the room is cleaned up, have a volunteer read aloud Deuteronomy 30:11-20. Reread the first part of verse 20: **"To choose life is to love the Lord your God, obey him, and stay close to him."** Then ask:

■ **What are specific ways to use our hands to obey God?**

■ **What are specific ways to stay close to God?**

Have someone record the suggestions. When the handprints and footprints are dry, have kids use markers to write ways to use their hands to obey God in the handprints, and ways to stay close to God in the footprints. Also have everyone write this sentence in one of the prints: "(Name) chooses life!"

DEUTERONOMY 31:1-8

THEME:
Leadership

SUMMARY:
Kids will experience their own leadership abilities by planning and completing a PROJECT that demonstrates that they're the future leaders of the church.

PREPARATION: Work with kids to plan an activity that lets them do things usually left to adults in the church. For example, leading a worship service in your church, at a nursing home, or at a soup kitchen; planning and giving a party in a children's hospital; putting on an open-air Christian concert; hosting an evangelistic

event for their non-Christian friends. You'll need Bibles when debriefing the activities.

Do everything it takes to make this project a success and a positive experience for the kids involved. After the project is completed, ask:

■ **How did you feel about taking leadership in this way?**

■ **What was scariest or most intimidating?**

■ **What was most rewarding?**

■ **What did you learn about yourself?**

Have a volunteer read aloud Deuteronomy 31:1-8. Ask:

■ **How do you suppose Joshua felt about taking over leadership from Moses?**

■ **How did you experience God's promise, given in verse 8, in our project?**

■ **What new leadership challenges do you think God might have in store for you?**

DEUTERONOMY 34:1-12

THEME:
Leaving a legacy

SUMMARY:
In this AFFIRMATION, kids will encourage one another by expressing positive things they'll remember about each other.

PREPARATION: Set up your meeting room like a funeral chapel. Drape a black cloth over a large box or table to represent a coffin, provide a flower arrangement or two, and set up chairs in rows. If you wish, have everyone come dressed in black. (Having a mock funeral adds an element of fun to this activity, but if someone in your group has recently been bereaved, you'll probably want to do the affirmation without the funeral setting. Use a "remembering each other theme" or "10-year reunion" setting instead.) Provide paper, pencils, and Bibles.

Have a volunteer read aloud Deuteronomy 34:1-12.

Say: **After his death, Moses was remembered as a great servant-leader of God. How do you think you'll be remembered? Today you'll get a chance to find out.**

Have each person write his or her name on the top of a sheet of paper. Pass the papers up and down the rows so that each person can write a sentence, phrase, or description of a positive quality or action that other people will be remembered for. When everyone has contributed to all the sheets, collect them and read them as eulogies. Ask:

■ **Which comment in your eulogy surprised you most? Which pleased you most?**

■ **What quality do you want to develop now to be remembered by later?**

JOSHUA

"Always remember what is written in the Book of the Teachings. Study it day and night to be sure to obey everything that is written there. If you do this, you will be wise and successful in everything."

Joshua 1:8

JOSHUA
1:1-9

THEME:
Passing the torch of leadership

SUMMARY:
Use this SKIT to help kids see that when God approves of a leader, he or she can be an effective one.

CONFIDENCE TO SPARE

SCENE: Two kids go bowling and discuss the upcoming year's events for their church youth group.

PROPS: Two chairs at a desk facing the audience, paper, and a pencil. You'll also need Bibles for the discussion after the skit.

CHARACTERS:
Jenna
Lyle

SCRIPT
(Throughout the skit, the two characters need to really look like they're bowling, preferably right toward the audience.)

Jenna: *(Rolls ball and watches it.)* So, anyway, Lyle, I'm really glad... *(Reacting to ball)* Yes! ...That you're the new president of the youth group.

Lyle: Thanks.

Jenna: *(Going to her seat to mark her score)* You know, I'm going off to State, and I was afraid there wouldn't be anyone responsible to continue all the stuff we started this year.

Lyle: *(Preparing to bowl)* Such as?

(He pauses and turns to look at Jenna while she speaks.)

Jenna: Oh, you know, the weekly activities, Pilgrim Playhouse in November, the Christmas clothing drive, Easter breakfast...

Lyle: *(Sigh)* I didn't realize there was so much to keep track of... *(Shrugs, then bowls.)*

Jenna: Whatsamatter? Getting cold feet?

(Lyle is trying all the body English he can to get his ball to go left, then right.)

Jenna: Come on, you weren't elected by accident.

Lyle: *(Smacks his forehead in frustration.)* A 7-10 split. It figures. *(Gets another ball.)*

Jenna: Come on, loosen up. You're gonna be a great group president!

Lyle: Oh, sure. I don't have a clue what to say or do at the next meeting. *(He bowls again.)*

Jenna: That's nothing. There are magazines and stuff that tell you how to hold meetings. *(Watching Lyle's ball)* Straight down the middle. Tough break. *(She stands and gets ready to bowl.)* What's important is that you've got the group's confidence, and you've got the sponsor's confidence, too!

Lyle: *(Surprised, sitting in his seat)* I do?

Jenna: Sure. Mrs. Quigley told me how relieved she was that you were gonna be the new president.

Lyle: *(As Jenna bowls)* She did?

Jenna: Yeah, she said she knew all the kids respected you...

Lyle: Really?

Jenna: And she knew that you'd

do your best. *(Looks down the alley at the pins.)* RATS! *(Gets another ball.)*

Lyle: Well, sure, I'll try hard to make the group even better.

Jenna: *(Bowls again.)* It's up to you to lead them forward, that's for sure. *(She watches her ball and shakes her head in disgust.)*

Lyle: A gutter ball. That's tough.

Jenna: Yeah, I think my winning streak just died in this frame. Put me down for two.

Lyle: *(Writes, then stands and prepares to bowl.)* Looks like we're tied. *(He bowls.)*

Jenna: Lyle, I know you're nervous, but remember, God will help you, and he can do anything.

Lyle: *(Reacting to the strike)* YESSS!

(Lyle and Jenna high five.)

Permission to photocopy this skit from *Youth Worker's Encyclopedia: OT* granted for local church use. Copyright © Group Publishing, Inc., Box 481, Loveland, CO 80539.

If you use this skit as a discussion starter, here are possible questions:

■ **How would reading Joshua 1:1-9 affect a leader like Lyle?**

■ **Why can a godly leader have such confidence?**

■ **In what way are you a leader?**

■ **Can the passage in Joshua help you? How?**

JOSHUA 4:1-24

THEME:
Remembering God's work in our lives

SUMMARY:
In this OVERNIGHTER, kids will participate in a 24-hour retreat or lock-in designed to create memories for the future and memorialize memories of the past.

PREPARATION: Publicize the retreat through handouts and bulletin announcements using various real-life "Remember when..." statements. For example, "Remember when Tom Olsen ran out of gas on the way home from the lock-in and five kids had to walk a mile back to church?" Interview parents, youth leaders, former Sunday school teachers, and potential retreat participants about significant memorable events to uncover material to use in your "Remember when..." statements.

If possible, secure videotapes or photos of past retreats, Sunday school programs, or other events in which the youth participated. (If you plan to show videos of past events, you'll need a videocassette recorder.) Have each participant bring a childhood photo taken between the ages of birth and 2. Ask each person to write his or her name on the back of the photo and to bring the photo in a plain envelope (for secrecy). You'll also need Bibles, paper, pencils, tape or thumbtacks (to display photos), and a small photo album to award as a prize.

Plan a retreat based on Joshua 4:1-24. Your goal for the weekend will be to help the participants realize the importance of memories from the past and the significance of creating memories for the future. Use the following ideas to make the retreat a memorable event:

COMMUNITY BUILDERS:

• Play a game from childhood such as Duck, Duck, Goose; Red Light, Green Light; or Simon Says. See who remembers the rules best.

• Create a memory-game tournament (using the game Concentration as a model). Split a deck of cards (so you have two of every number and face card) and shuffle them face down in rows. Have kids turn over two cards at a time, attempting to get matching cards (unmatched cards are turned face down again). See who can get the most matches.

• Set up a picture gallery using childhood photos of the teenagers who are present. Give each person a pencil and sheet of paper and have him or her attempt to name the person in each photo. Award a small photo album to the person who guesses the most correctly.

ACTIVITIES:

• Have kids read Joshua 4:1-24 then go on a memory hike to follow the example of the people in this passage. You'll need to prepare the hike ahead of time by leaving a

stone at each of five or six gathering places in the hike area.

Attach a two-fold message to each stone. The first part of the message should be a "memory-jogger," such as "Remember when we went on a servant event to Mexico." Organize your memory-joggers chronologically from the earliest activities of the group to the most recent. Have kids discuss ways they remember God working during those activities. The second part of the message should be directions to the next stone.

At each gathering place, have the group reminisce about the activity cited in the memory-jogger and then try to figure out where to go for the next stone.

• Show videos or photos of past events. Allow time to talk about what those events meant to participants.

• Prepare a Bible study focusing on Joshua 4:1-24 and its significance.

• Plan a "memory worship" in which kids remember and tell about God's saving acts in their own lives.

JOSHUA
7

THEME:
The consequences of our actions

SUMMARY:
Use this SKIT to help kids see that their actions influence others.

GOOD QUESTION

SCENE: An English class where a few students push the teacher to the limit.

PROPS: Chairs, desks, and books. You'll need Bibles for the discussion after the skit.

CHARACTERS:
Mr. Crenshaw
Mike
Trista
Kimi
Alan
Sondra

SCRIPT

(Class is in session. Mr. Crenshaw is in the middle of presenting some material.)

Mr. Crenshaw: Our next word for this week is voluminous, which, of course, means something that has great volume or is very big.

Mike: *(To Trista, in a loud whisper)* Like Mr. Crenshaw's lectures!

(Trista suppresses a laugh. Mr. Crenshaw notices.)

Mr. Crenshaw: *(Sharply)* Trista, is there something you would like to share with the class?

Trista: *(With a smirk on her face)* No.

Mr. Crenshaw: Well, then I suggest you keep quiet. Now, can anyone tell me what ambulatory means? *(Notices Mike raising his hand.)* Mike?

Mike: Let's see... ambulatory. Isn't that a bathroom in an ambulance?

(Everyone snickers.)

Mr. Crenshaw: *(Mad)* That's enough! Ambulatory means having the ability to get around. Now, no more nonsense! Our next word is crestfallen. Who

can define... *(He's interrupted by Trista's hand shooting up.)* OK, Trista?

Trista: *(She looks around, stands up next to her desk, and says seriously)* Crestfallen—the little blobs of blue toothpaste that collect and harden in the sink when you try to squeeze too much onto your brush—crestfallen.

(Trista primly sits down. The class erupts with laughter. Mr. Crenshaw looks about ready to explode.)

Mr. Crenshaw: That will be enough! You can all look up that one on your own! *(He tries something different.)* Let's review last week's words. Who can use temperamental in a sentence?

(Mike, Trista, and Kimi all raise their hands. Mr. Crenshaw looks relieved at Kimi.) Finally, someone who will give me a good answer. Kimi?

Kimi: *(Looks around at the others a little embarrassed. Giggles while responding.)* Um... when the teacher constantly loses his temper, a mental breakdown is sure to occur.

(Everyone else stares at Kimi, shocked. She never fools around in class. Then all of the kids laugh uproariously.)

Mr. Crenshaw: *(Boiling mad)* THAT'S IT! NO MORE! I don't have to put up with this kind of garbage! You all have an assignment for next Monday. I want a 20-page analysis of the book we've been reading! *(He picks up his teachers text and stomps out.)*

Mike: But it's WAR AND PEACE!

Trista: And we're only on chapter 3!

Alan and Sondra: *(They look at each other and say together)* What did WE do?

If you use this skit as a discussion starter, here are possible questions:

■ **How might the rest of the class feel toward Mike, Trista, and Kimi?**

■ **What would you do if you were in their class?**

■ **Read Joshua 7. How did Achan's actions affect others around him?**

■ **Why do you think God punished Achan's family?**

■ **What can you learn from the story of Achan?**

JOSHUA 7:1-12

THEME:
Priorities

SUMMARY:
Use this SKIT to help kids understand that when they're trying to accomplish something important, they've got to have their priorities in order.

FIRST THINGS FIRST

SCENE: A room where Jim is just finishing an exhaustive term paper.

PROPS: A real or cardboard personal computer, a desk, and a chair. You'll also need Bibles for the discussion after the skit.

CHARACTERS:
Jim
Bo

SCRIPT

(Jim is typing madly at a computer keyboard. He types for several seconds, nodding his head and stopping occasionally to rub his hands together with satisfaction.)

Jim: Yes...uh huh... all right...

(Bo enters and watches Jim for a few seconds before speaking.)

Bo: Boy, whatever you're working on must be really good!

(Jim doesn't notice him and keeps typing.)

Bo: I mean, you sure are throwing yourself into whatever you're typing there!

Jim: Huh? Oh, hi, Bo. *(Looking around)* Have you been here long?

Bo: Not really. Just long enough to see you basking in the warmth of your own incredible computer skills.

Jim: Computer skills? Hah! *(Dramatically, standing up)* My boy, I am just putting the finishing touches on my ticket to college! The end of a future of asking, "Paper or plastic?" The door to a new existence!

Bo: *(Looks around)* A new existence? Paper or plastic? What are you talking about?

Jim: *(Keeping it dramatic)* I've finished it! Done! Completamundo! Don't you see?

Bo: I see a guy who's been staring at a computer screen too long.

Jim: *(Chuckles and comes back to earth somewhat.)* Oh, don't worry about me. All I'm trying to say is that I've finished the term paper I've been working on! And...it's great!

Bo: Really?

Jim: Really. Before I wrote it, I showed Mr. Stevens my outline. *(Proudly)* He said it was such an original idea, if I combined it with my stellar writing skills, I was sure to get selected for the Bender Bakery Scholarship.

Bo: Bender Bakery? Aren't they the nice folks who brought Yid-Yah Toaster Pastries and Koo-Koo Cocoa Muffins to this great land of ours?

Jim: The very same. When I receive the scholarship for this bit of literary craftsmanship *(pats the computer gently)*, it'll be worth 2,000 smackers.

Bo: Wow! Two-thousand bucks?

Jim: Yup. *(Dramatic, Shakespearish)* Ah, good and noble Bo, my compatriot. I wilt not forget thee when I enjoyeth the campus life. *(He sits down at the computer again.)* Now all I have to do is save it to the disk and...
(The lights in the room turn off, then come right back on. Jim stares in horror at the screen. Bo looks innocently around.)

Bo: Huh... Wonder what that was... Must have been a power surge of some sort.
(No response from Jim, who continues to fix his gaze on the screen, eyes bugging out if possible. Bo looks curiously at the screen, just to see what Jim's staring at.)

Bo: Fey, Jim, that's kind of neat. How did you get the screen to do that? It looks like some sort of abstract artwork or maybe what you'd get if you sat a monkey at the computer for an hour and let him go at it. So *(slapping Jim on the back)*, where's this killer term paper you've been raving about?

Jim: *(Staring at the screen)* Gone.

Bo: Gone? What do you mean?

Jim: Gone. Finito. Kaput. History. That power surge must have wiped it out.

Bo: No way! Even I, humble Bo, know that you're always supposed to hook computers up to some sort of surge "thingy" before you do anything else.
(Jim puts his head in his hands in despair.)

Bo: So just push the right buttons, and it should come back.
(Bo, the ultimate computer illiterate, starts jabbing at the keyboard indiscriminately. Jim gets up and starts to leave.)

Bo: Where you going, Hemingway?

Jim: Oh... I thought I might go buy a surge protector.
(Jim exits. Bo freezes.)

If you use this skit as a discussion starter, here are possible questions:

∎ **Why is it so easy to get our priorities out of order?**

∎ **What particular areas do you have trouble prioritizing?**

∎ **Read Joshua 7:1-12. What does this passage tell us about getting our priorities in order?**

∎ **Why must God's commands always take precedence?**

∎ **What happens when we don't put them first?**

JOSHUA
15:1-12

THEME:

The importance of land to ancient Israelites.

SUMMARY:
In this LEARNING GAME, kids will play a variation of musical chairs to learn about the importance that the Israelites placed on land.

PREPARATION: Go to a local carpet store and ask for a donation of carpet squares. (These could be remnants or sample squares that merchants discard regularly.) You'll also need Bibles, a tape player, and music by a contemporary Christian artist.

In a large open space (fellowship hall or gymnasium), spread out the carpet squares so they're approximately four feet apart. Distribute enough squares so all but one person will have one.

Ask participants to wander in between the squares, not stepping on them as music is played on the tape player. When the music stops, have each person choose a nearby piece of "land" (a carpet square) and claim it by jumping onto it. The person who doesn't find a piece of land will be eliminated. Remove a carpet square and play again. Continue playing rounds until only one person is left standing on a carpet square. (To speed up the game, remove more than one carpet square each round.)

Redistribute carpet squares so everyone has one, then have kids sit on their squares for a brief discussion. Read aloud Joshua 15:1-12. Ask:

- ■ **What did you do to try to win this game?**
- ■ **How is that like the way people try to obtain land in real life? How is that different?**
- ■ **Why was land important to the Israelites?**
- ■ **How was land obtained?**
- ■ **Is land as important to us today? Why or why not?**
- ■ **What kinds of battles are fought over land today?**

JOSHUA
20:1-9

THEME:

Taking refuge in God

SUMMARY:
In this LEARNING GAME, a chair in the middle of an indoor playing space becomes a safety zone.

PREPARATION: You'll need a large, open meeting space or gymnasium. Place a single chair in the middle of the open space. You'll also need Bibles and a cardboard roll (empty wrapping-paper tube). Or you can create your own "bop tube" by rolling up and taping newspaper into a tube.

Tell teenagers you're going to play a version of Bop Tag with a safety zone. The person who is

"It" uses the bop tube (cardboard roll) to gently tap individuals. Kids who are tapped by the bop tube are out and must leave the game.

The chair in the middle of the room is the safety zone (anyone sitting in the chair can't be bopped). But only one person at a time may be in the safety zone. When another person comes to seek refuge in the safety zone, the person in the chair must move out into the playing area again. The object of the game is for It to bop all the players until there is only one person left in the safety zone.

After this game, have someone read aloud Joshua 20:1-9. Talk about how the safety zone in the game is like or unlike the cities of safety described in the passage.

JOSHUA
24:14-15

THEME:

Choose whom you'll serve.

SUMMARY:
In this DEVOTION, teenagers will discover how they serve "things" other than God. Then they'll learn to put God first.

PREPARATION: You'll need a collection of things such as a compact disc, loose change, a checkbook, pictures of friends, a poster of a movie star, books, an empty alcohol bottle, a pretty sweater, a leather belt, a pair of gold earrings,

a T-shirt with the name of an athletic team on it, and a cross on a chain. You'll also need Bibles, paper, and pencils.

EXPERIENCE

Display the items on a table near the center of the room. Ask the group to stand around the table and examine all the items without touching them. Then cover the table with a large tablecloth so none of the items show.

Give each person a sheet of paper and pencil. Ask kids to each write their names at the top of the paper and then list as many of the items on the table as possible in three minutes. At the end of three minutes, have teenagers pass their papers to their neighbors. Uncover the table and list the items as the kids check their neighbors' papers. Have each person record the number of items correctly listed on the top of the paper and return the paper to the original participant.

RESPONSE

Have teenagers give the person who listed the most items correctly a standing ovation. Then ask:

■ **What item did you list first?**

■ **Why do you think you listed that first?**

■ **Who listed the cross?**

■ **Why did you list the cross? Why didn't you list the cross?**

■ **Which things were easiest to remember?**

■ **How is your list an accurate representation of the things that are important in your life? How is it an inaccurate representation?**

Have a member of the group read Joshua 24:14-15. Ask:

■ **Why is it hard to put God before other things in life?**

CLOSING

Form a circle and pass the cross around the circle. As each person holds the cross, have that person say a prayer (silently or aloud), asking God to help him or her put God before all other things in life.

JUDGES

*"The angel of the Lord appeared to
Gideon and said, 'The Lord is with you,
mighty warrior!' "*

Judges 6:12

JUDGES
2:10-12

THEME:
Living a separate life

SUMMARY:
In this SKIT, a teenager tries to be just like the "cool" guy at school by mimicking his every move.

TWO PETES IN A POD

SCENE: Stella is sitting at a table reading the comics. Dance music is playing in the background.

PROPS: A table and chair for Stella. Pete is wearing a label around his neck, "Non-Christian Pete." Re-Pete has a label around his neck, "Christian Re-Pete," and a marker in his pocket. You'll need Bibles for the discussion after the skit.

CHARACTERS:
Stella
Pete
Re-Pete

SCRIPT
(Pete dances in with Re-Pete inches behind him, mimicking Pete's every move. This goes on for about 20 seconds before Stella begins to speak.)
Stella: *(Staring at Re-Pete)* Uh, Re-Pete, what are you doing?
Re-Pete: *(Still mimicking Pete, snaps at Stella.)* Sh! I'm concentrating!
Stella: On what?
Re-Pete: On doing exactly what Pete does.

Stella: Why?
Re-Pete: Because I want to be just like him.
Stella: Why?
Re-Pete: Because people think he's way cool.
Stella: Re-Pete?
Re-Pete: Yep?
Stella: You're a Christian, right?
Re-Pete: Yessum.
Stella: And Pete's not, right?
Re-Pete: Correctamundo!
Stella: Then, Re-Pete?
Re-Pete: Speak to me, baby!
Stella: Shouldn't you be dancing to the beat of a different drummer?
Re-Pete: *(Music stops, Re-Pete looks at Stella, pauses, realizes his mistake.)* Ya know, you're right! (Re-Pete gives one last up and down glance at Pete, takes out a marker from his pocket, and X's through the "Re" on Re-Pete. Walks off arm in arm with Stella. Music starts again, then Pete shrugs and walks off in opposite direction.)*

If you use this skit as a discussion starter, here are possible questions:
■ **Why would it be important for Re-Pete to stop trying to be like Pete?**
■ **How could Re-Pete pattern his life after Jesus?**
■ **Read Judges 2:10-12. What was the result of the Israelites' following the ways of the people around them?**
■ **What would your spiritual life be like if it mimicked your friends' attitudes and actions?**

■ **How can you balance your responsibility to reach out to non-Christians, yet maintain your separation from the world?**

JUDGES
6–7

THEME:
Dealing with sin

SUMMARY:
Kids will smash glass jars to symbolize dealing with their sins in this OBJECT LESSON.

PREPARATION: You'll need Bibles, sturdy burlap bags, small glass jars (that can be smashed), paper, pencils, safety goggles, and hammers.

Summarize Judges 6–7, in which God commanded Gideon to smash the altar to Baal and the idol of Asherah. Remind kids that only after Gideon had taken care of the sin in his own city did God begin to work through Gideon to free Israel from the Midianites.

As you tell Gideon's story, give each person a small glass jar, a sheet of paper, and a pencil. Have teenagers each write on their paper a sin (idol) that keeps them from being effective Christians. Have kids fold their papers and place them in their jars.

One at a time, have kids each bring up their jars and place them in a double-lined burlap bag. After someone places his or her jar in the bag, have the whole class pray that God would help that person deal with the sin listed on the paper. Then have that person put on the safety goggles and use a hammer to smash the jar through the burlap bag. Continue until each person has smashed his or her own jar.

Then have teenagers share how overcoming the sins on their papers can help them become effective Christians in the real-life world around them.

(**Note:** You might want to use newspaper in the burlap bags to help contain glass shards for easier cleanup. Also, be sure to empty bags after each glass-breaking to control mess.)

JUDGES
6:13-24

THEME:
Answering God's call

SUMMARY:
In this PROJECT, participants will answer a "call" to assist an elderly person or shut-in in the congregation by raking leaves, running errands, or shoveling snow.

PREPARATION: Collect names and needs of shut-ins, elderly individuals, or needy people in the congregation. (Lists should include names, phone numbers, and addresses.) You'll also need a hat or bowl, and Bibles.

As a group, read aloud Judges 6:13-24. Then ask:
■ **How did God call Gideon?**
■ **How does God call us?**

■ **How did Gideon answer God's call?**

■ **How can we answer God's call?**

■ **What are the characteristics needed to accept an "assignment" from God?**

Place pieces of paper with the names, addresses, and phone numbers of the elderly or shut-ins you've collected in a hat or bowl. Have each group member draw a name, then brainstorm things that could be done to help these individuals over the next three months. Ask each young person to call his or her shut-in within the next five days. Ask teenagers to offer their serving gifts to those shut-ins for the next three months. (You may want to limit the commitment to five serving activities with each shut-in.)

Have adult volunteers follow up with the shut-ins after seven days to ask about the services rendered—whether they were helpful and beneficial, and how well the servants performed their tasks.

Each time the group gathers, ask for reports on servant activity from the calls the youth group members have accepted.

JUDGES 11:1-10

THEME:
Reconciliation and trust

SUMMARY:
Participants will experience reconciliation and put their trust in the hands of another person in this DEVOTION.

PREPARATION: You'll need an equal number of red and black markers (enough for every teenager to have either one red or one black marker). You'll also need Bibles, face paints, and one paintbrush for every two people.

EXPERIENCE

Form two teams—team A and team B. Have teams form lines facing each other (so each person is facing a partner from the other team). Give everyone on team A a black marker and everyone on team B a red marker. Have team members roll up their sleeves. (Warn kids that they might get messy.)

Say: **We're going to have the "Great Color-Marker Fight of the Century." The object of this "fight" is to put marks on the arms of the most people on the opposing team with your color marker in 15 seconds. Please be careful not to mark on anyone's clothing! After you've been marked, sit down where you are to indicate you're out of the fight.**

Before beginning the contest, allow anyone who doesn't want to participate to stand off to the side.

RESPONSE

After this activity form pairs made up of one person from each team. Have pairs sit on the floor and discuss the following questions:

■ **What went through your mind as you "fought" against the opposing team members?**

■ **Those of you who decided not to participate, what made you want to avoid the fight?**

■ **What influences whether or not we fight in real life?**

■ **Now that the fight is over, what specific actions could we take to reconcile with our opponents on the other team?**

■ **What specific actions can people take to reconcile with each other after a fight in real life strains a relationship?**

■ **Why is it difficult to trust people who have hurt you in the past?**

■ **How can God help us overcome the distrust and hurt feelings that come when we fight with each other?**

CLOSING

Distribute face paints and brushes to each pair. Have each teenager paint a small design (flower, star, flag, sun) on the cheek of his or her "reconciled" partner. As partners are painting, read Judges 11:1-10 to the group. Then ask:

■ **Why did Jephthah have a difficult time trusting the elders of Gilead?**

■ **How did he later show them he had reconciled their differences?**

Close with a prayer of thanks to God for the example of Jephthah in Judges 11:1-10.

JUDGES 16

THEME:
Our source of strength

SUMMARY:

In this LEARNING GAME, teenagers participate in a mini-Olympic course to show their strength of mind and body.

PREPARATION: Gather mops for javelins (include a pail of water for each mop), garbage can lids for the discus, and other mini-Olympic resources. Prepare score cards to tally the results and bring a silly prize for the overall winner. Don't forget to bring Bibles.

Set up a mini-Olympics with at least five events (both physical and mental activities). Provide adequate time for each person to participate in each activity. Determine a scoring method for each activity and keep track to determine the overall winner of the mini-Olympics.

Here are some mini-Olympic event ideas:

• Hundred-Yard Dash—Have the participants hop backward instead of running.

• Javelin Throw—Have several wet mops in a pail and have participants toss them as far as possible.

• Broad Jump—Have participants jump a distance with their knees tied together with a pair of old (but clean) nylon pantyhose.

• Discus Throw—Using a garbage can lid as a discus, have participants each throw the discus. Award points according to the number of feet thrown.

• Riddles—Use "Riddles," found on pages 44–45 of *Youth Group Trust Builders,* by Denny Rydberg, Group Publishing, Inc.

• Answer That—Have kids compete to answer questions gathered from high school math, science, and history books. Award a point for each correct answer.

After the group has participated in your mini-Olympics, award a silly prize to the overall winner. Then ask:

■ **Which was easier—using your body or your mind?**

■ **How important is strength of body?**

■ **How important is strength of mind?**

■ **What is your source of strength in everyday life?**

Have someone read Judges 16. Then discuss the importance of Samson's physical and mental strength. Wrap up by asking:

■ **What does the story of Samson tell us about physical strength?**

■ **How can we apply that lesson to our daily lives?**

RUTH

"Where you go, I will go. Where you live, I will live. Your people will be my people, and your God will be my God."

Ruth 1:16b

RUTH 1

THEME:
The importance of family relationships

SUMMARY:
Teenagers will develop a CRE-ATIVE PRAYER using names of family members for each letter of the alphabet.

PREPARATION: Give each participant a sheet of paper with the letters of the alphabet written down the side. You'll also need Bibles.

Use this activity as a prayer opener or closing for a youth group gathering.

Remind teenagers that we have family members all around the world who are part of our extended families—uncles, cousins, in-laws, and so on. Give teenagers five minutes to think of as many relatives as possible who have names (or nicknames) beginning with each letter of the alphabet. Have kids write these names next to the appropriate letters of the alphabet.

You may want to give a prize to the person who has the most letters filled in at the end of five minutes.

Then lead everyone in "popcorn prayers" (or short, one-to-two sentence prayers), starting with the letter A and continuing through the end of the alphabet. Begin the prayer by saying: **God, today we are reminded that you gather us together in families. We know that** "family" means more than just our parents and our brothers and sisters. We pray for the needs of these family members beginning with. . . Have teenagers call out the names on their lists alphabetically.

After the prayer, ask:

■ **Were there family members you hadn't thought about for a long time on your list?**

■ **Who were they, and what memories do you have of them?**

■ **How did you feel when you heard different names being called out for prayers?**

■ **Why is it difficult to pray for some people?**

Have someone read aloud Ruth 1. Wrap up by asking:

■ **Why do you think that Naomi and Ruth were so close as mother and daughter-in-law?**

■ **What can we learn from their relationship that we can apply to our own relationships?**

RUTH 1:14-18

THEME:
Loyalty

SUMMARY:
In this SKIT, two dogs are discussing being loyal to their masters.

MAN'S BEST FRIEND

SCENE: Rex is standing by himself flipping a coin.

PROPS: Characters should wear

floppy ears and collars with name tags made out of poster board. You'll need Bibles for the discussion after the skit.

CHARACTERS:
Rex
Barney

SCRIPT

Rex: *(As he flips a coin)* Oh no! Heads again!

Barney: *(Walks up, scratching behind his ear.)* Hey, Rex, what's up?

Rex: Oh, I'm just deciding whether or not to stay with my master. *(Flips coin again.)* Oh no! Heads again! OK, best 27 out of 53.

Barney: Rex, of course you'll stay. You ARE a dog, you know. It's your nature.

Rex: I know, I know. I just wish I was more like a human sometimes. They get to DECIDE if they'll be loyal or not! *(Flips coin again.)* Another heads!

Barney: Yeah, but would you ever really WANT to decide to be disloyal to a loving master who knows much more than you and has your best interests at heart?

Rex: I guess you're right. Being a dog does have its advantages. *(Rex throws away the coin. Barney picks it up.)*

Barney: *(Picking up coin)* Hey, Rex, this is a two-headed coin!

Rex: I know, it makes decisions a lot easier.

(They begin walking off.)

Barney: Let's go chase cars or somethin'.

Rex: OK, but first I gotta find a dog biscuit—I'm starving!

Permission to photocopy this skit from *Youth Worker's Encyclopedia: OT* is granted for local church use. Copyright © Group Publishing, Inc., Box 481, Loveland, CO 80539.

If you use this skit as a discussion starter, here are possible questions:

■ **Is loyalty an important quality to have? If so, who should you be loyal to? Why?**

■ **Why is it so hard to be loyal to God? to friends? to family?**

Read aloud Ruth 1:14-18. Ask:

■ **Why do you think Ruth was able to make that promise to Naomi?**

■ **Is there anything you could be as loyal to? What?**

■ **Is it something you should be loyal to?**

RUTH
4:3-22

THEME:
God's family

SUMMARY:
In this PROJECT, teenagers will each create a "family tree."

PREPARATION: You'll need Bibles and a "family-tree" form for each group member. (You can find these at bookstores or make up your own by looking at family trees illustrated in study Bibles.) Talk to your pastor about featuring a different teenager's family each week in your narthex or fellowship hall.

Read together the genealogy of David, found in Ruth 4:3-22. Ask:

■ **Do you hear any names in this genealogy that are part of your family tree? Which ones?**

Tell the group that during the next three months, your congregation will highlight a different youth group family. Have teenagers research their own family history by using the family-tree form you provide.

Ask teenagers to interview parents, grandparents, and other relatives to get as much information as possible on their families.

In addition to their family trees, have kids list (on another sheet of paper) the discoveries they made while researching their family histories.

Each week, display a different family tree and "discovery notes" in the narthex or fellowship hall. During your church service, have a person who knows the featured family tell a positive story about that family.

1 SAMUEL

"God does not see the same way people see.
People look at the outside of a person, but
the Lord looks at the heart."

1 Samuel 16:7b

1 SAMUEL
1

THEME:
Waiting patiently
for God's timing

SUMMARY:
In this DEVOTION, kids antici-
pate opening wrapped presents
that represent God's gifts in our
lives, and they give a gift back to
God, just as Hannah did.

PREPARATION: Wrap several
boxes as presents (one for every
four to six people). Inside each box,
put an item that represents something that's tied to God's timing.
For example, a marriage license
could represent marriage, a rattle
or a diaper could represent a baby,
gold coins could represent heaven,
and so on. You'll also need Bibles, a
gift bag, and a pencil and paper for
each person.

EXPERIENCE
Form groups of four to six people
and have each group select a number from one to 10. (Make sure that
you have one gift-wrapped box for
each group.) Next, have representa-
tives from each group come to the
front and place themselves in
numerical order according to the
number they chose.

Say: **The first person in line
will choose a present, then the
next person will choose, and so
on, until each person has selected one. Then you'll take your
present back to your group and
wait until I say you can open it.**

RESPONSE
Ask a volunteer to read aloud
1 Samuel 1:1–2:11. Ask:
■ **Why was it hard for Hannah to wait for a child?**
■ **What are things you're currently waiting for God to "deliver" in your life?**
■ **What makes it hard to wait
for those things? What makes it
easy?**
■ **Would you have been willing to do what Hannah did?
Why or why not?**

CLOSING
Say: **You may now open your
presents. Inside you'll find an
item that represents something
God has asked us to wait for. In
God's perfect timing, these
things will be gifts to some of
us. In your group, brainstorm
what your item represents.**

After a minute or two, ask
groups to each tell what their item
is and what it represents. Then ask:
■ **How is the way we waited
before opening these gifts like
the way we must wait on God?**
■ **What's something you're
waiting for that you can give as
a gift back to God?**

Give kids each a pencil and
paper and have them list their gifts
to God. Place a gift bag at the front
of your meeting area. Then ask
kids to place their gifts in the bag.
As they place their gifts in the bag,
ask them to say a silent "offering"
prayer to God.

1 SAMUEL
2:12-17; 3:12-14

THEME:
Breaking the cycle
of poor parenting

SUMMARY:
Kids participate in a LEARNING
GAME that will help them understand how poor parenting can be
a hardship that God can use for
good.

PREPARATION: You'll need a six-
pack of soft drinks for every six
people in your group. (For example, if your group has 30 people,
you'll need five six-packs of soft
drinks.) The soft drinks need to be
the same flavor. You'll also need a
3-foot-long piece of rope for each
team of six, a roll of tape (to mark
the starting line), a clean ice chest,
and cups for everyone. Don't forget
Bibles.

Form teams of no more than six.
Give each team a six-pack of
soft drinks and a piece of rope.
Have each team form a line behind
a piece of tape and place the ice
chest about 30 feet from the line.
Next, have the first person in line
tie one end of the rope to the six-
pack and the other end to his or
her leg.

Say: **When I say "go," the first
person in line will run to the ice
chest, pull a soft drink out of
the six-pack, and pour it completely into the ice chest.** (Caution kids to be careful as they open
the soft drink cans.) **This could get**
messy, so be prepared for the soft
drink to spray forcefully out of the
can! Also remember that the
smoother you're able to run, the
less "explosive" the soft drink
will become, so try to run in such
a way as to move the six-packs
gently along the floor.

After the first person pours out
a can, he or she must run back to
the next person in line, untie the
rope, and re-tie it to the next person, who repeats the action.
Continue until you've poured out
all of your soft drink cans. The
first team to finish wins! Ready?
Go!

When kids finish, have each person fill his or her cup from the ice
chest. Have the team that won go
first.

Then ask a volunteer to read
aloud 1 Samuel 2:12-17; 3:12-14.
Ask:

■ **What made Eli a poor
father?**

■ **How does poor parenting
adversely affect kids today?**

■ **How did the soft drinks
tied to your foot hinder you in
the race?**

■ **How are the soft drinks
like poor parenting?**

■ **How can you turn the
hardships of poor parenting
into gifts that everyone can benefit from?**

Say: **Just as in the game, running the race in life is hard
when we have extra weight
attached to us. God is willing to
take any situation we have and
bring something good out of it.
He'll give us the power to break
the cycle and not repeat it with
our own families.**

Close by giving kids a chance to pray about their situations quietly. End the prayer time by asking kids to each tell God one reason why they're thankful for their parents.

1 SAMUEL
7:2-13

THEME:
Remembering God's goodness

SUMMARY:
In this OBJECT LESSON, kids will paint rocks with pictures of things God has provided for them in the past, so they'll feel encouraged about God's provision for the future.

PREPARATION: You'll need a small rock for each person, one large rock, puffy paints or colored markers, and Bibles.

Form groups of no more than four. Give each group several paints or markers and each person a rock. Then say: **This rock is called Ebenezer. Ebenezer means "God has helped us." Choose someone in your group to read aloud 1 Samuel 7:2-13.**

When the groups are finished, ask them to discuss:
■ **Why did the people of Israel place a rock on the ground?**
■ **Why is it important to remember what God has done for us in the past?**

■ **In what ways has God helped you in the past?**
■ **What will you need God's help for in the future?**

Have kids draw things, people, or symbols on their rocks that illustrate how God has provided for them in the past (for example, helping them pass a test, helping them make friends at a new school, or helping them get a job). After they're finished, have kids explain the symbols or pictures on their rocks to others in their group.

Ask teenagers to keep their rocks somewhere visible so they'll remember God's provision when facing tough times. Encourage them to keep adding pictures to the rocks as things happen—they could call it an "Ebenezer moment."

Close by pulling out a large rock and asking kids to each paint or mark one symbol of God's goodness on it. Keep this in your youth room as a group reminder of God's goodness.

1 SAMUEL
8:1-22

THEME:
Our way vs. God's way

SUMMARY:
Kids will participate in a CRE-ATIVE READING using traffic signs for God's warnings in Scripture.

PREPARATION: You'll need 12 sheets of white construction paper; masking tape; colored markers; seven tongue depressors or large, flat sticks; and Bibles.

Form six groups (a group can be one person). Give each group two pieces of construction paper, masking tape, markers, and one large tongue depressor. Assign each group one of the following traffic signs: One Way, No U-Turn, Caution, Bumps Ahead, Wrong Way, or Yield. Give groups five minutes to complete their signs.

When they're finished, say: **I'll read a story based on 1 Samuel 8:1-22. When you hear your sign mentioned in the story, stand up as a group, wave your sign, and shout out your warning.**

DEMANDING OUR OWN WAY

There once was a judge named Samuel. He was getting very old, so he decided to turn his responsibilities over to his two sons. The people cried out, **"Caution"** and **"Bumps Ahead"** because they knew that his sons were evil and would not judge them fairly.

So all the elders and the bigwigs got together to ask Samuel if he'd **Yield** to their desire to have a king. They knew that if they had his sons as judges, they'd definitely be going in the **Wrong Way.**

Samuel wasn't happy that the people wanted a king, for it was not the **One Way** that God had done things in the past. So, Samuel prayed to God and told him of their request. God granted them their request but told them to exercise **Caution,** for there would be **No U-Turn** allowed, and they couldn't go back to their old ways. He also told them that there would be **Bumps Ahead** because a king would take their sons into battle and force others into hard labor. The king would train their daughters as cooks and perfume sellers and take their best crops and grains.

Samuel **Caution**ed the people that this was the **Wrong Way,** but they did not **Yield** to God's warnings of the **Bumps Ahead.** So the people of Israel were given a king. However, it wasn't long before they admitted that they were going the **Wrong Way,** but **No U-Turn** was allowed. They wanted to go back to the **One Way** that God wanted. Sadly, it was too late, and the people of Israel suffered under the rule of a king, simply because they demanded their own way.

1 SAMUEL 10:8; 13:8-14

THEME:
Waiting on God

SUMMARY:
In this DEVOTION, kids will have to wait to move forward in a race, and they'll discover the rewards of waiting and doing things God's way.

PREPARATION: You'll need a deck of at least 20 green and 20 yellow 3×5 cards. (If you have more than

20 kids participating, you'll want to add one extra yellow card for each additional person.) You'll also need a pencil for each person, masking tape, and Bibles.

EXPERIENCE

Place two lines of tape on the floor about 20 feet apart. Have kids line up side by side behind one line while you stand at the opposite line holding the 3×5 cards.

Say: **Starting with the person on my far left, I will hold up a card for each person. Just like a traffic light, if it's green you may "go" three average steps, but if it's yellow you must wait for your next turn. I'll turn the cards quickly, so pay attention to which card is yours. The first person to cross this line wins. Ready? Go!** (Note: If you run out of cards just shuffle and start the deck over.)

RESPONSE

Ask:

■ **What was it like to get a green card? a yellow card?**

■ **What was hard about waiting for a green card?**

Ask a volunteer to read aloud 1 Samuel 10:8; 13:8-14. Then ask:

■ **Why did Saul make the sacrifice instead of Samuel?**

■ **What was wrong with doing that?** (Only priests were to perform sacrifices.)

■ **What were the consequences of Saul's impatience?**

■ **In your own life, what's something you feel impatient about or that you're beginning to lose hope about?**

CLOSING

Give kids each a yellow card and a pencil and have them write something they're losing hope about. Then ask them to pray silently, asking God for the strength to wait patiently.

1 SAMUEL
16:1-13

THEME:
Inner qualities of the heart

SUMMARY:
Throw a PARTY with a "heart" theme to celebrate the inner qualities that God thinks are important.

PREPARATION: You'll need to send out heart-theme invitations at least two weeks ahead of time, inviting kids to come to a "light-hearted" party featuring fun and food. (This might go over better at one of the kids' homes instead of the church.)

Organize parents or kids to bring heart-related foods, such as heart-shaped cookies, artichoke hearts, heart-shaped sandwiches or hamburger patties, heart candies, red punch, various fruits cut into the shape of a heart, and so on. Have kids bring chips, potato salad, or any other side dishes that go with your meal. Arrange chairs in a heart pattern for eating and serve the meal on heart-decorated paper products.

You'll also need newsprint, scissors, markers, red construction paper, a deck of playing cards (with enough cards in the suit of hearts to give one card to each person), and Bibles.

When kids arrive have them cut a heart-shaped banner out of newsprint, then have them each sign their names on it. Throughout the evening, encourage kids to think of "inner" qualities they appreciate about other youth group members and write those qualities next to their names.

Have kids each cut out a heart from red construction paper. Tell them they're not allowed to say the word "heart." If someone catches someone else saying "heart," the person caught must give up his or her heart to the "catcher."

Play "heart" Pictionary using words such as heart attack, coronary, heartthrob, and so on.

Have heart-theme prizes for the winners, such as candy hearts.

After dinner and games, gather everyone together and say: **Tonight we've put a lot of emphasis on the heart. In the Bible, God did, too. As we look at the Scriptures, we see that God was always concerned about what was in people's hearts. In fact, when God got ready to choose a king for Israel, he didn't look at resumes of the wealthiest, most successful, most handsome men in the region.**

Have a volunteer read aloud 1 Samuel 16:1-13, then ask:

■ **What did God look for in a king?**

■ **What would we look for in a king?**

■ **What kinds of inner qualities do you think are important to God?**

■ **Based on God's criteria, who do you know who would be "king" material?**

■ **Think about this for a moment: What would it take for you to be God's kind of king?**

As kids leave, hand each person a playing card in the suit of hearts as a reminder to make the inner qualities of the heart their first priority.

1 SAMUEL
16:7

THEME:
Trusting people

SUMMARY:
Kids will play a LEARNING GAME where they have to trust each other to win.

PREPARATION: You'll need equal numbers of paper slips marked with a blue or red marker, chairs, a sock, and Bibles.

As you welcome kids to the meeting, give each one a slip of paper marked with either a blue or red marker (prepare equal numbers of both). Tell kids not to reveal the color on their slips of paper. Create an open space in the middle of the room and place a chair for a goal at each end of the open space. Ask one person with a red slip and one person with a blue slip to each play goalie in front of one of the goals. Have the rest of the kids scatter throughout the open area.

Say: We're going to play a game called Toss the Sock. I've secretly divided you into two teams—the blue team and the red team (indicate the blue team's goal and the red team's goal). You're not allowed to show anyone else your slip of paper, and you're not allowed to move from your spot on the floor.

Say: The object of the game is to throw a sock to your teammates, getting the sock close enough to the opposing team's goal to throw it under and through the chair. Team members must each try to guard their goal any way they can.

Here's the catch: When you toss the sock to each other, you won't know which team each person belongs to because you don't have to tell the truth when someone asks which team you're on.

Start the game by rolling up a sock into a ball and throwing it to one of the kids. When three or four goals have been scored, stop. Ask:

■ How did you feel during the game?

■ Was it hard to trust people? Why or why not?

■ What emotions did you feel toward people you thought were friends but turned out to be "enemies"?

Read aloud 1 Samuel 16:7. Wrap up the game by asking:

■ How is not knowing who's on your team like not knowing who you can trust in life?

■ What are ways we gauge whether we can trust someone?

■ How does God gauge whether someone is trustworthy, according to this verse?

■ Is it possible for us to follow God's example? Why or why not?

■ How should we gauge who we trust in life?

1 SAMUEL
17:1-58

THEME:
Handling giants in our lives

SUMMARY:
In this DEVOTION, kids try to jump as high as a giant, only to learn that in order to slay giants, they need God's help.

PREPARATION: You'll need to make a 15-foot giant out of newsprint. Draw him with armor and make his face mean and ugly. He should look intimidating. You'll also need black markers, pens, tape, and Bibles.

EXPERIENCE
Securely tape your giant against a wall that's taller than 15 feet. Have each person line up five feet away from the giant with the black marker in his or her hand. Have each person jump at the giant, making a mark as high as possible. To defeat the giant, someone must make a mark on the giant's head.

After all kids take a turn, have them write their names by their marks (allow kids to stand on chairs, if necessary).

RESPONSE

Retell the story of David and Goliath in an exciting and dynamic way, using your Bible as a reference. When you're finished, ask:

■ **How is the way you tried to defeat the giant like or unlike the way David defeated Goliath?**

■ **In what ways did fighting Goliath help David rely upon God?**

■ **Why were the other Israelites afraid to depend upon God's strength?**

■ **What are some "giants" in your own life right now?**

CLOSING

Give kids each a pen and have them describe one "giant" they're facing in life on the 15-foot giant. When everyone is finished, have kids work together to make marks on the giant's head, then tear him down. Close by having kids pray for strength to slay their personal giants.

1 SAMUEL
17:38-49

THEME:

God uses what we have.

SUMMARY:
In this SKIT, a guy isn't sure how to tell his friend about Christ, so he gets some "advice" from other Christian friends.

THE WITNESS

SCENE: Four friends are at the park having a picnic. They're finishing up with their dessert—Jell-O.

PROPS: Blanket, picnic basket, bowls and spoons, paper towels, Jell-O, a small brochure or tract, a pair of 3-D glasses, and a videotape. You'll also need Bibles for discussion after the skit.

CHARACTERS:
Brad (wants to tell a particular friend about Christ)
Matt, Julie, and **Todd** (Brad's Christian friends who try to give him advice on how to tell his friend about Christ)

SCRIPT
(All are sitting on a blanket, eating their Jell-O, and having a good time. A picnic basket is in the center of the blanket.)

Julie: What a lunch! Having a picnic was a great idea! Glad I thought of it!

Matt: Actually, I thought of it.

Julie: But the Jell-O for dessert was my idea.

Matt: Yeah, but I picked the flavor.

Julie: So, I brought the spoons.

Matt: I thought of the bowls.

Julie: Lucky I got the paper towels.

Matt: *(Rolling his eyes then looking at Brad)* Hey, Brad, you've been kind of quiet. Something on your mind?

Brad: Oh, I've been thinking about my friend Steve. He's not a Christian, and I want to tell him about Jesus, but I really don't know how. I'm just not a very good speaker. I'm afraid I'll mess it all up.

Julie: *(Excitedly)* Oh, I know how

to help! Do you have a slide projector?

Brad: A slide projector? Nooo... but I guess I could borrow one from Mrs. Kelly's room. Why?

Julie: Well, if you put together a slide show about your life and add a lot of cool music, Steve will just have to become a Christian. You can start out with pictures of yourself when you were a little kid and talk about all the fun stuff you used to do. Then start talking about growing up and all the problems in life you've had to deal with. As the mood of the music changes, you'll be able to work in stuff about Jesus and how he can solve all our problems. I'll help you choose the music if you want. Mood music is very important.

Matt: *(Excitedly)* This is great! Do you have a shirt with an easily accessible pocket?

Brad: Yeah, but why?

Matt: 'Cause right after you show him the slide show, you can inconspicuously pull out this 3-D tract, "What Hell Is Like and Why You Don't Want to Go There." Here, you'll need to put these glasses on him when you hand him the booklet *(hands 3-D glasses to Brad)*. You can just sit there while he reads it if you want. You really don't have to do anything else. All the steps for becoming a Christian are listed in the back. Works every time.

Brad: *(Unsure)* I guess I could go change before I talk to him.

Julie: And when you're done, if he still hasn't become a Christian, show this video *(hands videotape to Brad)*. It's a tape of a bunch of superstar Christians who got together to play softball. It's pretty funny and has a lot of interviews with the players. He'll see what fun Christians can have and won't be able to resist joining us. And the best part about this whole thing is that you don't need to be there with him while he's looking at all this stuff. It might make him feel better if you hung around, but there's really no need. Telling people about Jesus is so simple these days. It's a wonder we don't have more people becoming Christians.

Brad: *(Hesitantly)* Wow, uh, thanks for all the advice, I guess.

Julie: Don't mention it. Good luck!

Matt: Yeah, I hope it all works out for you. Well, Julie and I gotta be going... drama club waits for no man.

Julie: Or woman. *(Julie and Matt walk away, leaving Brad and Todd with stunned looks on their faces.)*

Brad: *(Looking at Todd)* Man, I would never be able to think of all that stuff. God must want someone else to tell Steve about Jesus because I'm sure not equipped to do the job.

Todd: Have you tried just talking to Steve?

Brad: You mean without using anything? By myself? Me and him? Just talking? I'd botch it for sure.

Todd: I don't know, Brad. Steve respects you. I think he'll listen to what you have to say. I mean, if it were me, I'd listen to *you* more than I'd want to watch all those other things.

Brad: Yeah, I guess you're right. God probably wants to use me like I am. I mean, he did create me this way, huh?

Todd: Yeah. And besides—the last time I saw you use a slide projector you put all the slides in upside down.
(Both exit.)

If you use this skit as a discussion starter, here are possible questions:

■ **When have you felt unsure about sharing your faith?**

■ **What did you do?**

■ **Do you think God ever asks us to do things we're not capable of doing? Why or why not? Back up your answers with at least two Scripture passages.**

Read 1 Samuel 17:38-49. Ask:

■ **Do you think David felt led by God to do what he did?**

■ **Do you think he ever doubted he would defeat the giant?**

■ **If so, why do you think he fought him anyway? If not, why not?**

■ **Why do you think David picked five stones from the stream when he only needed one stone?**

■ **How does sharing faith compare to defeating a giant?**

1 SAMUEL 18–20

THEME:
Friendship

SUMMARY:
Kids will act out a modern version of David and Jonathan's friendship in this SKIT.

THE WONDER-FULL YEARS

SCENE: A narrator remembers a friendship from his youth.

PROPS: Five or six school books, two lunch bags with lunch in them, a table, six to eight chairs, paper, and pencils. You'll also need Bibles for the discussion after the skit.

CHARACTERS:
Narrator
David
David's Friend
Jonathan
four or five Students
Teacher
*(**Note:** "The wonder years" are synonymous with the three years kids spend in junior high. They're exciting, fearsome, and eye-opening years for most kids. But sometimes the wonder years aren't so wonderful. There are hard lessons to be learned. And there are looming challenges to overcome.*

That's what this narrated skit is all about. It's patterned after the hit TV show The Wonder Years.

To use it in your group, have the actors perform their parts in mime, responding appropriately to the narration. Have them "mouth" any actual words spoken by the kids or teacher in the narration. The skit requires some rehearsal, but far less than a normal drama. Spend 30 to 60 minutes practicing, then present the skit to the rest of the youth group or to the church.)

SCRIPT

(Narrator stands to the far right or left of stage, reading the skit dramatically, as one looking back on his life.)

I met Jonathan Priest in the fall of our eighth-grade year. His family had just moved to town from California or some weird place like that, so he didn't know anybody. And he acted like he didn't want to know anybody.

(David walks on stage with books under his arm. He's talking with a friend. Jonathan is offstage right. He also has books under his arm.)

Jonathan was quiet...kept to himself. After class, he'd leave fast and walk home alone. He didn't answer in class, and the teachers didn't call on him either. That was real strange.

(David waves goodbye to his friend and walks fast toward Jonathan. Jonathan walks aimlessly toward David.)

I'll never forget how we met.

(David and Jonathan collide. Books fly everywhere.)

It was one of those stupid accidents that is nobody's fault, really. You know—you get involved in something, and you just don't think.

(They pick up the books.)

I told him I was sorry and that the accident was real dumb of me. But he didn't say a thing. Not a

thing. Just looked away.

(Jonathan starts to walk away.)

"Look, guy, I said I'm sorry."

(Jonathan nods.)

Now I was getting angry. I mean, it wasn't my fault. If anything, he should've been looking where he was going.

"Hey, you," I demanded. "Aren't you going to say anything?"

"I'm s-s-s-sorry," he said.

The kid stuttered! Jonathan stuttered! Now it made sense. That's why he was so quiet in class. That's why the teachers didn't call on him. Because he stuttered.

I felt like a real jerk.

(David acts apologetic toward Jonathan.)

"Hey, now I really am sorry," I told him. "My name's David. What's yours?"

"J-J-J-Jonathan," he told me. "J-J-J-Jonathan P-P-P-Priest."

I invited Jonathan Priest to sit with me for lunch, and that's how our friendship began.

(The two sit at a table, take out lunch sacks, and eat while talking.)

It's really no big deal that kids stutter. Although, if you paid attention to some of the insensitive idiots in junior high school, you'd think it's a major handicap. They actually put kids down with speech defects.

I learned a lot from Jonathan that year. For one thing, patience. You've got to be patient with kids who stutter. And you can't tell them to talk slower or take a deep breath or any of those other things that people say when they're around stutterers.

You've just got to be quiet. Which is hard for a 15-year-old.

I also learned a lot of algebra from Jonathan Priest. He was brilliant in math, probably because he spent so much time with the books while the rest of us were talking.

(David and Jonathan study together.)

I just couldn't catch on to algebra, and spring finals were coming fast. When we weren't playing basketball or skating or going to movies, we were studying. We became best friends that year—Jonathan Priest and me.

(Stage is set up like a classroom—chairs in a row, teacher in front, six or eight students. Kids mime sitting at desks.)

Then came the big exam. I was supposed to study the week before, but baseball was starting that month, and the church group had a retreat the weekend before—so studying was on the bottom of my priority list. By the time the algebra final rolled around, I didn't know a square root from a plant root. And I was scared!

(David walks into class and sits next to Jonathan. The test begins.)

About halfway into the test, I began to get real scared—the prospect of remedial summer school didn't exactly thrill me. Then I looked over and saw Jonathan's answer sheet filling up beautifully. The teacher had turned away, so I nudged Jonathan and motioned for him to push his paper closer.

Jonathan shook his head.

"No way," he whispered.

I couldn't believe it! This was my best friend. My buddy. I taught him to play basketball and introduced him to all my friends. Now he wouldn't do a simple favor for me? Again I tried. Again, he shook his head "no."

Old Man Johnson, the teacher, saw me.

"David, what's going on back there? Do you want to be removed from this class?"

"Don't bother!" I said. And I slammed my book shut and got out of that place.

(David gets up and glares at Jonathan. Jonathan shakes his head sadly and looks back at his test.)

I waited for him after class, and was I angry!

(David angrily confronts Jonathan.)

Have you ever gotten into an argument where you knew from the start that you were wrong and the other person was right? One you were into so deeply that throwing up your hands and saying, "You're right—you're right," would be the ultimate defeat? That's the way this argument was.

I knew I was wrong for wanting to cheat on the test. I mean, the Bible tells you. Your parents tell you. Your conscience tells you. And Jonathan told me. Oh, did he tell me...

I started out with the dumbest line: "I thought we were friends." Like that was supposed to mean he should do any stupid thing for me in the name of friendship.

Jonathan let me know that real friends bring out the best in each other and that cheating on math tests is not exactly one of those best things.

He was right. I knew he was right, and he knew he was right. But I was backed into a corner. So I did the only thing a wounded, insecure 15-year-old could do. I hurt him bad.

"Jonathan," I said, "you're a real j-j-j-jerk!"

And that got him. It was a good clean shot that hit him where he hurt. His eyes filled up with tears, and he couldn't say a word. It was as though I'd blasted him in the gut. He just stood there for a few minutes; then he turned and walked away.

(Jonathan walks away.)

I've never forgotten that feeling. I felt low. Real low. Like scum. I tried calling after him, but he didn't turn. And I wasn't going to run after him. No way. I was too proud.

Things were never the same after that. We'd run into each other in the hall, and we'd nod, but we wouldn't talk. I couldn't look at him, and he wouldn't look at me. The hurt was too deep. He found other friends, and I got on the basketball and track team, so we didn't hang around together.

The next summer his family moved back to California. When I was in college, I learned that Jonathan had been drafted and went to Vietnam, where he was killed.

I wish this story had a happy ending. Sometimes it takes a lot of pain to grow, and I'll have to admit that Jonathan Priest helped me grow. I learned that when you have a good friend,

you have to take the hard words from him as well as what you want to hear. And I learned that when you've made a fool of yourself, you've got to admit it. You've got to ask for forgiveness and get on with the business of being friends.

And most of all, I learned that there's nothing as precious as a good friend. Nothing.

(David exits.)

For a discussion after the skit, have kids skim 1 Samuel 18–20 to get familiar with the story. Then, form pairs and have partners discuss:

■ **What similarities do you see in the friendship of the characters in the skit and the friendship described in 1 Samuel 18–20?**

■ **What are three things you need to be a good friend to someone like Jonathan was to David?**

Close with a prayer, thanking God for the gift of friendship.

1 SAMUEL 20:1-42

THEME:
Developing strong friendships

SUMMARY:
On this RETREAT, kids will be challenged to develop good friendships.

PREPARATION: Plan four Bible study sessions based on Jonathan and David's example of friendship in 1 Samuel 20:1-42.

Use the following themes to structure the retreat:

Friday Night: love deeply— Explore ways kids can show their friends that they love them in tangible ways, even when it's tough.

Saturday Morning: be willing to sacrifice—Have kids discuss what it means to make a sacrifice for someone and what Christ's sacrifice means to them.

Saturday Night: always speak well of your friend—Get kids talking about the importance of integrity in their speech and the dangers of gossip and slander.

Sunday Morning: keep your promises—Have kids examine the importance of doing what they say (use Scriptures from Proverbs on remaining true to your word).

If possible, choose a place for your retreat where everyone can stay in close quarters—a large cabin would be ideal. Involve kids in activities that build and strengthen friendships. For example:

• Form teams to make the meals.

• Form pairs or trios for exploration hikes or devotions.

• Plan cooperative, not competitive, games.

• Assign each person a secret pal and prayer buddy.

• Encourage kids to come up with unique decorations for their rooms.

• Post friendship-related Scriptures in prominent places.

Close the weekend with kids each doing something nice for their secret pals, then have them reveal themselves to each other. Have secret pals pray together for each other to become better friends. Gather everyone together and have kids each finish this sentence: "This weekend I've learned _____ about being a better friend."

1 SAMUEL
24:1-22

THEME:
Respecting authority

SUMMARY:
On this ADVENTURE, kids will tour a police station and gain an appreciation and understanding of the duties of a law enforcement officer.

PREPARATION: You'll need to call ahead to your local police station and organize a tour. Make sure you're specific about the kinds of things you'd like included in your visit; for example, a full tour of the facilities, an overview of a police officer's job description, what it takes to become a police officer, a ride in a police car, what happens to someone when they're "brought in," and so on. You'll also need doughnuts, hot chocolate, and Bibles.

Plan to tour your local police station. For fun, give kids doughnuts and hot chocolate when they arrive at the church before they go to the police station.

Say: **To some of us, dough-nuts are all we think about when we think about police officers.** Today we'll expand our thinking and gain a deeper respect for what these people really do each day to protect us.

After the tour gather back together for a time of debriefing. Read aloud 1 Samuel 24:1-22, then ask:

■ **How did David show respect for the authority over him?**

■ **Why is it hard to show respect for authority some-times?**

■ **What did you learn today that has helped you have more respect for the police officers in our area?**

■ **Why do you think God cares if we respect those who have authority over us?**

■ **What's one thing you can do to respect the authorities in your life?**

Close your day together by pray-ing for the people who serve as policemen and policewomen in your city.

1 SAMUEL
25:4-35

THEME:
Revenge doesn't pay.

SUMMARY:
Kids will participate in an "intergalactic" LEARNING GAME to discover the consequences of taking revenge into their own hands.

PREPARATION: You'll need two large cardboard refrigerator boxes (you can find these at an appliance store), several newspapers, large colored markers, several blindfolds (you can use bandannas, scarves, or towels), and Bibles.

Form two teams. Name one team the Starship Enterprise and the second team the Romu-lans. Give each team a refrigerator box, colored markers, and an ample supply of newspapers. Have each team decorate its refrigerator box to depict its identity.

Say: **We find ourselves at yet another confrontation between the Starship Enterprise and their arch rivals, the Romulans. The Romulans have initiated this attack because they're looking for revenge. Each team member will be blindfolded and will have five minutes to wad up newspaper bombs and throw them into the opponent's starship. At the end of five min-utes, the team with the most**

bombs in its starship explodes and loses.

Have each person put on a blindfold. As soon as all of the Romulans have put on their blindfolds, have each team begin to make newspaper bombs. In the midst of the rustling papers, secretly remove the blindfolds from members of the Starship Enterprise team. Say: **Load phasers and commence firing!**

After five minutes, have the Romulans remove their blindfolds and have both teams count the bombs in their starships. Obviously, the Romulans will be the losing team. Gather the teams together and ask:

■ **Do you feel that this game was fair? Why or why not?**

■ **How did it feel to be a Romulan?**

■ **How did it feel to be part of the Starship Enterprise?**

■ **What are the typical consequences of revenge in real life? Explain.**

Have a volunteer (or several) from the Starship Enterprise read aloud 1 Samuel 25:4-35. Have members of the Starship Enterprise team pair up with members of the Romulan team. Then ask the following questions and have partners discuss them one at a time. Have volunteers share their discoveries with the whole class. Wrap up the game by asking:

■ **What revenge did David want to take and why?**

■ **Why did Abigail stop David from taking revenge?**

■ **What did David have to lose if he took revenge into his own hands?**

■ **Why is it hard for us to give up our right to take revenge?**

■ **Do you believe revenge is sweet? Why or why not?**

2 SAMUEL

"He [David] said: 'The Lord is my rock, my protection, my Savior.' "

2 Samuel 22:2

2 SAMUEL
1:17-27

THEME:
Reputation

SUMMARY:

Teenagers will create new identities for themselves on a weekend RETREAT and learn how quickly they can establish a new reputation.

PREPARATION: You'll need to plan and advertise a "come-as-you-might-be" retreat. Invite another youth group, one that your kids aren't familiar with, to join you on the retreat. Choose a "neutral" site for the retreat, away from either group's church and bring supplies as needed for the activities you choose. You'll also need Bibles, tape, paper, and pencils.

Invite your kids to a "come-as-you-might-be" retreat. To attend the retreat kids must each do the following:

• create a new identity that includes a name, family background, personality, and personal tastes (in clothing, hairstyle, music, hobbies, interests, and anything else they can think of);

• become that person from the time they leave for the retreat until the closing debriefing at the retreat; and

• respond to others on the retreat as if they'd never met them before that day.

Kids will have a chance to become whoever they want for the retreat. And don't forget to tell them that they'll be spending the weekend with complete strangers!

Begin the retreat with crowd-breakers and games that'll help kids meet one another. Remind kids they must play their roles until the end of the retreat. Have the kids make name tags that include a self-description. To help kids learn new names, form teams of five then give teams each five minutes to write down on paper as many words as they can by combining letters from their first and last names.

During the retreat, play volleyball, softball, and other sports that'll give kids a chance to interact and act out their identities. Play board games and Trivial Pursuit-style games at night to bring kids together. Through it all, remind kids to act in accordance with their new personas.

Plan your theme on the topic of reputation or character building. Use the lives of King Saul and his son, Jonathan, as your biblical foundation. Focus the retreat on 2 Samuel 1:17-27. Have kids compare and contrast Saul's and Jonathan's reputations, then examine David's lament for Saul and Jonathan in the passage. (A helpful resource is Gene Edwards' book *A Tale of Three Kings: The Study of Brokenness,* which is a story of the relationships between Saul, David, and Absalom.)

After each study session, form discussion groups of four or five kids and have them discuss "in character" what they've learned.

Close the retreat with a debriefing session. Have kids form a circle. Tape a sheet of paper to each person's back. Then give kids each a pencil and have them wander around the circle, writing words that describe each person's personality. After 10 or 15 minutes, have kids sit down and remove the papers from their backs. Tell kids it's now OK to resume their normal personalities and names.

One by one, have teenagers say how they felt when they read the words written about them and then give a short description of their real personalities (invite those who know the teenagers to add details). Ask kids to each explain why they chose the identities they did. Ask:

■ **What did you like or dislike about the person you became?**

■ **What did you like or dislike about the others on our retreat?**

■ **Was it hard to become a different person? Why or why not?**

■ **What are characteristics of the person you became that you're going to continue?**

■ **Did you feel more secure or less secure knowing that you began the retreat with a "clean slate"?**

Have kids hold hands in a circle, then have them each close in prayer by asking God to develop positive characteristics in them.

2 SAMUEL 3:13-16

THEME:
Respect for others' relationships

SUMMARY:
In this LEARNING GAME, kids will try to break up established pairs by dragging one partner outside of a circle.

PREPARATION: Draw or tape a large circle in the center of your meeting room or gym. You'll need Bibles.

Have kids pair up and sit within the large circle you've made. Ask them to link arms firmly at the elbow. Say: **You're now joined to your partner. The only way you can be separated from your partner is if one of you is dragged out of the circle. The partner who is dragged outside of the circle must leave the circle and his or her partner behind.**

Choose one pair to be "pair wreckers." Their job is to separate partners from each other by dragging one partner out of the circle. Once a pair wrecker successfully drags someone out of the circle, he or she should link up with the partner that remains in the circle. The ousted person should then attempt to split up another pair.

Continue until every partnership has been tested or until kids lose interest. Don't declare winners or losers, and don't refer to the activity as a game. Also, don't suggest that those within the circle should resist separation.

After the activity, have all the kids sit in a circle. Ask:

■ **How did you feel when you and your partner were being pulled apart?**

■ **How did you feel when you saw others being pulled apart?**

■ **Did you feel protective of your partner? Why or why not?**

■ **Did you feel dependent upon your partner? Why or why not?**

■ **How strongly did you struggle to stay together?**

Read aloud the story of Michal's being taken away from her husband (2 Samuel 3:13-16). Then ask:

■ **How do you think the three main characters in this story—David, Michal, and Paltiel—felt?**

■ **How are those feelings like those you felt during our activity?**

■ **What would you have done that Paltiel didn't?**

■ **Is it ever right for someone to separate two people in a marriage, dating, or friendship relationship? Why or why not?**

2 SAMUEL
6:1-9

THEME:

Being angry with God

SUMMARY:
In this DEVOTION, teenagers identify ways people deal with anger and decide whether it's possible to be angry with God and still maintain a loving relationship with him.

PREPARATION: You'll need pencils, paper, and Bibles.

EXPERIENCE

Form groups of two to five. Give groups 20 minutes to create 30- to 60-second commercials advertising a product that will help people express or deal with their anger. They might advertise such things as a punching dummy, a two-sided mask with contrasting smiling and angry faces, a compact disc of brain-soothing music, or a "Don't get mad—get even" do-it-yourself survival kit. Kids will need to make outlines or write scripts for their advertisements, so give each group paper and pencils. Also tell kids they can use props if they wish.

After 20 minutes have groups each present their commercials. (If you have access to a video camera, videotape the commercials for the showing.) Then ask:

■ **Which products provided answers to help people deal with their anger in a positive way?**

■ **Which would help you?**

■ **Did the commercials portray anger as a positive or negative emotion?**

■ **Do you believe it's OK to be angry? Why or why not?**

RESPONSE

Designate four corners of the room as "furious," "angry," "a little miffed," and "I'm cool." Say: **I'll read a story to you from 2 Samuel 6:1-9. Occasionally I'll pause to get your reactions to what's happening in the story. When I pause, go to the corner that best expresses how you feel about what I've read.**

Read the story, pausing after verse 7 and after 8 for kids to move to the corner that best represents their degree of anger. Give kids in each corner a moment to discuss with one another how they feel and why. Then ask a volunteer from each corner to say why they feel as they do. There are no right or wrong answers, so encourage kids to express their opinions freely.

Say: **Tell about a time when you've been angry at God.** Allow kids time to respond. Then ask:

■ **Is it ever appropriate to be angry with God?**

■ **How do you think God responds to us when we're angry at him?**

■ **How might we express our anger and still keep our relationship with God strong?**

CLOSING

Close the meeting by forming groups of three, then asking them to each pray together about situations that have produced anger in their lives, especially anger at God.

2 SAMUEL 11:1–12:24

THEME:
Sin

SUMMARY:

In this LEARNING GAME, teenagers are given a clue to a secret story and must figure out the rest of the story.

PREPARATION: Be prepared to tell a story from your own life about how you learned to deal with sin. You'll need Bibles.

Challenge the group to unravel a brain teaser. You'll provide the situation, and the kids must figure out the story behind it. They may ask you only "yes" or "no" questions.

Here is the situation: **She came out of the water, and he died.** Repeat the clue several times—it's the only information you'll provide, other than "yes" or "no" answers to their questions. The solution to the brain teaser is the story of David's sin with Bathsheba. Bathsheba came out of the water, and that eventually led to the death of her husband, Uriah, the Hittite.

Tell kids they'll figure out the brain teaser more quickly if they confine their questions to facts they already know. For example, they might assume the woman is coming out of a lake or a river, and that's not the case. Also, tell kids to concentrate on broad questions rather than specifics. For example, it's better to ask, "Did he die a violent death?" rather than "Was he shot in the head?"

From your clue, kids must figure out that the story is about a king who sees a woman bathing, then has an affair with her, resulting in her pregnancy, and ending with the king ordering the death of the woman's husband. After the story is discovered, tell kids your story is actually the true story of King David, Bathsheba, and Uriah.

Form trios and have groups familiarize themselves with the

story in 2 Samuel 11:1–12:24. Then have trios discuss the following questions:

■ **Why did David choose to deal with his sin the way he did?**

■ **How would David's plan have worked if he hadn't been exposed by Nathan?**

■ **If he'd ended his deception sooner, how would this story have ended differently?**

■ **How could David have handled this situation differently, and what would the consequences have been if he did?**

■ **How do you deal with your own sin? Is it like or unlike the way David dealt with his?**

Listen to kids' answers without judging them right or wrong. Then tell about a time you learned how to deal with your own sin. Conclude by reading aloud Psalm 51, David's prayer of repentance over his sin with Bathsheba.

2 SAMUEL 15:1-12

THEME:

Betrayal

SUMMARY:

This active DEVOTION is in a *Donahue* talk show format, with two kids role-playing David and Absalom as guests, and the rest of the kids asking questions and offering their opinions about Absalom's betrayal.

PREPARATION: The week before your meeting, assign the roles of David and Absalom to two teenagers. Ask them to study their characters' lives in 2 Samuel, especially 15:1-12, and be prepared to be guests on a talk show. Set up your meeting room like a talk show set, with three chairs in the front and the rest of the chairs facing them. You'll need a microphone (even if you don't have a sound system in your room) and Bibles.

EXPERIENCE

Holding the microphone, say: **Welcome to our show. Let me introduce you to our special guests today. On my right is David, King of Israel. This shepherd's son has done great things. He killed a lion and a bear to protect his sheep, knocked off the giant—Goliath— with a single stone, and is an accomplished musician.**

On my left is David's son, Absalom. He's already killed a man, been in exile for three years, and for five years did not see his father. He's since been reunited with his father. As you can see, he's one of the most handsome men alive. Let's give a warm welcome to our guests. (Pause for applause.) **Before we begin, let me give you a little more background on these two.**

Read aloud 2 Samuel 15:1-12. Then say: **Absalom is conspiring to take over his father's kingdom. We've asked the two of them to meet here on our show, so Absalom could explain why he plans to betray his father, the king.**

Conduct the interview as a typical talk show host. Carry around your microphone and encourage the audience to ask questions and make comments. Keep the interview lively by asking questions like these that stimulate discussion:

■ **Absalom, what have you been up to?**

■ **What's the deal with this so-called betrayal plan?**

■ **Don't you care about your dad?**

■ **What was it like growing up as his son?**

■ **David, to what extent do you blame yourself for your son's betrayal?**

■ **Do you think the mistakes you've made in your life have set a bad example for him?**

■ **What do you think of your son now?**

■ **Do you still love him?**

RESPONSE

Ask the audience:

■ **What can be done to restore this father/son relationship?**

■ **Is it too late? Why or why not?**

■ **What have you learned about restoring your own broken relationships?**

Encourage kids to offer solutions on how to restore this broken relationship and broken relationships in their own lives.

CLOSING

Conclude the interview by asking both David and Absalom where their relationship will go from here. Ask them to each decide whether the solutions offered by the audience could change their relationship.

2 SAMUEL 18:9-33

THEME:
A parent's love

SUMMARY:
In this PROJECT, parents and teenagers build a "walk of love" as a testimony to their love for one another.

PREPARATION: You'll need to pick a special place on your church grounds to pour a small concrete slab. If possible, enlist the help of someone with cement-pouring experience. Gather 2×4s to use as forms in pouring the concrete. Ask kids to each bring an empty plastic milk container with the top cut off. Have parents bring saws, hammers, nails, shovels, and wheelbarrows. You'll also need bags of ready-mix concrete and Bibles. Ask for volunteers to fix breakfast for the parents and teenagers.

(**Note:** Tell participants they'll be making footprints in cement, so they might want to wear old shoes.)

Host a parent/teen breakfast on a Saturday morning at your church. Make sure that teenagers whose parents can't come are adopted by other adults so they can participate.

After the meal, tell or read aloud the story of Absalom's death and David's grief (2 Samuel 18:9-33). Explain how Absalom made himself David's enemy, but David loved his son anyway.

Have parents and teenagers

work together to make forms out of the 2×4s for pouring the concrete. Have participants dig out a walkway, create a frame out of the boards, forming the shape of your concrete slab or walkway. Then pour water in a wheelbarrow and open your concrete bags. Have kids, one by one, fill their milk containers with the mix and pour it into the wheelbarrow.

As they do, say: **The concrete mix represents Absalom's rebellious acts—some were small, some were big, but all together they caused destruction in his relationship with his dad. The wheelbarrow represents David's love** (mix the concrete and water). **David's love absorbed Absalom's sin. And the more he absorbed that sin, the stronger his love became.**

Assign a small section of the frame to each teenager present. When the concrete is mixed, have teenagers pour and smooth it into the section of the frame assigned to them.

After the concrete has hardened a little, ask parents to put their footprints in it as if taking one step. Then have teenagers do the same, representing the shared love between parents and teenagers.

Have each family write their last name along the side of their assigned section. This "walk of love" will be a lasting reminder of the love between parents and their kids.

2 SAMUEL
22:2-25

THEME:
Enemies

SUMMARY:
In this OBJECT LESSON, teenagers will listen as the leader reads a Scripture passage about David praising God, and they will choose an object that best represents the emotions they feel.

PREPARATION: You'll need a box of tissues, a baseball-sized rock, a balloon, a belt, and Bibles.

Have your group form a circle by holding hands. Then have them drop their hands but stay close enough to each other to pass items to one another. Place a box of tissues, a baseball-sized rock, a blown-up balloon, and a belt in the center of the circle. One by one, hold up each item and ask:

■ **What emotion or situation could this item represent?**

There are no right or wrong answers. If kids seem stumped, offer a few ideas to get them thinking. For example, the tissue could represent illness or sorrow. The rock could represent hard times, anger, or stability. The balloon could bring thoughts of a party, or freedom, or happy feelings. The belt could mean support or possibly punishment.

Say: **I'll slowly read 2 Samuel 22:2-25. As I read, pass the balloon clockwise from one** person to the next. Don't be in a hurry, but keep the item moving. Listen to the words I'm reading, and if an item in the center of the circle better represents those words, get that item and pass it on instead of the one you have. Read the passage slowly, giving kids time to change items from the center of the circle.

When you've completed the passage, have the kids sit where they are. Encourage them to open their Bibles to 2 Samuel 22:2-25 and have them each read aloud a verse. When you get to sections of the Scripture where someone changed the item being passed, stop and ask why.

After the passage has been read and discussed, ask:

■ **What pattern do you see in this Scripture passage?**

■ **What is the significance of this pattern?**

■ **What have you learned that might help you in your everyday life?**

To close, have kids sing their favorite praise songs. Sing the songs as an expression of the strength God gives us when we praise him. (Check out *The Group Praise & Worship Songbook* as a resource.)

2 SAMUEL 23:8-39

THEME:
Appreciating "mighty people" in our lives

SUMMARY:
In this PROJECT, teenagers will each make a scrapbook about people who've had a positive influence on them.

PREPARATION: You'll need card-stock paper, colored pens or markers, plastic term paper covers, and Bibles.

Say: **Second Samuel 23:8-39 is a listing of David's "mighty men." These are the people who made a difference in his life by giving him guidance and strength, as well as fighting beside him. We all have "mighty people" in our lives who've done the same for us. It's important that we recognize these people and thank them for helping us. That's what this project is about.**

Read aloud 2 Samuel 23:8-39. Then ask:

■ **What kind of people might qualify as mighty people in our lives?**

Kids might give examples like people who taught them important lessons about life, encouraged them the most when they were down, said just the right thing when needed, believed in them no matter what, inspired them to take action or change, or made some significant contribution in their lives.

Give kids each a stack of card-stock paper, a plastic cover, and a pen or marker. Ask them to each make a list of the mighty people in their lives. Help them get started by sharing your own list.

Then have kids use the paper and plastic covers to put together "Mighty People" scrapbooks. Encourage teenagers to include pictures, cards, letters, newspaper articles, and written descriptions of the mighty people in their lives.

In two weeks, have kids bring their scrapbooks back to the group and describe what they've collected. Then encourage kids to share their scrapbooks with the important people in their lives.

2 SAMUEL 24:1-25

THEME:
Faith

SUMMARY:
In this SKIT, two guys are looking in trash bins for Christmas gifts. A discussion ensues, questioning the motives of the gift giver.

FREE GIFTS!

SCENE: Two guys, Gene and Kevin, are driving in a car on their way to the mall to shop for Christmas gifts.

PROPS: Two chairs (car seats), a trash can, a pair of socks, a box of candy, and a wrapped package with a pair of boxer shorts inside. You'll also need Bibles for the discussion after the skit.

CHARACTERS:
Gene
Kevin

SCRIPT
(Gene opens car door and sits in passenger seat.)
Kevin: Hi, Gene.
Gene: Hey, Kevin.
Kevin: *(Beginning to drive)* Thanks for coming with me. I hate Christmas shopping by myself.
Gene: Yeah, me too. Where we goin'?
Kevin: I thought I'd cruise on over to the mall first and see what I could find.
Gene: Good idea. Do you know what you're looking for?
Kevin: Sort of. Most of the gifts I get are even a surprise to me. Never know what you're gonna find at the mall.
Gene: Know what you mean. When I shop, I just go up and down the aisles until I find something that catches my eye.
Kevin: I guess in a way that's how I shop, too.
Gene: *(Pointing out the window)* Hey, Kev, you missed the parking lot entrance to the mall.
Kevin: Yeah, we're going around the back.
Gene: I didn't know they had an entrance around there.
Kevin: Oh, they don't. But that's where we're going to do our shopping.
Gene: The only things back there are trash bins...
Kevin: I know.

Gene: Kevin, I think I'm missing something here.

Kevin: *(Both getting out of car and looking around)* Well, this is where I do all of my Christmas shopping every year. You can find some pretty cool things in the trash bins back here.

Gene: And you give this stuff away as Christmas gifts?

Kevin: Yeah. And the beauty of the whole thing is that people don't usually know the difference. They think I went out and spent a lot of money on them, and I don't tell them any differently.

Gene: Of course not.

Kevin: *(Walking over to the trash can)* Well, let's start shoppin'! Hey, hey, hey! I just got here, and I've already hit the jackpot. Look at these! *(Holds up a pair of socks.)*

Gene: You're gonna give those to somebody as a gift?

Kevin: Sure. One wash, with a little bleach of course, and they're as good as new! *(Looks deeper in trash can and pulls up a half-empty box of candy.)* Wow, this can has a bonanza of gifts in it. My mom loves this kind of chocolate.

Gene: You can't give that to your mother! It's a half-eaten box of chocolates!

Kevin: Of course not! I'm not that dumb. I'll find a smaller box to put them in so it looks like I bought them.

Gene: You're kidding, right?

Kevin: Well, I'm not going to give them to her like this!

Gene: No, I mean about this whole thing. You really don't "shop" here do you?

Kevin: Sure. Why not?

Gene: What you're doing doesn't bother you?

Kevin: Why should it bother me?

Gene: Because you're making people think you sacrificed something for them when you really didn't. Everybody loves to buy things on sale, but you're going a little too far. It might be a little different if you didn't have any money, but you do. You're not being thrifty, you're being cheap!

Kevin: Oh, people don't care.

Gene: What if you found out your brother's and sister's presents were all brand-new from the store but yours were from a trash can out back?

Kevin: My parents wouldn't do that; they love us all just the same. Anyway, what you don't know won't hurt you.

Gene: Would you do that to me?

Kevin: Of course not, you're my best friend.

Gene: Kevin, did you get me something for Christmas?

Kevin: Sure did. It's in the car. *(Brings out a wrapped package with Gene's name on it.)* I know it's early, but go ahead and open it up.

Gene: *(Opens package.)* Hey, great, glow-in-the-dark Goofy boxer shorts. Kevin, how come there's no tag or stickers on these?

Kevin: Uh... I took them off before I wrapped them. Yeah.

Gene: Kevin, why is there someone's name written inside the waistband?

Kevin: That would be the, uh, new, um, designer label... Besides, Gene, it's the thought that counts.

Gene: *(Thinking)* Yeah... I know. *(Both exit.)*

If you use this skit as a discussion starter, here are possible questions:

■ **How would you feel if you received a "gift" but later on found out that it actually came from a trash bin? Explain?**

■ **Read 2 Samuel 24:1-25. Why wasn't David willing to sacrifice burnt offerings to God that didn't cost him anything?**

■ **Do you think God asks sacrifices of us? If so, what kind? If not, why not?**

2 SAMUEL 24:15-16

THEME:
When God is sad

SUMMARY:
In this PROJECT, teenagers will put together a book called *What Grieves God's Heart?* using articles they cut out of newspapers.

PREPARATION: You'll need newspapers, legal-size paper, scissors, glue, markers or pens, a stapler, and Bibles.

Ask a volunteer to read aloud 2 Samuel 24:15-16. Then ask:

■ **Why did God feel sad?**

■ **How could an all-powerful, all-knowing God be sad?**

■ **How did God express the sadness in his heart?**

Form pairs and give each pair a newspaper, legal-size paper, scissors, glue, and a marker or pen. Ask pairs to search their newspapers for stories that would make God sad. Have them cut out the articles, glue them on legal-size paper, then write below each article what about the story might make God sad.

After 30 minutes or so, gather back together and staple the pages with a front page that reads "What Grieves God's Heart?"

Form a circle to close in prayer. Pass the "book" around the circle. As kids receive the book, have them each pick out something that grieves God's heart and pray about that situation. When everyone has prayed, close by thanking God for his care and concern for us.

2 SAMUEL 24:18-25

THEME:
Friendship and sacrifice

SUMMARY:
In this SKIT, teenagers illustrate how true giving involves sacrifice.

THE UNGIVING GIVER

SCENE: Tom is sitting in a classroom before the class begins. His classmates are sitting around him, also preparing for the school day ahead.

PROPS: A couple sheets of paper, a folder, two pencils, and a paper bag with some cookies in it. You'll also need Bibles for the discussion after the skit.

CHARACTERS:

Tom (an outgoing, talkative teenager)
Mike (a student)
Sarah (a student)
Becky (a student)
Gary (a student)
Judy (a student)

SCRIPT

Tom: Hey, Mike! How you doing? Heard you had that 27-hour bug that was traveling around. Bad stuff! Heard it caused terrible headaches, lots of stomach pain, made you throw up this stuff that looked like ...

Mike: *(Rolling his eyes)* Stop! Unless you want to find out firsthand what it looked like!

Tom: Sorry. I guess you still look pretty bad. Maybe you should turn and face Sarah over there, you know, in case you still have germs or any recurring symptoms! *(Feeling sorry for Mike)* Anything I can get you?

Mike: I could really use the lecture notes from the last few days. The semester test is coming up on Friday.

Tom: No problemo, buddy! *(Turns to Becky.)* Becky, Mikey needs your notes from last week. *(He reaches over and takes them from her folder and gives them to Mike.)* There you go. Don't say I never gave you anything!

Sarah: Tom, what's the possibility of getting a ride home with you today? My car's in the shop, and I won't have time to get to work if I ride the bus.

Tom: Always glad to help out. Gary, you got your wheels here? *(Gary nods.)* Good. Why don't you give Sarah a ride home after school. It would really help us out.

Gary: Sure.

Tom: Good man, I knew I could count on you.

Sarah: *(Embarrassed)* Tom!

Tom: No, it's OK, Sarah. I don't mind helping you out in a time of desperate need! After all, what are friends for?

(Judy is sitting behind Tom and breaks the point of her pencil. He turns to see what happened.)

Judy: Oh, no! What'll I do now?

Tom: Nothing to fear, I'm here! *(Turns to Mike.)* Mikey, since I gave you those notes, the least you can do is lend Judy your pencil. *(He takes Mike's pencil from his hand and gives it to Judy.)* Just remember, Judy-O, when your "#2" is broken, I'm your #1! *(He winks at her boastfully.)* Whoa! Everyone clam up—class is ready to start.

(Tom focuses his attention forward as he helps himself to the cookies out of Judy's lunch bag. The others shake their heads in disgust.)

If you use this skit as a discussion starter, here are possible questions:

■ How helpful do you think Tom really was?

■ How would you describe Tom's friendship to those around him?

■ If you were to meet Tom today, what would you say to him about his method of giving to others?

Ask a volunteer to read aloud 2 Samuel 24:18-25. Then ask:

■ Why did David insist on buying the threshing floor rather than taking it for nothing?

■ What difference do you think it would've made to God if David had offered a sacrifice that cost him nothing?

■ Do we have the same attitude about giving to God? Why or why not?

■ What does it mean to be a true friend to God or others?

1 KINGS

"Obey the Lord your God. Follow him by obeying his demands, his commands, his laws, and his rules that are written in the teachings of Moses. If you do these things, you will be successful in all you do and wherever you go."

1 Kings 2:3

1 KINGS
2:1-4

THEME:
Goals

SUMMARY:
In this DEVOTION, teenagers will compare a goal in an activity to David's goal for Solomon.

PREPARATION: For every two people, gather 12 cotton balls, two bowls, a spoon, and a blindfold. You'll also need a watch (either digital or with a second hand) and Bibles.

EXPERIENCE
Briefly discuss what a goal is. Talk about games that use the term "goal" to describe a score, such as hockey or soccer. Explain that you're going to give everyone a goal to strive for in the next few minutes.

Form pairs. Have one member of each pair put on a blindfold. Tell the non-blindfolded partner to remain totally silent until you give the signal that it's OK to talk. Place a spoon, an empty bowl, and a bowl containing 12 cotton balls in front of each blindfolded partner.

Explain that the goal is for the blindfolded partner to move the cotton balls from one bowl to the next within a minute and a half, using only the spoon. The other partner can only watch (in agony and frustration) for the first minute.

Time the event with a watch. After one minute, tell the sighted

partners they can begin coaching with words, but cannot touch the spoons, bowls, cotton balls, or their partners. Call "time" after another 30 seconds. Then let kids remove their blindfolds. Have partners count their cotton balls and report how close they came to their goal.

RESPONSE
Have pairs join together to form groups of no more than four. Have foursomes discuss the following questions. Have the oldest person in each foursome report his or her group's answers to the first question, the second oldest report answers to the second question, and so on. Ask:
■ **What went through your mind as you attempted to accomplish your goal in this activity?**
■ **What helped you accomplish your goal?**
Have the youngest group member read aloud 1 Kings 2:1-4. Then ask:
■ **How would you describe David's goal for Solomon in 1 Kings 2:1-4?**
■ **What do you think Solomon could have done to accomplish that goal?**
■ **What can we learn from David's advice to Solomon about setting goals?**
■ **What can we learn from our activity to help us accomplish David's goal for Solomon in our own lives?**

CLOSING
Close by leading the group in this prayer: **Lord, we don't know what lies ahead. But we do**

know that your hand will guide us, and your love will support us. Help us to set goals that are pleasing to you and to hang in there until we accomplish them. In Jesus' name, amen.

1 KINGS
2:1-4

THEME:
Being remembered

SUMMARY:
In this SKIT, two mice are trying to decide what to put on their deceased friend's tomb.

FAMOUS LAST WORDS

SCENE: Two mice are standing over their dead mouse friend (who is lying down, feet stuck in the air, and holding a chunk of cheese).

PROPS: Either draw or use small strips of poster board for whiskers. Buckteeth can also be made out of poster board.

CHARACTERS:
Chip
Chuck
Herbert

SCRIPT
(Chip and Chuck are standing over the body of Herbert, speaking in squeaky mouse voices.)
Chip: Poor Herbert. I told him that cheese didn't look quite right.
Chuck: What was the last thing he said?
Chip: "Hey, this tastes funny!"

Chuck: No, I mean, what's the last significant thing he said? You know, something to remember him by?
Chip: I don't really know.
Chuck: How do you think he'd want to be remembered? We've gotta think of something to put on his tombstone. He sure didn't leave us much to go on.
Chip: How about "Don't eat the cheese"?
Chuck: No, something more endearing like "Just call me 'Squeaks.' "
Chip: That's good, but it doesn't really say who he was... You know, what he was about. What would you want your last words to be?
Chuck: "That stupid cat is as slow as my gran..."
Chip: No, really. What would you want everyone to think of you after you died?
Chuck: I guess I've never really given it much thought. I am just a mouse, ya know. How would you want to be remembered?
Chip: I don't know. But if you're at my funeral, make me look real good!
Chuck: Chip?
Chip: Yeah, Chuck.
Chuck: Mice don't lie.
Chip: Good point. *(Pauses.)* Chuck?
Chuck: Yeah, Chip.
Chip: If you're at my funeral...
Chuck: Yeah?
Chip: Keep your mouth shut.
Chuck: Ditto.

If you use this skit as a discussion starter, here are possible questions:

■ **If you were able to choose what your last words on earth would be, what would you say?**

■ **How do you want people to remember you?**

Read 1 Kings 2:1-4. Tell kids these are some of the last words of David to his son Solomon. Ask:

■ **Do you think Solomon gave special attention to David's last words?**

■ **If so, why do you think last words are so important?**

■ **If your friends were deciding what was going to be on your tombstone, what do you think they would say?**

■ **Is it what you want to be known for? Why?**

1 KINGS 3:5-14

THEME:
The desire to do the right thing

SUMMARY:
Kids play a LEARNING GAME designed to help them explore what's really important.

PREPARATION: You'll need fake money (in varying dollar amounts) for each person. Cut different-colored pieces of paper into dollar-shaped strips (each color can represent a different denomination). You'll need a chalkboard or overhead projector and a list of at least 20 "important things," such as owning a new Porsche, becoming a movie star, making the winning touchdown at the Super Bowl, winning the lottery, and so on. Add a few less tangible items, such as good health, a long life, and a happy marriage, but be sure to include "wisdom to know right from wrong" on your list. Don't forget Bibles.

Using the chalkboard or overhead projector, show kids the list of items they can "purchase." Give each teenager $100 in fake money. Tell your teenagers that they'll be able to purchase the items with their fake money. The catch is that you cannot grant two people the same item. Teenagers will need to bid against each other for the items they want.

Describe the rules for bidding: **Money cannot be exchanged or given to other group members. You may buy as many items as you can successfully bid for, but two people cannot own the same item.**

Have teenagers start bidding on the listed items. Award the purchased items to kids by writing each item on paper and giving it to the highest bidder.

After the bidding is done, form a circle and have every other person in the circle (starting with the person on your right) answer the first question. Then have the kids who didn't answer the first question answer the second. Continue this way until you've discussed all the questions. Ask:

■ **Why did you bid on the items you did?**

■ **What items seemed to have more benefits to you than others?**

■ **How did your wisdom affect your bidding choice?**

■ **How did you feel when you weren't able to have all the items you would have liked?**

■ **Which item on the list do you think a truly wise person would have bid the most for?**

Ask someone to read 1 Kings 3:5-14.

Say: **In this passage God gives us a picture of a young man who had the opportunity to ask God for anything he wanted. This young man asked for godly wisdom.**

Invite teenagers to repeat with you Solomon's words (1 Kings 3:7-9) as a closing prayer to God.

1 KINGS
3:16-28

THEME:
Wisdom

SUMMARY:
In this PROJECT/ MUSIC IDEA, kids create an opera to illustrate how to seek wisdom in a tough situation.

PREPARATION: You'll need pencils, paper, Bibles, costume pieces (such as hats, bathrobes, and towels for turbans), and props as needed. (Props can be real items or made from cardboard.)

Have teenagers read 1 Kings 3:16-28. Then form pairs and have partners take turns answering the following questions. Allow no more than 30 seconds for each partner to answer each question. Ask:

■ **How would you have handled the situation in this passage if you were Solomon?**

■ **Where did Solomon get the wisdom to handle this tough situation? Explain.**

■ **What are difficult situations you face?**

Form drama groups of at least three people. Tell kids to choose one or more tough situations they face and create a short "opera" describing that situation and how to wisely resolve it. Encourage kids to have fun creating their operas and to plan on singing them (with high-pitched voices and lots of vibrato) for the whole group.

Teenagers will need to write a script, select costumes and props, and choose roles for their mini-operas. When groups are prepared, have them present their operas. Expect plenty of laughs.

When groups are finished with their presentations, have teenagers talk about how God gives us wisdom to handle difficult situations like those depicted in the operas.

1 KINGS
8:22-39

THEME:
God's attributes

SUMMARY:
Kids will explore God's attributes and write a psalm listing those attributes in this DEVOTION.

PREPARATION: You'll need ledger-sized paper or card stock, felt-tip pens, and Bibles.

EXPERIENCE
Form groups of no more than four. Assign each group at least one of the verses in 1 Kings 8:22-39. Say: **Each group has a portion of a fantastic prayer that Solomon offered. This prayer is filled with descriptions of God. Read your assigned passage and write a short psalm (song, verse, or poem) of praise that declares at least one of the attributes described by Solomon.**

Give each group supplies then allow five minutes for kids to create their psalms. Then have groups each read their psalms aloud prayerfully, one after the other in order of the verses they were assigned.

RESPONSE
Have kids disband their groups and form new groups of no more than four. Ask the following questions and have kids answer them before sharing their insights with other groups. Ask:

■ **What was it like to create a psalm based on this passage?**
■ **How did it feel to hear these psalms offered as prayers to God?**
■ **How is that like the way we feel when we learn about God through Scripture?**
■ **Which of the characteristics of God do you feel affects you most?**
■ **How do you feel when you're faced with God's majesty?**

CLOSING
Close with a "praise-a-thon" or time of worship and singing praise to God. You might want to consult *The Group Songbook* or *The Group Praise & Worship Songbook* for songs to use during the praise-a-thon.

1 KINGS
11:1-13

THEME:
Guarding against sin

SUMMARY:
Through this OBJECT LESSON, kids will discover that sin often leads to a tangled mess.

PREPARATION: You'll need a large room, a ladder, several rolls of the same color of yarn, two 3×5 cards for each teenager, tape (you may also want to use pushpins), and Bibles.

Before kids arrive, prepare the room in the following manner. On half of the cards, write a number. (Don't duplicate numbers.) Create "result" cards from the remaining blank cards. On one-third of the blank cards, list a sinful activity (such as taking drugs, blaspheming God, or murder). On another third of the cards, write "try again," and on the remaining third write "eternal reward."

Tape a long piece of yarn (long enough to stretch across the room) on each numbered card. Then attach the cards to the wall with tape or a pushpin. Using a ladder, thread the yarn across the room, above the reach of the teenagers, to the wall on the other side. When you reach the other side, fasten the end of the yarn to the wall and tape a numbered card to each yarn end. (Keep track of which number matches which card.)

When you've attached a result card to each numbered card, one by one untape each result card and weave the yarn in and out of other strands. Then retape the result card on the wall. (Repeat this for each set of cards.) The idea is to create a maze of yarn that kids have to follow but cannot touch.

As kids start to arrive, assemble them outside of the meeting room. Say: **Today you're going to be part of a living object lesson on how sin can get us tangled up. When I open the door, you must select a numbered card and follow that number to its end. If you arrive at a "sin" card, you're out of the game. If you arrive at a "try again" card, you may follow another numbered card. Each person to arrive at a card marked "eternal reward" is a winner. You cannot touch the yarn or follow a path someone else is already following.**

When everyone is finished, form trios and have kids discuss the following questions:

■ **What was it like to follow unknown paths in this object lesson?**

■ **How is that like or unlike the way we follow paths in life?**

■ **How is the way we got tangled up in this maze like the way people get tangled up in sin?**

Have a volunteer read 1 Kings 11:1-13. Ask:

■ **How did Solomon get himself tangled up in sin?**

■ **Why did such a wise person allow himself to get messed up in this situation?**

■ **What are the "strings" that tangle up Christians today?**

To close, have kids form pairs. Say: **Tell your partner about one thing that can tangle you up in life. Then pray for your partner to discover God's wisdom in that area.**

1 KINGS
13:11-25

THEME:
The consequences of lying

SUMMARY:
In this OBJECT LESSON, teenagers will "taste" the consequences of lying.

PREPARATION: On a table in the center of the meeting room, place paper cups and plastic spoons, two or three pitchers of water (depending on the group's size), a bowl of sugar, and a bowl of Tabasco sauce. You'll also need Bibles.

Give each person a paper cup and a plastic spoon and have everyone gather around the table in a circle. Ask kids to fill their paper cups halfway with water.

Say: **We're about to conduct a highly sophisticated test to determine how well you were in control of your words last week. Your fresh, pure cup of water represents your life at the start of last week—before you had a chance to do good or evil with your speech. Listen carefully to my instructions:**

• **If you complimented someone this past week, put a small amount of sugar in your cup.** (Allow kids to add sugar.)

• **If you apologized to someone, put a small amount of sugar in your cup.** (Allow kids to add sugar.)

• **If you told the truth when it might've been easier not to, put a small amount of sugar in your cup.** (Allow kids to add sugar.)

• **If you told a family member or friend how much you love him or her, put a small amount of sugar in your cup.** (Allow kids to add sugar.)

Have teenagers stir their concoctions and ask for volunteers to drink the sweetened water. (You should have no problem finding volunteers.) Encourage everyone to at least taste the water.

Say: **Well, it looks like many of you passed the first portion of our test impressively. But let's see how you do in the second half.**

Give kids each fresh cups and ask them to fill them halfway with water. Tell kids they must try to be brutally honest with themselves in the second half of the test. Say:

• **If you tricked someone this past week, put in a small amount of Tabasco sauce.** (Allow kids to add Tabasco.)

• **If you lied to someone in any way, put in a small amount of Tabasco.** (Allow kids to add Tabasco.)

• **If you were insensitive to friends or family, put in a small amount of Tabasco.** (Allow kids to add Tabasco.)

• **If you passed along a rumor or spoke of someone in a negative way, put in a small amount of Tabasco.** (Allow kids to add Tabasco.)

• **If you told someone (including your parents) only part of the truth about something and kept secret other information you knew about the topic, put in a small amount of Tabasco.** (Allow kids to add Tabasco.)

Again, have kids stir their concoctions and ask for volunteers to drink their water. (This time you'll probably have fewer takers!) Even so, encourage everyone to at least taste the water.

Have kids raise their cups as you ask the following questions. Give kids a few seconds to think after each question and tell them you'd like to hear lots of interesting responses. When one teenager shares an answer, teenagers who thought of the same answer and have nothing more to add can lower their cups. When all cups are lowered, ask the next question and repeat the process. Ask:

■ **What feelings did you have about drinking the water mixed with sugar? Tabasco sauce?**

■ **How are those feelings similar to the feelings you have after you've been honest or dishonest in your speech?**

■ **If these two cups of water reflect the kinds of words you used this past week, how do you feel about the results of our test?**

Read aloud the story in 1 Kings 13:11-25. Then wrap up the experience by asking:

■ **What's your first impression of the old prophet who lied to the "man of God"?**

■ **How do the consequences of the old prophet's lies compare to the consequences you faced at the end of our test?**

■ **What are the consequences of lying to friends, family, God, or others?**

■ **What can we learn from this story in 1 Kings 13:11-25 about the consequences of lying?**

1 KINGS
17:1-7

THEME:
God is our provider and protector.

SUMMARY:
Kids honor their parents at a PARTY and acknowledge God as their provider.

PREPARATION: Help teenagers plan a meal, create and mail invitations, make decorations, and develop a program for a party to honor their parents. Don't forget Bibles.

Have a volunteer read 1 Kings 17:1-7. Then ask:

■ **How does God provide for us?**

■ **How can we demonstrate our thankfulness to God for his provision?**

Say: **To express our thankfulness for God's provision, we're going to prepare a party to thank those who've provided for our daily needs—our parents.**

Have kids set a date for the party, then let them each choose an activity they'd like to help with in preparation for the party (such as making invitations or decorations, shopping, cooking, serving food, selecting entertainment, or cleaning up after the party).

Let teenagers know they can invite any person who provides for them (parents, stepparents, guardians, other relatives). Then have kids personalize the party for the people they've invited. For example, teenagers might

• create personalized place mats for each parent that include messages of love and thanksgiving;

• write notes thanking God for providing parents to fulfill their physical and emotional needs; and

• give parents door prizes that offer services, such as a free car-wash, free back rub, or making them a meal of their choice.

1 KINGS
17:7-24

THEME:
Trusting God

SUMMARY:
Teenagers will create a video PROJECT illustrating the widow's faith described in this Bible passage.

PREPARATION: You'll need one video camera for every four kids, a few costumes (such as shawls or towels), props (such as jars of flour), a videocassette recorder, a television, and Bibles.

Form groups of no more than four. Have groups read 1 Kings 17:7-24 and then brainstorm a way to re-create the events of that passage.

Give groups at least 30 minutes to determine their plans, choose costumes and props, and practice their presentations. Encourage kids to add elements to their sto-

ries that might have happened to the widow. For example, her son or friends might have given her a hard time for sacrificing her last bit of food for a stranger.

To increase the variety in the productions, assign each group a slightly different angle on the project. For example, one group could do its presentation as a documentary, another as a news story, another as a home movie, and so on. Have kids come up with unusual angles.

When groups are ready, videotape their productions. Then have groups gather and watch the results. After watching the videos, ask:

■ **What are examples of difficult sacrifices Christians sometimes must make?**

■ **What does this story teach us about obeying and trusting God?**

■ **Following the example of the widow in the story, how can you better trust God?**

1 KINGS
18:16-40

THEME:
God's power

SUMMARY:
In this PROJECT, kids will script and perform a "freeze-frame" drama of Elijah's encounter with the prophets of Baal.

PREPARATION: You'll need paper, pencils, various costumes, and props (such as a couple of charcoal grills, newspapers, matches, and a bucket of water). You'll also need a camera, film, and Bibles.

Ask a volunteer to read 1 Kings 18:16-40. Then distribute paper and pencils. Ask each person to write on his or her paper what 1 Kings 18:16-40 says about God's power and why it's important for us today.

After a couple of minutes, say: **Today we're going to create a freeze-frame drama to demonstrate God's reality and power.**

Form groups of no more than four and have teenagers share their written insights and talk about how God's power is shown today. Next have groups use the costumes and props you've provided (and others they can think of) to create a freeze-frame "living picture" of a scene from the Bible passage. Encourage teenagers to use every group member in their scenes.

When groups are ready, take a picture of each frozen scene. Then have groups each create a freeze-frame picture of a modern situation where God's power is evident today. Once again snap photos of these scenes.

If you're using a regular camera, have someone take the film to a one-hour developer, while kids enjoy a party waiting for the results.

Post the finished photos around the room. Then have kids wander silently around the room, stopping at each photo to pray. Have teenagers pray for God's power to be evident in the world and for the strength to stand up against ungodly forces.

1 KINGS 19:1-9

THEME:
Encouragement

SUMMARY:
In this AFFIRMATION, teenagers will be God's messengers of encouragement to others in the church or their neighborhoods.

PREPARATION: You'll need paper, pens, markers, tape, and various other supplies depending on the stations you set up. Don't forget Bibles.

Create signs using paper, markers, and tape, then set up "encouragement stations" around the room, such as

• The Cookie Encouragers—At this station group members make a batch of cookies and deliver them to a family they feel needs uplifting.

• The Mailbox Encouragers—At this station group members write letters and notes of affirmation, thanksgiving, and encouragement and send them to people who need a kind word.

• The Good-Deed Encouragers—At this station kids plan and perform good deeds such as washing a car, mowing a lawn, raking leaves, shoveling snow, or some other kind act.

Form pairs and say: **Tell your partner the last encouraging thing someone said to you. Explain how you felt about what was said.**

Ask a volunteer from each pair to tell the rest of the group what encouraging words they and their partners heard. Say: **We all like and need encouragement. This is especially true when things aren't going very well. Let's see how God encouraged Elijah during a particularly difficult time.**

Have a volunteer read 1 Kings 19:1-9. Then have teenagers select one of the encouragement stations to visit. Have teenagers who have gathered at each station decide who they'll affirm then make plans to carry out their tasks.

Send groups out to do their deeds of encouragement. Afterward, have each group report back. Ask:

■ **How did it feel to do encouraging things for others?**

■ **How did people respond?**

■ **How are our encouraging words like the encouraging words and actions the angel expressed to Elijah?**

1 KINGS
19:1-18

THEME:
Silence

SUMMARY:
In this CREATIVE READING, kids will learn the importance of listening to the still, small voice of God.

PREPARATION: You'll need construction paper in a variety of colors, newsprint, tape, paper, markers, pencils, and Bibles.

Use markers and newsprint to create the following color chart and tape the chart to the wall:

"Black—Pray silently."

"Purple—Hug someone."

"Brown—Sit down."

"Blue—Read the passage."

"White—Write insights on your paper based on what you read."

Give kids each a sheet of paper and a pencil. Say: **I'm going to give you instructions for this activity using only the colored paper and a few written words. During this time we may not speak to each other. Simply follow the instructions as I give them to you.**

Use the following steps to lead kids through a silent Bible study about listening to God. Hold up the colored slips of paper as indicated and write the words that follow on newsprint. Allow time after each instruction for kids to silently complete the activity.

Step 1: (Brown) (Blue) "1 Kings 19:1-3"

Step 2: "How does Elijah feel?" (White)

Step 3: (Blue) "1 Kings 19:4-8"

Step 4: "What is God trying to say to Elijah?" (White)

Step 5: (Blue) "1 Kings 19:9-13"

Step 6: "Where was God's voice?" (White)

Step 7: (Blue) "1 Kings 19:14-18"

Step 8: "What did God say to Elijah?" (White)

Step 9: "When have you felt alone?" (White)

Step 10: "How can God help us when we're feeling alone?" (White)

Step 11: (Purple)

Step 12: "How can we hear the still, small voice of God?" (White)

Step 13: (Black)

1 KINGS
19:8-12

THEME:
Listening to God

SUMMARY:

In this DEVOTION, teenagers will experience a discipline of silence and note how God speaks to them.

PREPARATION: You'll need pencils and paper for each teenager. You'll also need a television, compact disc or cassette player, radio, and Bibles.

EXPERIENCE

Bring in a television, compact disc or cassette player, and radio.

Turn all the machines on and turn them up to a loud volume. Very quietly try to explain what you would like the teenagers to do (read 1 Kings 19:8-12 and talk about what it means to listen to God).

Naturally, most kids will not be able to hear you. After a couple of minutes, turn off the noise.

RESPONSE

Read 1 Kings 19:8-12 to teenagers. Ask:

■ **How difficult was it for you to listen to me when I first gave you instructions?**

■ **How is listening to me with all the noise in the background like listening to God's still, small voice? How is it unlike listening to God's still, small voice?**

Say: **We're going to try the same thing Elijah tried. We're going to have a discipline of silence for the next half-hour.**

Take your Bible, a pencil, and paper, and go off where you can be by yourself.

Don't talk to anyone. Spend the entire time reading the Bible, praying, and simply waiting quietly for God to speak to you. Take notes about anything you learn from your silent time.

CLOSING

After 30 minutes, signal teenagers to return. Have volunteers share their notes with the whole class. Ask:

■ **What's it like to be alone with God?**

■ **What do you learn about yourself when you're alone?**

Close by asking teenagers to commit themselves to a designated time of quiet with God this week.

Have teenagers tell a partner what their plan is for quiet time with God. Then when you meet again next, have volunteers tell about their quiet times and what they discovered about God and themselves.

Encourage teenagers to plan frequent quiet times in the coming year.

1 KINGS
19:14-21

> ### THEME:
> The value of friends
>
> ### SUMMARY:
> In this PROJECT, teenagers will interview other Christians about their friendships.

PREPARATION: You'll need 3×5 cards, pens, and a tape recorder for each group of three or four teenagers. You'll also need Bibles.

Form groups of no more than four and have the youngest person in each group read aloud 1 Kings 19:14-21. Next have foursomes discuss these questions:

■ **Why do you think God wanted Elijah to find a new friend in Elisha?**

■ **When have you felt like Elijah? How might (or did) making a new friendship help you in a situation like that?**

■ **How does it make you feel to know that God encourages us to have close relationships with others like the one he encouraged Elijah to build with Elisha?**

Say: **Elijah found out that having a godly friend like Elisha was a positive, God-encouraged thing. Now let's take part in a project to help us explore more about what having good Christian friends can mean to us today.**

Give each group a tape recorder. Have groups go out and interview Christians about their friends.

Have teenagers ask questions or describe situations, such as the following:

■ **Who do you consider your spiritual friends or leaders?**

■ **Describe a time when you were helped, encouraged, or uplifted by Christian friends.**

When kids return, have them play the recorded interviews for the whole group. Ask:

■ **What are the common attributes of friendship?**

■ **What do these interviews tell us about the value of friendship?**

Distribute 3×5 cards and pens. Have teenagers each list on their cards the name of a Christian friend they respect and like.

Then take a moment and have kids each pray for the friend listed on their 3×5 cards. Invite teenagers to take their cards home and post them in a place where they'll be reminded to pray often for their friends.

1 KINGS
22:1-40

> ### THEME:
> Advice
>
> ### SUMMARY:
> Kids will experience getting good and bad advice in this LEARNING GAME.

PREPARATION: You'll need Bibles, paper, pencils, and 3×5 "advice" cards (enough for each person to have one). Divide the cards into thirds. On one-third of the cards write "good," on another third write "neutral," and on the other third write "bad."

After kids arrive, ask:
■ **If eight doctors diagnosed you as having cancer, but a ninth doctor said you didn't have cancer, who would you believe? Why?**

■ **How would your answer be different if the ninth doctor was the only one of the 10 who was an expert in cancer detection?**

Have teenagers read 1 Kings 22:1-40 and discuss with two other people how they'd summarize the passage.

Then have kids list things they could use some good advice about; for example, "What college should I go to?" or "What should I do if a friend invites me to a party where I know kids will be taking drugs?"

After teenagers have listed a few ideas, shuffle the advice cards and deal one to each person. Have a volunteer read aloud one of the ideas where advice is needed. Then call on someone in the group to give advice for that situation based on the card he or she is holding. If that person is holding a "good" card, he or she is to give good advice for the situation. If the person is holding a "neutral" card, he or she should give useless advice. If the person is holding a "bad" card, he or she should give bad advice.

Call on three or four people to read their situations. With each new situation, collect the advice cards, reshuffle, and repeat the process. Wrap up the activity by asking:

■ **How does it feel to get bad advice?**

■ **How does it feel to get worthless advice?**

■ **Why is it sometimes difficult to hear the truth?**

2 KINGS

"Where is the Lord, the God of Elijah?"

2 Kings 2:14b

2 KINGS
1:2-8

THEME:

The importance of seeking God

SUMMARY:
Kids learn the importance of seeking God by searching for a silver dollar or other special coin in this LEARNING GAME.

PREPARATION: You'll need enough white cloth blindfolds for everyone, markers, Bibles, and a silver dollar or other special coin.

Form pairs. Say: **In this race one person in each pair will search blindfolded for a lost coin, while the other observes and makes sure his or her partner doesn't get hurt. Then you'll switch roles and do the activity again.**

Tell the observers they're not to speak to or guide their blindfolded partners. After all pairs have a blindfolded partner, place the coin somewhere in the room and say: **Go!** Have blindfolded kids keep searching until someone finds the coin. Then repeat the activity a few more times, allowing partners to switch roles.

Afterward have partners pair up to form foursomes for the following discussion questions:

■ **How did you feel while searching for the coin blind-folded?**

■ **How did you feel as the observer?**

■ **How is this experience like seeking God?**

Ask a volunteer to read 2 Kings 1:2-8.

Say: **It's easy to seek out the known, touchable, and obvious things to help us when we're in need. It isn't always easy to reach for God, who we can't see or touch. Yet God wants us to seek him by faith during difficult times.**

Give each teenager a marker. Ask kids to write their pledges to seek God during difficult times on their blindfolds. Encourage kids to carry their blindfolds as a reminder that God is with them.

2 KINGS
2:1-11

THEME:
Commitment

SUMMARY:
Kids will reaffirm their commitment to God in this PROJECT by making a "commitment covenant" and choosing someone in the group to whom they'll be accountable.

PREPARATION: You'll need paper, markers, and Bibles.

Form a circle. Explain that this activity is about commitment. Determine whose birthday is closest to today. Starting with that person and then going in clockwise order, ask each person to read one verse from 2 Kings 2:1-11 aloud until the entire passage is read. Then ask:

■ **What statements or actions are repeated in the passage?**

■ **Why do you think Elisha responded that way?**

Say: **Commitment is an agreement or pledge to do something in the future. When we became Christians, we pledged to follow Christ wherever he leads.**

Form pairs and give them two sheets of paper and a marker. Ask teenagers to reaffirm on paper their commitment to God. Have kids write the following statement on their paper:

"I reaffirm my commitment to you, God, by pledging to do _____ next week."

Ask teenagers to each fill in the blank and draw a line for their signature, the date, and a witness' signature (their partner's) and phone number. After teenagers complete and sign their covenants, have their partners sign them and fill in their phone numbers. Encourage teenagers to call their partners during the next week to see how they did on their pledges. Have them ask questions like:

■ **How did you feel after keeping or not keeping your commitment to God last week?**

■ **How is that like or unlike God's commitment to us?**

■ **How will you respond to your commitments in the future?**

Ask teenagers to close by praying with their partners.

2 KINGS 2:1-14

THEME:
Trust and friend-ship

SUMMARY:
Teenagers participate in this PROJECT involving trust and create a puppet play based on friendship.

PREPARATION: You'll need a large cardboard box, enough white socks and markers for everyone, and Bibles.

Form a tight circle. Ask for a volunteer to step into the middle of the circle. Have the teenagers in the circle stand facing inward with their hands in front and one foot back to give them better leverage. Tell them that they'll be trying to keep the volunteer from falling.

Make sure the volunteer is standing straight, with eyes closed and arms folded over his or her chest. Then ask the volunteer to fall toward the circle. Pass the volunteer around the circle and then set him or her upright. Give each person a chance to be in the middle of the circle.

Form trios to discuss the following questions. After asking the questions, have volunteers share their groups' insights with the whole group. Ask:

■ **How did it feel when you fell toward the circle?**

■ **How did it feel to help catch the person in the middle?**

■ **Read aloud John 15:13. How is this trust exercise like the passage in John?**

■ **How important is trust in a friendship?**

Form groups of no more than five. Give each person a white sock and a marker and tell each group to read 2 Kings 2:1-14.

Ask each group to write a short puppet play based on the scriptural friendship they read about in 2 Kings. Have kids use markers to make hand puppets out of the socks.

Cut a large, square hole out of a cardboard box to use as a puppet stage. Then have each group perform its creative work for the rest of the teenagers.

2 KINGS
4:1-7

THEME:
God will provide.

SUMMARY:
In this ADVENTURE, kids will learn how God provides for our needs by doing a "God-provides" video scavenger hunt.

PREPARATION: You'll need at least two video cameras, a television and videocassette recorder, popcorn, and Bibles.

Form two groups. Give each group a video camera and explain that they're going to participate in a "God-provides" video scavenger hunt. Tell groups they have 30 minutes to videotape as many situations, people, and places as they can where God provides for a need. Determine the boundaries for the scavenger hunt (such as within walking distance of your meeting place). Then provide teenagers with examples such as a bird eating, someone helping a customer load grocery bags into a car, a local mission, or a food pantry. Then turn them loose.

After the scavenger hunt, gather everyone together and have groups report on how they did. Then ask the following questions one at a time. Have three or four people answer each question and try to have everyone answer at least one of the questions (don't call on the same people each time). Ask:

■ **How did you feel during this experience? Explain.**

■ **Were you surprised at the many ways God provides for our needs? Why or why not?**

■ **What does this experience tell us about how God meets our personal needs?**

■ **Is it easy to trust God to meet your needs? Why or why not?**

Ask a volunteer to read 2 Kings 4:1-7. Say: **It's sometimes difficult to see how God meets our needs in a world where we take so much for granted. But God is faithful and provides for us just as he did for the woman and her family in the Scripture reading. We need only to trust God and do our best.**

Close the experience by bringing out the popcorn and watching the videos.

2 KINGS
4:8-17

THEME:
Hospitality

SUMMARY:
In this PROJECT, teenagers will learn what it means to extend hospitality to others by forming a hospitality committee.

PREPARATION: You'll need paper, pencils, and Bibles.

(**Note:** This project works well with a youth council or with a core of teenagers who hold leadership positions in the youth group.)

Form a hospitality committee in the youth group and ask kids to commit to at least one year of service on the hospitality committee.

At your first meeting, pray for God's guidance and blessing. Then ask a volunteer to read 2 Kings 4:8-17. In groups of no more than three, have kids discuss these questions:

■ **Why do you think the Shunammite woman was concerned about Elisha?**

■ **In what ways did she show hospitality to him?**

■ **How would you describe Elisha's reaction to the hospitality of the Shunammite woman?**

■ **How do people today respond to hospitable actions?**

Distribute paper and pencils to everyone, then have trios write down their answers to the next question:

■ **How can we, as a committee, be like the Shunammite woman and show hospitality to others in our church and in our community?**

Kids might answer the previous questions with ideas like "Welcome visitors and invite them to sit with us during Sunday school," "Start our own thrift store that collects and then gives away quality used clothes to those who need them," "Volunteer at a homeless shelter once a week (or month)," "With our parents' permission, volunteer our homes to house guest speakers, missionaries, or other youth groups when they're in town," "Take meals to the families of youth group members who are sick," or "Join a workcamp project to repair low-income housing." Remind kids that they're brainstorming, so no answer is too outlandish.

After each group has several ideas, invite the person with the most buttons in each group to report his or her group's answers. Then, as a large group, decide on two or three ideas to implement in the coming year.

Have kids assign roles to make sure the hospitality programs they've decided on will happen. For example, kids might designate a meals coordinator who keeps track of what food is needed and finds volunteers to prepare it, or they might select an information coordinator who's responsible for contacting any outside agencies (such as a homeless shelter).

When the hospitality committee's year is up, hold an evaluation meeting to reflect on kids' experiences in hospitality. Have kids reread 2 Kings 4:8-17 and discuss questions such as:

■ **On a scale of 1 to 10 (10 being best), how would you rate your experience as a member of the hospitality committee? Explain.**

■ **Was your experience what you expected it to be? Why or why not? What could have made it better?**

■ **How did we follow the example of the Shunammite woman in the hospitality projects we completed?**

■ **What reactions do you remember most from people who received our hospitality? Why did those reactions impress you?**

■ **How will your experience on this hospitality committee affect the way you live from day to day in the coming year?**

(Note: If your kids are interested in joining a workcamp to repair low-income housing, you might want to get information from Group Workcamps, Box 599, Loveland, CO 80539, (303) 669-3836, extension 4437.)

2 KINGS 5:1-14

THEME:
Doing things God's way

SUMMARY:
In this SKIT, a cook receives a recipe over the phone for cheesecake from a master chef. The only problem is, the cook doesn't get it quite right.

IT'S A PIECE OF CAKE

SCENE: Bob is on the phone with the master chef, Jacques, getting instructions for cheesecake.

PROPS: Two telephones. You'll also need Bibles for the discussion after the skit.

CHARACTERS:
Jacques (master chef away on vacation)
Bob (his replacement)

SCRIPT
(Bob dials Jacques' number. Jacques picks up the phone.)

Jacques: *(With heavy French accent for the whole skit)* Allo?

Bob: Hi, Jacques? I hate to disturb you, but I've got a problem. I need to make a cheesecake for the Bendini party, but I can't find your recipe. They asked specifically for your cheesecake. Can you give it to me over the phone?

Jacques: But of course. Do you have le pen?

Bob: *(Looks around, can't find one.)* Uh, no, but I'll just yell the directions back to the kitchen.

Jacques: Tres bien. For le crust, crush 8 graham crackers into leetle-bitty pieces and mix zem with ½ cup of sugar and 4 tablespoons of butter.

Bob: *(Covering mouthpiece with hand and yelling to the kitchen)* Crush about 10 saltine crackers and mix it with 1 cup of flour and 2 tablespoons of lemon juice! *(Uncovering mouthpiece)* OK, I got it.

Jacques: *(Slowly and deliberately)* In a separate bowl, mix together 24 ounces of cream cheese, 1 cup sugar, and 5 egg yolks.

Bob: *(Covering mouthpiece)* Mix in 24 ounces of sour cream, a teaspoon of sugar, and 6 egg shells! *(Uncovering mouthpiece)* OK, go ahead.

Jacques: Beat the 5 egg whites until leetle-bitty stiff peaks form, then fold them into the mixture. Pour it into a pan and bake at 375 degrees for about an hour, turning it about every 15 minutes.

Bob: *(Covering mouthpiece)* Scramble the 6 eggs and put them in a blender with the crust. Pour contents in a baking dish and bake at 200 degrees for 30 minutes! *(Uncovers mouthpiece.)*

Jacques: That's it! When the time is up, take it out of the oven and Voila!—a cheesecake like no other. Did you get all of that?

Bob: Yep, I made a few small changes, but I'm sure it will come out just like yours.

Jacques: I have complete confidence in you! I'm sure you will make me proud!

Bob: Oh, your cheesecake will be the talk of the town. If there's any left, I'll save you a piece.

Jacques: Merci. Goodbye!

Bob: 'Bye! *(Hangs up the phone and pats himself on the back.)*

If you use this skit as a discussion starter, here are possible questions:

■ **Why is it important to do things God's way?**

■ **Does God give us freedom to be creative? Explain.**

■ **What are some of the explicit instructions God has given us about how we should live our lives?**

■ **Read 2 Kings 5:1-14. Why was it necessary for Naaman to wash himself in the river when God could just as easily have healed him?**

■ **What do you think would have happened had Naaman not fully followed God's directions?**

2 KINGS
5:1-19

THEME:
Faith and obedience.

SUMMARY:
In this ADVENTURE, kids will participate in a blind trust-walk to learn the importance of active obedience.

PREPARATION: You'll need Bibles, newsprint, markers, and masking tape.

Tell kids the theme of this activity, then form groups of four to six. Explain that everyone will spend the next 10 minutes participating in a blind trust-walk.

Ask kids to pair up within their groups. One person will act as guide; one will act as the blind person. The blind person must close his or her eyes and "trust" the guide. The guide must lead the blind person around the building (and even outside if weather permits) to experience different things.

For example, the guide could

have the blind person put his or her hands in water from the drinking fountain, go up or down stairs or on an elevator, or touch a sculpture or plant in the building. You might even suggest that guides take their partners for a short run. (But for safety, caution them to carefully hold on to their partners while running.)

Have kids go on their trust-walks for about five minutes. Then have partners switch roles and repeat the activity.

After teenagers finish their experiences, have them gather in their groups of four or six. Give each group a sheet of newsprint, a marker, Bibles, and a piece of masking tape. Ask:

■ **How did it feel being the blind person? the guide?**

■ **Did you open your eyes? Why or why not?**

Ask a volunteer in each group to read 2 Kings 5:1-19.

Then have groups discuss the following questions and write their responses on newsprint:

■ **How is our experience like what Naaman went through in his search to be healed?**

■ **How does Naaman's response after being healed set the example for how we should respond?**

■ **What will you do this week to express your faithful obedience to God?**

When the small groups have finished, ask them to tape their responses to the wall and explain them to the entire group.

To close, have everyone form a circle and read aloud 2 Kings 5:14 as a reminder that faith and obedience go hand in hand.

2 KINGS
6:13-17

THEME:

God's unseen protection

SUMMARY:
In this ADVENTURE, teenagers will learn about God's protection when they experience a simulated rainstorm while blindfolded in a tent.

PREPARATION: You'll need one or more large tents, a garden hose with a nozzle, blindfolds for everyone, and Bibles. Set up the tent(s) outside your meeting place in advance but don't let kids know about them.

After the group gathers for the meeting, announce that today everyone will experience God's unseen protection. Ask a volunteer to read 2 Kings 6:13-17. Then give teenagers each a blindfold.

Ask everyone to line up single file and put on the blindfolds. Then lead the blindfolded group outside and into the waiting tent(s). So that kids don't know they're entering a tent, have adult sponsors hold open the door and guide kids as necessary.

Then turn on the hose and give the tent(s) a good hard spray. After the initial shock, ask everyone to remove their blindfolds. If the entire group fits into one tent comfortably, continue the lesson inside the tent. If not, gather everyone back in your regular meeting place and ask:

■ **How did you feel when you heard the sound of water battering the tent?**

■ **Were you surprised about not getting wet? Why or why not?**

■ **How is not seeing what protected you like the experience of the young man in the Bible story?**

Say: **Although we don't see God's protection every day, God is always keeping watch over us.**

2 KINGS 8:1-6

THEME:
God rewards faithful obedience.

SUMMARY:
Kids affirm each other's successes and make certificates of congratulations for each other at this PARTY.

PREPARATION: You'll need colored 8½×11 paper, construction paper, scissors, glue, markers, felt-tip pens, colorful stickers, a portable stereo system, Christian tapes or compact discs, and Bibles. Provide plates, napkins, cups, and ice for the party. Ask kids to bring snacks, baked goods, and beverages.

Have kids help you prepare the snacks and choose music to listen to for a time of community-building and fun. After things are set up, say: **Today we're going to** celebrate everyone's recent successes! Explain that this isn't a contest to see who's performed the greatest but an opportunity to affirm each other's accomplishments.

Form groups of two or three. Ask teenagers to tell their group members about a recent accomplishment. Using colored paper, construction paper, and stickers, have kids each make a "certificate of congratulations" for one of their group members (one certificate per person).

When everyone's created a certificate for someone in their group, form one large group again. Have the creators of the certificates present them to the people they were created for. Ask everyone to applaud (the louder the better) after each presentation. After the presentations, ask a volunteer to read 2 Kings 8:1-6.

Have kids re-form their small groups to discuss the following questions:

■ **How did it feel to be recognized by your peers for your accomplishments?**

■ **How is your experience like the woman in the Scripture passage who was rewarded for her faithfulness to God?**

■ **What will you do this week to show God your faithful obedience?**

Say: **God is pleased with us when we faithfully obey. Let's celebrate that faithfulness!**

Encourage kids to affirm each other for their successes. Continue with the party and have kids eat snacks and drink beverages.

2 KINGS 11:1-3

THEME:

Helping those with limited abilities

SUMMARY:
In this PARTY, teenagers will help each other through a simulation where some group members can't use arms, eyes, or legs.

PREPARATION: You'll need Bibles, two or three blindfolds, and a stack of construction paper squares. (You should have red, yellow, blue, and green squares with twice as many green squares as the total of the other colors.) You'll also need refreshments (snacks and beverages) to serve at the party, which should be set up in an extra room or fellowship hall ahead of time.

Give teenagers each a construction paper square (randomly distribute the colors as kids arrive) and tell them that today's lesson is about helping those who can't help themselves. Announce that goodies have been provided for them in the extra room or fellowship hall for their enjoyment. Then have teenagers take out their construction paper squares, and explain that the colors represent their simulated physical condition:

Red—No arms (you may not use your arms).

Yellow—Blind (you must be blindfolded).

Blue—No legs (you may not use your legs).

Green—You have no physical limitations.

Explain that the object is for everyone to get to the other room to enjoy the refreshments. The "catch" is, the "green" people are responsible to help those who hold the other colors. Provide blindfolds for the blind and say: **Let's go eat refreshments and have a good time.**

After 15 minutes (or when the kids have each had a chance to enjoy the snacks), declare everyone healed and gather them together.

Form pairs and have partners discuss the following questions before sharing their insights with the whole class:

■ **How did you feel being disabled in this exercise?**

■ **How did you feel as one of the people without physical limitations?**

■ **How is this like the way you handle situations at school, work, or at home? How is it unlike the way you handle situations?**

■ **What does this say about how we ought to treat those who have limited abilities?**

Ask a volunteer to read 2 Kings 11:1-3.

Say: **The baby in the story couldn't help himself. It took someone who was willing to look out for his welfare. God asks us to have that same attitude toward others who have limitations.**

Close with a prayer asking God to give everyone a heart of compassion for those with limited abilities. Then continue the party.

2 KINGS
12:4-16

THEME:
Serving God

SUMMARY:

In this PROJECT, teenagers will serve God by creating "missions calendars."

PREPARATION: You'll need paper, pens or pencils, markers, rulers, and a sample four-week calendar for each group of four or five kids.

(**Note:** It may be helpful to photocopy a blank calendar format for convenience.) You'll also need a table with a basket and Bibles.

Form groups of four or five. Give each group the supplies and announce that you're creating "mission calendars," which will be used in the following weeks to raise money for missions. Show kids a sample four-week calendar and ask them to use their imaginations to create their own calendars.

Have kids list a creative, money-making idea in each calendar space. The following are some ideas:

• Did you go to work or school today? Some don't have that opportunity. Donate 50 cents.

• Give 10 cents for every pair of glasses in your home.

• Donate 5 cents for every television and radio in your home.

• Give a penny for every piece of sports equipment you own.

Explain that this is an opportunity for serving God and building up his kingdom. A week before the project ends, remind teenagers to bring back their calendars and the money they've collected.

At your scheduled meeting, ask teenagers to hold on to the money until later in the program. Have a volunteer read 2 Kings 12:4-16. Then ask:

■ **How did you feel about donating your money to this project?**

■ **Did you find it easy or difficult? Explain.**

■ **How was this experience like that of the people in the Bible story who were charged with repairing the temple?**

Say: **Your act of service this month will be to build up God's kingdom much like the temple was built up and repaired in the passage. Your loving service to God will bless many.**

For the closing, place a basket on the table and ask teenagers to form a circle around the table. As they place their donations in the basket, pray: **God, bless these gifts to your service.** After kids have all placed their donations in the basket, say: **Amen.** Decide as a group where to donate the money.

2 KINGS
13:20-21

THEME:
The influence of a godly life

SUMMARY:

In this AFFIRMATION, kids will learn what effects a godly life has on others after a person passes away.

PREPARATION: Have teenagers bring in the obituary sections of their local newspapers. You'll also need paper, markers, newsprint, masking tape, and Bibles.

Form groups of three or four. Give each group a sheet of newsprint and a marker. Make sure each group has at least one obituary section. Give teenagers five minutes to list on the newsprint as many interesting facts about the people in the obituaries as they can. After they've completed the activity, have teenagers tape their findings on the wall. Then ask each group to share discoveries.

Have teenagers write their answers to the following questions on a sheet of paper, then discuss the answers in their groups.

■ **How did you feel about what you read in the obituaries?**

■ **Who has influenced your life the most? How has that person influenced you?**

Re-form the large group. Ask a volunteer to read 2 Kings 13:20-21, which tells about how Elisha influenced others even after his death.

Say: **The way we live can influence or impact those around us. What people remember about us can bring them closer to God and life, or lead them away from God.**

Ask teenagers to gather back in their groups. Give each group paper and markers (enough for each member). Ask teenagers to write an "epitaph" for each member of their group (one epitaph per person). Explain that an epitaph is what a person would like to be remembered for. Encourage kids to write positive things about other group members. Then have groups read their epitaphs to the whole group. Display the papers around the room as reminders for kids to make wise choices about how to live so each will be remembered in positive ways.

Close with a prayer.

2 KINGS
17:7-18

THEME:
Sin

SUMMARY:
Kids will use Chinese handcuffs in this OBJECT LESSON to experience how sin latches on and doesn't let go.

PREPARATION: You'll need Bibles and five Chinese handcuffs (finger cuffs) for every two people. If you can't find Chinese handcuffs, you can use thread. You'll need a spool for each pair.

Form pairs. Give each pair five Chinese handcuffs. Ask one person in the pair to be "sin," the other to be the "victim." Explain that each person will get a chance to play both parts.

Have the person playing sin place one handcuff on the victim's forefingers. Then ask the victim to attempt to get free without ripping the handcuff. Then have sin add a second, third, fourth, and fifth handcuff to the victim's fingers. Each time, the victim must attempt to break free from the Chinese handcuffs. Then have partners switch roles and repeat the activity.

(**Note:** If you can't find Chinese handcuffs, have sin tie a thread loosely around the victim's wrists. Then have victims attempt to break free from the thread. Repeat this five times, doubling the amount of thread each time.)

Afterward, ask pairs the following questions. Allow discussion time before having volunteers share their partners' insights. Ask:

■ **How did you feel when trying to get loose from the Chinese handcuffs?**

■ **How is this experience like sin in your life?**

Ask a volunteer to read 2 Kings 17:7-18.

Say: **If you allow sin into your life, its hold will increase as you continue in that sin. God offers freedom from sin and safety if we follow his commands.**

Give each teenager a Chinese handcuff (or a length of thread) to take home as a reminder that sin causes bondage.

2 KINGS
20:1-11

THEME:
Prayer

SUMMARY:
Kids will experience the power of prayer through a CREATIVE PRAYER service.

PREPARATION: Before teenagers arrive, set up the room with an altar surrounded by chairs. On the altar, put two candles, a Bible opened to 2 Kings 20:1-11, and a basket. You'll also need index cards, pencils, Bibles, a cassette player or portable compact disc player, and a copy of John Michael Talbot's album *Come to the Quiet* or some other instrumental meditative music.

Begin playing the music with the lights dimmed (or off) and the candles lit before kids arrive. It may be helpful to meet in another part of the building such as a prayer chapel.

As the teenagers enter the room, ask them to remove their shoes and take a seat around the altar. After everyone is seated, explain that this is a creative prayer service. Give each person an index card and a pencil. Ask each person to write a prayer request (they don't have to sign their names). After everyone is finished, ask each person to place his or her card (face down) in the basket. Repeat as a group: **"Hear our prayer, oh Lord,"** as each card is placed in the basket. After all the cards are in the basket, allow kids to silently come up to the altar, turn over a card, and offer a prayer for the request listed.

After 10 or 15 minutes, turn on the lights and ask:

■ **How did you feel when you entered the room?**

■ **How did you feel during the service?**

■ **What was it like to pray for yourself? someone else?**

Say: **When we pray, we develop a closer relationship with God. And there is power in prayer.**

Listen to this example from 2 Kings 20:1-11.

Read 2 Kings 20:1-11.

Close by having the group form a circle for a moment of silent prayer, ending with "amen."

2 KINGS
22:8-10

THEME:
Discovering God's Word

SUMMARY:
In this LEARNING GAME, kids discover God's Word in a treasure hunt.

PREPARATION: You'll need at least two Bibles (to hide), ribbon (to wrap around each Bible), clues (prepared ahead of time and put on numbered index cards), a bag of bite-sized candy bars, and the Scripture passage from 2 Kings 22:8-10 printed on index cards (enough for everyone).

Before the meeting, hide two or more Bibles (wrapped in ribbons) somewhere in the church. Determine what clues you'll use to lead kids to the hidden Bibles. (Plan to have at least four clues for each hidden Bible.) Use Scripture verses as clues to direct teenagers to various places in the church building as they search for the Bibles. For example:

• Galatians 6:14 could be used to direct kids to a cross.

• Genesis 8:20 could lead kids to the altar.

• James 1:23 could lead kids to a mirror.

• Luke 11:10 could lead kids to a door.

• John 6:35 could lead kids to the kitchen.

• Judges 16:3 could lead kids to a gate.

• Psalm 30:4 could lead kids to the choir loft.

• Ecclesiastes 1:13 could lead kids to a classroom.

Write your clues (the Bible references) on index cards. Then attach a candy bar to each clue and place the clues around the church in reverse order. For example, you'd start by placing clue number 4 (which leads to the Bible). Then you'd hide clue number 3 that leads to clue number 4. Continue until you're left holding clue number 1, which initiates the search, for each hidden Bible.

When kids arrive, form groups according to the number of Bibles you hide (one group for each hidden Bible). Explain that each group will receive a clue at the start and must solve that clue to find the next clue and so on, until their group finds that particular Bible hidden somewhere in the building. Tell groups they must bring back the correct number of candy bars along with their Bibles to show that they found all the clues. After answering any questions kids might have, give groups their first clues and send them on their treasure hunts.

After the activity, have a volunteer read 2 Kings 22:8-10 from a newly discovered Bible. Then ask groups to discuss these questions:

■ **How did you feel when you found your clues and the Bible?**

■ **How might this experience be like Hilkiah's when he found God's Word in the temple?**

■ **Now that you've discovered God's Word, what do you plan to do with it?**

Say: **God's Word is like a hidden treasure suddenly found. It's worth more than gold but is useless unless it's read.**

Form a circle for your closing and give each person an index card with the passage on it. Encourage teenagers to discover God's Word in a new way by reading it often.

2 KINGS
23:1-3

THEME:
Discovering God's will

SUMMARY:
In this CREATIVE READING, kids learn that one way to discover God's will is to know God's Word.

PREPARATION: You'll need Bibles, concordances, paper, newsprint, a marker, tape, index cards, and pencils. Using a marker, write out each of the following Scripture passages (but without the references) on a sheet of newsprint: Psalm 119:105; Ephesians 5:17; Romans 12:2; 2 Timothy 2:15; Psalm 119:160; and Psalm 37:23. Number the Scriptures as you list them.

Form groups of four. Give each group a concordance, a Bible, paper, and pencils. Tape newsprint on a wall to display the Scriptures.

Ask groups to use their concordances to determine where each Scripture can be found in the Bible. (You may need to show kids how to use a concordance if they're not familiar with this tool.) As groups find the references, have them list each reference on their papers. When groups have found all the passages, have them shout out together what each reference is. Have someone write these next to the Scripture passages on the newsprint.

Then have kids form new groups consisting of people who weren't in their original groups. Ask the following questions and have the person whose birthday is nearest to today answer the first question. Then rotate around the group so each person answers at least one question. Ask:

■ **How did you feel while searching for the reference that matched the Scripture passage?**

■ **How is this kind of search like the search we have for God's will in our lives? How is it unlike our search?**

■ **What did you discover about God's will in these passages?**

■ **What will you do as a result of your discovery?**

■ **How does the Bible help us discover God's will?**

Read aloud 2 Kings 23:1-3.

Say: **One of the best ways to know God's will is to read God's Word—the Bible.**

Give teenagers each an index card and on one side of the card ask them to write a covenant with

God to read the Bible during the next week. On the other side of the index card, have kids write Psalm 119:105 as a reminder that God's Word contains God's will.

2 KINGS
24:18–25:21

THEME:
Sin

SUMMARY:
Kids will realize that sin separates us from God in a simulation LEARNING GAME.

PREPARATION: You'll need newsprint, masking tape, markers, Bibles, and a set of at least three questions that require a Bible to answer. An example of the type of question you might ask is "Who is the king described in 2 Kings 24:18-20 and what was his behavior before God?"

Form two groups and have them sit on opposite sides of the room. Group 1 will represent people who are separated from God because of sin, and group 2 will represent people who are not separated from God.

Post the questions on the wall. Give each group newsprint, markers, and masking tape. Explain that group 1 isn't allowed to use the Bible. Give Bibles to members of group 2 and ask both groups to answer the questions.

Allow about seven minutes to complete the activity. Then ask:

■ **What was it like to have access to the Bible in answering the questions?**

■ **What was it like if you didn't have access to a Bible?**

■ **How is this experience like being separated from God as a result of sin? How is it unlike being separated from God?**

■ **What does this activity say about how we should respond to God in our daily living?**

Have volunteers read 2 Kings 24:18–25:21. Then close by having kids pray silent prayers of confession, asking God to forgive them for their sins and to guide them away from sinful actions.

1 CHRONICLES

"Lord God, you have treated me like a very important person."

1 Chronicles 17:17b

1 CHRONICLES 1:1–2:15

<table>
<tr><td>

THEME:
Spiritual heritage

SUMMARY:
In this PROJECT, teenagers will write thank-you letters to their oldest living Christian relatives.

</td></tr>
</table>

PREPARATION: For each person, you'll need paper, an envelope, a stamp, a pen or pencil, and a Bible. If possible, call your group members' parents the week before you meet to find out the names and addresses of their oldest living Christian relatives.

Have kids form a circle. Then ask:

■ **What do you know about your family's ancestors?**

■ **Where are your ancestors from?**

■ **Do you have any famous ancestors? Were they Christians?**

Read 1 Chronicles 1:1–2:15 together as a group. As kids look it over, have them shout out names they recognize. Make sure they see the direct connection from Adam to Abraham to David. Ask:

■ **What are some of the benefits of having a Christian heritage?**

Instruct kids to think of their oldest living Christian relatives. Have a few share who these people are. Say: **For some of you, your oldest living Christian relative might be a parent or even yourself!**

Pass out a sheet of paper and a pen or pencil to each person. Tell teenagers to each write a short thank-you letter to their oldest living Christian relatives. (If kids have no older Christian relatives, have them write short notes to the "family" of Christians who may come after them, telling them about the hopes they have for future generations of Christians in their families.)

Be especially sensitive to kids from blended families and adoptive families. Stress that a spiritual relative might not be a blood relative—he or she could be someone who's played an important spiritual role in our lives. If you collected names and address from kids' parents, hand these out on strips of paper. Hand out envelopes and have kids address them. Provide stamps so kids will be sure to mail them. (Kids who wrote notes to their own Christian descendants can seal their letters in envelopes and keep them in scrapbooks or photo albums.)

Close with prayer, thanking God for the relatives before us—and after us—who live for him.

1 CHRONICLES 6:31-32

<table>
<tr><td>

THEME:
Worship

SUMMARY:
In this MUSIC IDEA, kids will form small groups to write praise songs, then teach them to the whole group.

</td></tr>
</table>

PREPARATION: You'll need paper, pencils, and Bibles. Also, bring a variety of items that could be used as instruments (traditional instruments, such as a tambourine, or creative instruments, such as a half-full jar of peanuts to shake, an empty bottle to blow in, or bottle caps to "click").

Read aloud 1 Chronicles 6:31-32, then ask:
■ **What does it mean to worship God?**
■ **When do we worship God?**
■ **How is our worship different from the worship of the people in the Old Testament?**
■ **What must a song contain to be considered a worship song?**

Tell kids they're going to write worship songs. Encourage them by saying that people who write worship songs are just regular people who want to express themselves to God.

Form groups of no more than five. Say: **The easiest way to write a worship song is by starting with the tune of a song you already know. In your groups, decide on a tune, then write new words to uniquely express your praise or worship to God.**

Explain to kids that their words can thank God for things, quote verses from the Bible, or just talk about who God is. Distribute paper and pencils so groups can write down the songs they create.

After about 10 minutes, have groups each sing their songs, teaching them to the whole group. As each group sings, have a few volunteers add rhythm by playing the instruments you brought.

If a couple of the songs really turn out well, sing them again in the future as a way for group members to express their hearts to God.

1 CHRONICLES 11:10-25

THEME:
Radical commitment

SUMMARY:
Teenagers will run across an open space while blindfolded in this ADVENTURE.

PREPARATION: Safety is the key for this activity. You'll need either an empty gym or a large, flat field or parking lot. (If you use a field, make sure the ground is flat, hard, and smooth.) You'll need Bibles and one blindfold for every four kids.

Take your group to the "Radical Run" location and form teams of four. Tell them you're going to have them try something that every person is capable of doing but that no one will find easy. Let them know it will take full commitment.

Explain to kids that they'll be blindfolded, then asked to run across the area at full speed. Participants' level of commitment will show clearly in their willingness to actually run—not walk or trot.

Have one person from each

team go to the far end of the running area. Give them strict instructions to tell their teams' runners when to stop. Make sure they understand the importance of this role.

Have each team blindfold one person, then point him or her in the right direction and say "go!"

Declare a winning team, then bring the group back together and read aloud 1 Chronicles 11:10-25.

(Note: For a safer variation of this activity, eliminate the blindfolds and have kids run backward instead.)

Say: **Here were some of the most radical people in the entire Bible: Jashobeam, Eleazar, Abishai, and Benaiah. These guys had such a high commitment to David, they went against all odds to do some radical things for him.**

Have kids discuss the following questions in their teams. Then have volunteers share their team members' insights with the whole group. Ask:

■ **How were the experiences of these four people like the experience we just had running blindfolded?**

■ **What does it mean to have "radical" commitment to God?**

■ **How would your life have to change for you to consider yourself "radically committed"?**

■ **Do you want to live radically for God? Why or why not?**

After kids answer the question, have them pray for each other to close out the activity.

1 CHRONICLES 14:8-17

THEME:
Following God

SUMMARY:
Kids will bake brownies together using different recipes in this OBJECT LESSON.

PREPARATION: You'll need access to an oven and a stove. For each group, you'll need a photocopy of a recipe from the "Recipes" handout (p. 161), the ingredients listed, a 2-quart saucepan, and spoon, measuring utensils, and a 9×9×2-inch baking pan. You'll also need Bibles.

Form three groups. (Groups should be no smaller than two and no larger than 10.) Give group 1 recipe #1 (ingredients only) and instruct them to go to the kitchen and make something. Tell them they have only seven minutes to complete their task. Send an adult leader to go with them—but don't allow the leader to offer any help. While group 1 is gone, play a game with the remaining groups. (Check out *Great Group Games for Youth Ministry* for game ideas. The book is available from Group Publishing.)

When group 1 returns, send in group 2 with recipe #2 (ingredients and measurements but no instructions) to accomplish the same task in seven minutes. Again, play a game with the remaining groups while group 2 is gone.

(continued on p. 162)

RECIPES

Directions: Photocopy and cut apart this handout for use in the 1 Chronicles 14:8-17 activity.

Recipe #1

margarine or butter
unsweetened chocolate
sugar
eggs
vanilla
all-purpose flour
salt

Recipe #2

½ cup margarine or butter
2 squares (1 ounce each) unsweetened chocolate
1 cup sugar
2 eggs
1 teaspoon vanilla
½ cup all-purpose flour
¼ teaspoon salt

Recipe #3: Fudgy Brownies

½ cup margarine or butter
2 squares (1 ounce each) unsweetened chocolate
1 cup sugar
2 eggs
1 teaspoon vanilla
½ cup all-purpose flour*
¼ teaspoon salt

Heat oven to 350°. Heat margarine and chocolate in 2-quart saucepan over low heat until melted; remove from heat. Mix in sugar, eggs, and vanilla. Stir in remaining ingredients. Spread in greased baking pan, 9×9×2 inches. Bake until brownies begin to pull away from sides of pan, 20 to 25 minutes; cool. Cut into 1-inch squares.

*If using self-rising flour, omit salt.

"Fudgy Brownies" recipe reprinted from *Betty Crocker's Cookie Book* with the permission of General Mills, Inc.

When group 2 returns, send in group 3 with recipe #3 (the full recipe), again allowing them seven minutes. This time the adult leader can offer all the help he or she wants—especially suggesting they get started melting the chocolate and margarine right away.

After group 3 returns, have members from each group read aloud 1 Chronicles 14:8-17, keying in on the theme "Doing things God's way." After reading the passage, say: **One key to David's success was his complete obedience to God's direction.**

Ask:

■ **How is God's way of doing things sometimes different from our way?**

Ask kids to give examples of times when a Christian teenager might prefer to do things his or her own way rather than God's way.

After about 20 minutes, take your whole group down to the kitchen to check on their creations. Explain the instructions each group had, then ask the people in the first two teams:

■ **How did you feel about making up your own instructions? What difference did it make?**

Have kids sample each product and give their reactions to the whole group. Then sample the brownies made by the third group. Wrap up the experience by asking:

■ **How is what happened to our first two recipes like or unlike what happens to us as Christians when we don't follow God like we should?**

■ **How can we become better at "doing things God's way" this week?**

1 CHRONICLES 17:1-6

THEME:

Being a suitable dwelling place for God

SUMMARY:
In this SKIT, a student is discussing with his friend how he is trying to set up house inside his body so that Jesus will have a comfortable place to live.

MAKE YOURSELF AT HOME

SCENE: Joel is going over his shopping list out loud while walking down the sidewalk on his way to the toy store. There he bumps into Faith.

PROPS: You'll need a piece of paper for a shopping list and a Bible for the discussion afterward.

CHARACTERS:
Joel
Faith

SCRIPT
(Joel is walking down the sidewalk preoccupied with his shopping list.)

Joel: Let's see ... Table, chair—wait—better make that "chairs" in case he wants to have guests over. Plates, sofa ...

Faith: Hi, Joel! Where are you going?

Joel: *(Slightly startled)* Huh? Oh, hi, Faith. I'm going to the toy store.

Faith: What for?

Joel: To buy some more dollhouse furniture.

Faith: What on earth for?

Joel: To swallow.

Faith: You've been EATING doll furniture?

Joel: No—swallowing it. Don't want it to get damaged on the way down. Jesus wouldn't like it.

Faith: 'Scuse me?

Joel: Well, you gotta figure if Jesus is living inside me, he'll need a place to hang his hat, so to speak. And I figure he wouldn't want to use broken furniture. Nothing but the best for Jesus! Hey, what size batteries should I swallow for the microwave?

Faith: Joel, you don't need to swallow any batteries.

Joel: How silly of me! Of course I don't! Jesus could run the microwave on his own power.

Faith: No, no, no! Joel, Jesus doesn't live in you like that.

Joel: What do you mean?

Faith: You know, physically. Jesus doesn't live in you physically. It's a spiritual kind of thing.

Joel: You mean …

Faith: Yep, you've been swallowing that furniture for nothing.

Joel: Hmm. I was just trying to make him comfortable. Well, maybe somebody down there will get some use out of all that stuff. By the way, do you know where there's a water fountain around here?

Faith: Got a lamp stuck in your throat?

Joel: No, I need to fill the pool.

Faith: Joel?

Joel: Yeah?

Faith: *(Starts to say something, then stops.)* Never mind. The fountain's over there.

(Joel walks off as Faith points to the side. Faith stands gawking at Joel for a few seconds, shaking her head in disbelief, then walks off in the opposite direction.)

If you use this skit as a discussion starter, here are possible questions:

■ **How does God live inside us?**

■ **Read 1 Chronicles 17:1-6 and 1 Corinthians 3:16-17. Why did David feel it was important to build God a temple?**

■ **How does God dwell among us now as opposed to Old Testament times? Why do you think it has changed?**

■ **If you were going to build God a temple, what would it look like?**

■ **If you are God's temple, what should your life be like?**

1 CHRONICLES 17:16-27

THEME:
Humility

SUMMARY:
In this CREATIVE PRAYER, teenagers will write prayer letters to God, then read them corporately in humble positions.

PREPARATION: You'll need paper, pencils or pens, and Bibles.

Have your group read David's prayer to God found in 1 Chronicles 17:16-27. Make sure they understand that when David says, "your servant," he's referring to himself.

Say: **One of the keys to David's success was his humility. He knew that God was in control and that anything good was because of God.**

Pass out a sheet of paper and a pencil or pen to each person. Explain that writing out prayer letters to God is often a great way to clear our thoughts and become humble before God.

Ask your group to quietly, in an attitude of prayer, write a prayer letter to God, expressing his greatness and power—using the same tone David used. Make sure your kids know their letters don't have to be very long.

After a few minutes, ask:

■ **If you went before a great leader and wanted to be humble before him or her, how might you express this with your body?**

Tell kids they're going to express their humility to God by reading their prayer letters in front of the group. Then suggest they all assume a humble position, such as kneeling. Make sure you join them. Ask kids to lead each other in prayer by reading their prayer letters aloud.

1 CHRONICLES 21:1-24

THEME:
The effects of sin

SUMMARY:
In this LEARNING GAME, kids' actions will affect other players.

PREPARATION: You'll need a large room; several large, strong rubber bands; a stopwatch or clock with a second hand; and a Bible.

Form teams of no more than five. Tell kids they're going to play a game in which one team will compete at a time.

Bring the first team to the center of the room and have team members stand in a circle. Place a strong rubber band around the ankles of kids standing next to each other so that every person is attached to the people on either side.

Now tell team members that their task is to walk as a team toward a wall. The team that gets to a wall in the shortest amount of time wins.

Before the first team starts, say: **Oh, and two more rules: You can't talk or make any sounds. If I hear one word or even a grunt or giggle, you'll be redirected toward the farthest wall at that point. And if you break a rubber band, you must stop while I replace it, but the clock will continue to run.**

On "go," start the clock. Stay near the team so you can hear if anyone makes a noise. If a noise is made or a word is spoken, clearly instruct the team to change direction toward the farthest wall.

When the first team finishes, give team members a round of applause, then bring up the next team and repeat the activity. Continue until all teams have completed the task. Declare the winning team, then form trios and have them discuss the following questions:

▪ **How did your actions affect others in this game?**

▪ **When do your actions in real life affect others?**

▪ **What are examples of times when a teenager's negative actions affected other people's lives?**

Read aloud 1 Chronicles 21:1-24. Make sure kids understand what's taking place in this passage—that David's sin against God had significant effects on other people's lives. Then ask:

▪ **When we sin, who's affected by the results?**

▪ **What are examples of sins we commit that hurt others?**

Close with prayer, asking God to give us courage and strength to resist sin and to forgive us for how our sins have affected other people's lives.

1 CHRONICLES
22

THEME:
Serving God

SUMMARY:
Kids will practice serving others in this ADVENTURE.

PREPARATION: You'll need Bibles.

Read aloud 1 Chronicles 22. Point out that David and Solomon had completely different roles. Solomon was the one who actually got to build the temple for God—a great honor. But God valued David's service and Solomon's service equally. Ask:

▪ **Which do you think is better in God's eyes: to rake leaves for an elderly person or to build houses for homeless people? Explain.**

▪ **How do you think God measures our success?**

Form groups of no more than four and have each group brainstorm a way to serve others (that can be accomplished in your available time). Encourage kids to think of ways to serve each other, people in the neighborhood, or family members. After groups have brainstormed their ideas, call everyone together.

Say: **Although people often measure success externally, God measures success according to the condition of our hearts. So when we're serving him, it's not what we do so much as our attitude in doing**

it. So whether we "build tem-
ples" or just "fight battles" to
survive, the important thing is
that our hearts are right.

Have groups tell what act of service they've brainstormed. Then
send groups out to serve in the
ways they've planned. When kids
return, have them discuss whether
their serving actions were more
like David's or Solomon's. Remind
teenagers to maintain their serving
attitudes throughout the week and
to look for new ways to serve with
a right heart.

2 CHRONICLES

*"Now [God] give me wisdom and
knowledge so I can lead these people in
the right way..."*

2 Chronicles 1:10a

2 CHRONICLES 1:7-12

THEME:
Wisdom

SUMMARY:
In this AFFIRMATION, kids will thank teachers for their wisdom by decorating T-shirts for them.

PREPARATION: Ask participants to each bring an extra-large, white T-shirt. Explain that this will be given as a gift, so it should be new or in good shape. You'll need a sheet of newsprint, puff paints or fabric paints of various colors, a stack of old newspapers, and a Bible.

Ask teenagers to define "wisdom." When the group has decided on a definition, write it on newsprint so everyone can see it.

Say: **Using this definition of "wisdom," think of a teacher or another person who has taught you wisdom.**

When each person has thought of someone, tell kids they'll be making "thank-you" T-shirts for these people. Have kids put several sheets of newspaper inside the T-shirts they've brought to keep the paints from going through the fabric onto the other layer of cloth.

Have kids use the paints to decorate the T-shirts with words, pictures, or other symbols. Encourage teenagers to think about lessons they've learned from their teachers as they work on the T-shirts.

When kids have completed their T-shirts, have a volunteer read aloud 2 Chronicles 1:7-12. Then ask:

■ **What would you have asked for if God had made this offer to you?**

■ **How have you sought wisdom in your life?**

■ **In what areas of your life would you like to have more wisdom?**

■ **How can you become more wise?**

Encourage kids to deliver their T-shirts within the week. Close with prayer, having kids thank God for the people for whom they've made the shirts and asking God for more opportunities to gain wisdom.

2 CHRONICLES 1:7-13

THEME:
Following the desires of your heart

SUMMARY:
In this SKIT, contestants of a game show tell about the desires of their hearts.

WHAT IN THE WORLD DO YOU WANT?

SCENE: Contestants Buddy and Suzanne are sitting. The announcer, Wally, is standing off to the side. Zack, the host, is standing in the front with a microphone and a big, cheesy smile on his face.

PROPS: You'll need two chairs, '70s disco-type clothes for Zack, a microphone for Wally to hold, and Bibles for the discussion afterward.

CHARACTERS:
Zack Zuckerman—game show host (has annoying "used-car salesman" voice)
Wally Paper—game show announcer (has annoying "used-car salesman" voice)
Buddy—game show contestant
Suzanne—game show contestant

SCRIPT

Zack: *(Speaks fast, like a radio DJ.)* Hi, ladies and gentlemen, and welcome to WHAT IN THE WORLD DO YOU WANT? In case you're a new viewer, let me go over the rules of our game. We ask our two contestants to tell us their little ol' hearts' desires and then we grant them! But we not only grant a heart's desire, we also look into the future and tell our contestants what their desires will bring them in the long run. They then have one chance either to keep their desires or change their minds. Now our first contestant is Suzanne from Fullerton, California! Suzanne, tell us nice and loud what's the one thing you desire more than anything!

Suzanne: Well, I want to live my life for God no matter what I'm involved in.

Zack: Really!? Well, to each her own! Wally Paper, tell her what she's won!

Wally: *(Offstage)* Well, Zack, I'm glad you asked 'cause Suzanne will raise a Christian family and stay true to her God while at the same time going through vari-

ous life struggles. She'll die an old woman and leave behind a lot of people who love and miss her. She'll then go to heaven, where she'll spend eternity with God and experience joys we can't even imagine.

Zack: Well, Suzanne, do you want to keep your desire or change your mind?

Suzanne: I'll keep my desire.

Zack: I've got a million bucks here in my pocket that says you'll change your mind.

Suzanne: Sorry, Zack, I'm keeping my desire.

Zack: Very well! Enjoy! Now our second guest is from Del City, Oklahoma. Ladies and gentlemen, welcome Buddy! *(All clap for him.)* Now, Buddy, tell us what YOUR heart's desire is.

Buddy: Well, sir, I want to have all the money in the world at my disposal so I can do anything I want to do, whenever I want.

Zack: *(To audience)* Now THAT'S what I call desire! Wally, tell him what he's won!

Wally: Again, I'm glad you asked, Zack, 'cause Buddy's got a lot comin' to him. Buddy, you'll be the envy of your block with the comfortable life you're about to lead. You'll have enough money to do whatever you want, whenever you want to do it.

Zack: Well, well, well, Buddy. What do you think about that?

Buddy: *(Excited)* Sounds great! Will I live to be an old man?

Zack: Sure you will!

Buddy: Will I have lots of friends?

Zack: Buddy, with all your money, you can buy any friends you need!

Buddy: What happens after I die?

Zack: What does it matter, Buddy? You'll get what you want while you're on earth. That afterlife stuff will take care of itself.

Buddy: *(Contemplating)* Um, I think I want to change my mind.

Zack: What? And miss out on all the fun that pleasing yourself can bring you?!

Buddy: Uh, yeah.

Zack: OK, Buddy, name your poison!

Buddy: I think I want to have the same desire Suzanne has.

Zack: Funny thing—most people say the same thing once they see where their desires will lead them. Buddy, are you sure this is what you want?

Buddy: Oh, yeah. Quite sure.

Zack: All right! Well, folks, thanks for joining us and remember only you can decide: *What in the World Do You Want?*

Permission to photocopy this skit from *Youth Worker's Encyclopedia: OT* granted for local church use. Copyright © Group Publishing, Inc., Box 481, Loveland, CO 80539.

If you use this skit as a discussion starter, here are possible questions:

■ **Are desires in and of themselves good, bad, neither, or both? Explain.**

■ **What are examples of good desires? bad desires?**

■ **What are the desires of your heart—good and bad?**

■ **Do you think you would be more or less willing to pursue those desires if you knew where they would take you in life? Explain.**

■ **Read 2 Chronicles 1:7-13.**

Why do you think Solomon's request pleased God?

2 CHRONICLES 2:12-14

THEME:
Using talents for God

SUMMARY:
Kids will try to guess each other's secret talents in this AFFIRMATION.

PREPARATION: For each person, you'll need a sheet of construction paper, a marker, small gummed stars, and a 24-inch length of yarn. You'll also need a few hole punchers and a Bible.

Give each person a sheet of construction paper, a marker, several small gummed stars, and a 24-inch length of yarn. Provide hole punchers for kids to create placards to wear around their necks.

Have kids each write on one side of their placards their names and the sentence "I'm a talented person!" On the other side, have them each secretly write three talents they have. For example, group members may write things like "athletic ability," "ability to make friends easily," or "ability to laugh in any situation."

Have kids wear their placards name-side out. Give kids 10 minutes to walk around and try to guess the talents on the other side of each person's placard by writing their guesses on the name side of the person's placard. For each correct guess, the person who guessed correctly receives a gummed star to place on his or her placard. The person with the most stars is named the best "talent scout" and wins a round of applause.

When the activity is finished, have kids each tell what their secret talents are, as well as the talents other people wrote on their placards. Ask:

■ **Are you surprised by how many talents you have? Why or why not?**

■ **What's one talent you have that you enjoy using for God?**

Read aloud 2 Chronicles 2:12-14. Ask:

■ **How did Huram-Abi use his talents for God?**

■ **How can you be more like Huram-Abi?**

2 CHRONICLES 10:1-19

THEME:
Following good advice

SUMMARY:
In this PROJECT, kids will interview others in search of good advice.

PREPARATION: You'll need a video camera (or a tape recorder if you don't have access to video) and Bibles.

Have kids form groups of no more than five. Read aloud 2 Chronicles 10:1-19. Then have kids discuss these questions in their groups:

■ **Why did Rehoboam choose the advice he did?**

■ **What was the result of his choice?**

■ **Who are you most likely to go to for advice? Why?**

Explain that everyone will be participating in a project on the topic of good advice. The project is to interview people of all ages, asking them about good advice. Kids should use questions such as the following:

■ **What's the best advice you've ever received and why?**

■ **Tell about a time when you wish you'd followed someone's advice.**

■ **What advice can you offer teenagers today?**

Have group members work together to accomplish these tasks:

• Determine what questions to ask.

• Find people of all ages to interview.

• Arrange times for these people to be interviewed on camera.

• Record the interviews.

When the project has been completed, have everyone gather to watch (or listen to) it. Afterward, have kids share what they've learned and what advice from the video (or audio) they hope to follow.

2 CHRONICLES
14:8-15

THEME:
Calling to God for help

SUMMARY:
In this MUSIC IDEA, kids search for songs that call to God for help.

PREPARATION: You'll need a variety of hymnals and songbooks, pencils, paper, and Bibles.

Have kids form teams of no more than three. Give each team a Bible, a sheet of paper, and a pencil. Have kids assign the following roles within their teams: reader, writer, and speaker. Teams with less than three members may assign two roles to one person.

Have the readers read 2 Chronicles 14:8-15 to their team members. Ask:

■ **When do you feel like calling out to God for help as these people did?**

■ **Have you ever called to God through a song? If so, when?**

Say: **We're going to have a song-finding contest. You'll be looking for titles of songs that call to God for help, such as "I Will Call Upon the Lord," and "Change My Heart, Oh God," or lines from songs, such as "Please be near me to the end" from "Thy Word."** Think of the songs together and have your writers list them. Look for **songs you think other teams won't list.**

Allow each team to select one hymnal or songbook as a resource (although teams can list songs not found in their books), then begin the search. After five minutes, call time. Have each speaker read one song from his or her team's list. If another team has that song listed, both teams (and any other teams with that song) must cross the song from their lists. Have speakers continue until all lists have been read. The team with the most songs remaining on its list wins.

Congratulate the winners. Then ask that team to select one song from its list and lead everyone in singing the song to close.

2 CHRONICLES
20:6-12

THEME:
Prayer

SUMMARY:
In this CREATIVE PRAYER/CREATIVE READING, kids will add their own prayers to that of Jehoshaphat.

PREPARATION: You'll need pencils, paper, and Bibles.

Distribute pencils and paper. Say: **Second Chronicles 20 tells of the people of Judah, who are about to go to battle against the Moabites and Ammonites. In** verses 6 through 12, we read the prayer of their king, Jehoshaphat. He begins by praising God, telling how powerful and wonderful he is. Think of one thing about God you'd like to praise him for and write this in one sentence on your paper.

Allow a moment for kids to do this, then continue. Say: **Jehoshaphat then thanks God for what he's done for them in the past. Think of one thing God has done for you and write this in one sentence.**

When kids have done this, continue. Say: **Then the king reminded God of his promise to hear them and save them when they called for help. Think of one promise God has made, whether to love us, send Jesus, or another promise you know about, and write this in your next sentence.**

When kids are done, say: **Finally Jehoshaphat asked for help. Think of one situation in which you need God's help. This should be something you'd be willing to share aloud. Then write one sentence asking God for help in this situation.**

When everyone has completed this, have kids stand in a circle. Begin reading the prayer of Jehoshaphat as written here. Each time you stop, have kids go around the circle and read the sentence prayers they've written.

Say: **"Lord, God of our ancestors, you are the God in heaven. You rule over all the kingdoms of the nations. You have power and strength, so no one can stand against you."**

Have kids read their prayers of praise.

Continue: **"Our God, you forced out the people who lived in this land as your people Israel moved in. And you gave this land forever to the descendants of your friend Abraham. They lived in this land and built a temple for you."**

Have kids read their prayers thanking God for what he's done.

Continue: **"If trouble comes upon us, or war, punishment, sickness, or hunger, we will stand before you and before this temple where you have chosen to be worshiped. We will cry out to you when we are in trouble. Then you will hear and save us."**

Have kids read their prayers of promise, then continue: **"But now here are men from Ammon, Moab, and Edom. You wouldn't let the Israelites enter their lands when the Israelites came from Egypt. So the Israelites turned away and did not destroy them. But see how they repay us for not destroying them! They have come to force us out of your land, which you gave us as our own. Our God, punish those people. We have no power against this large army that is attacking us. We don't know what to do, so we look to you for help."**

Have kids read their prayers asking for help.

Say: **Jehoshaphat was so confident that God would answer his prayer that he thanked God before they even went to battle. He said, "Thank the Lord,** because his love continues forever." **Let's close our time of prayer by saying these words of thanks together.**

Repeat the prayer of thanks together.

2 CHRONICLES 26:16-21

THEME:
Pride

SUMMARY:
In this LEARNING GAME, kids will compete to be the best braggart.

PREPARATION: You'll need a Bible.

Have kids form a circle. Say: **We're going to determine who's the best person here by having a bragging contest. We'll go around the circle and each person must complete the following sentence: "I'm the best because . . ." What you say may be true, such as "I'm the best because I got the highest score in my class on a test this week." Or it may be a lie, such as "I'm the best because the Phoenix Suns tried to recruit me for their team last week." Listen to what others say because we'll be voting for the best braggart.**

Begin the bragging yourself, then have kids take turns telling others why they're great. After you've gone around the circle, have kids vote for the top four braggers. Then have these four go into the championship round. Give them one more chance to tell everyone a new reason why they're the best. After this round, have everyone vote once more to determine the group's best braggart.

Have the winner read 2 Chronicles 26:16-21 to the rest of the group. Ask:

■ **Uzziah was a powerful king. What was his attitude toward God after he became great?**

■ **When we think we're the best, whether it's true or not, what's our attitude toward God and others like?**

■ **What's it like to be around someone who's prideful?**

■ **When do you have a problem with pride?**

■ **Perhaps you've heard the saying "Pride goes before a fall." How was this true for Uzziah? How is it true for us today?**

Close by taking turns going around the circle again, but this time in prayer. Have kids complete the sentence "God, you're the best because..." and brag to God about himself.

2 CHRONICLES
30:6-12

THEME:
Telling others
about God

SUMMARY:
In this PROJECT, kids will prepare a message about God to
share with others.

PREPARATION: You'll need a Bible.
Kids may need to gather other supplies as they determine the needs of
the project.

When kids have gathered, ask:
∎ **How have you felt about
telling others about God?**

When kids have responded, say:
**Let's read about a king who
wanted everyone to turn to God.**
Read aloud 2 Chronicles 30:6-12.
Then form groups of no more than
five. Have groups discuss the following questions and share insights with the whole group. Ask:
∎ **How do the messengers'
feelings compare with your feelings about telling others to turn
to God?**
∎ **How are we like or unlike
King Hezekiah and his messengers?**
Say: **Even though many people laughed at the king and
his messengers, some people
turned to God. As a result, the
king and the land enjoyed a
time of great success. We can
be like this king and send a
message about God to others.**

Explain that the goal of this project is to send a message about God
to others. Have kids brainstorm
what kind of message this will be.
For example, they could create a
skit and present it at a park or
other public place. Or they might
want to visit people who've left the
youth group or church and invite
them to return.

When kids have determined
what they'll be doing, help them
organize their project and take
action. If some feel unsure about
the response they'll get, encourage
them with the story of Hezekiah's
messengers.

2 CHRONICLES
32:6-8

THEME: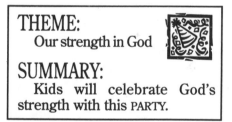
Our strength in God

SUMMARY:
Kids will celebrate God's
strength with this PARTY.

PREPARATION: You'll need pencils or pens, a package of bubble
gum, a rope, a bowl filled with at
least 40 uninflated balloons, a "barbell" cake (two round cakes with
black frosting joined by a foil-cov-
ered dowel), candy, fruit juice, and
a Bible.

When kids arrive, tell them the
theme of this party is
"strength." Then lead them in several of the following games and
activities:

•**Tongue Twisters**—Place several pencils or pens on a table. Time kids to see who is fastest at picking up one using only his or her tongue (no lips). Award the person with the strongest tongue a package of bubble gum.

•**Tug of War**—Try various combinations of groups, such as guys against girls, leaders against kids, freshman against seniors, and so on.

•**Lung Power**—Have kids form two teams. Place a large bowl of uninflated balloons at the front of the room. The first person on each team must take a balloon, blow it up, then sit on it to pop it. Then the next person takes his or her turn. The first team to pop 20 balloons wins. (If your group has more than 40 members, form three or more teams.)

For refreshments, serve a barbell cake, super-strength "vitamins" (M&M's or jelly beans), and power punch (any fruit juice).

When you've finished the games and refreshments, read aloud 2 Chronicles 32:6-8 and ask:

■ **What would it be like to rely on God in battle like this?**

■ **What kinds of strength does God offer for battles today?**

■ **When do you find yourself relying on your own strength instead of turning to God?**

■ **What makes it hard or easy to rely on God's strength?**

Have kids form groups of no more than six.

Say: **Think of an area of your life in which you need to rely on God's strength instead of your own. Perhaps you need emotional strength to deal with a difficult relationship. Or you**
may need physical strength because of sickness or injury.

Ask the person wearing the most blue in each group to share first. Then have that person's group members lift him or her up off the ground and in unison repeat Hezekiah's words: "We have the Lord our God to help us and to fight our battles." (You may want to write this on newsprint and tape it in a prominent place.) Have group members continue sharing and lifting each other up both physically and with words of encouragement.

2 CHRONICLES 34:29-33

THEME:
Renewing our commitment to God

SUMMARY:
In this LEARNING GAME, kids will compare symbols of commitment to their actions in real life.

PREPARATION: You'll need Bibles.

Have kids form groups of no more than five. Say: **The goal of this game is to find objects you have with you or objects around the room that represent commitment. For example, a ring might represent a commitment to a special friend, or a letter jacket might represent a commitment to your sports team. You have three minutes to find as many objects as possible.**

Begin the search and call time at three minutes. Have groups each tell how the objects they've selected represent commitment. When each group has shared, have a volunteer read aloud 2 Chronicles 34:29-33. Ask:

■ **What objects do we have that represent our commitment to God?**

Say: **Carrying around Bibles or wearing crosses might let a few people know about our commitment to God, but our actions let people know how true our commitment is.**

Ask:

■ **What actions did the people in this story do and promise to do to show their commitment?**

■ **What do your actions show about your commitment to God?**

■ **What kind of agreement could our group make that would demonstrate our commitment to God?**

Have the group work together to decide upon a symbol, such as a special handshake, slogan, or cheer, that would remind them of their commitment to God. Then have each person share one area in which he or she would like to make a new commitment to God. After each person tells about this commitment, have the rest of the group offer encouragement by demonstrating the group symbol.

EZRA

"The Lord our God has been kind to us."

Ezra 9:8b

EZRA
1:1-7

THEME:
The value of home and memories

SUMMARY:
In this DEVOTION, teenagers bring objects from home that are valuable and special to them.

PREPARATION: Call group members ahead of time and tell them to each bring the most important single object they can find from their rooms. You'll also need Bibles.

EXPERIENCE
After teenagers arrive, form groups of three or four. In their groups, have teenagers display their objects and explain the personal value of their possessions to their partners.

Then ask small groups to discuss the following questions. Allow time for discussion before having volunteers share their insights with the whole class. Ask:

■ **What criteria did you use in selecting your object?**

■ **What other objects might you have brought if you were allowed more items? Explain.**

■ **How do the items we own contribute to making your house a "home"?**

■ **Besides material goods, what makes your home special and valuable to you?**

RESPONSE
As a group, read Ezra 1:1-7. Then say: **For 70 years, the Jews had** been away from their home as captives within a foreign land. These verses tell about the Jews' first opportunity to go home and be a nation again. Ask:

■ **How would you feel about being away from home for several decades?**

■ **What things would you miss about home? Would the objects you selected today still be as important? Explain.**

■ **What would be the first thing you'd do when you finally returned home?**

■ **According to these verses, what were some of the things the Jews did to prepare for returning home? What things did they look forward to?**

CLOSING
Encourage teenagers to discuss in their groups what items they'd select if they were to be gone for 70 years, but assured of certain return. Close with a prayer, focusing on the value of faith, family, and future.

EZRA
4:1-5

THEME:
Dealing with opposition

SUMMARY:
Teenagers will play a LEARNING GAME in which one group tries to prevent the other from completing a newspaper structure.

PREPARATION: You'll need several newspapers, masking tape, wooden matches, and Bibles.

Form two groups. Give one group newspapers and masking tape and instruct them to build a newspaper wall at least 6 feet high and 15 feet long. As the first group begins to build, tell the second group that its job is to disrupt the construction. Tell teenagers in this group that they may not throw objects at the wall or physically touch the structure to tear it down, but they may hinder the construction in other, creative ways.

Allow several minutes for this activity, then read Ezra 4:1-5. Form pairs consisting of one member from each group. Have partners discuss the following questions, then tell the whole group what they discussed. Ask:

■ **What was it like to have your construction disrupted?**

■ **How might your feelings be similar to the Jews' experience in rebuilding the temple?**

■ **Is opposition always a bad thing? Why or why not?**

■ **What personal opposition have you had, as a Christian?**

■ **How have those who don't understand your faith disrupted your life?**

■ **When faced with opposition, what options do you have? Which one would God desire of you?**

Give each person a wooden match. Have partners take turns lighting their matches and sharing one "hot" area of opposition in their lives as the match burns. Then have partners pray for each other that God will reveal an opportunity to escape or endurance to overcome the situation.

EZRA
9:1-15

THEME:
Marrying a non-Christian

SUMMARY:
In this SKIT, a dog and a cat fall in love and try to work out their differences with the aid of a marriage counselor.

LOVE AT FIRST BITE

SCENE: A dog and a cat are in the office of a marriage counselor, trying to work through potential problems in their upcoming marriage.

PROPS: Three chairs, a desk, a notepad, a ball of yarn, a dog biscuit, whiskers for Phyllis, a dog collar for Hercules. You'll need Bibles for the discussion afterward.

CHARACTERS:
Phyllis (the cat)
Hercules (the Saint Bernard)
Dr. Van Lint (the counselor)

SCRIPT
(Dr. Van Lint is sitting at his desk. Hercules and Phyllis walk in and sit down.)

Dr. Van Lint: Good afternoon, folks. How can I be of assistance to you today?

Hercules: We'd like to talk to you about our upcoming marriage.

Phyllis: We're supposed to tie the

knot in a few months, but we're starting to have some doubts.

Dr. Van Lint: What sort of doubts?

Phyllis: We're just so different from each other.

Hercules: I'm always ready to play, but a lot of the time she just wants to be left alone. And her incessant purring drives me crazy!

Phyllis: *(With an angry look)* My purring? MY purring?! What about your barking and slobbering and shedding and howling and chewing on sticks? Huh? What about those things?

Hercules: Yeah, well, at least I keep my claws out of the furniture!

Dr. Van Lint: OK. Calm down now. Nice kitty. Nice doggy. *(He gives Hercules a dog biscuit and Phyllis a ball of yarn.)* Here, maybe this will help.

Phyllis: I'm sorry. It's just that sometimes I feel like we're from different worlds, and I wonder if we'll ever make a marriage work.

Dr. Van Lint: I kind of wonder the same thing. What makes you think you can be happy together?

Phyllis: What do you mean?

Dr. Van Lint: *(Looking at Phyllis)* I mean, in case you haven't realized, you're a cat, and he's a dog.

Hercules: *(Threatened)* And?

Dr. Van Lint: Annnd... cats and dogs are usually very different. You know, dogs chase cats, cats chase mice, mice eat cheese, birds eat worms, lions chase antelope, big fish chase little fish... Are you getting the picture at all?

Hercules: So you're trying to say

that we're just too different?

Dr. Van Lint: Exactly!

Phyllis: But couldn't we both change and try to become more like each other?

Dr. Van Lint: *(Looking at Phyllis)* Do you want to become more like a dog? *(Looking at Hercules)* Do you want to become more like a cat?

(Phyllis and Hercules look up and down at each other for a minute.)

Hercules: *(To Dr. Van Lint)* Maybe we should think about it some more.

(Phyllis nods in agreement.)

Dr. Van Lint: Good idea.

(All exit.)

If you use this skit as a discussion starter, here are possible questions:

■ **If you were Dr. Van Lint, what advice would you have given to Hercules and Phyllis?**

■ **Read Ezra 9:1-15. Why do you think God wanted Israelites to marry only other Israelites? Do you think that law can be applied to Christians today? Explain.**

■ **What are the arguments for and against marrying non-Christians?**

■ **Is it OK for Christians to be partners with non-Christians in other areas, such as business?**

■ **Are there types of relationships with non-Christians you should avoid? Explain.**

NEHEMIAH

"I prayed to the God of heaven."

Nehemiah 1:4b

NEHEMIAH
1:1-11

THEME:
Prayer

SUMMARY:

In this CREATIVE PRAYER, teenagers will discuss the benefits of purposeful prayer.

PREPARATION: You'll need a large piece of cork board with a paper target, several blindfolds, darts (preferably one for each person), markers, paper, and Bibles.

Set up a piece of cork board and designate it as a target. Make sure your target area is relatively free of breakables—especially windows. Form groups of four or five teenagers and give each group one blindfold and a dart for each member. Have groups each blindfold a member and guide him or her to the target area for one toss at the target. After each throw, have groups blindfold another member to toss a dart. Repeat the process until everyone's tossed a dart.

After all the groups have thrown their darts, say: **It's difficult to throw darts blindfolded. Yet, many people today toss prayers to God just as we tossed these darts. Nehemiah, however, chose a more focused approach to prayer. Nehemiah's Jewish friends were in trouble back in Jerusalem, and the wall surrounding the city was in ruins. Nehemiah prayed a purposeful prayer—that is, a prayer aimed with eyes wide open and at a specific target.**

Instruct teenagers to regroup and read Nehemiah 1:1-11. Then have kids list times when Nehemiah prayed a focused prayer and things he did to show his concern for the situation. Have kids discuss and answer the following questions as a group:

■ **What does the manner and content of Nehemiah's prayer tell you about him?**

■ **Why was it important for him to be so specific?**

■ **How can we be more specific in our prayer lives?**

Allow several minutes for discussion. Then pass out paper and markers and have teenagers each draw a target and write in the bull's eye a specific situation that needs God's immediate attention. Give teenagers each another dart and, after a moment of personal, silent prayer for their target areas, have them throw their darts at their newly created targets. Close with a group prayer.

NEHEMIAH
2:11-18

THEME:
The value of each group member

SUMMARY:

Teenagers will brainstorm and formulate a plan in this OBJECT LESSON to find "missing" or "lost" youth group members.

PREPARATION: On a large piece of white butcher paper, draw a brick wall and write in each brick the name of every teenager who's been to one of your group's meetings in the last year. Post the paper wall for kids to see as they arrive. You'll also need a black marker and Bibles.

Invite teenagers to observe the wall and make any comments about the listed names. Then explain that this wall represents the entire youth group (encourage them to find their own names). Using a black marker, roughly color over the following categories of people (asking the teenagers to help choose the names to blacken):
• those absent from the present meeting (for any reason),
• those who attend another church program but not youth group,
• those who never come, and
• any other "category" necessary (the only bricks remaining should be those of that evening's attending teenagers).

The wall will now look like a shadow of its former self. As a group, read Nehemiah 2:11-18. Then ask:

■ **How is our youth group wall like the one Nehemiah found in Jerusalem?**

■ **How do you think Nehemiah felt when he saw the wall? How are your feelings similar or different?**

■ **Why is every brick in our wall important to God?**

As a group, brainstorm specific ideas to encourage "absentees" to become regular group members.

Choose one or two of the ideas and discuss with your group the logistics of each one. Spend time in prayer for both the plan and each teenager in your wall—present or absent.

If you have time, ask teenagers to attach notes to bricks of those in attendance, citing positive reasons that person is important to the group. Keep the wall up for the coming weeks but replace the blacked-out names of those who attend in the coming weeks with fresh, new bricks listing their names.

NEHEMIAH
4:1-3, 9-14

THEME:
  Standing against ridicule

SUMMARY:
  In this SKIT, a basketball player considers not returning to the game because some fans for the other team are calling him names.

STICKS AND STONES

SCENE: It's halftime, and Coach is talking about the game to one of his players in the locker room.

PROPS: You'll need a bench, a basketball, and Bibles for the discussion afterward.

CHARACTERS:
Coach
Kyle

SCRIPT

(Kyle is dejected, his head hanging down as he begins to talk to his coach.)

Kyle: Coach, I don't think I can play the second half.

Coach: *(Surprised)* What's wrong? Did you pull or twist something? We need you out there.

Kyle: I know, Coach, but, well... they called me names.

Coach: Huh?

Kyle: You know, the fans—they were calling me names. Especially when I scored. I just don't think I can take it anymore.

Coach: *(Incredulously)* You don't think you can play because people from the opposing team called you names?! What did they call you that was so bad?

Kyle: Well, they called me a weasel. But that's not all. They also said things like "Pass it behind you!" "Look out!" and "Don't step out of bounds!" *(Sigh)* But the worst one was "Foul!" And, Coach, I wasn't fouling anybody out there. Why do they hate me so much?

Coach: *(In a firm but understanding voice)* Kyle, they're from the opposing team! They'll do anything to help their side win! The only reason they're saying so many things to you is that you're doing a great job. They're trying to make you lose your nerve. They'd be cheering for you if you were messing up and helping their team out.

Kyle: But what if some of the things they're saying are true? I mean, what if I really am a weasel?

Coach: You are not a weasel.

Kyle: Yeah, says you. There are a lot more of them who say I am one!

Coach: Kyle, think about it. Do they want you to win?

Kyle: *(Thinks.)* Well, I guess not.

Coach: Of course they don't. They're for the other team. If they could help their side win by calling you names, do you think they would?

Kyle: Yeah, I guess you're right. But how do I not let them bug me?

Coach: Kyle, don't listen to them. Listen to me. If you're doing something wrong, I'LL tell you. If you're not sure what to do, look at ME, and I'LL guide you. I want you to win. THEY don't. They aren't on your team.

Kyle: Thanks, Coach. And I'm sorry I let them get to me.

Coach: That's OK. It's easy to do when there are hundreds of them and only one of me. Just remember that nobody wants you to win more than I do and nobody knows what to do for this team more than I do. Well, it's time to go win a game.

Kyle: *(Excited)* Let's do it!

(They both begin to walk off.)

Coach: I think you look much more like a badger anyway.

If you use this skit as a discussion starter, here are possible questions:

∎ **What are some things you might be ridiculed about for following Christ? How do you deal with that?**

∎ **How can you turn ridicule**

into something positive?

■ How do you deal with criticism when it comes from other Christians? Do you think they always have your best interest at heart? Explain.

■ Do you have others' best interests in mind when you criticize them? How can you help them know it?

■ Read Nehemiah 4:1-3, 9-14. How did the Jews react to ridicule about rebuilding Jerusalem's wall? How do you think the Jews felt while rebuilding? Explain.

■ What message can you draw from this passage that will help you when you are being ridiculed for doing something right?

NEHEMIAH 5:1-12

THEME:
Struggling for economic stability

SUMMARY:
Teenagers perform a contemporary CREATIVE READING—using candies for currency—about the economic hardships of Nehemiah's people in Jerusalem.

PREPARATION: Each teenager will need a small cup of 10 candy pieces, such as M&M's, and a photocopy of the "Creative Reading for Nehemiah 5:1-12" handout (p. 187). You'll also need to place a bowl on a small table or desk somewhere in the room. Select two adult leaders to be the "President" and "Nehemiah." Form five different groups or give each group part to one person. For added meaning, plan to serve a surprise pizza party immediately following the reading. You'll also need Bibles.

Explain to group members that you'll be doing a reading based on Nehemiah 5:1-12 that's a contemporary retelling of the passage. Then give everyone a photocopy of the "Creative Reading for Nehemiah 5:1-12" handout (p. 187). After the reading, form groups of no more than three. Have the oldest person in each trio read Nehemiah 5:1-12 from the Bible. Then have trios discuss these questions:

■ What can we learn from this reading and this passage?

■ How can we trust God in the midst of economic struggles?

■ How can we practice trusting God for our economic needs this week?

NEHEMIAH 8:1-8

THEME:
God's Word

SUMMARY:
In this OBJECT LESSON, teenagers will experience the importance of Scripture.

CREATIVE READING FOR NEHEMIAH 5:1-12

All Guys: We have many sons, and we're starving. We need pizza!

All Girls: We have many daughters, and we're hungry. We need pizza!

President: *(Chanting)* I want your candies! I need your candies! I love your candies!

Group 1: But we've sacrificed market profits for you—here, have three candies. *(Each group member gives President three candies.)*

Group 2: And we've sold our cars for you—here, have three candies. *(Each group member gives President three candies.)*

Group 3: And we've mortgaged our homes—here, have four candies. *(Each group member gives President four candies.)*

Group 4: And we've had yard sales for you—here, have a candy. *(Each group member gives President one candy.)*

Group 5: And we use supermarket coupons—here, have another candy! *(Each group member gives President one candy.)*

President: *(Chanting)* I want your candies! I need your candies! I love your candies!

Group 1: But we've had to borrow candies to pay your taxes. *(Each group member takes two candies from another group and gives them to President.)*

Group 2: And our whole family has to work to pay your taxes. *(Whole group gives a total of three candies to President.)*

Group 3: And we've sold our house, our car, our television... *(Whole group gives a total of five candies to President.)*

Group 4: And we've maxed out our credit cards. *(Whole group gives a total of five candies to President.)*

Group 5: And we already give most of our paycheck! *(Each group member gives seven candies to President.)*

President: *(Chanting)* I want your candies! I need your candies! I love your candies!

Group 1: Without candies, we can't buy pizza... *(Group wails.)*

Group 2: Without pizza, we can't feed children... *(Group wails.)*

Group 3: Without children, we can't get more candies... *(Group wails.)*

Group 4: Without more candies, we'll all starve... *(Group wails.)*

Group 5: Pepperoni! Sausage! Beef and olives! Extra cheese!

Nehemiah: Hold on, Mr. President! You're enslaving your own people through your taxes. It's not right. Fear God and stop your taxing! Give back their homes, cars, and candies.

President: You're right. Tax breaks on the house... and maybe PIZZA! *(President gives back the candies in equal amounts.)*

PREPARATION: You'll need to secure a room that can be darkened as much as possible. Also, you'll need a candle for each teenager, matches, and Bibles.

Give each person an unlit candle and lead them to a dark room. As you enter, give one person a Bible already opened to Nehemiah 8:1-8. Encourage kids to sit in a circle and, once settled, ask the preselected person to read the passage (which should be impossible if the room is dark enough). Allow the person to struggle, then light your own candle and repeat the request. Again, he or she should have difficulty reading. Light another person's candle and repeat your request. Continue this process until every candle is lit. If the person still can't read the passage, turn on the lights. Ask everyone:

■ **How did you feel when the Scripture was being read in the dark?**

■ **In what way is light important to reading? What purpose does it serve?**

Read Nehemiah 8:1-8 again and ask:

■ **Why did Ezra believe reading the Book of the Teachings was so important?**

■ **How long did Ezra read the Teachings to the people? How did the people respond?**

■ **Why is it important that we comprehend God's Word?**

■ **Is it enough merely to know about God? Why or why not?**

Have kids brainstorm Scripture passages that are difficult to decipher. Then form teams to explore those passages in detail by using

Bible study materials, concordances, and the insights of people in your church who are good students of the Bible. Close in prayer, thanking God for the Bible.

NEHEMIAH
9:5-37

THEME:
Remaining faithful

SUMMARY:
Teenagers will go on a "patriotic" RETREAT that focuses on America, its history, and its future.

PREPARATION: To make this retreat fun, create a setting exploding with patriotism. Plan on using lots of parade music. Decorate with red, white, and blue banners and presidential photos. Prepare meals such as hamburgers and fries, apple pie, and Coca-Cola. Publicity might include mini-flags containing retreat information. Gather supplies as needed for the activities you choose. You'll also need Bibles.

Encourage teenagers to come to this retreat dressed as someone from 100 to 200 years ago. As kids arrive, play parade music or patriotic hymns. Play games like Name That President or Wheel of History (using historical-event puzzles).

Or play good old American games with patriotic names, such as Yankee Doodle Dodge Ball;

Valley Forge Volleyball (in a swimming pool); or Paul Revere Relays, in which teenagers ride piggyback to accomplish deeds such as balancing a cup of tea or dribbling a "cannon" ball (basketball).

During a discussion time, read Nehemiah 9:5-37 and talk with teenagers about the rise and fall of the nation of Israel. Ask kids to note similar conditions between present-day America and the Jews of Nehemiah's time. In groups of no more than five, have teenagers paraphrase the passage or create dramatic sketches or musical numbers. Write encouraging letters to the president (1600 Pennsylvania Ave., Washington, D.C. 20500). And spend time praying for the president, Congress, our nation, and our churches.

NEHEMIAH
12:27-30

THEME:
Celebrating life

SUMMARY:
In this ADVENTURE, teenagers will go to a local sporting activity and interview (on video or audio cassette) celebratory fans to record examples of "celebration."

PREPARATION: You'll need a video camera or cassette recorder for every four to five teenagers. Plan to take kids to an athletic event such as a college or high school football, basketball, or baseball game. You'll also need Bibles.

Take your group to the athletic event. Meet for a few minutes before the event and read Nehemiah 12:27-30. Ask kids to describe the joy the Jews must have felt in finally completing the wall.

Form groups of four or five and provide each group with either a video camera or cassette recorder. Have groups interview fans in the stands and record significant "celebrations" by the crowd throughout the evening. Interviews might address such topics as

■ **How do you support a team in bad and good times?**

■ **What do you do to celebrate a team's success?**

■ **Why do you enjoy celebrating about your team?**

Afterward, replay the interviews and discuss the value of celebration. Identify high points and memories from the event. Compare the joy of winning a contest to building a wall of protection. Then, in pairs, thank God for good times and the opportunity to celebrate life.

ESTHER

"Then I will go the king, even though it is against the law, and if I die, I die."

Esther 4:16b

ESTHER
2:1-17

THEME:

Beauty

SUMMARY:
Teenagers will enjoy the "sweetness" of positive AFFIRMATION and learn the importance of seeing both inner and outer beauty.

PREPARATION: You'll need three chocolate kisses for each person and Bibles.

Give each person three chocolate kisses, then read Esther 2:1-17. Explain how Esther's Jewish background could be threatening inside the throne room of a foreign king and also how Esther evidently possessed both outer and inner beauty.

Have kids find partners and sit face to face. Then encourage each person to think of a physical, outer attribute that makes his or her partner attractive (such as hair, style of dress, or a skill or ability). Have kids unwrap a chocolate kiss and feed it to their partners as they share attributes.

After each partner has shared, repeat the process but have each person identify an inner quality that makes his or her partner attractive (such as a personality trait, humor, or intelligence) and share another chocolate kiss. Then read Galatians 5:22-23 and repeat the process one more time, but have teenagers encourage their partners by describing a spiritual quality from Galatians that makes that person attractive to both God and humans as they share the last chocolate kiss.

End this activity by having partners pray for each other, thanking God for the unique beauty they've been given, inside and out.

ESTHER
3

THEME:

Prejudice

SUMMARY:
In this SKIT, two friends discuss their attitudes about people who are different from them.

A CASE OF THE BLUES

SCENE: Terra and Jeni take a break from shopping to talk about life.

PROPS: You'll need shopping bags, a yellow armband, a green armband, a blue armband, and Bibles for the discussion afterward.

CHARACTERS:
Terra (wears a blue armband and has a bad attitude)
Jeni (wears a green armband and has a good attitude)
Heather (wears a yellow armband)

SCRIPT
Terra: Whew! *(Plops down on chair.)* What a sale!

Jeni: I'm so tired, and my feet are killing me! But it was worth it to get these great new school clothes.

Terra: Yeah, we'll definitely look the best. People won't even be looking at those snobby Yellows.

Jeni: *(Sighs.)* Terra, not this again. Why are you so against Yellows?

Terra: Don't get me started...

Jeni: I just don't get it. I mean, in fourth grade you were like best friends with Katrina. It didn't matter then that she was a Yellow and you were a Blue. Why does it matter now?

Terra: Jeni, you just don't know them like I do. They all think they're so great, but they're really stupid. Don't you hate how pushy they are and how they always flaunt their new clothes?

Jeni: Terra! Those are total stereotypes! You talk like they're all the same! You only know a couple of Yellows, and you don't even spend that much time with THEM! How can you hate a whole group of people when you don't even know them?

Terra: It doesn't matter. They're all the same. I don't have to know them all.

Jeni: OK, then what about Jesse Ritter? He tutored you in algebra until you got an A. And he didn't even get paid for it! What about Mrs. Easley, who used to give us rides to church all the time? Terra, you met one Yellow you didn't like, and now you hate them all.

Terra: *(Sees Heather coming, eyes get wide.)* Oh, great. Here comes Heather, queen of all Yellows. Better hang on to your bags, Jen.

Jeni: Terra, you're such a... *(Stands up to greet Heather.)* Heather! Hi! How's it going?

Heather: Good. Wow, the mall's really crowded today.

Jeni: Yeah, there's an awesome sale over at Harris'—50 percent off almost everything. It's a zoo, but it's worth it!

Heather: Sounds like something I can't pass up. Looks like you cleaned 'em out, Terra!

Terra: *(Looking away)* Uh huh.

Heather: Well, I'd better get over there. See you guys in school! *(Exits.)*

Terra: *(Waits until Heather is gone.)* Yellows are so fake.

Jeni: *(Stands up.)* Terra, I'm so sick of hearing about how much you hate Yellows. When you decide to lose this attitude, give me a call. I'm going to go find Heather. *(Exits.)*

Terra: *(Sits in silence for a few seconds.)* I hate Greens.

If you use this skit as a discussion starter, here are possible questions:

■ **What's your first impression of the characters in this skit? Explain.**

■ **Read Esther 3. How were the people in this skit like or unlike the people described in this passage?**

■ **What can you do this week to avoid falling into the trap of prejudice like Haman and Terra?**

ESTHER
3:13; 4:12-16

THEME:
Speaking out for God

SUMMARY:
Teenagers will study different faiths and then carry their Bibles visibly for one week in this AD-VENTURE.

PREPARATION: For each person, you'll need Bibles, a pencil, and paper.

Take your kids to a busy shopping center. Give kids each a pencil and a sheet of paper, then tell them to observe people in the mall, noting their jewelry and clothing—items that might reveal something about what they believe. Allow one hour for teenagers to accomplish this task.

Afterward, return to the church or a group member's home and discuss the following questions:

■ **What did you discover about people based on the symbols they wore?**

■ **How does what people outwardly wear reflect what they inwardly believe?**

■ **Is it easier to wear a "state-ment" than to say it aloud? Explain.**

As a group, read Esther 3:13; 4:12-16. Explain how Esther was faced with revealing who she really was (a Jew) to a pagan king who could easily kill her. Then form pairs and have partners discuss the following questions. Have volunteers then share their partners' insights with the whole group. Ask:

■ **What would motivate Esther to give up her life for her people?**

■ **Is it easier to wear a "world-ly" slogan than to reveal your identity in Jesus Christ? Explain.**

■ **How far would you be willing to go for your faith?**

■ **Where would be the most difficult place for you to share your faith? Explain.**

■ **In what areas of our society today do we need more people willing to risk all in order to save a few?**

Challenge teenagers to carry their Bibles visibly in the coming week *everywhere* they go. Encourage teenagers to write in a personal journal about their experiences—good and bad—as they boldly share their faith in God. At your next meeting, provide time for teenagers to tell about their experiments and the opportunities they had to talk about their faith. Close in prayer, inviting God's strength and courage.

JOB

"The Lord gave these things to me, and he has taken them away. Praise the name of the Lord."

Job 1:21b

JOB
1:1–2:10

THEME:
Trusting God in
hard times

SUMMARY:
In this DEVOTION, kids will
react to one another as victims
of various disasters or trials.

PREPARATION: Print the following "roles" on 3×5 cards:
• Farm and home were lost in a
flood.
• Home and all belongings were
destroyed in a fire.
• Family was killed in an auto
accident.
• Home was burglarized.
• Family member is dying of
cancer.
• Lost your job a week before
Christmas.
If possible, think of a different
role for each student; otherwise
simply repeat these six. You'll need
one role card for each person, tape,
and Bibles. A tape player and blues
music are optional.

EXPERIENCE

Form a circle. Walk around behind teenagers and tape a role card
on each person's back so that others may read the role. Say: **I'm giving you each a role to play for a
few minutes, although you don't
know what it is. I will tell you
that each of you has become the
victim of some sort of disaster or
bad circumstance. Take a few
minutes and mingle with one**
**another, treating others as if they
really were in those roles. But
don't give their roles away.**

Allow about five minutes for kids
to interact with one another. This is
a good time to play some blues
music. Then have teenagers sit
down and read their role cards.

RESPONSE

Form pairs and have partners
discuss the following questions:
■ **What was your first reac-
tion to your role?**
■ **What are some feelings that
you might have under these cir-
cumstances? Explain.**
■ **How might you feel toward
others? toward God?**
■ **How did others respond to
you? What did they say?**
■ **How did their words make
you feel?**
Have pairs read Job 1:1–2:10.
Then ask:
■ **Would you react more like
Job or Job's wife? Why?**
■ **Why is it difficult to trust
God in hard times?**
■ **What is one reason we can
trust God in the hardest times?**

CLOSING

Have partners share prayer
requests and commit to praying for
each other in the coming week.
Then close by singing "Trust and
Obey," which can be found in *Songs*,
compiled by Yohann Anderson.

JOB
6:1-13

THEME:
Discouragement

SUMMARY:
Teenagers will encourage one another and compare the effect to blowing up a balloon in this AFFIRMATION.

PREPARATION: You'll need enough party-sized balloons for everyone, felt-tip markers, and Bibles.

Form trios and have a volunteer in each trio read aloud Job 6:1-13. Have trios discuss these questions:
■ **How is Job feeling in this passage?**
■ **When was a time when you felt that way?**
■ **What helps you get through discouraging times?**
■ **How can you help others through their discouraging times?**
Give each person a balloon and give each trio a felt-tip marker. Instruct everyone to draw a happy face on his or her balloon.
Say: **You're going to blow up your balloons now, but don't blow them up all at once. I want you to go around your group and encourage one another by completing the sentence "I'm glad you're here today because..." After someone encourages you, put two puffs of air into your balloon. Go around your group a few times until everyone's balloon is full.**

Allow a few minutes for kids to encourage one another and blow up their balloons, then instruct them to tie off their balloons. Ask:
■ **How is discouragement like a deflated balloon?**
■ **How did encouragement change the balloon?**
■ **In what ways does encouragement change you?**
Have trios share ways that they'd like to encourage people during the coming week.

JOB
14:1-2

THEME:
The temporary nature of life

SUMMARY:
In this ADVENTURE, kids will be challenged to view life with a different perspective by visiting a cemetery.

PREPARATION: Try to locate a cemetery with above-ground headstones, if possible. You'll need pencils, paper, and Bibles.

Car pool to a local cemetery. Upon arriving, remind kids that a cemetery is a place for respectful, appropriate behavior.
Pass out pencils and paper, then say: **Take about 15 minutes to walk around the cemetery alone. Look at the headstones and markers and write down the shortest life span, the longest life span, and any inter-**

esting comments you see. No one is allowed to speak until we meet back here in 15 minutes.

Send kids out, making sure that they're by themselves. In 15 minutes, gather together and ask:

■ **What was the longest life span? the shortest?**

■ **What were some of the interesting comments on the headstones?**

■ **How did you feel when you found someone who had a long life span? a short life span?**

■ **How did you feel as you walked around the cemetery? Why?**

Form groups of no more than four. Have a volunteer from each group read aloud Job 14:1-2. Ask:

■ **After walking through the cemetery, what do you think this passage means? Explain.**

■ **If you knew the exact day that you would die, would you live your life differently? How?**

■ **What is one thing that you want to be remembered for and why?**

■ **What can you do to achieve that?**

JOB
19:25-27

THEME:
Longing for God

SUMMARY:
In this MUSIC IDEA, kids will compare contemporary love songs with Christian music that talks about loving God.

PREPARATION: Gather a wide variety of contemporary love songs. You may want to ask kids or leaders to bring in copies of their favorites the week before this activity. Collect a variety of Christian music—praise, worship, contemporary, or hymns. Again, ask kids or leaders to bring in some of their favorites ahead of time. You'll also need a tape player and Bibles.

Form a circle. Say: **I have some music here that I want you all to listen to. Regardless of your taste in music, listen for what the artists are saying through their words.**

Play about 30 to 45 seconds of a few mainstream love songs, then ask kids to describe the messages in the songs.

Say: **Now I'm going to play some different music. Again, I want you to listen for the messages in the songs. Your taste in music isn't important here, just what's being said.**

Play about 30 to 45 seconds of a few Christian songs, then ask kids what the artists are saying through their words.

Afterward, ask:

■ **What were some similar themes in the music?**

■ **How could you tell that some songs were Christian music and some weren't?**

Have a volunteer read aloud Job 19:25-27. Ask:

■ **Can a Christian's longing for God be compared to one person's love for another? Explain.**

■ **When is a time that you've longed for God?**

■ **How does music help us express that desire?**

Close by singing praise songs that express a longing for God. Turn out the lights so that kids can focus on God.

JOB
21:1-26

THEME:
Justice

SUMMARY:

In this ADVENTURE, kids will visit a courtroom to listen to the punishments given to people who break the law, then they'll decide whether those punishments are just.

PREPARATION: You'll need to arrange for your kids to visit a criminal court. You'll also need paper, pencils, and Bibles.

Take kids to watch a morning or afternoon session of a criminal court. Give teenagers paper and pencils, and ask them to write answers to these two questions after each punishment is handed down:

■ **Was the punishment fair? Why or why not?**

■ **What would have made the punishment fair?**

After the court session, gather your kids in a circle somewhere in the court building. For each case you witnessed, have kids vote on whether or not the punishment was fair. Ask a representative from those who vote yes and those who vote no to explain their feelings.

Then read aloud Job 21:1-26. Ask:

■ **Why do some people pay for bad deeds, while others don't?**

■ **In our society, are most people punished fairly for the wrong things they've done? Why or why not?**

■ **How does God respond to people who do wrong things?**

■ **Do you ever feel like Job did—that some people get away with the wrong things they do? Explain.**

To close, ask kids to think about a time they did something wrong but weren't punished for it. Ask them to pray about that situation, asking God for forgiveness.

JOB
21:7-21

THEME:
When evil people succeed

SUMMARY:

Teenagers will take part in a CREATIVE READING that deals with the fact that sometimes life isn't fair.

PREPARATION: Choose four readers and give each one a photocopy of the "Creative Reading for Job 21:7-21" handout (p. 199). Reader 1 should stand apart from the rest. Reader 2 needs to be a girl, and Reader 3 needs to be a guy.

Have your volunteers perform the reading at Sunday School or a midweek youth meeting. Afterward, close with the following questions:

(continued on p. 200)

CREATIVE READING FOR JOB 21:7-21

Reader 1: Why do the wicked live on?

Reader 2: *(Incredulously)* ...She cheats and gets an A. I study and get a C minus.

Reader 3: *(As if in conversation)* ...Steroids! So now he's starting this week while I sit the bench.

Reader 4: Look, I'll just call in sick, and we'll go to the lake. Like anyone will know.

Reader 1: Their homes are safe and free from fear. They sing to the music of tambourine and harp.

Reader 3: I worked out all summer while he partied. So how come I'm the one on second-string?

Reader 4: Let someone else pick up the slack at work. I need to work on my water skiing.

Reader 2: And she's got a different guy for every night of the week! *(Sighs.)* Maybe I should lower my standards a little?

Reader 1: They spend their years in prosperity.

Reader 4: Hey, another promotion! And a raise!

Reader 2: *(Looks to God.)* It's just not fair!

Reader 3: *(Looks to God.)* It's just not fair!

Reader 1: Yet they say to God, "Leave us alone! We have no desire to know your ways."

Reader 2: She used to be so close to you, God.

Reader 3: And then he makes jokes about me going to Bible study.

Reader 4: They need God like a crutch and act so self-righteous.

Reader 1: Let his own eyes see his destruction; let him drink of the wrath of the Almighty.

(Readers 2 and 3 walk offstage. Reader 4 suddenly looks up with a terrified look.)

Reader 1: When his allotted time comes to an end...

Reader 4: *(Yells.)* No! It's not fair! *(Covers head with hands and freezes.)*

■ How does it feel when the wicked succeed?

■ How can we deal with it when they do?

■ What are wrong ways to deal with the success of evil people?

JOB
32:6-10; 33:8-17

THEME:
Wisdom for the young

SUMMARY:
In this AFFIRMATION, kids will "spy" on peers so they can list those people's wise actions or words.

PREPARATION: Dress as a spy for this activity (a brimmed hat and a trench coat make for a good costume). You'll need a small note pad and a pencil for each person. Inside each note pad, write a group member's name. You'll also need Bibles.

Put note pads and pencils in the pockets of your spy costume. When kids arrive, sneak into the room as if you were a spy. Sneak around the room giving each person a note pad and pencil (make sure you don't give someone a note pad with his or her own name).

Then say: **Today's meeting is top secret. Don't open your note pad until I tell you to and don't say anything about what's written inside it. Your mission, should you decide to accept it, is to spy**

on the person whose name is written in your book. But I don't want you to uncover the usual, embarrassing stuff about that person. Here's a clue to what I'm expecting you to find out.

Read aloud Job 32:6-10 and 33:8-17. Then ask:

■ **Who can guess what information I'm expecting you to discover?**

After a few guesses, say: **Elihu didn't speak up because he didn't think he had any wisdom to offer Job. But the more he listened, the more he realized he did have something to offer.**

Your mission is to spy on your designated person for a month, listing everything you can find out about the wise decisions, actions, or words of your person. In one month, we'll meet to debrief your mission, and I'll ask you to stand and read the information you've collected.

OK, you may now look at the name of your assigned person. Let's synchronize our watches and plan to meet back in this room one month from now.

Sneak out of the room, get out of your costume, and continue your meeting.

During the next month, creatively remind kids each week about their secret mission through anonymous phone calls or unsigned letters. In one month, meet to debrief with your kids. Wear your costume again.

Have kids come up one by one to tell what they've discovered about their assigned people. Have them read aloud what they've written but not reveal the identity of their people until they've finished describing the wise deeds. After each person is revealed, have kids give that person a standing ovation.

JOB
38:1–40:5

THEME:
God's greatness

SUMMARY:

In this PROJECT, kids will create birds using various materials, then compare their creations to God's.

PREPARATION: You'll need feathers, newspapers, cardboard or poster board, masking tape, quick-drying glue, rubber bands, wire, scissors, staplers, and any other "building" materials you can gather. You'll also need an inexpensive cap with a feather in it (for a prize) and a Bible for each person.

Pile your supplies in the middle of the room and have kids sit in a circle around the pile. Place newspaper in front of each person. Then say: **Today your challenge is to create a bird that can fly. You can use any of the materials in front of you. You have 15 minutes. And the person whose bird flies the farthest wins a special prize. Ready? Go!**

After 15 minutes, put a masking tape line on your meeting-room floor and have your kids stand behind it. Then one at a time, have them launch their birds. Keep track of whose bird flies the farthest. Give that person a cap with a feather in it.

If possible, take kids outside to search for real birds. When you find them, ask kids to take two minutes to silently observe everything they can about the birds. Then return to your meeting room. (If you can't observe real birds, ask kids to close their eyes for two minutes and imagine a real bird. Challenge them to think of how the bird looks, what it sounds like, how it moves, and so on.)

Have kids sit in circles of no more than six per circle. Then have kids discuss the following questions in their circle groups. Ask:

∎ **How are the birds we created like real birds? How are they different?**

∎ **What would you need to create a real bird?**

∎ **What feelings did you have as you created your bird?**

∎ **What was it like to launch your bird into flight?**

∎ **How might God's feelings have been similar when he launched his first bird into flight?**

Have kids take turns going around their circles and reading aloud two verses from Job 38:1–40:5. Continue until they finish reading the Scripture passage. Then ask:

∎ **If you'd been Job, how would you have felt after God spoke these words to you?**

∎ **What was God's purpose in saying all of this to Job?**

■ **Think about the bird you created and the bird God created—what are the fundamental differences between you and God?**

Say: **When we understand the greatness of God, one natural response is to worship him. Let's do that now.**

Close by gathering everyone in one large circle and singing two or three worship songs to God.

JOB
38–41

THEME:
God's sovereignty

SUMMARY:
Kids will participate in a SKIT that helps them see the importance of understanding God's sovereignty.

COACH

SCENE: Sean questions the new basketball coach.

PROPS: Chairs for the team, paper (four to six sheets), and a clipboard for Coach.

CHARACTERS:
Coach Johnson (preferably a bigger guy)
Sean (cocky, somewhat whiny)
Team (four to six other guys or girls)

SCRIPT

Teammate 1: Hey, did you guys hear who's going to be our new coach? Mike Johnson!

Teammate 2: Mike Johnson! You mean THE Mike Johnson? Olympic gold medalist? NBA All-Star? MVP of the NBA?

Teammate 1: Yep, THE Mike Johnson. *(Looks offstage.)* Here he comes now!

Coach: *(Enters, carrying a clipboard.)* Hi, guys.

Team: Hey, Coach.

Coach: Why don't you all have a seat, and we'll get started.
(Team sits down.)

Coach: I'm Coach Johnson, and I'll be working with you this week, helping you prepare for the upcoming playoffs. Now I've seen your game films, and I think we can make some effective changes that will make you guys state champions.

Sean: *(Enters the room and speaks to a nearby teammate, loud enough for all to hear.)* What does this clown know about basketball? Why does he think he's so great?

Teammate 3: Shhh!

Coach: Let's start by going over your positions. McNeil, you're center, right? Grant, you're guard. Michaels, you're forward.

Sean: Aw, man, why's he putting me at guard? I like to play forward. I'm better at forward. This is gonna stink!

Teammate 4: Shhh!

Coach: *(Hands out sheets of paper.)* These are some plays we're going to be working on this week. We'll go over them on paper, then learn them on the court.

Sean: *(Looking at paper)* These are horrible! They'll never work! Other teams will be walking all over us in the playoffs, I'm sure!

Who invited this joker to our practice?

Teammates 3 and 4: Shhh!

Coach: I've also arranged for you to play Westview first, instead of Lakeside. That way we can work on our strategies more thoroughly.

Sean: Westview? Westview took state last year! We can't beat them! This guy's gonna cost us the championship!

Team: SHHH!

Sean: I've had enough of this! I'm not going to be on a losing team, led by some guy who knows nothing about basketball! I'm outta here! *(Exits.)*

Coach: What's wrong with him?

Teammate 1: Oh, he just doesn't know who he's playing ball with.

If you use this skit as a discussion starter, here are possible questions:

■ **What was Sean's problem in this skit?**

■ **How might his response be different if he knew who the coach was?**

Read Job 38–40. Ask:

■ **What does this passage say about God's sovereignty?**

■ **Why was it important for Job to know "who he was playing ball with"?**

■ **When do we need to remember God's sovereignty?**

JOB 42:1-6

THEME:

Knowing God intimately

SUMMARY:
In this DEVOTION, participants will go to an ice-cream shop to learn the difference between knowledge and experience.

PREPARATION: You'll need to locate an ice-cream shop that your group will visit during this activity. You'll also need paper, pencils, money for ice-cream, Bibles, and an instant-print camera with film.

EXPERIENCE

Take your kids to a nearby ice-cream shop (one with plenty of flavors to choose from). Have each person pick out his or her favorite ice-cream flavor, and then use the instant-print camera to take a picture of it. (If you can't round up an instant-print camera, have kids simply make mental pictures of their favorite flavors.) Then gather your kids in a circle outside the ice-cream shop. Give them each paper and a pencil and ask them to take one minute to write descriptions of their favorite ice-cream flavors as they look at their pictures.

Next take kids back into the ice-cream shop to order cones or cups of their favorite flavors. Gather back together and have kids write new descriptions of their favorite flavors as they eat.

RESPONSE

Form partners by having teenagers who chose different kinds of ice-cream pair up. Then have partners discuss the following questions:

■ **How are the two descriptions you wrote different?**

■ **How did tasting your favorite flavor help you describe it better?**

■ **How would your opinion of your favorite ice-cream flavor be different if you couldn't taste it?**

Have a volunteer read aloud Job 42:1-6, then ask:

■ **How is our ice-cream experiment similar to Job's experience in learning to know God?**

■ **What's the difference between knowledge about God and knowing God?**

■ **What must we do to really know God?**

CLOSING

Have kids each turn over their pictures and write three things they can do in the next month to "taste" God. (If you didn't use real pictures, just have kids write on blank paper.) Then have each person tell about one idea he or she listed. Commit to checking back with kids about their ideas in one month.

JOB
42:7-13

THEME:
Forgiveness

SUMMARY:
In this CREATIVE PRAYER, kids will bury rocks that have sins written on them.

PREPARATION: You'll need fist-sized rocks, markers, and Bibles. You'll also need to find a place where you can dig a small hole on or near your church grounds (if you can't do this at your church, go to a leader's home or to a wooded area).

Ask kids to close their eyes and think of at least one person who's hurt them. Prod them to remember not only what the person did, but how it was done. Then give kids each a fist-sized rock and a marker. Have them write on their rocks words that describe what the people who sinned against them did; for example, "betrayed," "lied," or "stole." Tell kids not to reveal the people's names, though.

Then have kids each choose a partner and discuss the following questions:

■ **When you look at the words on your rock, how do you feel?**

■ **Is it easy or difficult for you to get over the hurt this person caused you? Explain.**

■ **How is this rock like the feelings you have about the person who sinned against you? How is it different?**

Take teenagers to your digging site and have them line up single file. One by one, have them each come forward and help dig a hole by removing one shovelful of dirt. When everyone has had a chance to dig, form a circle and gather around the hole.

Say: **It's time to forgive the person your rock represents. As we stand here in silence, take whatever time you need to talk to God about your feelings toward this person. Then ask God to give you the strength to forgive. When you're ready, come forward to the hole and throw your rock in it.**

When kids finish, have them line up single file and one by one put back a shovelful of dirt into the hole, burying the rocks.

Then read aloud Job 42:7-13. Say: **God honored Job's forgiveness of his friends, and he honors your forgiveness today. If it's appropriate in your situation, I challenge you to tell the person your rock represents about your decision to forgive him or her.**

PSALMS

"The Lord is my Shepherd..."

Psalms 23:1a

PSALM 3

THEME:
God helps us in times of need.

SUMMARY:
In this LEARNING GAME, kids will experience what it feels like to be helped in the midst of a struggle.

PREPARATION: Bring confetti, squirt guns, noisemakers, and an umbrella or rain slicker to the meeting. You'll also need Bibles.

Have kids stand in two lines facing each other. Arm them with confetti, squirt guns, and noisemakers. Have the first person in line walk down the middle of the "gauntlet," while all the other kids throw confetti, squirt their squirt guns, and use their noisemakers. Say: **If you want help when you're walking down the gauntlet, all you have to do is yell "Help!" and someone will help you.**

When the person yells "help," rescue him or her by using an umbrella or rain slicker as a shield. Have kids each take a turn walking through the gauntlet.

Read aloud Psalm 3, then ask:

■ **What went through your mind as you were walking through the gauntlet?**

■ **What did you notice about yourself when you were a part of the gauntlet?**

■ **What was it like for you to be able to call for help and be** shielded from the attack?

■ **How does God help us through life's trials?**

■ **When and where can you call for God's help and protection?**

PSALM 8

THEME:
Praising God

SUMMARY:
In this CREATIVE READING/CREATIVE PRAYER, kids will use Scripture to create a prayer of praise to God.

PREPARATION: You'll need two sheets of newsprint, tape, a marker, and Bibles.

Help kids make Psalm 8 their own prayer of praise. Tape two sheets of newsprint to a wall. Ask kids for other words that mean "wonderful." Write these words on one sheet of newsprint. Then ask kids to name things God has made. Write these words on the other sheet of newsprint.

Next read Psalm 8 aloud in the New Century Version. Pause after you read the word "wonderful" in verse 1. Have kids shout out the words on the first sheet of newsprint during the pause. Then resume reading. Pause again after you read, "I see the moon and stars..." in verse 3. Have kids shout out the words on the other sheet of newsprint. Then resume reading once more.

When you read the last verse, pause after the word "wonderful" and have kids shout out the words on the first newsprint again.

Close by having everyone shout together "amen!"

PSALM
8:3-9

THEME:

People are God's crowning creation.

SUMMARY:
Kids will perform a CREATIVE READING of Psalm 8:3-9.

PREPARATION: Make four photocopies of the "Creative Reading for Psalm 8:3-9" handout on page 209.

Select four volunteers to be the readers, then have them stand in a line in front of the group to perform this creative reading based on Psalm 8:3-9.

PSALM
13

THEME:

Expressing ourselves to God

SUMMARY:
In this PROJECT, kids will create an "expressing booth" to express themselves to God.

PREPARATION: Collect materials to build the expressing booth: a large appliance box or donated wood from a local lumber yard, an an old phone (if you can find one), spray paint, and colored markers. Kids will need to bring in personal items—such as posters, stickers, artwork, and crafts—to decorate the booth. You'll also need Bibles.

Lead your group in building an "expressing booth." Use a large appliance box or donated wood from a local lumber yard to build a booth that resembles a phone booth. Have kids decorate it any way they like—let them personalize it with posters, stickers, artwork, and crafts, or use spray paint and colored markers to create positive graffiti. If you can, find an old phone to put in the booth to make it look functional.

After you finish building the expressing booth, have kids each take a turn inside the booth expressing something positive about the group (if you have a phone in there, have them say their affirmations into the phone). For example, kids might say, "I like the way we all care about each other," or "I always have a great time when I come to youth group." Make sure the rest of the group gathers around the booth to hear the positive comments.

After everyone has had a turn in the expressing booth, have kids pair up and read Psalm 13. Ask:

■ **When we want to talk to God, how do we do it?**

■ **Do you ever cry about something to God? Why or why not?**

(continued on p. 210)

CREATIVE READING FOR PSALM 8:3-9

Reader 1: I look at your heavens, which you made with your fingers. I see the moon and stars, which you created. But why are people important to you? Why do you take care of human beings?

Reader 2: I love summer! I love the sun, the sand, the waves, the babes!

Reader 3: Rock climbing is killer. I love the feeling of just me and the rocks—the feeling of "do or die."

Reader 2: Snow does it for me—and lots of it. If I could ski every day, I would.

Reader 4: But none of those things are as awesome as what God created last...you and me. God thinks we're cool. He loves us even when we ignore or hate him.

Reader 1: You made them a little lower than the angels and crowned them with glory and honor. You put them in charge of everything you made. You put all things under their control: all the sheep, the cattle, and the wild animals, the birds in the sky, the fish in the sea, and everything that lives under water.

Reader 2: The God of the universe, who created everything there is, has time to care about *me?*

Reader 3: Doesn't he have better things to do?

Reader 4: God put me in charge of the things he created?

Reader 2: Did God know what he was doing? Wasn't God taking a big risk?

Reader 3: How am I doing with that responsibility?

Reader 4: How do I treat the earth?

Reader 2: How do I treat my school?

Reader 3: How do I treat my parents?

Reader 4: How do I treat my body?

Reader 1: Lord our Lord, your name is the most wonderful name in all the earth!

All: Thank you, God, for trusting us with what you made.

All: Thank you, God, for caring about us so much.

All: Thank you, God, for loving us enough to send your Son to die for us.

■ **What kind of mood are you usually in when you talk to God? Explain.**

■ **What kinds of things do you have a difficult time talking to God about?**

■ **Why does God want us to express ourselves to him?**

Say: **Because this is an expressing booth, you can feel free to express anything you want to God—whatever is in your heart.**

Have kids gather in a circle around the booth. One at a time, have them enter the booth and express something to God (aloud or silently).

Then close by reading aloud Psalm 13:5-6. Say: **We can say whatever we want to God, whenever we want, because God already knows our thoughts and concerns.**

PSALM 16:5-6

THEME:

God is all we need.

SUMMARY:

Kids will play a LEARNING GAME that challenges them to quickly finish sentences that begin with "All you need..."

PREPARATION: Bring a soft object to throw, such as a Nerf ball or a wadded-up pair of (clean) socks. You'll also need Bibles.

Have kids stand or sit in a circle. Say: **Let's play a game called All You Need. I'll begin a statement and throw the ball to someone in the circle. Whoever catches the ball must finish the statement.**

For example, if I say, "All you need to make spaghetti is..." and I throw the ball to you, you might say, "boiling water," and then throw the ball to someone else who might say, "meatballs," and then throw the ball to someone else, and so on. I'll interrupt you with different statements, so don't be concerned if you don't get to answer every statement. Make sure everyone is included in the ball throwing.

Include these statements:

• **All you need for a good party is...**

• **All you need to fix a flat tire is...**

• **All you need for a great concert is...**

• **All you need for a perfect weekend is...**

• **All you need to be popular is...**

• **All you need to make friends is...**

• **All you need for peace is...**

• **All you need to get to heaven is...**

When the game is finished, read aloud Psalm 16:5-6. Then ask:

■ **What was easy about this game? What was difficult?**

■ **What was easy about thinking of the ingredients for the last statements (popularity, making friends, peace, heav-**

en)? What was difficult?

■ **What kinds of things last forever? only a short time?**

■ **Why is God all we need?**

Close in prayer by passing the ball, with each person completing the following prayer: "Lord, you're all I need for..."

PSALM 19:1-4

THEME:
God reveals himself through creation.

SUMMARY:
In this daylong ADVENTURE, kids will study creation in many different ways to learn how God reveals his character through his creation.

PREPARATION: Rent a contemporary movie on video. (Get permission to show the video from the video producer since it will be a public showing.) You'll also need a television, videocassette recorder, and Bibles. Borrow artwork, crafts or jewelry from people you know.

Plan a day adventure for your kids that includes some or all of these ideas:

• Watch a scene from a movie *without* the sound turned up. Challenge kids to follow the story just by what they see. Specifically, have them get a feel for the characters by watching their facial expressions and body language. Have them write down what happened in the scene. Then go back and watch the scene with sound to see who got it right.

• Take a walk through your church grounds or neighborhood and point out things you see, such as a rock, flower, book, key, puppy, cotton ball, spider, piece of candy, or newspaper. Ask kids to tell how each object might symbolize something about themselves. For example, a rock might symbolize strength, or a puppy might symbolize warmth or unconditional love.

• Go somewhere to study creations other people have made (art in a gallery; art books at a local library; artwork, crafts, or jewelry from people you know; or graffiti in a telephone booth). Ask kids to find a partner, choose one piece of art (craft, jewelry, or graffiti), and brainstorm a list of characteristics about the creator that are revealed by the creation. For example, with a lavish piece of jewelry, kids might list "likes doing things in a big way."

• Create sand sculptures at a local park's sandbox. Then ask kids to decide what each sculpture reveals about its creator.

Afterward, gather everyone together. Read aloud Psalm 19:1-4, then ask:

■ **How is God revealed through creation?**

■ **What can other cultures learn about God from his creation?**

■ **What "stories" are the heavens telling?**

■ **We are God's creation. How does God reveal himself through us?**

PSALM
20

THEME:
Expressing our
feelings to God

SUMMARY:
In this CREATIVE PRAYER, kids
will use body language to help
express their feelings to God.

PREPARATION: You'll need Bibles.

Sometimes kids have trouble
seeing prayer as a way of expressing themselves. Here's an
activity that puts a twist in their
prayers and enhances their sense
of expression.

Ask kids to space themselves at
least an arm's length from one
another. Say: **Our prayers express
our feelings to God. Some
prayers ask for God's help, forgiveness, or wisdom in dealing
with a situation. Think about a
prayer you want to say to God
and use body language to express your prayer. For example,
if you want to tell God you're
afraid, you may curl up in a ball.
Or if you want to praise God, you
may lift your hands.**

Encourage kids to move beyond
just bowing heads or kneeling.
Read aloud Psalm 20, then say:
Amen. Have kids form a circle.
Ask:

■ **What were you trying to
express through body language
in your prayer?**

■ **How did your body language affect the way you felt**
during the prayer?

■ **Why is it important to
express ourselves in new ways
to God?**

PSALM
23

THEME:
God is our good
shepherd.

SUMMARY:
In this OVERNIGHTER, kids will
explore Psalm 23 through a
series of activities that evoke the
feelings expressed in each
verse.

PREPARATION: You'll need pizza
ingredients (which kids will find on
a scavenger hunt), bandannas or
something for blindfolds, paper,
pencils, tape, and Bibles.

Invite kids to an overnighter that
features activities tied to Psalm
23:

• **Verse 1**—To explore the idea
that God has everything we need,
say: **We're going to make pizza
tonight, but I didn't bring all of
the ingredients. What do we
need to make pizza?** Have the
kids list the ingredients.

You'll probably want to make
sure the following are included in
kids' list of ingredients: ready-
made pizza dough (such as Boboli
or Pillsbury pizza dough), pizza
sauce from a can or jar (you can
also use spaghetti sauce), plenty of

mozzarella cheese, and pizza toppings, such as pepperoni or sausage.

Next, say: **Your job is to go out and find these ingredients, scavenger-hunt fashion, so that we'll have something to eat tonight. Get into groups of two or three people. You have 20 minutes to find your ingredients.** Divide the ingredients by listing them on pieces of paper and give each group a list.

When everyone returns, read aloud Psalm 23:1 and ask:

■ **What was hard about this scavenger hunt? What was easy?**

■ **How did you feel when you were on the scavenger hunt?**

■ **How was the scavenger hunt like Psalm 23:1? How was it unlike the Psalm?**

Have kids prepare the pizzas then eat them.

• **Verses 2-5**—Have kids pair up. Say: **Stand in front of your partner and pretend that you're looking into a mirror. Make a series of facial expressions that match your partner's expressions and actions.** Have kids do this for two minutes. Next, have volunteers pass out blindfolds.

Say: **Now get into trios. One of you must put on a blindfold, one will be the "mirror" partner, and one will be the "eyes" for the blindfolded partner. The eyes will tell the blindfolded partner what movements to do to match the mirror partner.**

Have kids do this for two minutes and then switch, so everyone gets a chance to be the blindfolded person and the eyes.

Have the kids remove their blindfolds and sit in a circle. Read aloud Psalm 23:2-5 and ask:

■ **When you first started this activity—with just two people and no blindfold—what was hard about it? What was easy?**

■ **How did the activity change when the blindfold and the guide were added?**

■ **What would the activity have been like had there not been a guide?**

■ **How was this activity like how God guides us? How was it unlike how God guides us?**

• **Verse 6**—Have kids tape one sheet of paper onto their backs. Have kids go around to each person and write on the paper one reason they think that person is a blessing. When kids are finished, have them sit in a circle. Read aloud Psalm 23:6. Have kids each read a few items listed on their papers. Then have them close in prayer, thanking God for his blessings and for helping them to be a blessing to others.

PSALM
29

THEME:
God's powerful voice

SUMMARY:
In this ADVENTURE, kids will record sounds of "powerful" things and compare them to God's powerful voice.

PREPARATION: Bring several tape recorders with built-in or plug-in microphones (or have kids bring their own). Make sure the recorders have batteries. You'll also need blank cassettes (one for each group of three) and Bibles.

Form groups of three and give each group a tape recorder and a blank tape. Tell groups to go out into the surrounding neighborhood to record as many powerful sounds as they can—for example, a jackhammer, a loud engine, or a barking dog. Ask kids to also *look* for evidences of God's power while they're out. Have them return to your meeting place in 30 minutes.

When everyone returns, ask kids to play back their sounds. Challenge the group to guess what the sounds are and why they're powerful. Then read aloud Psalm 29. Ask groups to discuss the following questions:

■ **What do you think the "voice of the Lord" sounds like?**

■ **How would God's voice compare to the sounds you recorded?**

■ **Why does God's voice have the power that it does?**

■ **How or what can God's voice create? destroy?**

PSALM 30:5

THEME:
Joy

SUMMARY:
In this OBJECT LESSON, kids will enjoy breakfast and discuss how their perspective has changed overnight.

PREPARATION: You'll need yellow and orange construction paper, felt-tip pens, scissors, and Bibles. You'll also need ingredients for a light breakfast (to be held the morning after a youth meeting).

Before the youth meeting, use yellow and orange construction paper to cut out a moon (yellow paper) and a sun (orange paper) for each group member. Write the words to Psalm 30:5 on each moon. Pass out the paper moons during the meeting, then read aloud Psalm 30:5.

Say: **Write on your moon one problem you're struggling with. Spend five minutes praying about that problem. Then take the moon home with you and put it under your pillow. Bring it back here tomorrow morning for a special "joy" during the morning breakfast.**

The following morning, prepare a light breakfast for kids. Be sure to include plenty of orange juice (tell kids the juice represents sunshine) and sing joyful songs. Pass out a paper sun to each participant. Say: **Read the problem you** wrote about on your moon. On your sun, write how your perspective on that problem has changed overnight.

Reread Psalm 30:5. Talk about God's ability to make everything new in our lives and what joy that newness brings.

PSALM 32:7-9

THEME:
God's guidance

SUMMARY:
In this ADVENTURE, kids get clues to a secret location they must find, and along the way, they learn the importance of God's guidance.

PREPARATION: Pick a location for your adventure and tell everyone to bring a few dollars for a fast-food snack. You'll need Bibles.

Decide on a location for your adventure, then make clues to fit that location. For example:

• It's within three miles of the church.

• The manager's name is Maurice.

• There's an E in the name.

• There are 15 parking spaces

• They have more salt in their shakes than on their fries.

Form teams of three or four. (Make sure each team has transportation if your chosen location is too far to walk.)

Say: **On this adventure you'll need to find a location in town such as a fast-food restaurant, an ice-cream parlor, or a doughnut shop. I'll give you five to 10 clues** (similar to the ones listed below) **to help you find it.**

You'll need a 15-minute head start, so you can go to the destination and wait. Have teams then compete to see which one can figure out where the destination is and get there fastest (without speeding while driving).

Once everyone arrives at the location, have kids enjoy a snack. Then read aloud Psalm 32:7-9. Wrap up the adventure by asking:

■ **How was this adventure like how God leads and guides us? How was it unlike how God leads us?**

■ **How would you describe God's directions for your life?**

■ **Why do we need God's direction in our lives?**

■ **How could this adventure have been easier? more difficult?**

■ **What would make God's direction easier to follow?**

PSALM 33:1-3

THEME:
Music

SUMMARY:
In this OBJECT LESSON, kids will organize rocks into sculptures to explore views about various kinds of music.

PREPARATION: You'll need a supply of small rocks or pebbles (preferably with smooth surfaces), several bottles of all-purpose glue, acrylic paints, paintbrushes, 3×5 pieces of cardboard, and Bibles.

Set the supplies on a table and ask kids to sit around the table. Read aloud Psalm 33:1-3. Say: **Music means something different to each person. But what does it mean to God? Use the materials on this table to create rock sculptures that represent what you think your favorite kind of music means to God.**

For example, if you like rock and you think God's excited about rock music, you could make a big exclamation point out of rocks. Or, if you think God disapproves of the music you like, you could spell "no" with your rocks. Use a cardboard base as a foundation for your sculpture.

While the sculptures are drying, ask group members to guess what other kids' sculptures represent. Then have the sculptors explain what their sculptures mean and why they think God feels a certain way about their favorite music.

PSALM 33:6-9

THEME:
God's power

SUMMARY:
In this OBJECT LESSON, kids will discover how different objects get their "power" and discuss how God's power is different.

PREPARATION: You'll need several old broken appliances (check a thrift store or ask church members for donations) and enough tools for kids to work on the broken appliances. Also, bring a working blender, ice cream, milk, and chocolate syrup. Don't forget Bibles.

Have kids try to "fix" the appliances by taking them apart and putting them back together. Ask teenagers to brainstorm about modern conveniences that we take for granted, such as electricity, running water, plumbing, or grocery stores. Have them discuss what life would be like without these things. Then ask:

■ **What's necessary to make these appliances work?**

■ **How would our lives be different without electricity or other power sources?**

■ **Could we survive without these power sources? Why or why not?**

Have someone read aloud Psalm 33:6-9, then ask:

■ **What kind of power does God have?**

■ **Is God's power necessary**

for the earth to "run"? for us to "run"?

■ **What would happen if God's power weren't available for us to use?**

■ **How would that change our lives?**

■ **How can God's power influence our daily lives?**

In closing, pull out a working blender and have kids make milkshakes. Then have them each thank God for his power and how it gives us life.

PSALM
37:2-7

THEME:
Faith

SUMMARY:
In this mini-ADVENTURE, kids will find things that require faith to "work" and compare what they learn to their faith in God.

PREPARATION: Bring Bibles.

Have kids find a partner. Then have pairs find one thing in the surrounding area (in the church or on church grounds) that requires faith for it to work—for example, running water, a balloon, a dry sponge, a glass, or an unopened soft drink can. Give pairs 10 minutes to find their "faith items" and return to the meeting area.

When pairs return, have them each tell about their items. But first they must ask the rest of the group, "Do you have faith that...?" (They

should personalize the question to their specific items.) Then have them show the group what they found.

Say: **Faith is built into our everyday life.** Have someone read aloud Psalm 37:2-7, then ask:

■ **What are other things we have faith in?**

■ **How is our faith in those things, and in the things you found, like our faith in God? How are they unlike our faith?**

■ **How can we have faith that God will keep his promises?**

■ **Describe a time when your faith in God has helped you.**

■ **How can having faith in God change our lives?**

PSALM
40:6-10

THEME:
Proclaiming God's love

SUMMARY:
In this PROJECT, kids share God's love with others by passing out Life Savers and "love notes" from God.

PREPARATION: You'll need Life Savers, blank index cards (enough to give each person four cards), a hole puncher, pens, items for decorating the note cards (such as colored markers, stickers, and glitter), yarn, and Bibles.

Have someone read Psalm 40:6-10 to the group. Ask:

■ When is the last time you told someone about God's love?

■ Why do others need to know that God loves them?

Say: **In response to this passage, today we're going to write "love notes" from God to give to others.**

Give each teenager four index cards. Have teenagers fold the cards in half, lengthwise, to make note cards. On the outside of the card, have kids write, "I want to be your Life Saver!" On the inside, have them write a Bible verse that expresses God's love and forgiveness, such as Numbers 14:18a; John 3:16; John 11:25; or Romans 5:8. Have kids decorate their note cards using markers, stickers, and glitter. Then have kids punch a hole in the corner of each note card, put a piece of yarn through the hole, and tie the yarn to a Life Saver.

Car pool to a nearby children's hospital, orphanage, homeless shelter, or nursing home, and have teenagers distribute their note cards. (Some institutions may prefer that you call ahead to make any necessary arrangements.)

After the Life Savers are distributed, gather everyone in a group and ask:

■ **How did it feel to share Christ with others?**

■ **In what ways might people react to the message that God loves them?**

Say: **God wants us to do more than attend church. God wants us to tell others about his love, righteousness, and forgiveness. Think about how you can share Christ with someone else this week.**

PSALM 42:1-2

THEME:
Desiring God

SUMMARY:
In this DEVOTION, teenagers will compare their desire for God to a deer panting for water.

PREPARATION: You'll need 15 saltine crackers and a cup of water for each person. You'll also need Bibles.

EXPERIENCE

Have kids sit in a circle on the floor. Give saltine crackers to each teenager. Say: **We're going to conduct a little experiment today to find out how many crackers it will take to make you thirsty. When I say "go," eat all your crackers quickly. Ready? Go!**

After kids have eaten their crackers, say: **Raise your hand if you'd like a cup of water right now.** (But don't give anyone water yet.) Have group members who don't raise their hands eat five more crackers, then ask them the same question again. (Again, don't give anyone water.) Repeat the process one more time, giving five more crackers to those who aren't thirsty. (Still don't give anyone water.)

RESPONSE

Form trios, then ask:

■ **How is your desire for water different now, compared to before eating the crackers?**

■ **What would you do to get a drink right now?**

■ **How long would you want to go without drinking anything?**

Have someone read Psalm 42:1-2. Ask:

■ **You can tell when a deer is thirsty because it pants. How can you tell when you're thirsty for God?**

■ **In your groups, share a time when you were thirsty for God.**

■ **How does God quench our thirst for him?**

CLOSING

Give everyone a cup of water but instruct them not to drink it yet. Have trios share praises to God in the form of a toast and then drink together. Dismiss by singing "As the Deer," which can be found in *The Group Songbook* (Group Publishing).

PSALM 46:1-3

THEME:
Trusting God in times of trouble

SUMMARY:
In this OBJECT LESSON, kids will observe a candle in a water balloon to see how God surrounds them.

PREPARATION: Buy water balloons and small birthday candles. Pick a location by a water hose or a faucet to do this lesson. You'll also need Bibles.

orm groups of no more than three. Give each group a water balloon and a birthday candle. Have teenagers put the candles inside the balloons (carefully, so as not to puncture them), then fill the balloons with water. Tell group members to leave a little air inside the balloons when tying them.

Say: **Let's pretend our balloons are each individual "worlds," and our candles are people living in the worlds. Let's create "earthquakes" and see how our candles respond.**

Have trios sit in circles on the floor and carefully roll their balloons back and forth. Tell kids to observe what their candles do as the balloons are rolling. After a minute or two, have trios stop rolling the balloons to discuss these questions.

■ **What did you notice about your candle as it rolled inside the balloon?**

■ **What was the function of the water inside the balloon?**

Have a volunteer read Psalm 46:1-3. Ask:

■ **How is this passage like the candle in the balloon?**

■ **How is God like the water in the balloon?**

■ **When do you feel like your world is being shaken?**

■ **How can Psalm 46:1-3 encourage you when it seems like your world is being shaken?**

Say: **Though we feel like the water being shaken in the balloon, we can easily be the floating candle if we put our trust in God. God is like the water, softening the "earthquakes" of our lives and surrounding us with love.**

PSALM
49:1-11, 15-20

THEME:
Relying on God, not money, for security

SUMMARY:
In this LEARNING GAME, teenagers discover that God is the only one who can provide security.

PREPARATION: Cut circular or square tokens (about 2 inches in diameter) out of construction paper. You'll need four tokens and a small rock for each person. Put several fans in front of a table and gather enough Bibles for half the group.

Give each teenager four tokens and a rock and have everyone form pairs.

Say: **These tokens represent money. The object of this game is to collect the most money. Hide your tokens in one hand and place your rock in the other. Then take turns trying to pick which hand your partner's hiding his or her tokens in. If you guess correctly, you can take your partner's tokens. After you both have a turn, find new partners and repeat the process. Ready? Go.**

Have teenagers play for two or three minutes. Then stop the action and tell group members to sit down and count their money. After teenagers have tallied their tokens, ask the top five token-holders to come up front. Ask:

■ **What did you think your chances were of winning the game?**

■ **How does it feel to have so much money?**

Have these same five kids place their money and their rocks on a table in front of the fans. Turn the fans on so that their tokens blow away.

Have one of the "winners" read Psalm 49:1-11,15-20. Ask everyone:

■ **What does this passage say about our priorities?**

■ **Were your priorities in this game similar to those in real life? How?**

■ **How might Psalm 49:1-11, 15-20 encourage you to live your life differently?**

■ **What comfort can you draw from realizing that money doesn't last?**

Close saying: **God, the rock, will always be there for you and will not be tossed by a passing wind. God is always there for you no matter how much money you have or make, no matter what you win or lose. As Psalm 49:15 says, "But God will save my life and will take me from the grave."**

PSALM
50:4-23

THEME:
God is the ultimate judge.

SUMMARY:
In this ADVENTURE, kids observe a courtroom to get an idea of how we'll be judged by God for our actions.

PREPARATION: Call the local courthouse to set up a day and time to visit a courtroom. Plan to be there long enough to observe a few different cases. Recruit drivers to car pool to and from the courthouse. You'll need paper, pencils, and Bibles.

M eet at church. Make sure each person has paper and a pencil to take notes, then drive to the courthouse. Observe the courtroom and the cases taking place that day. Tell the kids to pay close attention to the judge and the way he or she acts.

Return to church to discuss your observations. Have teenagers read Psalm 50:4-23 quietly to themselves. Then wrap up the adventure by asking:

■ **What did you observe about the judge in the courtroom?**

■ **In what ways is God similar to the judge we saw? In what ways is God different?**

■ **Why do judges require respect?**

■ **What is God's attitude toward the wicked in Psalm 50:16-22?**

■ **Although God is the ultimate judge, how does that show us his love?**

PSALM
51

THEME:
Forgiveness

SUMMARY:
In this PROJECT, teenagers will have the chance to ask God's forgiveness and "see" their sin disappear.

PREPARATION: You'll need Bibles, paper, and one disappearing-ink pen (or disappearing ink and a toothpick to use as a pen) for each group of four. (Check your local novelty or toy store for disappearing ink.)

F orm groups of no more than four. Say: **After David sinned by committing adultery with Bathsheba, the prophet Nathan came to talk to David. He told David that, because of his sin, one of David's children would die. David wrote Psalm 51, pleading that God would spare the life of his child.**

Have a member of each group read aloud Psalm 51 to his or her group, then ask:

■ **How did David respond to his sin?**

■ **When you do something wrong, do you respond the same way David did? Why or why not?**

Give each group paper and a disappearing-ink pen (or disappearing ink and a toothpick to use as a pen). Say: **On your paper write one thing you'd like to ask**

God's forgiveness for. Then fold the paper immediately and pray silently for God to forgive and cleanse you.

Reread Psalm 51:6-9. Ask:

■ **How can David be so confident God will forgive him?**

■ **How can you be sure God will forgive you?**

■ **How does that make you feel?**

Have kids unfold their papers (the ink should have disappeared by now). Say: **Keep this blank piece of paper as a reminder of God's forgiveness and also as a reminder to confess your sins.**

PSALM 51:1-15

THEME:
God's forgiveness and renewal

SUMMARY:
In this CREATIVE READING, kids will read a modern version of Psalm 51:1-15 to help them understand how God can forgive, cleanse, and renew them.

PREPARATION: Make a photocopy of the "Creative Reading for Psalm 51:1-15" handout (p. 223) for each person. Choose three people to read the numbered sections (with the tone of voice indicated), then lead the group in the reading. Afterward, sing the praise song "Create in Me a Clean Heart," which can be found in *The Group Songbook* (Group Publishing).

PSALM 56:10-11

THEME:
Trust

SUMMARY:
In this LEARNING GAME, kids will experience what it means to trust someone.

PREPARATION: You'll need Bibles, a blindfold and a wet sponge for every two people, and an open area.

Play this game on a hot summer day when everyone is wearing casual clothes. Gather everyone in an open area, such as a gymnasium or outside on the grass. Warn everyone that they'll be getting wet during this game.

Form pairs. Blindfold one person in each pair and give him or her a wet sponge. Tell the sighted partners they'll act as guides. On "go," have the blindfolded kids throw sponges at other group members by following their sighted partners' verbal commands, such as "Right! Left! Duck! Run! Throw the sponge!" The sighted kids can't touch their blindfolded partners.

After sponges are thrown, have sighted kids verbally guide their blindfolded partners to any sponge on the ground and continue the action. If either partner gets hit by a sponge, both partners are out. The object is to be the last pair left. Every two or three minutes, have partners switch roles and play again.

(continued on p. 224)

CREATIVE READING FOR PSALM 51:1-15

Whole Group: O loving and kind God, forgive me. Have pity on me and take away the traces of my actions. Wash me, cleanse me from this guilt. Let me be clean again. For I admit my awful actions...

Speaker 1: *(Almost whispering)* Lying to my teacher...

Speaker 2: *(Almost whispering)* Yelling at my mom...

Speaker 3: *(Almost whispering)* Putting down my brother and sister...

Speaker 1: *(Almost whispering)* Cheating on my test at school...

Speaker 2: *(Almost whispering)* Thinking of myself first...

Speaker 3: *(Almost whispering)* Having a bad attitude...

Whole Group: I thought what I did wouldn't hurt anyone. But it did. It hurt you. You saw it all even though I thought no one was looking, even though I thought no one noticed. You were watching the whole time. You are rightly disappointed in me.

Speaker 1: *(Reflective but firm, as if remembering)* You, God, deserve honesty from the heart.

Speaker 2: *(Reflective but firm)* Sincerity.

Speaker 3: *(Reflective but firm)* Truthfulness.

All Speakers: Give me the wisdom to do these things! Cleanse me again. And after you've dealt with me, help me to be joyful again. Don't keep looking at my sins. Erase them from your sight.

Speaker 1: *(Excitedly)* Create in me a new, clean heart, O God!

Speaker 2: *(Excitedly)* Filled with clean thoughts and right desires!

Speaker 3: *(Excitedly)* And the will to do what is right in your eyes!

Whole Group: Don't keep me from your presence. Don't take your Holy Spirit from me. Restore to me again the joy of your salvation and make me willing to choose to obey you.

Speaker 1: *(Confidently)* Then I will teach others about you...

Speaker 2: *(Getting an idea)* Like my friend at school...

Speaker 3: *(Getting an idea)* Or the person next door...

Speaker 1: And they...

Speaker 2: Like me...

Speaker 3: Will confess and return to you.

Whole Group: You alone, God, can rescue me, save me, forgive me, and cleanse me. Then I will lift my voice to sing of your forgiveness. How I will praise you.

Clean up the area then gather in a dry spot for a discussion. Have pairs join together to form groups of no more than four. Ask these questions:

■ **What were your reactions to being blindfolded and trusting your partner to lead you?**

■ **How does this compare to what you feel when you trust God to guide you—even though you can't see God?**

■ **What made it difficult for you to follow your partner's guidance? What made it easy?**

Ask a volunteer in each group to read aloud Psalm 56:10-11. Have groups discuss the following questions. Then have each volunteer share his or her group's insights with the whole class. Ask:

■ **What does this passage say to you about trusting God?**

■ **What makes is difficult for you to trust God's guidance? What makes it easy?**

■ **How does God guide us today?**

Ask teenagers to share a time when they trusted God. Then have groups join together for prayer, asking God to help them trust in him.

PSALM
57

THEME:
God's faithfulness

SUMMARY:
Kids compare paper hearts to God's faithfulness in this DEVOTION.

PREPARATION: Cut enough hearts out of blue and red construction paper for each person to have one of each color. You'll also need glue and Bibles.

EXPERIENCE
Pass out one red and one blue heart to each person. Say: **The blue heart represents you, and the red heart represents Jesus. Glue the blue heart and the red heart together.**

When everyone is finished, form pairs. Allow a few minutes for pairs to share prayer requests and praises with one another. Then tell the kids to try to separate the blue and red hearts in such a way that neither heart has the opposite color paper on it (it's nearly impossible).

RESPONSE
Ask pairs the following questions:

■ **What happened when you tried to separate the two hearts?**

■ **Why did some blue paper stick on the red heart and some red paper stick on the blue heart?**

Have partners read Psalm 57 together. Ask:

■ **How is God's faithfulness like glue? How is it unlike glue?**

■ **What bonds us together with Jesus?**

CLOSING
Have partners share their definitions of God's faithfulness then offer a prayer of thanks that Jesus will never be separated from us.

PSALM 61:1-4

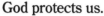

THEME:

God protects us.

SUMMARY:
Kids go on a RETREAT that helps them understand how God protects them.

PREPARATION: Pick a safe location for your retreat where group members can sleep outside without a tent. For example, you might use the church lawn, someone's large back yard, or a campground. Bring Bibles, tents (enough to sleep half of the group members), and food and beverages (including marshmallows for a campfire snack and breakfast the next morning) for everyone.

Announce the date for your retreat. Ask all those attending to bring a sack lunch (it will actually be eaten for dinner) and a sleeping bag. Be sure to mention that some kids will be sleeping without a tent. Form two groups from those who sign up.

Gather enough tents (either have the congregation donate some or rent some from a sporting-goods store) for one group to sleep in. Recruit adult volunteers to prepare the menu and help out with the retreat.

On Friday afternoon, meet at the church. Car pool to the location of your retreat. Upon arrival, announce the names of those kids sleeping in tents. Have everyone set up camp.

Afterward, have kids eat their sack lunches. If time permits, play games until bed or have a campfire and roast marshmallows.

In the morning serve breakfast. After breakfast, gather all the kids together. Ask the kids without tents:

■ **What did you first think when you found out that you didn't get to sleep in a tent?**

■ **What was it like to be without a tent?**

Then ask the kids with tents the following questions:

■ **What did you first think when you found out that you got to sleep in a tent?**

■ **What was it like to be inside the tent?**

Read Psalm 61:1-4. Then ask everyone:

■ **How is God like a tent to those who know and love him?**

■ **What does God want to protect us from?**

■ **How does God shelter us or provide us with a feeling of safety?**

Close by singing "Hiding Place."

PSALM 66

THEME:

Praising God

SUMMARY:
Plan a PARTY to celebrate the awesomeness of God.

PREPARATION: Pick a day to have your party. Publicize the party by putting up posters around the church. Make photocopied fliers announcing the theme, date, time, and location of the party (enough for each person to have one). You'll also need pens, pencils, 3×5 cards, a cassette tape player, contemporary Christian music (preferably praise music), and Bibles.

Two weeks before your party, pass out pencils and photocopied fliers that have all the party information on it. The flier should also include a blank space for each person to write his or her favorite attribute of God, such as God's faithfulness, kindness, mercifulness, wisdom, compassion, or power.

Say: **Bring something to the party to share with everyone else that represents your favorite attribute of God. For example, if your favorite attribute is God's faithfulness, you might bring peanut butter sandwiches because they really stick to you. Or you might bring chocolate chip cookies to represent God's sweet spirit, or a bottle of Gatorade to represent God's power to meet our physical needs.**

At the party, use pens and 3×5 cards to have teenagers create labels, explaining what each food and drink item represents. For example, a label for pumpkin bread might read "bread of life."

Select four volunteers to read Psalm 66, each reading five verses with much expression. Ask:

■ **How does this passage make you feel toward God?**

■ **Why do we often forget the awesomeness and excitement of God?**

■ **How can we remember God's awesomeness?**

Have teenagers share praises of things they're thankful for. Play contemporary Christian music that praises God's awesomeness. A good choice is "Awesome God" by Rich Mullins, which can be found in *The Group Songbook* (Group Publishing).

PSALM 70

THEME:
God's timing

SUMMARY:
In this CREATIVE PRAYER, teenagers will pray for things that happen during different hours of the day.

PREPARATION: Make four small posters that have a time of day written on them. For example, you might have a poster for 8:30 a.m., one for 3:00 p.m., one for 7:30 p.m., and one for 10:00 p.m. You'll also need Bibles.

Have kids read Psalm 70 quietly to themselves. Then form four groups and have them discuss the following questions:

■ **What do you think David was feeling when he wrote this?**

■ **What do you do when you feel that way?**

■ **How does prayer help you through those times?**

Then give each group a poster with a time of day written on it. Say: **Think of something that happens at your assigned time that you could pray about. For example, for 3:00 p.m. you might pray that you'd have the courage to talk to your friend about Jesus. For 7:30 p.m. you might pray for diligence to get all your studying done. For 10:00 p.m. you might pray for everyone to get home safely from a school social.**

Give groups ample time to pray. Rotate the posters so everyone has a chance to pray for each hour.

To close, pray together thankfully that God's timing is not our timing—that God's timing is much better than ours. Ask for the patience we need in waiting for our prayers to be answered.

PSALM
77

THEME:
God's ever-present strength

SUMMARY:
In this DEVOTION, teenagers will create footprints to emphasize God's presence in tough times.

PREPARATION: For each person, you'll need an adult-sized shoe box filled with about one inch of clean sand. Sand can be collected from a park or purchased at a plant nursery (about $2 to $3 per 50 pounds—enough for about 10 shoe boxes).

You'll also need enough plaster of Paris to make a foot mold for each person. You can purchase plaster of Paris from a craft or school-supply store (about $4 per 4.4 pounds—enough for about 10 footprints). Be sure to seal the container to keep the mix from hardening.

When planning, be aware that it will take over one hour for the footprints to dry. The process can be quickened by placing the boxes near a warm source.

For each group of four, you'll need markers, newspaper, a basin of warm water, a washcloth, a towel, and Bibles.

Before the devotion, write the following questions on newsprint or a blackboard:

■ **How did you feel as you listened to Psalm 77?**

■ **What words or phrases in this psalm stood out to you? Explain.**

■ **What message was the psalmist trying to get across?**

■ **Is that message important to us today? Why or why not?**

EXPERIENCE
Form groups of no more than four and distribute the following supplies to each group: the boxes of sand, markers, newspaper, mixture of plaster of Paris, a basin of warm water, a washcloth, and a towel. Have each group read aloud Psalm 77 then discuss the questions on the newsprint or blackboard.

After about five minutes, have groups come together to share what they discovered from the psalm. Say: **Each of us have felt like this before. We've felt alone. Yet we have someone who is**

always with us every step of the way.

Have kids return to their small groups. Have each group member remove a shoe and sock and step into a box of moist sand, creating a footprint. Then have another group member pour in the plaster of Paris mixture to make a mold. Ask kids not to brush off their feet when they're finished.

When everyone has made a footprint, say: **One of our most hidden places is our feet. We hide them all day in shoes. We may feel uncomfortable having them exposed right now. Yet feet are powerful allies. They carry us and sometimes help us carry others. Right now, I want each of you to pair up with the person next to you and wash that person's foot.**

RESPONSE

After everyone has had his or her feet washed, have pairs join together to form foursomes.

Have groups of four discuss the following questions then report their insights to the whole group. Ask:

■ **What was it like washing someone else's foot?**

■ **What was it like having your own foot exposed and washed?**

■ **How does this relate to our reading from Psalm 77?**

■ **When have others been there to carry you?**

■ **When have you carried someone else?**

CLOSING

Form a circle. Close with a sentence-completion prayer. Have teenagers simultaneously fill in the name of someone they'll "walk" with in prayer for the following week. Tell them to think of someone who is hurting and, during the prayer, to fill in the blank with that person's name.

Pray: **Lord, you know that** (name) **is hurting this week, and I commit to walk with** (name) **in prayer.**

When the plaster of Paris footprints are dry, have kids autograph each other's footprints by writing one reason that person is fun to "walk" through life with. Then have kids keep their footprints as reminders that God—and our Christian family—can carry us through tough times.

PSALM 82

THEME:
God's grace

SUMMARY:
In this PROJECT, teenagers and adults will work together to plant a garden for an inner city soup kitchen or food pantry.

PREPARATION: You'll need Bibles and gardening resources.

Together with teenagers in your youth group, contact the director of a local soup kitchen or food pantry to learn which types of fresh vegetable and fruit donations are most useful to their organization. Once you have a good list to chose from, talk with experienced gardeners in your congregation to determine which vegetables and fruits can be effectively grown in your area. (Remember, it's OK if you choose to grow only one vegetable or fruit, such as corn, tomatoes, or melons.)

Once you've determined what you want to grow, find a plot of land your youth group can use to grow the produce. If possible, use a section of the church grounds. If that's not possible, ask congregation members to consider loaning part of their land for the project. You'll need to secure the help of at least one gardening expert in your congregation who will act as an adviser and guide for the kids as they tackle this project.

You'll also need things such as gardening tools, equipment, supplies, and seeds or seedlings. Ask congregation members to donate these items.

When you and your youth group are ready, call a special meeting with kids and interested adults. Tell group members about this project to help the needy people in your area. Ask kids and adults to commit to seeing the project through from start to finish. Assign various people responsibility for collecting and keeping track of tools and equipment, scheduling, and overseeing the project.

Begin the farming process as spring approaches. As kids work from week to week, surprise them often with drinks and other treats.

At harvest time, gather all the participants together on the land.

Have a volunteer read aloud Psalm 82. Discuss how growing the garden for those in need is like "defending the rights of the poor" or "saving the weak and helpless." As a part of the ceremony, harvest the crop and wash it. Then present it to the director of the soup kitchen or food pantry with a rousing round of applause.

PSALM 84

THEME:
Longing for God

SUMMARY:
In this CREATIVE READING, kids will perform a "reader's theater" paraphrasing Psalm 84.

PREPARATION: You'll need three photocopies of the "Creative Reading for Psalm 84" handout (p. 231). Give the three photocopies to recruited readers the week before the reading so they can become familiar with the script. These teenagers will also be responsible for creating simple movements to involve the entire group in their reading; for example, flexing muscles like a bodybuilder for the word "strength," bowing to the ground for the word "Lord," and making praying hands for the word "church."

Before the reading, form three groups and assign each reader to a different group. Have readers inform their groups of the creative movements they'll act out during the reading.

For the performance, have the readers stand in a triangle with their backs to each other. Have the three groups encircle the trio, with each group facing its reader-leader, ready to act out the phrases that will be read.

PSALM 89

THEME:
Godly qualities

SUMMARY:
Kids will compare godly and ungodly characteristics as they relax and gaze at God's creation in this OBJECT LESSON.

PREPARATION: You'll need 100 marbles, 12 wooden blocks, masking tape, markers, a Bible, and two or three pitchers filled with water. Find a scenic outdoor location for this activity.

Form five groups. Give one group a Bible, give the second group masking tape and markers, give the third group 12 wooden blocks, give the fourth group 100 marbles, and give the fifth group two or three pitchers filled with water.

Find a level area and have the groups sit in clusters. Have the members of group 1 (the group with the Bible) take turns reading aloud sections of Psalm 89 (verses 1-10, 11-18, 19-29, 30-37, 38-45, and 46-52) until the entire psalm is read. After the

reading of each section, have other teenagers call out the qualities of God (either named or alluded to) in the passage. For example, kids might say "love," "loyalty," or "all-powerful."

As teenagers call out the godly qualities, have members of group 2 (the group with the masking tape and markers) write those qualities on separate strips of tape. Then have members of group 3 (the group with the blocks) attach the masking tape strips to their blocks.

When all the blocks have qualities taped to them, have kids set the blocks firmly on the ground to form a foundation.

Next, have teenagers think of human qualities that are the opposite of the godly characteristics they listed. For example, they might say "hate," "disloyalty," or "abusive power." Have the members of group 4 (the group with the marbles) use the marbles to form the initials of the words they list. Tell the group to place these initials on the blocks (or on the ground next to the blocks).

When all groups have finished, instruct group 5 (the group with the pitchers of water) to pour the water over the blocks and marbles. (The marbles will move, while the blocks will remain in place.) Once the water is poured, ask:

■ **What was it like to write human qualities with marbles?**

■ **How did you feel when the water washed away the human characteristics?**

■ **Why do you think the godly qualities were less likely to be moved?**

■ **How does this object lesson relate to our lives today?**

CREATIVE READING FOR PSALM 84

Reader 1: Almighty Lord, how awesome are the places you dwell.

Reader 2: I always want to be with you, Lord.

Reader 3: Everything in me wants to be where you are.

Reader 2: My soul grows weak when I'm not with you.

Reader 1: My heart cries when you seem far away.

Reader 3: Even my body would die if you didn't give me life in your presence.

Reader 2: But I know you will never abandon me.

Reader 1: I can see how you care for the birds. They have homes and food and freedom.

Reader 3: How much more you care for me, Lord God Almighty.

Reader 1: Going through life with you is awesome!

Reader 2: It's awesome because you give me strength.

Reader 3: It's awesome because you help me overcome bad times.

Reader 1: It's awesome because you can make even the worst times turn out good. It's awesome because you really care about me.

Reader 3: It's awesome because I trust you.

Reader 1: One day of walking with you is better than a thousand days of walking alone.

Reader 2: Lord, you are like sunshine on warm days and like a refuge in stormy weather.

Reader 3: Lord, you are my king and my God.

All: Lord God, our lives are blessed because we trust in you.

PSALM 90

THEME:
Time

SUMMARY:
In this PARTY, teenagers examine time and learn how "growing older" might affect their lives.

PREPARATION: Ask teenagers to invite their parents and other older guests to attend the party. Be sure they include people in their 70s and 80s, if possible. For fun in keeping with the "time" theme, decorate the party room with a variety of clocks. Encourage teenagers and guests to bring watches and unique clocks to the party. Decorate a cake like a clock face.

You'll also need beverages and paper products to serve the refreshments, newsprint and markers or a chalkboard and chalk for the brainstorming session, and Bibles.

As guests arrive, lead them in games and community-building activities that focus on time. For example, have timed relays or play Pictionary, constantly emphasizing the time.

Play time-oriented songs, such as "Rock Around the Clock" by Bill Haley and the Comets, "Time Is..." by DC Talk, or "It's Time" by Wayne Watson. During the party, ask individuals from various age groups if they'll serve on a panel of experts later in the day. Have a "timed" eating session (such as four minutes and 37 seconds) during which party-goers can eat the refreshments.

At some point in the evening, read aloud Psalm 90. Form mixed groups of five or six and have them search the passage for phrases that emphasize time. Write these on newsprint or a blackboard.

Then call the panel of experts to the front of the room and ask:

■ **What it was like to be a teenager during the time when you grew up?**

■ **What do you remember about the first time you heard the story of Jesus?**

■ **How has your faith in Jesus grown over time?**

Allow time for attendees to ask the panel any other questions they might have that relate to time and growing older.

End the party by reading Psalm 90:12, 14-17 as the closing prayer.

PSALM 91:9-13

THEME:
Angels watching over us

SUMMARY:
Kids will participate in a SKIT that depicts how angels watch over us in difficult times.

ANOTHER LOVELY DAY

SCENE: Matt takes a typical walk to the bus stop.

PROPS: Backpack and two chairs. You'll also need Bibles for the discussion after the skit.

CHARACTERS:

Matt (can't see or hear Angel or Bartholomew)

Angel (wears a white T-shirt and pants)

Nasty Guys (two shady-looking thugs, troublemakers)

Drug Dealer (similar to Nasty Guys)

Trevor (can't see or hear Angel or Bartholomew)

Bartholomew (dresses like Angel)

SCRIPT

Matt: *(Kneeling, hands folded, and eyes closed)* ... and protect me today, God. Keep me from things that might harm me or turn me away from you. Amen.
(Matt gets up, picks up backpack, and walks out the door. Angel follows.)

Angel: Well, Matt. Another big day! I hope you remembered that algebra homework.

Matt: Oh no! I forgot to do my algebra homework! I'll try to finish it in study hall.

Angel: Uh oh, trouble ahead! Two shady-looking guys. Matt, you wait here. I'll be right back!
(Hurries over to Nasty Guys.)

Matt: Oh, gross. I stepped in gum!
(Stops to wipe off shoe.)

Angel: Hey, guys. You really don't want to hurt that innocent-looking sophomore over there. In fact, I think you might find something more interesting over in that direction. *(Points away from Matt.)*

Nasty Guy 1: Man, there's nothing happening on this street. Let's check out the action over

there. *(Points same direction Angel did.)*

Nasty Guy 2: Yeah, I got a bad feeling about this corner all of a sudden.
(Both leave. Angel returns to Matt.)

Angel: Sorry about the gum, Matt. But it's safe now, so let's go. We're almost at the bus stop.
(Two of them walk a little way, then Matt sits down on one of the chairs.)

Matt: Maybe I can start that algebra before the bus comes.

Angel: Oh no. Drug dealer at nine o'clock. Just be quiet, Matt. I'll take care of him.
(Angel stands in front of Matt with folded arms while Dealer walks by.)

Dealer: *(Muttering)* Coulda' swore I saw someone here.

Angel: Sorry. We're not interested! Now, Matt, about that algebra...
(Trevor enters with Bartholomew.)

Trevor: Hey, Matt. What's up?

Matt: *(To Trevor)* Aw, just trying to do this algebra homework that I forgot last night.

Angel: Bartholomew! How are things?

Bartholomew: *(To Angel)* Pretty good. Just the usual stray dog, reckless car, and adult bookstore to contend with. But a beautiful morning, wouldn't you agree?

Trevor: *(To Matt)* Yeah, I almost forgot about my algebra, too. Luckily I remembered to do it after youth group last night. It's not too hard. You should be able to finish it by third period.

Angel: *(To Bartholomew)* I couldn't agree more. The Boss has really outdone himself this time!

Matt: I hope so. Look at this, I stepped in gum this morning!

Trevor: Whoa, that's so weird! Me, too!

(Angel and Bartholomew look at each other and smile.)

Angel: Yep, it sure is a lovely day!

If you use this skit as a discussion starter, here are possible questions:

■ **What does this skit say about the role of angels in our lives?**

■ **Read Psalm 91:9-13. Do you believe angels take an active role in watching over us? Why or why not?**

■ **How might your perspective on life be different if you knew angels were watching over you?**

PSALM 94

THEME:
Punishment

SUMMARY:
In this LEARNING GAME, kids will enact trials in which the defendants are both the victim and the accused.

PREPARATION: Set up the meeting room like a courtroom. You'll need Bibles and a photocopy of the "Dockets" handouts (p. 236-238) for each group of young people.

Have teenagers form groups of no more than eight. Have each group read aloud Psalm 94. Ask:

■ **What do you think when guilty people win in court? When the victim loses or is abused?**

■ **When have you experienced injustice?**

Instruct the groups that they'll be recreating courtroom cases in which the victim and the accused will be involved. Each group will have a prosecution lawyer, a defense lawyer, a judge, a victim, an accused, and witnesses (at least one witness for both prosecution and defense).

Give each group a photocopy of the "Dockets" handout. Allow the groups about 15 minutes to assign roles and to create their cases. Then have groups each present their cases.

Allow each case to develop for 15 to 20 minutes. After closing arguments by the prosecution and defense, have the observing group members act as the jury and determine the verdict. Then begin another case.

After the last case, gather everyone together and ask:

■ **What was it like being part of a trial?**

■ **How did you feel when the verdicts were read?**

■ **What role was the easiest to play? the hardest? Explain.**

■ **How might God judge these cases?**

Close the meeting by reading aloud Psalm 94:1-3.

PSALM
95:6-7

THEME:

Time with God

SUMMARY:
Kids will learn about the importance of spending time with God by spending time with each other in this DEVOTION.

PREPARATION: For each group of four, you'll need a clock or a watch. You'll also need paper, pencils, and Bibles.

EXPERIENCE
Form groups of no more than four. Give each group a clock or a watch. Then have group members each take one minute to learn as much as they can about the other kids in their group.

After members of each group have had a chance to get acquainted, distribute paper and pencils to each person. Have kids in each group write what they remember about the other kids in their group. Then have teenagers each take one more minute to ask questions or confirm information on their paper.

RESPONSE
Ask:
■ **How much did you learn about each other in the first minute?**
■ **Did you learn anything new in the second minute? What?**
■ **What might you learn about each other if you had five min-utes a day to spend talking together?**

Form pairs. Have pairs read aloud Psalm 95:6-7. Ask:
■ **What does this passage say about spending time with God?**
■ **What are ways we can spend time with God?**

CLOSING
Have pairs choose one way they'll spend time with God every day this week. Then have partners commit to check up on each other during the week to see how their commitment is going.

Have partners seal their commitments with a closing prayer.

PSALM
96

THEME:

Worship

SUMMARY:
In this MUSIC IDEA, teenagers will perform creative interpretations of Christian music as an expression of worship to God.

PREPARATION: The week before this activity, tell kids to wear something special—clothes that have a special meaning to them (a favorite outfit) or represent something they care about (such as a Scottish kilt, a cheerleader uniform, an American Indian outfit, or street person's clothes). Tell kids they'll take part in a fashion show to model these clothes.

(continued on p. 239)

DOCKETS: CASE 1

The Case: A college student, who was driving under the influence of alcohol, plowed into a crowd of elementary school children. Two children were killed and a third suffered injuries that left him or her paralyzed.

Victim: A 9-year-old who will never walk again.

Accused: A 20-year-old with two previous convictions for drunken driving. The last arrest was three months ago. The accused is presently serving a sentence of community service and court-ordered–substance-abuse counseling (including weekly Alcoholics Anonymous meetings). This individual comes from a family with an alcoholic mother.

Prosecution: The goal is to convince the jury that the accused is guilty of recklessly endangering the lives of people by driving while impaired. As a result of this negligence, two are dead, and one is injured permanently. The objective is to obtain a sentence of two counts of second-degree murder and one count of attempted murder.

Defense: The goal is to convince the jury of the victim's innocence. The chief argument will center around the issue of alcoholism. Alcoholism is a disease, and the accused cannot be responsible for the results of a disease. Likewise, being from an alcoholic home trained the accused to become an alcoholic.

Judge: The goal is to keep order in the court, allow both the prosecution and the defense to present their cases, and keep the trial from lasting more than 20 minutes. The following pattern must be followed:

- opening arguments from prosecution and defense,
- presentation of prosecution's case with witnesses,
- presentation of defense's case with witnesses,
- closing arguments from prosecution and defense, and
- deliberation and verdict by the jury.

Witnesses: At least one witness is needed for both the prosecution and the defense.

The chief witness for the prosecution can be a police officer who arrested the accused. This witness can testify that the accused was both legally drunk and has a history of alcohol abuse. Other witnesses could be a bartender who served drinks to the accused, a child in the crowd who saw the accused's car approaching, or a doctor who would talk about the effect of alcohol on the body.

The chief witness for the defense can be a psychologist who will state that alcoholism is a disease. Other witnesses could be the accused's father telling of the history of alcohol use in the family, a college roommate who can testify that the accused is a decent person, or an Alcoholic's Anonymous member who can testify to the difficulty of stopping the abuse of alcohol.

Jury: The goal is to determine guilt or innocence and the appropriate sentence. In addition to the evidence, the jury needs to consider the biblical principles found in Exodus 21:12-14; Numbers 14:18; Proverbs 20:1; and Proverbs 23:29-35.

DOCKETS: CASE 2

The Case: A young teenager is caught outside a supermarket with a loaf of bread, a jar of peanut butter, and several other small grocery items. The teenager had not paid for these items. When the police investigated, they discovered the teenager was a member of a homeless family living in a station wagon. The teenager stole the food to feed two young siblings who hadn't eaten in three days.

Victim: A supermarket that is part of a national chain of stores (profits the previous year were more than $500 million).

Accused: A 13-year-old whose family is homeless. The teenager is being charged with shoplifting $22.79 worth of food.

Prosecution: The goal is to gain a conviction for shoplifting. The intent is to see that the young person pays for the stolen items plus court costs. In addition, the store wants the teenager sent to a juvenile detention center.

Defense: The goal is to show that the teenager stole in order to survive. The family is homeless because the government cut the program that paid for the family's rent. Their landlord evicted them, and since they were without a mailing address, they weren't able to receive food stamps. They've exhausted their options with social organizations, such as food pantries and the Salvation Army.

Judge: The goal is to keep order in the court, allow both the prosecution and the defense to present their cases, and keep the trial from lasting more than 20 minutes. The following pattern must be followed:

• opening statements by prosecution and defense,

• presentation of prosecution's case with witnesses,

• presentation of defense's case with witnesses,

• closing arguments by prosecution and defense, and

• deliberation and verdict by the jury.

Witnesses: At least one witness is needed for both the prosecution and the defense.

The chief witness for the prosecution can be the security guard who saw the teenager take the food and stopped him or her outside the store. Other witnesses could be a shopper who saw the theft, the store's business manager who could tell how much shoplifting costs the consumer, or the landlord who evicted the family for not paying their rent.

The chief witness for the defense can be the father or mother who could tell about the family's hunger and despair from being homeless. Other witnesses could include a homeless-shelter manager who could tell of their policies and the plight of the homeless, the family's social-service caseworker who could tell that the family had no options of support left through the government, and another homeless person who could tell of the dangers—both physically and mentally—of living on the street.

Jury: The goal is to determine guilt or innocence and the appropriate sentence. In addition to the evidence, the jury needs to consider the biblical principles found in Deuteronomy 12:19-21; Ruth 2:2-7; Matthew 12:1-8; and 2 Thessalonians 3:10.

DOCKETS: CASE 3

The Case: A teenager is expelled from school for repeatedly telling others about Jesus while at school. The teenager has talked to several people during lunch, taped Bible tracts to lockers, and read the Bible aloud during study hall. The teenager has been suspended twice before for similar activities.

Victim: A high school with 1,500 students. The school's principal has repeatedly stated that there will be no religious activity during school hours.

Accused: A 15-year-old who is an active member of a local church. The teenager is being supported by the youth group of the church he or she attends and by his or her parents (although neither is forcing the teenager to talk about Jesus in school).

Prosecution: The goal is to show how the teenager's behavior violates federal laws regarding the separation of church and state. The hope is for the jury to accept the school's expulsion of the teenager.

Defense: The goal is to demonstrate that the school's policies violate the teenager's right to freedom of speech. The hope is to have the student returned back to school.

Judge: The goals are to keep order in the court, allow both the prosecution and the defense to present their cases, and keep the trial from lasting more than 20 minutes. The following pattern must be followed:

• opening arguments from the prosecution and defense,

• presentation of prosecution's case with witnesses,

• presentation of defense's case with witnesses,

• closing statements from the prosecution and defense, and

• deliberation and verdict from the jury.

Witnesses: At least one witness is needed for both the prosecution and the defense.

The chief witness for the prosecution can be an atheist student who is offended by the overtly Christian activities. Other witnesses could be the study hall teacher who has reprimanded the accused, an American Civil Liberties Union member who will describe the accused's behavior as a violation of the other students' rights, and a school board member who can verify that the principal's action is consistent with the board's policies.

The chief witness for the defense can be a student who attends church with the accused and can testify that the principal is targeting and harassing the accused. Other witnesses could include a youth minister who will describe the problems of today's youth and their need for spiritual guidance, the accused's parents who will testify that their child is not a discipline problem, a teacher who will verify that the teenager is a good student, or a Christian activist who will defend the accused's behavior as an acceptable behavior.

Jury: The goal is to determine guilt or innocence and the appropriate sentence. In addition to the evidence, the jury needs to consider the biblical principles found in Matthew 10:28-31; Matthew 28:18-20; and 2 Timothy 4:2-5.

For each group of four to six, you'll need a cassette player and a cassette tape containing one example of current contemporary Christian music. (If you're not sure which music groups to pick, ask the music salesperson at your local Christian bookstore for suggestions.) You'll also need a New American Standard (NAS) Version Bible.

Form a circle. With soft, upbeat music playing in the background, have teenagers take turns stepping into the center of the circle to explain why their outfits are special to them.

After all the teenagers have shared their feelings, read aloud Psalm 96 (if possible, use the NAS Version). Then say: **What we wear can say a lot about us—our likes, dislikes, and personalities. In Psalm 96, the psalmist compares worship to putting on "holy attire" (verse 9, NAS). Today we're going to try an experiment in worship by putting on "holy attire" through music.**

Form groups of four to six. Give each group a cassette player and a contemporary Christian music tape.

Say: **For the next 10 minutes, listen to the songs from the Christian tape you've been given. Choose the song you like the most and use that song as the basis for a pantomime, drama, or creative dance that illustrates the song's message. You can play a portion of it or the entire song, but the presentation must last at least one minute. We want this activity to worship God, show your group's creativity, and allow us to learn more about this song.**

Have groups spread out so they don't interrupt each other. When time is up, have groups each share their presentations. After each presentation, have groups explain why they chose the presentations they did.

Thank groups for their creativity. Encourage them to borrow the music they used in their presentations and continue to worship God through music the following week. Close the activity by having kids take turns reading aloud all of Psalm 96.

PSALM
101

THEME:
   Affirming volunteers

SUMMARY:
   In this AFFIRMATION, ongoing photographic activity will affirm those special people who serve the youth group.

PREPARATION: Decorate a bulletin board in the meeting room with the theme "Our Super-Serving Saint." Create youth group "service coupons" to give to the chosen servants. (The coupons will allow group members to give something back to the people who are always giving to the group.) Coupons should offer services such as a carwash, yardwork, or a window washing.

You'll also need Bibles, paper, slips of paper, a jar, pens, tape, an instant-print camera, and film.

Use Psalm 101 as a "job description" for the volunteer workers in your youth program. Then as a way of thanking the volunteers for filling the description outlined in Psalm 101, each time they volunteer time, energy, or items to the youth program, place their names in a special jar. Once a month at the youth meeting, draw a name from the jar. Then do each of the following activities:

• Have the group create and sign a thank-you card to give to the person. Place a service coupon inside the card.

• Car pool to the person's home and serenade him or her with a song, such as "Jesus Loves You."

• Take a photograph of the youth group surrounding the person, then present the person with the thank-you card and service coupon.

When you return to the meeting room, tape the photo to the bulletin board under the theme "Our Super-Saving Saint." Have the group gather around the picture and read aloud Psalm 101. Offer a prayer of thanks for that volunteer.

PSALM 103

THEME:
Christian growth

SUMMARY:
Young people will go on an OVERNIGHTER that focuses on developing the whole person.

PREPARATION: Plan a retreat based on Psalm 103. Recruit the following professionals (or their equivalents) to help design and staff this event as needed:

• a dietitian to plan wholesome meals and snacks,

• an aerobics instructor to design low-impact exercises,

• a pastor to design spiritually provoking worship services and discussions,

• a psychologist/social worker to discuss emotional issues, and

• a clown to develop games and social activities.

You'll need Bibles and the various supplies and equipment needed for each activity. You'll also need access to a typewriter and a photocopier.

Begin the event by having the clown lead 30 minutes of games and group-building activities that focus on the themes found in Psalm 103:1-4. Then have an aerobics instructor lead 30 minutes of fun exercises to emphasize the truth in Psalm 103:5—"He satisfies me with good things and makes me young again, like the eagle."

After the exercise period, have the pastor lead a discussion that compares the good things God gives us with the so-called good things offered by the world.

After the discussion (and a healthy snack), have kids break into five groups to create a celebration based on various parts of Psalm 103:8-18. Assign a different portion of the passage to each group (verses 8-9, 10-11, 12-14, 15-16, and 17-18), and have the group design and lead a different part of the celebration based on its assigned passage. Tell groups they can structure their parts of the celebration any way they want, as long as they effectively communicate the message found in their passages.

The next morning after breakfast, lead kids in reading aloud Psalm 103:19-22. Then have kids brainstorm an exhaustive list of ways they can praise God in their daily lives. After the event, type up the list, photocopy it, and distribute it to teenagers as a reminder to always be looking for new ways to worship God in their daily lives.

PSALM 104

THEME:
Creation

SUMMARY:
In this SKIT, teenagers will explore the controversial argument of evolution vs. Creation.

THE WORK OF GOD'S HANDS

SCENE: Justin changes the topic of his biology paper.

PROPS: Two chairs, books, a Bible, and a bell. You'll also need Bibles for the discussion after the skit.

CHARACTERS:
Morgan
Justin

SCRIPT

(Morgan is lying down across two chairs, her head on a pile of books, half asleep. Justin enters.)

Justin: Morgan? Hey, Morgan! *(Shakes her.)* Wake up! The bell's about to ring for first period.

Morgan: *(Yawns and stretches.)* Hmm? Oh, thanks, Justin.

Justin: What's up? Why so tired?

Morgan: I was up all night working on Mr. Long's biology paper. Darwin's theory of evolution... How boring. The first paragraph alone is enough to put anyone to sleep.

Justin: Yeah, I know. That's why I did mine on Creation.

Morgan: Creation? You mean you supported Creation?

Justin: Morgan, I tried and tried to write that stupid paper on evolution. I tried to support the idea that we came from monkeys or squid or some form of algae... but I couldn't!

Morgan: But you have to—that's the assignment, Justin!

Justin: I know it's the assignment. But it just didn't make sense. Think about it, Morgan. Think about little, tiny ants and how they know how and when to get food. Think about the ocean and all the fish and stuff that live there. Think about us—how complicated our bodies are. All this great stuff doesn't equal the idea that it all began with some "big bang."

Morgan: Well, Mr. Long thinks that it does, and he's the one grading your paper. You know, you could get an F for not following the instructions.

Justin: Yeah, I know. But I figure that the instructions said to write a paper explaining Darwin's theory of evolution, and I couldn't explain it. So I wrote a paper on what I believe. The world's an incredible place, Morgan. I know that someone made it that way—it didn't just happen.

Morgan: You're right about the world being a pretty incredible place. But how do you support a paper on Creation?

Justin: Well, for starters, I switched textbooks. *(Holds up Bible.)*

(Bell rings, and the two exit.)

Permission to photocopy this skit from *Youth Worker's Encyclopedia: OT* granted for local church use. Copyright Group © Publishing, Inc., Box 481, Loveland, CO 80539.

If you use this skit as a discussion starter, here are possible questions:

■ **How do you suppose Justin's paper will be received by his teacher?**

■ **Why is there such a controversy about evolution vs. Creation?**

■ **Read Psalm 104. What elements from this psalm might support Justin's paper?**

■ **Why is it important for Christians to believe God created the world?**

PSALM 107: 8, 15, 21, 31, 43

THEME:
God's loving help

SUMMARY:
In this DEVOTION, teenagers will create a paper "quilt" that illustrates God's work in their lives.

PREPARATION: For each group of four, you'll need pencils and markers, tape, and a Bible. For each person, you'll need five red paper hearts.

EXPERIENCE
Form groups of no more than four. Give each group a Bible, pencils or markers, and tape. Give each person five red paper hearts. Instruct the groups to read aloud Psalm 107:8, 15, 21, and 31. Ask:

■ **What do you notice about these verses?**

■ **What reasons can you think of for repeating something four times?**

Say: **Much of the Bible contains stories of ways God works in the lives of his people. Now it's your turn to share ways God has worked in your life. On each of your hearts, write one way God has been involved in your life.**

When everyone has finished, share your hearts with each other.

RESPONSE

When everyone is ready, ask:

■ **What are the common ways God has shown you his love?**

■ **What are the unique ways he has touched your life?**

■ **What is it like to share your story?**

■ **What feelings did you have when you heard someone else's story?**

■ **How can you show your love to others?**

Read aloud Psalm 107:43, then ask:

■ **What are ways we can remember God's love in our lives?**

CLOSING

Have teenagers in each group tape their hearts together to form a unique paper-heart quilt (see diagram). After the quilts are made, have each group place its quilt on the floor and form a circle around it. Then ask group members to share one way the other members in the group have shown God's love to them.

When all groups have finished, have them bring their quilts to the center of the room. Tape the quilt edges together to form one "master" quilt. Reread Psalm 107:43. Close by singing "Blest Be the Tie That Binds" or something similar.

PSALM 118:8-9

THEME:
Trusting God

SUMMARY:
In this DEVOTION/ PARTY, kids experience disappointment and learn to place their trust in God.

PREPARATION: You'll need invitations for everyone in your group. For the event, you'll need a block of ice; a tub large enough to hold the ice; "strange" snack foods, such as green beans, pickles, and onions; and "real" snack food that can be served during the party. Don't forget Bibles.

EXPERIENCE

One week ahead of time, invite kids to a party the next week. During the week, send postcards publicizing the party. Make it appealing, offering surprising food and unexpected entertainment.

On the day of the party, place a block of ice in a tub and prepare the strange snack foods (pickles, green beans, and onions) for serving. As kids arrive, explain that the promised entertainment will be sitting around and watching ice melt. Have kids form a circle around the ice tub, then bring out the strange snack foods. As kids are complaining about the "food and fun," ask:

■ **How does this party match your expectations?**

■ **What other things cause us to be disappointed in life?**

RESPONSE

Form pairs and have partners discuss the following questions:

■ **Who do you trust the most in your life? Why?**

■ **When has a friend disappointed you or let you down?**

Have a volunteer read Psalm 118:8-9 aloud. Ask:

■ **Why do we often go to friends before we go to God?**

■ **How is the way you were disappointed by this party like the way people often disappoint you?**

■ **Why can we count on God more than we can count on friends?**

CLOSING

Say: **Sometimes people let us down. But God never will.**

Bring out the real party foods and enjoy a fun time together as a living reminder that, while people often let us down, God is trustworthy.

PSALM
119:4-5, 9-11

THEME:
God's Word

SUMMARY:

In this LEARNING GAME, kids will discover how important it is to not only have God's Word, but to follow it.

PREPARATION: You'll need various treats, such as cookies and brownies, and something to drink. Arrange these on a table before anyone arrives. You'll also need Bibles.

As kids arrive, don't allow them to eat anything. Say: **In order to get any of the treats, you must follow me around for the next 15 minutes.**

Then lead teenagers in a game of Follow the Leader, taking them to a variety of places while doing active things.

For example, you might lead kids in running, exercising, playing Ring Around the Rosy, climbing a tree, standing on their heads, or doing cartwheels. If teenagers complain of being tired or not wanting to do an activity, remind them of the snack reward.

After 15 minutes, stop the game and let the kids enjoy the snacks and drinks. Then ask:

■ **Why was it hard to follow me the whole time?**

■ **When your parents tell you to do something, why is it sometimes hard to do what they say?**

Have a volunteer read aloud Psalm 119:4-5. Then form trios and have them discuss the following question:

■ **How do you think God feels when we don't obey his Word? Explain.**

Have a second volunteer read Psalm 119:9-11. Then form new trios and have them discuss the following question:

■ **What does it mean to "take God's Word to heart"?**

Say: **God has great things in store for us if we follow him.**

Reread verse 9 and close in prayer, asking for strength to follow God's important "directions."

PSALM
121:1-8

THEME:

God is our help.

SUMMARY:
In this DEVOTION, kids learn that God is their source of help.

PREPARATION: You'll need Bibles and plenty of chairs.

EXPERIENCE

Arrange chairs in a row, across the full width of the meeting room. When kids arrive, have them remain on one side of the room.

Challenge teenagers to get the whole group to the other side without touching the chairs in any way. Allow time for teenagers to experience the need for help and encourage them to work as a team. If necessary, give kids a few hints to meet the challenge (such as stacking things on top of chairs so they won't touch the chairs while going over them, or having kids carefully help a small group member over the chairs).

RESPONSE

Form pairs and have partners discuss the following questions. Ask:

■ **How did you feel when I first gave you the instructions?**

■ **Why was it necessary to help each other?**

Read aloud Psalm 121:1-8. Have kids brainstorm situations that were tough for them to go through.

■ **How can these verses help**

when we go through seemingly impossible situations?

Now have partners pair up in foursomes to share their insights about the questions.

CLOSING

Say: **We all go through tough times. But Psalm 121:1-8 reminds us that the Lord is always near to help us.**

Have kids pray for each member of their foursomes and then think of one way they can help each other during the coming week (such as assisting with homework, giving someone a ride, or shopping for a friend).

PSALM
130:3-4a

THEME:

God's forgiveness

SUMMARY:
In this AFFIRMATION, kids will affirm God's forgiveness by acting out a "courtroom drama" where they forgive each other.

PREPARATION: You'll need Bibles, 3×5 cards, pencils, chairs, and a podium. Arrange chairs in a courtroom setting (a row of chairs at the side for the jury, one center chair for the accused, and a podium for the judge).

When the group arrives, choose two or three kids to be the accused then have them leave the room until directions are given to the judge and jury. Choose one teenager to be the judge and instruct him or her to say, "You are forgiven" when you ask for the verdict. Then use the rest of the group as the jury and instruct them to say, "Guilty as charged" when asked for their decision.

Have the accused teenagers return to the room. Give each of them a 3×5 card and a pencil and ask them to write something they've done or said that they regret. Let them know it will be read aloud. Collect the cards and explain that kids will act out a courtroom scene.

Set up the scene for the accused teenagers by describing what "crime" they're being accused of (read from their cards). Then have the accused teenagers explain the events and what happened. Encourage kids to be honest and to describe the regrettable experience in detail. After a minute or so, ask the jury for its verdict. Then ask the judge for the final verdict. Repeat this process for all the accused kids.

Have a volunteer read aloud Psalm 130:3-4a. Ask:

■ **How is this courtroom drama like the message of this passage?**

■ **How do you feel when you've done something wrong?**

■ **How does God's forgiveness make you feel?**

Close in prayer, thanking God for forgiving our sins.

PSALM 136:1-9

THEME:

God's love endures forever.

SUMMARY:

This CREATIVE READING will help kids realize that God's love is constant.

PREPARATION: You'll need at least 16 kids for the reading. (If you have fewer than 16 group members, have several people read more than one part.) Make photocopies of the "Creative Reading for Psalm 136:1-9" handout (p. 248) for each person and have everyone stand in a circle.

Explain that each person, in turn, will read a narrative part and that whenever the word "forever" is spoken during the reading, everyone, in turn, will echo the word.

For example, whenever a reader says "forever," the teenager standing to his or her left will echo "forever," then the teenager standing to the echoer's left will do the same thing, and so on, until everyone in the group has echoed the word. Also, each time the word "love" is spoken, everyone must draw in to the center of the circle for a group hug. If your group is smaller than 16, go around the circle more than once for the readings.

PSALM
138:6-8

THEME:

God's love and power

SUMMARY:
In this OBJECT LESSON, kids choose apples from a pile and compare an apple's uniqueness to their own.

PREPARATION: You'll need Bibles and a supply of apples (enough for everyone in your group, plus a few extras in case you have visitors).

Read aloud Psalm 138:6-8 then say: **This passage describes God's love and power for us, the "apples of his eye."** Place the apples in the center of the room. Ask teenagers to sit in a circle around the apples. Have each kid choose an apple and study it carefully. After a minute or so, have teenagers return their apples to the center of the circle. Mix them up and then see if kids can find their original apples.

When everyone has an apple, ask:

■ **Are you sure that you have your original apple?**

■ **What special markings or colors does your apple have that help to identify it?**

■ **How are we like these apples?**

Say: **Even though we're each unique like these apples, we all have the same access to God's love and power.**

Ask a volunteer to read Psalm 138:6-8. Have kids turn to a partner to discuss the following questions:

■ **Why do you suppose God made each of us so unique?**

■ **How have you experienced God's love and power uniquely in your life?**

■ **How can Psalm 138:6-8 encourage you this week?**

Encourage kids to take home their apples and place them in prominent places as reminders of what they learned during this activity.

Before dismissing, form pairs and have partners pray for each other that God will begin to fulfill his purpose in their lives. Then thank God for love that endures forever.

PSALM
139:1-6

THEME:

God knows us.

SUMMARY:
In this OBJECT LESSON, kids will design clown faces and learn that no matter what "faces" they put on, God knows the true person.

PREPARATION: You'll need an adequate amount of clown makeup or face paint, soap and water, petroleum jelly (or some other makeup-remover cream), old towels, and Bibles.

Form groups of two to four. Assign each group a station,

(continued on p. 249)

CREATIVE READING FOR PSALM 136:1-9

Reader 1: Give thanks to the Lord for he is good.

Reader 2: God's love *(group hug)* endures forever.

(Each person in the circle, beginning with Person 3 and ending with Person 2, echoes the word "forever.")

Reader 3: Give thanks to the God above all gods.

Reader 4: Give thanks to the Lord above all lords.

Reader 5: God's love *(group hug)* endures forever.

(All echo the word "forever.")

Reader 6: God alone does great wonders.

Reader 7: God's love *(group hug)* endures forever.

(All echo the word "forever.")

Reader 8: By his understanding, God created the heavens...

Reader 9: Spread out the earth upon the waters...

Reader 10: And made the sun and the moon...

Reader 11: The sun to watch over the day...

Reader 12: The moon and stars to watch over the night.

Reader 13: God's love *(group hug)* endures forever.

(All echo the word "forever.")

Reader 14: The God who is all these things and did all these things

Reader 15: Has a love *(group hug)* for us

Reader 16: That endures forever!

(All echo the word "forever.")

equipped with clown makeup or face paint. Have foursomes each choose a group member to be a clown. Then explain that the other group members have three minutes to create a face on their clown (clowns must not help with makeup) that resembles a "face" kids sometimes put on at home, school, work, or church. The object is to see which group creates the best clown face.

After three minutes, stop the activity. Have group members vote on the clowns that look most like the faces kids sometimes wear at home, school, work, or church. Then have groups discuss the following questions:

■ **How are these clown faces like the faces we put on at school, home, church, and work? How are they unlike our faces?**

■ **Why do people put on different faces?**

■ **What kinds of faces do they wear?**

Say: **We've all worn different faces—to impress others, because we feel embarrassed, or because we feel pressure to act a certain way.** Have a volunteer read Psalm 139:1-6, then ask:

■ **How does God see you?**

■ **Why did the psalmist think it was wonderful that God knew him so well?**

Close by joining hands and thanking God for knowing the true person inside each of us. Have clowns take off their makeup with petroleum jelly (or makeup-remover cream) then wash with soap and water.

PSALM 139:7-10

THEME:
God is everywhere.

SUMMARY:
In this scavenger hunt ADVENTURE, kids will spend time in a wide variety of places and realize that God's presence is everywhere.

PREPARATION: Provide everyone with a Bible and a photocopy of a "places" list. The list should include the following ideas:

• Go to the highest point you can think of (climb a tree, or go to the top floor of a building).

• Go to the lowest point you can think of (a tunnel, ditch, or someone's basement).

• Go to the quietest place you can think of.

• Go to the loudest place you can think of.

• Go to a homeless shelter or a hospital.

• Go to the sanctuary and pray silently for three minutes.

• Go to any other interesting places you can think of.

You'll also need transportation and adult volunteers to drive and be group leaders.

Form at least two groups and give everyone photocopies of the "places" list. Explain that kids have 45 minutes to go to as many places as they can before regrouping at your meeting place. (Adult drivers will need to provide transportation to each place.)

Explain that at each place, kids are to search for "evidence" of God's presence. The entire group must participate and be prepared to explain where they went and why.

When everyone has returned, have volunteers from each group describe the various places they went and explain why they went there. Then ask:

■ **Of the places you went, where did you feel God's presence the most? Explain.**

■ **Where did you feel God's presence the least? Explain.**

■ **Read Psalm 139:7-10. How do these verses affect your attitude about God's presence?**

Say: **It doesn't matter where we go or what we do—God will be there. God is everywhere.**

Close by having kids thank God for being with us at all times and in all circumstances.

PSALM 139:13-16

THEME:
God is the potter.

SUMMARY:
In this OBJECT LESSON, kids will create inventions and compare their inventions to God's creations.

PREPARATION: You'll need Bibles, paper, pencils, and a supply of modeling clay.

Give kids a ball of modeling clay and have them use the clay to create unusual "inventions." Suggest that kids invent a new tool, toy, or appliance. Allow five minutes for kids to create their inventions.

As kids work, say: **Inventing something new can be thrilling. That's just the way God feels about his greatest creations— each of us.**

Give kids each a sheet of paper and a pencil. Have teenagers write the name and purpose of their inventions on their papers. Ask the rest of the group to guess each invention's name and purpose before having the creator reveal the true name and purpose.

Then form groups of three and give each group a sheet of paper. Read aloud Psalm 139:13-16. Have groups brainstorm to write one sentence summarizing the verses. Have a volunteer from each group read aloud his or her group's summary. Ask:

■ **How are you—God's creation—like your invention?**

■ **How are you different from your invention?**

■ **What does it mean to be unique?**

■ **How did it feel to create something?**

■ **How do you think God feels about creating us?**

PSALM 139:13-16

THEME:
Growing up

SUMMARY:
Teenagers will hold a "You must have been a beautiful baby" PARTY to celebrate growing up.

PREPARATION: You'll need pink and blue decorations, stuffed animals, baby toys, baby bottles, cookies and milk, several jars of baby food (remove the labels or provide blindfolds for kids to have a taste test), plastic spoons, paper, pencils, string, tape, and Bibles. Also, have kids bring their baby pictures to the party.

Decorate your room with pink and blue decorations, lots of stuffed animals, baby bottles, and baby toys all around. Serve cookies and milk for refreshments.

Number the baby pictures and tape them to a wall. Tape a sheet of paper next to each one. Attach a pencil on a string to each sheet so kids can write on the paper. Throughout the party, have teenagers write their guesses as to who the baby in the picture is.

Have a baby-food taste test to see if kids can identify the contents of unmarked baby food containers (or have kids form pairs and feed one another baby food while blindfolded). Have kids play baby-oriented games, such as a crawling relay like Toddler Tag (played on the knees) or who can do the best crying-baby imitation. Play "baby" music, such as "You Must Have Been a Beautiful Baby," "Baby Face," and Amy Grant's "Baby, Baby."

During the party, take a few moments to share Psalm 139:13-16 as a reminder that God knows and cares about who they're becoming.

PSALM 141:3-4

THEME:
Guarding your speech

SUMMARY:
Teenagers will go on a "clean speech" OVERNIGHTER/RETREAT to learn the importance of watching what they say.

PREPARATION: Publicize the "guarding your speech" overnighter with posters shaped like a mouth. Serve healthy snack food for the retreat (such as fruits and vegetables) in addition to your regular meals. Also gather prizes, such as toothpaste, toothbrushes, dental floss, mints, and breath spray. Don't forget Bibles.

Plan an overnight retreat based on Psalm 141:3-4. Encourage kids to say only what is kind and necessary during the event. Tell your kids that you'll reward people who keep the best watch over their words.

Play games centered around the

"guarding your speech" theme. For example, have kids hold their tongues while communicating strange messages, or see who can be silent the longest. Award prizes (toothpaste, toothbrushes, dental floss, mints, and breath spray) to those people who practice positive speech habits (such as saying "please," "thank you," and "excuse me") and who encourage each other with kind words.

Focus your Bible study times on Psalm 141:3-4. Between games, snacks, and Bible studies, have kids spend a few minutes in quiet prayer.

Close the retreat with a morning worship service, during which teenagers talk about the difficulty in keeping watch over speech.

As kids arrive, pass out the slips of paper randomly and allow 15 minutes for interaction and for them to play out these roles. Then have teenagers sit in a circle. Ask:

■ **What was it like to be in the loving group? the proud group?**

■ **What real-life experiences does this activity remind you of?**

■ **Why do people sometimes fail to respond to love?**

Have a volunteer read Psalm 147:10-11. Say: **God has showered each of us with love beyond measure. Like us, God doesn't want his love to be ignored. God wants our faith and trust.**

Close by praying that group members will continually trust in God's love.

PSALM 147:10-11

THEME:
God's love

SUMMARY:
In this LEARNING GAME, kids will dramatize the difference between being "loving" and "proud."

PREPARATION: You'll need a slip of paper for each person. On half the slips write, "You're exceptionally loving. Shower everyone with love and kindness." On the other half write, "You're proud. If anyone says something kind, ignore them. You don't need their praise." Don't forget Bibles.

PSALM 150:1-6

THEME:
Praising God

SUMMARY:
In this PARTY/ MUSIC IDEA, kids will experience the joy of praising God.

PREPARATION: Publicize the party with posters about two weeks in advance. Gather as many musical instruments as possible, from small children's instruments to adult marching-band instruments. The more unique the instruments, the better. You'll also need snacks and beverages, Bibles, and cassette tapes as prizes.

During the party, involve kids in all sorts of musical-praise activities. Base the event on Psalm 150:1-6. Have a karaoke contest, play musical chairs, and give a musical quiz. Award cassette tapes as prizes.

Create a band by having kids play musical instruments they're familiar with. Pick a song that they should all know, such as "When the Saints Go Marching In" or another popular marching-band song.

During the party, serve snacks and beverages. Have a volunteer read aloud Psalm 150:1-6 and emphasize that praise doesn't have to follow a special pattern or be done in a traditional way. Music is one of many ways to praise God.

Close the party by gathering together and reading Psalm 150:1-6 in unison. Remind teenagers that praising God is something anyone can do, at any time and any place. End with a "praise prayer" by having everyone stand in a circle and shout in unison, "We praise you, God. Amen!"

PROVERBS

"Trust the Lord with all your heart, and don't depend on your own understanding. Remember the Lord in all you do, and he will give you success."

Proverbs 3:5-6

PROVERBS
2

THEME:
Seeking wisdom

SUMMARY:
In this CREATIVE READING, kids will perform an echo pantomime about the value of seeking wisdom.

PREPARATION: Familiarize yourself with the "Creative Reading for Proverbs 2" handout (p. 256). Make two photocopies of the reading, highlighting the parts for group 1 on one copy and the parts for group 2 on the other. Select two volunteers to lead the pantomime actions, designating one leader for each group. Give leaders their appropriate copy and practice the actions with them sometime before the actual reading.

Before the meeting begins, tape a sheet of newsprint to the wall. You'll need a marker and Bibles.

Form two groups, designating them group 1 and group 2. Have kids stand. Tell teenagers to follow their group leaders' actions as you read the script. Once members of one group complete an action, they are to freeze, while the members of the other group perform their action. Encourage kids to be completely silent during this activity.

When reading the script, read with feeling and keep a pace that allows time for the groups to mimic their leaders and to comprehend the passage.

After completing the pantomime, form groups of four. Have each group read Proverbs 2 and then come up with its own definition of wisdom. Have groups share their definitions with the other groups. Then ask:

■ **What are the benefits to having wisdom?**

■ **What might happen if we choose to reject wisdom?**

■ **Where can we find wisdom?**

■ **How does wisdom help us do what's right?**

Form a circle. Have kids brainstorm areas in their lives where they can use God's wisdom. List these areas on the newsprint taped to the wall. Conclude by asking God to give wisdom in these listed areas. Give kids time to pray silently for wisdom in dealing with personal areas of their lives.

PROVERBS
3:5-8

THEME:
Trusting God to lead us

SUMMARY:
In this hiking ADVENTURE, kids will discover what it means to trust a map—and the map maker—to lead them on the right path.

PREPARATION: Choose a location for a day hike (preferably a location with many connecting trails) and obtain a trail map for that location (or make your own). Tell kids to

(continued on p. 257)

CREATIVE READING FOR PROVERBS 2

SCRIPT	GROUP	ACTIONS
Wisdom.	1	*Raise hands upward.*
Listen carefully to it.	2	*Cup right hand behind right ear.*
Cry out for it.	1	*Raise face up and put fists at sides.*
Beg for it.	2	*Kneel on both knees, raise face, and fold hands together at chest.*
Search for it like silver.	1	*Look right, look left, and raise right hand to eyebrows.*
Hunt for it like hidden treasure.	2	*Stand up, look left, look right, and raise left hand to eyebrows.*
Then you will understand respect for the Lord.	1	*Kneel on one knee, bow head, and fold hands together at chest.*
And find that you know God.	2	*Raise hands and face to heaven.*
Only the Lord gives wisdom, knowledge, and understanding.	1	*Stand up, point up, and slowly bring hands to heart.*
Like a shield, God protects the innocent and faithful.	2	*Make an X with arms in front of body.*
Wisdom will help you do what's right.	1	*Raise arms, lower arms, then hit left palm with right fist.*
Wisdom will protect and guard you.	2	*Raise fists in boxing posture.*
It will keep you from the wicked.	1	*Raise both arms in front, palms facing front.*
Wisdom will help you be good and do what is right.	2	*Raise arms, lower arms, then hit left palm with right fist.*
And you will live in God's land.	1 and 2	*Kneel on both knees and bow head.*

bring a lunch, snacks, a full water bottle, and sturdy walking shoes. You'll need to bring the same supplies for yourself and a Bible. Plan for transportation to and from the hiking location.

When kids arrive, make sure they each have the required supplies: a lunch, snacks, a full water bottle, and sturdy walking shoes. Transport kids to the hiking location. Before hitting the trail, teach kids how to read the trail map. Show them which lines represent trails, which trail you'll be following, and landmarks along the way, such as creeks or hills. Encourage kids to drink plenty of water throughout the hike.

Form pairs. During the hike, give each pair a turn to lead the group. Give the leading pair the map. Rotate leaders throughout the day, giving each pair 30 minutes to lead (or less, depending on the size of the group and length of the trail). Tell leaders to let the rest of the kids try to find the path on their own, correcting them only when they're about to make a wrong turn.

When you've traveled half the distance, find a place to have lunch and discussion time. Have pairs discuss the following questions, and offer their insights to the whole group. Ask:

■ **As leaders, how did it feel to lead the group along an unfamiliar path with only a map to guide you?**

■ **As a group, how did it feel to have the leaders correct you when you almost made a wrong turn?**

■ **How did you know whether to trust the map?**

■ **How do you think the map maker determined that this was the way to go?**

■ **How do we know we'll reach our destination by following this map?**

Read aloud Proverbs 3:5-8. Ask:

■ **How can we trust the Lord to make our paths straight?**

■ **How is trusting God like trusting the map we're following today?**

■ **What are landmarks we can use to determine whether we're on the path God wants us to travel?**

■ **Why do we sometimes end up getting lost when we trust our own path?**

■ **When was a time in your life when your path didn't seem straight or you couldn't discern where it was at all? Explain how you found your way through.**

Say: **A map is a bird's-eye view of the area, looking down from the sky onto the trail. To complete our hike, we must trust that the map maker has seen the terrain and knows it better than we do. In the same way, we need to trust God, who can see our lives from a more complete perspective.**

Continue your hike. As you walk, encourage teenagers to tell their partners about times God made straight paths in their lives.

PROVERBS
4:20-27

THEME:

Perseverance

SUMMARY:
In this OBJECT LESSON, kids will discover perseverance by attempting to walk a line while looking through the wrong end of binoculars.

PREPARATION: You'll need chalk, a yardstick, binoculars, Bibles, and licorice strings for a snack.

M eet at the parking lot or an inside area where you can make a chalk line on the floor. Ask group members to use chalk and a yardstick to draw a straight line about 8 feet long.

Ask two volunteers to read aloud Proverbs 4:20-27. Then have group members take turns looking through the large end of binoculars while trying to walk along the chalk line (one foot in front of the other). This will be difficult at first, but with patience and perseverance, it can be done.

After everyone has had a chance to walk the line, discuss these questions:

■ **How is living the advice given in the Scriptures like walking the chalk line seen through the binoculars?**

■ **Why is it difficult to walk the chalk line?**

■ **Why is it difficult to walk the Scripture line—to live the advice given to us in the Bible?**

■ **What do we have to do to stay on the chalk line? Scripture line?**

■ **What are some of the most difficult Scripture lines to follow?**

■ **Why are they difficult?**

Have everyone line up single file and walk heel-and-toe to the snack table. Serve licorice strings and remind everyone that walking the straight line of faith—living the advice of the Scriptures—can be done with patience and perseverance.

PROVERBS
6:20-23

THEME:

Following parents' instructions

SUMMARY:
In this OBJECT LESSON, kids will run a race in the dark with a flashlight and discuss how parents' teaching sheds light on life.

PREPARATION: Set up a simple obstacle course with stacked paper cups, a strip of tape stretched out between two chairs, cardboard boxes as tunnels, a chair with empty half-gallon milk cartons standing on it, rows of inflated balloons taped to the floor, a table with a blanket thrown over it, and pyramids of empty soft drink cans.

Create the obstacle course in a room that can be made completely dark. Consider covering windows and door cracks with black construction paper. Make the course easy enough so kids won't get hurt in the dark. Have extra tape and inflated balloons available so you can quickly reconstruct the obstacle course if a team destroys it. Collect a flashlight, a stopwatch, Bibles, and a pen and sheet of paper for recording team times.

Form teams of four. Explain that each team, one person at a time, will run the obstacle course in the dark with the aid of the flashlight. Each team member will run through the obstacle course and, after completing it, will run back to the starting line (by going around—not through—the course) to give the flashlight to the next runner. The team with the fastest cumulative time wins. Add five seconds for each obstacle hit by a team member. Turn off the lights and let the race begin.

When all teams have completed the race, have teenagers form new groups consisting of people from different teams. Have teenagers discuss the following questions in their groups and share their insights with the whole group. Ask:

■ **What was it like running this obstacle course with only a flashlight to help you?**

■ **What are obstacles you face every day?**

Have everyone read Proverbs 6:20-23 in unison, then ask:

■ **How are parents' instructions like a light?**

■ **How do we know when our parents are giving us good advice to follow?**

■ **If your parents aren't available to give good advice, how do you find a role model you can trust?**

Say: **This week, whenever you turn on a light, remember the value of following your parents' wisdom.**

PROVERBS
10:8-14, 19-21, 31-32

THEME:
Wise and foolish speech

SUMMARY:
Kids examine the effects of their speech in this language LEARNING GAME.

PREPARATION: Bring the board game Taboo to your meeting (borrow the game from a friend or congregation member, or purchase it from a local toy store). Before the meeting, familiarize yourself with the rules of the game so you can explain them to the kids.

Form two teams. Explain the instructions of the game to the teams and have them play the game for a half-hour. After playing the game, ask:

■ **How did it feel to be "buzzed" for words you weren't supposed to say?**

■ **How did you keep control over what you said in the game?**

■ **In this game, the consequences of saying a taboo word were getting buzzed and losing a point. What are the consequences of carelessly speaking in real life?**

Form trios and have each member of the trio read one of the following verses: Proverbs 10:8-14, 19-21, and 31-32. Then have group members work together to summarize the themes of their passages and put them in one sentence. Ask:

■ **In these verses, what are the differences between someone who speaks carefully and someone who speaks carelessly?**

■ **What are real-life examples you see of people speaking carefully or foolishly?**

■ **In the game, saying too many words may mean losing a point. How is this like verse 19?**

■ **How can we develop good speaking habits in our lives?**

Close by asking kids to think of situations in which they're tempted to speak without thinking. Encourage teenagers to think of wise words they can say in these situations. Pray with the group, asking God to help group members speak wisely and to "buzz" them when they say taboo words.

PROVERBS 11:13

THEME:
Gossip

SUMMARY:
This LEARNING GAME helps kids understand how easily gossip spreads and that trustworthy people don't gossip.

PREPARATION: You'll need paper, pens, a marker, newsprint, tape, and Bibles.

Form a circle. If you have 14 people or more, form two circles and have both circles follow your instructions. Give each teenager a pen and sheet of paper. Tell kids to each write down a secret about themselves. Explain that this secret should be something no one in the room knows but also something that they wouldn't mind having people know. For example, someone might write, "I won my fourth-grade spelling bee" or "I have a birthmark in my bellybutton."

After everyone has written a secret, tell kids to fold their papers in half (covering their secrets) and write their names on the outside.

Say: **We're going to play Pass the Secret. The goal is to accurately communicate all the secrets we wrote on our papers to everyone in the circle by whispering them to each other. Here's how this game works:**

When I say "go," turn to the person on your right, whisper your secret to that person, and give him or her your folded paper. (You'll have to take turns whispering and receiving the secrets from those around you.)

After you receive a whispered secret from the person on your left, quickly whisper it to the person on your right, passing along the accompanying paper as well.

Because we'll all be passing notes and whispering secrets at the same time, this could get confusing, but do the best you can to keep up. When you receive the paper that has the name of the person to your right on it, write the whispered message that accompanied the paper next to the person's name. Then return

the paper to its original owner.

When kids understand the rules, say "go" to begin the game.

After the game, have group members compare the wording of their original secrets to the whispered messages written next to their names. Have volunteers share how their secrets changed or remained the same. Then ask:

■ **What surprised you about the way your secret returned to you?**

■ **If you weren't sure what someone whispered to you, how did you decide what to tell the person on your right?**

■ **How did you feel when you realized that you didn't tell someone's secret correctly?**

Have everyone read Proverbs 11:13 in unison, then ask:

■ **What is gossip?**

■ **How does gossip start?**

■ **What's it like to keep a good secret?**

■ **What does it mean to you when a friend keeps a secret?**

■ **When might it be dangerous to keep a secret?**

■ **How is telling a secret like this different from gossip?**

Conclude the activity by creating a "confidentiality contract" for your group. Have kids suggest the trust level they'd like the group to maintain. Also ask them to provide ideas on how to protect the information shared in the group. Write their ideas on the newsprint. Revise the ideas into a coherent and concise statement that all group members sign. Then post the agreement on the wall as a reminder of the group's commitment to honor everyone's confidentiality.

PROVERBS
12:1; 13:18, 24

THEME:
Spiritual discipline

SUMMARY:

This OVERNIGHTER/RETREAT is a wacky sports camp that helps teenagers focus on the meaning of and the need for spiritual discipline.

PREPARATION: Plan the event to be 24 hours long, starting on a Friday evening. Before the overnight retreat, collect the necessary supplies for each of the games and discussions. You'll need up to four adult volunteers to help coordinate and assist with activities. Don't forget Bibles.

Prepare wacky "athlete numbers" (like the ones track and field athletes wear) for each teenager by writing numbers such as 7.5, π, $x \neq 9$, ≈ 6.049, and the square root of 2. Collect safety pins so kids can fasten their numbers on their shirts.

Recruit up to four adult leaders to serve as coaches. They'll encourage kids to do their best at the various events. Plan snacks (including drinks), breakfast, and lunch. You'll also need money for a pizza party at the end of the retreat.

For Friday night, create a Room Trivia Game consisting of 10 questions based on information that can be found in the room. List the questions and make photocopies of the list for each person. For example, ask questions such as the number of people wearing mismatched socks, the two people who are dressed the most alike, the color of the toilet paper dispenser in the bathroom, the number of posters hung in the room, and the person wearing the most jewelry.

FRIDAY EVENING

Begin the event at 7:00 p.m. (Tell kids to eat dinner before arriving.) As kids arrive, give each person a number to pin on his or her shirt.

Begin the sports camp by singing the National Anthem and then introducing the coaches. Say: **This is a very special sports camp. We'll be training for new events to be held in the upcoming Olympics. You can never prepare too early. Competing in these events takes discipline.**

Form up to four teams (one team per coach). Then introduce the first event—the Room Trivia Game. Say: **This game requires writing speed and accuracy, mental quickness, and sprinting capabilities. We'll do a few warm-ups to prepare ourselves so we won't sprain our brains or contract writer's cramp.**

Conduct warm-up exercises. For example, kids could compute simple equations as quickly as possible (such as 9 + 13 = ?), write their signatures in the air, and do quick sprints across the room. Have the coaches give the kids tips along the way.

Form one large group, hand out the Room Trivia Game, and give kids 20 minutes to complete it.

When everyone is finished, check the accuracy of the kids' answers by polling the entire group.

Then prepare the group for the Bean Marathon. Give up to four adult leaders each a bag of beans and tell them to find hiding places for themselves. They'll give a bean to each teenager who finds them and performs the task described by the leader. Tasks could include singing the "ABC Song" or making up a poem about sports.

Have kids form pairs. Tell them that they have an hour to get as many beans as they can. To get beans, they have to find adult leaders and perform whatever task the adult leaders ask of them. Darken the building and give the adult leaders 15 minutes to find hiding places. Then allow an hour to play the game.

Afterward, return to the meeting room for snacks and free time. Then encourage kids to go to bed because all good athletes need their rest.

SATURDAY MORNING

After breakfast, prepare the teenagers for their "septathlon" (like a decathlon but with seven events). Do silly warm-up exercises (have kids suggest the exercises), and then lead them in the septathlon.

The events of the septathlon are as follows:

• **The Chair-Scooting Race:** Give each kid a chair. See who can scoot his or her chair across the width of the room the fastest.

• **Water-Balloon Shot Put:** Form pairs. Each pair is given six water balloons. The object is to throw the balloons as far as possible. One person in the pair is the thrower and the other is the marker. The thrower throws the balloon, and the marker runs to the point of impact. With a tape measure, measure the distance of the throw from the thrower to the marker.

• **Toothpick-Javelin Event:** Give each teenager a toothpick. Tell kids to put the toothpicks in their mouths with one end sticking out. To compete, the kids blow the toothpick as far away from themselves as they can. Whoever blows it the farthest wins. (Caution kids to be careful not to inhale the toothpicks when they prepare to blow.)

• **The Football 440:** Have kids form trios. Place two chairs about 15 feet from one another. Each trio has to kick a football one lap around the chairs, alternating kickers. The trio with the fastest time wins.

• **Box-Building Contest:** Form teams of four. Give all teams 15 minutes to build the highest structure they can out of empty boxes.

• **Box-Building Demolition:** Give all teams of four a stack of newspapers. Players form newspaper wads and try to demolish their opponents' buildings by launching newspaper wads at the structures. The team with a structure (or part of it) left standing wins.

• **Three-Legged Long Jump:** Have group members find partners who are roughly equal in size. Give each pair a piece of twine long enough to tie their ankles together. Lay a 2-foot-long piece of masking tape on the ground; this will be the point from which kids jump. Caution kids to be careful and work together in order to avoid falling. With a tape measure, measure the distance from the tape to each pair's landing spot. The longest jump wins.

After completing the septathlon, serve lunch.

SATURDAY AFTERNOON
After lunch, allow an hour of free time and then take the group to a local park or to your church's parking lot. Bring snacks and drinks with you. Have kids create their own rules for a game of kickball. For example, they may decide to run the bases backward, have five bases and a home plate, or pair up (as in the Three-Legged Long Jump) and play the game in pairs.

Return to your room for a discussion time. Ask:

■ **If last night's and today's activities had been serious events, how would you have prepared to compete against other people?**

■ **Who is your favorite athlete?**

■ **What do you think he or she does to be as good an athlete as possible?**

■ **What are other areas of life that require the discipline of an athlete?**

Have kids form trios. Have each person in the trio read one of the following verses: Proverbs 12:1; Proverbs 13:18; and Proverbs 13:24. Then have teenagers summarize their verses for their trio members. Ask:

■ **What does the word "discipline" mean to you?**

■ **What do you think spiritual discipline means?**

■ **How do we become spiritually disciplined?**

■ **According to the verses we just read, what happens to those who love discipline? to those who ignore discipline?**

Have kids brainstorm a list of things they can do to become spiritually fit. While you're holding the discussion, have a couple of the adult leaders prepare for the pizza party. Have them order the pizza so it will arrive when you're finished with your discussion. End the retreat with a prayer asking God to help kids continue to apply what they learned at the retreat in the weeks to come.

PROVERBS
12:17-20

THEME:
   Being an honest witness

SUMMARY:
   In this OBJECT LESSON, kids will attempt to recollect the images on 10 pictures.

PREPARATION: You'll need paper, 10 pictures (preferably ones with lots of details), pencils, and Bibles.

Form groups of three. Give each group paper, a pencil, and a Bible. Place the groups an equal distance from you. Say: **I'll hold up 10 pictures. Look carefully at them and try to remember as many details as possible.**

Hold up each picture for two seconds. After each picture, tell groups to determine what they saw and to write it on their papers. After all 10 pictures have been shown, show them again so groups can compare their answers to what's actually in the pictures.

Award 5 points for each correct guess. Award 5 points for honest answers, such as "We don't know" or "You went too fast." Ask:

■ **Was it hard to admit you didn't know what some of the pictures were? Why or why not?**

■ **When is it important to be sure about what you say?**

■ **Why is it sometimes important to say, "I don't know"?**

■ **How important is it to be honest in all situations?**

■ **Is honesty always rewarded?**

Have groups read Proverbs 12:17-20. Then have them write, in their own words, what it means to be honest according to these verses. Ask volunteers from each group to share their answers with the whole group. Ask:

■ **What does the Bible say about honesty?**

■ **How can we apply these lessons to our lives?**

PROVERBS
15:1

THEME:
   A gentle answer calms anger.

SUMMARY:
   In this SKIT, a brother and sister must deal with angry feelings.

ASHLEY'S ANSWER

SCENE: Ethan angrily confronts his sister.

PROPS: Books, a table, and chair. You'll also need Bibles for the discussion after the skit.

CHARACTERS:
Ethan (very angry, shouting)
Ashley (younger sister, reading a book)
Reader

SCRIPT

Scene 1

Ethan: *(Enters, slams door, and throws books on table. Looks around.)* Ashley! ASHLEY! *(Sees her sitting in a chair across the room.)* There you are, you little creep! I can't believe you turned me in today! Do you know what this means for me?

Ashley: Ethan, wait...

Ethan: No, I won't wait! I have detention for the rest of the semester, thanks to you! Detention! And since I'll be in detention, I won't be able to play baseball this year! But did you think of that? No, you only thought about yourself! You're so selfish!

Ashley: I'm selfish? I'm selfish! You're the one who cheated on your biology midterm! You think since you're "big man on campus" you can get away with anything! Well wake up, Ethan. You're just like the rest of us!

Ethan: I'm nothing like you! I wish I wasn't even related to you! I can't stand you!

Ashley: Well that goes both ways because I can't stand you, either. As far as I'm concerned, we're not related! You're such a jerk! *(Ashley exits in a huff. Ethan exits opposite direction.)*

Reader: A gentle answer turns away wrath, but a harsh word stirs up anger.

Scene 2

(Ashley re-enters, sits in same place, and begins reading a book.)

Ethan: *(Enters again, slams door, and throws books down.)* Ashley! ASHLEY! *(Sees her.)* There you are, you little creep! I can't believe you turned me in today! Do you know what this means for me?

Ashley: Ethan, wait...

Ethan: No, I won't wait! I have detention for the rest of the semester, thanks to you! Detention! And since I'll be in detention, I won't be able to play baseball this year! But did you think about that? No, you only thought about yourself! You're so selfish!

Ashley: *(Quietly)* They were pretty rough on you, huh?

Ethan: Of course they were rough on me! I got turned in for cheating on a midterm! They weren't going to pat me on the back and hand me a medal, were they?

Ashley: So you think that cheating was wrong, too?

Ethan: I know it's not right. But I was failing! If I'd failed that test, my grades wouldn't have been good enough to stay on the baseball team. It seemed like the only way, Ash.

Ashley: Ethan, I'm sorry I told on you. It's just that I knew it was wrong. And I knew that you knew it was wrong. What about studying? Or getting a tutor? Or doing extra credit to get your grade back up? You had other options, but you took the easy way out. Maybe I shouldn't have told...

Ethan: No, you shouldn't have!

Ashley: But you're my big brother. I didn't want to see you doing things the wrong way. I'm sorry it turned out so badly.

Ethan: Yeah, I know. Just next time, let me make my own decisions. I'll live with the choices I make. Deal?

Ashley: Deal.

(Ethan exits. Ashley goes back to her book.)

If you use this skit as a discussion starter, here are possible questions:

■ **What did you notice about the two ways this situation was acted out?**

■ **How did Ashley's response affect Ethan?**

■ **Read Proverbs 15:1. What's difficult about giving a "soft answer" when facing another person's anger?**

■ **What are the benefits of giving a soft answer?**

■ **What changes would you need to make this week that would enable you to follow the wisdom of Proverbs 15:1?**

PROVERBS 16:1-9

THEME:
Setting goals

SUMMARY:
Use this time-line PROJECT to help kids understand the importance of committing all they do to the Lord.

PREPARATION: You'll need a large roll of butcher paper (enough for each group member to have a piece 4 feet long), colorful markers, pens, glue, old magazines, scissors, and Bibles.

Have kids each take a piece of butcher paper and make future time lines for their lives, noting goals they expect to reach at certain ages. For example, their goals may be making the school basketball team at age 13, owning a car at age 16, or graduating from high school at age 18.

Then have kids decorate their time lines with personal drawings, magazine pictures, or any other creation representing their goals. For example, a picture of Michael Jordan could represent the basketball goal, a picture of a Ferrari could represent the car goal, or a picture of a person in a cap and gown could represent the graduation goal. When they've completed their projects, form a circle and have kids set their time lines in front of them. Ask:

■ **What makes these goals appealing to you?**

■ **How do you plan to reach your goals?**

■ **What mini-goals do you need to reach before you can reach your ultimate goal?**

■ **How do you know these are good goals for your life?**

Have kids open their Bibles to Proverbs 16:1-9. Go around the circle, having kids read one verse each until they've read the whole passage. Say: **These verses state that our plans will succeed when we commit them to the Lord. Look at your time lines.** Then ask:

■ **How are your goals in line with God's goals for your life?**

■ **What adjustments might you have to make to get them in line with God's goals?**

■ **What are examples in your past of when your goals were in line with God's? What are examples of when they were not?**

Encourage kids to post their time lines on their bedroom walls as reminders of their goals.

PROVERBS 17:17

THEME:

A friend loves at all times.

SUMMARY:
In this SKIT, a girl deals with the distractions that make it hard for her to be a friend in time of need.

AT ALL TIMES

SCENE: Tori goes to the best friend for some support.

PROPS: A phone, a sweater, a magazine, and a tape recording of a ringing phone. You'll also need Bibles for the discussion after the skit.

CHARACTERS:

Desiree (best friend of Tori's, but a social butterfly)
Tori (upset, depressed, sniffling)
Angela (a friend of Desiree's)

SCRIPT

(Desiree is sitting on the floor, looking at a magazine, and talking on the phone.)

Desiree: I can't believe he did that! What a jerk! But didn't we all warn her about him? It's not like...
(Tori knocks on door.)
Desiree: Come in! *(Continues talking on the phone.)* It's not like I'm surprised or anything. Oh hi, Tori. I'm talking to Cindy about... *(Notices that Tori is upset.)* Are you OK?
Tori: *(Shakes head.)* Uh uh.
Desiree: Cindy, I gotta go. I'll call you back later. 'Bye. *(Hangs up.)* Hey, what's wrong? *(Stands up and gives Tori a hug.)*
Tori: *(Crying, sniffling)* Drew and I broke up last night.
Desiree: Oh, I'm so sorry. What happened?
Tori: Well, we went out last night and everything was great until...
(Knock at the door.)
Desiree: Come in!
(Angela enters with a sweater.)
Desiree: Oh hi, Ang.

Angela: Here's your sweater that I borrowed last weekend. Thanks a million. It looked so good with my pink skirt. *(Noticing Tori)* Hi, Tori. *(Comfortingly)* Hey, girl, are you OK?

Tori: No, it's...

Angela: *(To Desiree)* Anyway, I wanted to see if you had a blouse that would go with those black pants that Mollie gave me for Christmas.

Desiree: You know, I have this excellent blouse, but I lent it to Mollie last week. You'll have to get it from her.

Angela: OK, well, I'd better jet. Nice to see you, Tori. Catch you later, Des.

(Angela exits.)

Desiree: *(To Tori)* Sorry. Now you said that everything was going great until...

Tori: Until we got to the movies, and he saw this girl from Ranchero High. It's the same girl that went to homecoming with Brady... She's gorgeous!

Desiree: I know who you mean.

Tori: Drew saw her and...

(Phone rings. Desiree sits on floor to answer it.)

Desiree: Hello? Oh, yeah, Cindy told me about it! But are you surprised? I mean we warned her about him, didn't we? And then she goes and wears that... *(Looks at Tori and stops talking.)* Um, can I call you back later? I'm kind of busy. Thanks, 'bye. *(Hangs up.)* Sorry. You saw the girl from Ranchero...

Tori: So Drew saw her and starts talking to her. Next thing I know, she's sitting with us in the movie! I was so mad! They were all buddy-buddy, too! So we

leave the movie and...

(Phone rings again. Desiree looks at it.)

Tori: Go ahead and answer it.

Desiree: No, I have a better idea. Let's go out back behind that big tree where we used to hide when we were little. Then we can have some peace and quiet.

Tori: *(Hugs Desiree.)* Thanks, Des.

Desiree: Hey, that's what friends are for, right?

(Girls exit. Phone is still ringing.)

If you use this skit as a discussion starter, here are possible questions:

■ **Read Proverbs 17:17. How does the sentiment of this verse compare to the attitudes we saw in the skit?**

■ **When is it easy for you to reflect Desiree's attitude?**

■ **When is it easy for you to reflect the attitude described in Proverbs 17:17?**

■ **How can you show a friend "love at all times" this week?**

PROVERBS
17:17

THEME:
Friendship

SUMMARY:
Kids will celebrate friendship at this PARTY.

PREPARATION: Tell kids to bring snacks, such as chips, dip, and drinks. You'll need upbeat contemporary Christian music, a cassette tape player, a roll of twine, Bibles, and one hymnal or songbook for every two kids at the party.

Also prepare two large paper bags full of old clothing items, such as hats, large pants, shirts, scarves, gloves, jackets, and large pairs of shoes. Make sure that both bags contain the same items. Place each bag on a chair.

Play fun, upbeat contemporary Christian music in the background throughout this event. Form pairs. If you have an uneven number of kids, pair kids with adult leaders. Give each pair a piece of twine to tie their ankles together, as if running a three-legged race. Once partners are tied together, explain the rules for the party.

Say: **We're on the buddy system for the evening. Anything you wish to do and anyplace you go, must be with your partner. If you wish to eat food, go ahead, but your partner must feed you. The only place you are allowed to be without your partner is in the bathroom. Let the fun begin!**

During the party, divide the kids into two groups, keeping pairs together. Set up the two chairs with clothing bags and run a relay race in which each pair has to run to its team's chair, pick two items of clothing out of the bag, and dress each other in that clothing. Have each pair do the "Hokeypokey" acting as one person (one person does all the right-side actions while the other does the left-side actions).

Sing songs that require clapping and hand motions, again having each person act as one side of the body. Take a snack break and remind kids that they must feed each other.

Have each pair find one or two more pairs and discuss Proverbs 17:17. Tell teenagers to share times when someone acted as a loving friend toward them and how they've been a loving friend to others. Conclude the evening by handing out one hymnal or songbook per pair. Tell kids to find songs about friendship with Jesus, then have everyone sing these songs as a group.

PROVERBS 18:13

THEME:
Listening

SUMMARY:
In this OBJECT LESSON, kids will listen to each other with cotton in their ears.

PREPARATION: You'll need newsprint, markers, cotton balls, tape, and Bibles.

Title a sheet of newsprint "Listening Blockages" and tape it to a wall. Ask kids to brainstorm reasons people have trouble listening; for example, not paying attention or thinking about what they're going to say or do next.

Give kids each the same number of cotton balls as there are items listed as listening blockages. Also distribute tape. Tell kids that the cotton balls represent the items they listed, then have them gently tape the cotton wads over their ears.

Form pairs. On another sheet of newsprint, write these instructions: "In a normal voice, tell your partner what you did last week." After partners have tried to communicate with each other, have kids remove their cotton balls and recount to their partners what they heard. Ask:

■ **How did it feel to listen to your partner with cotton in your ears?**

■ **How is the cotton in your ears like the listening blockages we listed earlier?**

Have volunteers read aloud Proverbs 18:13. Ask:

■ **What does this verse say about listening?**

■ **Why do you think listening to our friends is important?**

PROVERBS 21:2-3

THEME:
Obeying God

SUMMARY:
In this DEVOTION, kids will consider the difference between doing what's right in people's eyes and doing what's right in God's eyes.

PREPARATION: Bring a remote control with you to the meeting (or create one by covering a necklace gift box with construction paper and drawing rewind, fast forward, play, pause, and stop buttons on it). Also prepare a list of tempting situations, such as the opportunity to cheat on a test, shoplift, disobey a parent, drink at a party, and other similar situations.

EXPERIENCE

Recruit volunteers to participate in a remote control role-play. Describe one of the tempting situations and tell the kids to role play how their peers would handle the situation. For example, kids may act out a shoplifting scene where one person is a store manager who looks away, two other people are scheming to take compact discs, and another person is deciding whether to join the other two.

Hit the play button (say "play" aloud) and allow kids time to act out the scene. When the kids come to a decision point, for example, whether or not to take the CDs, press the pause button (call out "pause") and ask the rest of the group how the actors should conclude the role-play. The actors then act out the group's consensus. Recruit more volunteers to act out a new situation. Hit the rewind button (call out "rewind") and have kids "rewind" the role-play so they can come to a new conclusion.

RESPONSE

Ask kids to stand and have them read Proverbs 21:2-3 in unison. Ask the following questions one at a time, and after someone gives a response to a question, he or she may sit down. After each response, have all group members who have nothing further to add sit down. Continue soliciting responses until everyone is seated. Then ask the next question and repeat the process. Ask:

■ **In the role-plays, how did people justify their actions?**

■ **How do you see this every day at school, home, or with your friends?**

■ **What is it like for you to act out obedience to God in the face of peer pressure?**

■ **When you have tough choices between doing what your friends want to do and what God says is right, how can you remain obedient?**

CLOSING

Pray with the teenagers for strength to obey God even when others disagree. After the prayer, have kids form a circle and put their hands in the middle. Tell them that on the count of three everyone will raise their hands and cheer, "God's ways always!" Then lead the closing cheer.

PROVERBS
23:17-21

THEME:
Peer pressure

SUMMARY:
Kids learn through this OBJECT LESSON that those we choose to "join" or associate with make an impression on us.

PREPARATION: You'll need a large container of crayons (thick crayons work best) and a plain white sheet of paper for each teenager. You'll also need Bibles.

Give each kid a sheet of paper and a crayon. Tell kids they have 10 minutes to collect 10 "impressions" of the meeting area, inside and outside, by placing the paper over objects such as carpet, a heater grate, or a keyhole and rubbing the crayon over the objects to pick up their patterns. Tell kids to list each item on the other side of the paper. When they return, have them take turns guessing where everyone got the impressions on their papers.

Say: **Sometimes we're like this paper, allowing others to make impressions on us. Like the pressure the crayon and the object make on the paper, our friends sometimes pressure us to look and act certain ways.** Ask:

■ **How can we determine the pattern that will appear on our papers?**

■ **How can we avoid patterns that we don't want on our papers?**

■ **What has happened to the crayon as a result of this process?**

Form pairs and tell partners to read Proverbs 23:17-21 to each other, alternating verses. Have pairs discuss the following questions, and then share insights with the whole group:

■ **What are ways we can avoid negative peer pressure—the temptation to join our friends in disobeying God?**

■ **Why are we sometimes attracted to what our friends are doing?**

■ **Even though the crayon made an impression on the paper, the paper made an impression on the crayon. How can we make positive impressions on our friends?**

Close with a prayer asking God to make his impression on all group members and enable group members to make God's impression on others.

PROVERBS
25:6-7a

THEME:
Pride

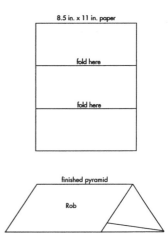

SUMMARY:
This DEVOTION helps kids understand pride and humility.

PREPARATION: You'll need enough paper and pens for kids to have one of each, tape, a stack of old newspapers, a table, and Bibles.

EXPERIENCE
Tell kids to each take a pen and a sheet of paper. Have your teenagers fold their papers into thirds and tape the open edge so it will stand up like a pyramid (see diagram). On the outside of the pyramid, have kids write their names. Then tell the group that they'll be playing a version of King of the Hill. The object of the game is to be the person with his or her pyramid on the table when time runs out.

Kids will knock other players' pyramids off the table by hitting them with newspaper wads. Whenever kids knock another person's pyramid completely off the table, they get to put their own cards on the table again (if theirs were knocked off). Play this game for 10 minutes.

RESPONSE
Ask:
■ **How did you like having your pyramid on top of the table?**
■ **How did it feel to have it knocked off?**
■ **How did it feel to knock someone else's pyramid off the table and replace it with your own?**

Have kids form pairs. Tell pairs to read Proverbs 25:6-7a to each other, with one person reading verse 6 and the other reading verse 7a. Then have them discuss the following questions:
■ **What do these verses say about instances when we feel proud and lift ourselves to a place of honor?**
■ **What are modern-day situ-**

ations to which these verses apply?

■ According to this passage, what should our attitude be in situations where we have opportunities to look good in front of others?

CLOSING

Form a circle around the table. Say: **Close your eyes and imagine a situation this week in which you may wish to lift yourself up. Now think of a way to lift someone else up instead and to be humble before God. Pray silently that God would remind you to be humble in that situation this week.**

Close by singing "Humble Thyself in the Sight of the Lord."

(**Note:** Other verses in Proverbs which deal with the theme of pride are Proverbs 3:34; Proverbs 11:2; Proverbs 16:18-19; Proverbs 18:12; and Proverbs 29:23.)

PROVERBS
25:21-22

THEME:
Loving our enemies
SUMMARY:
Kids perform a CREATIVE READING about loving those who are hard to love.

PREPARATION: Make four photocopies of the "Creative Reading for Proverbs 25:21-22" handout (p. 274).

Recruit four kids to read. Have Readers 1, 2, and 3 stand in a group and Reader 4 stand apart as the narrator. Put Reader 1 between 2 and 3, with 2 and 3 turned slightly away from Reader 1 (as if 2 were on one shoulder as the evil conscience and 3 were on the other as the good conscience). Give readers time to practice the reading before they perform it. When they're ready, use the reading during a youth meeting or a Sunday-morning worship service.

PROVERBS
26:18-19

THEME:
Sincerity
SUMMARY:
In this AFFIRMATION, kids will learn to share sincere compliments with each other.

PREPARATION: Obtain a toy dart gun with suction-cup darts (you can purchase a set at most toy stores). You'll also need index cards, markers, masking tape, Bibles, and a blindfold.

Form groups of four. Have groups read Proverbs 26:18-19 and discuss the following questions:

■ What are situations in which we tell others that we're "only joking" or "just kidding" about something?

(continued on p. 275)

CREATIVE READING FOR PROVERBS 25:21-22

Reader 1: I'm so angry! Aaron totally humiliated me in front of my friends! I can't ever trust him again! He's so cruel to me.

Reader 2: I've seen him do that to you before. If I were you, I'd stay away from him for good. You can't count on him!

Reader 3: I don't know. You may want to give him another chance. Don't shut the door on him. You never know when someone will change.

Reader 1: All I know is that he's hurt me for the last time. I'll just ignore him. Let him live his life; I'll live mine.

Reader 4: If your enemy is hungry, give him food to eat...

Reader 1: Can you believe it? Aaron had the nerve to ask me to share my lunch with him! After all that he's done to me, he wants to take my sandwich, too!

Reader 2: I wouldn't give him anything. Why let him take advantage of you? He's never given you anything but grief. Keep your sandwich to yourself.

Reader 3: You never know what his circumstances are. Maybe there's a good reason for him to be so hungry. Besides, if you can show him a little kindness, perhaps you'd make a difference in his life.

Reader 1: I don't know what to do. I don't want to let him take advantage of me. But I also don't want him to starve. Maybe I could give up a sandwich just once.

Reader 4: If your enemy is thirsty, give him water to drink.

Reader 1: And listen to this: I got the last Coke out of the vending machine, and Aaron has the guts to ask me if he can have it.

Reader 2: I wouldn't give it to him. You were there first and paid for it with your own money. Why should you give it to him? I wouldn't even give it to him if he offered to pay me back for it. He can just go find the drinking fountain.

Reader 3: Who cares if he returns the favor? Who cares if he pays you back? You never know when a little kindness can melt someone's heart or open them up to God.

Reader 1: A Coke is a luxury, for him and for me. I suppose I can get a drink at the water fountain myself. But will he even understand why I'm making this little sacrifice?

Reader 4: In doing these things, it will be like heaping burning coals on his head...

Reader 1: Wow! Aaron actually said "hello" to me in the hall and in a nice tone of voice! Maybe showing some kindness does make a difference.

Reader 2: Don't get your hopes up. He's just using you again!

Reader 3: Don't give up hope. The Lord is using you to reach him.

Reader 1: Looking back on it, I suppose I would do it all over again.

Reader 4: And the Lord will reward you.

■ Why do we say "only joking" or "just kidding"?

■ How do you feel when someone says "only joking" or "just kidding" to you?

Say: **It's important that we give each other sincere encouragement. When we put someone down, even if we say, "I was only joking," we can harm that person emotionally. This week let's practice "shooting darts of affirmation" to those around us.**

Have everyone sit in a circle and give each teenager an index card and marker. Tell teenagers to secretly write a positive word that describes the person to their right; for example "enthusiastic," "joyful," or "funny." While kids are writing, draw a grid like the one in the diagram on a window or a blackboard (use erasable markers). Make sure there is at least one space on the grid for each person in the class. Then collect the cards, shuffle them, and tape them on the grid with the affirmation words showing.

Choose a volunteer to shoot the first dart. Blindfold the volunteer, give that person the gun, and let him or her shoot it at the grid. When the dart lands on or near a word, have the person who wrote that word reveal who the word describes and explain why the word describes that person. Then turn that card over, write "wild card" on it, and tape it back on the grid. Let another teenager shoot the gun and repeat the process. If someone hits a wild card, he or she gets to choose any word left on the grid, and the person who wrote it shares who it is about and why. Continue until all cards have been turned over.

grid

3 x 5 card

funny	kind	creative	thoughtful
WILD CARD	happy	WILD CARD	musical
smart	athletic	friendly	WILD CARD
giving	WILD CARD	sweet	strong

PROVERBS 28:13-14

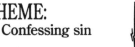

THEME:
Confessing sin

SUMMARY:
Kids confess their sins in this CREATIVE PRAYER.

PREPARATION: Hold the meeting in a room that offers a variety of hiding places. If the room is big and lacks places to hide, create hiding places by bringing in refrigerator boxes, blankets, and chairs. You'll also need Bibles.

In preparation for prayer, have teenagers create hiding places for themselves (one person per hiding place). Tell them to remain in the room so they can hear you. Once kids have created their places and hidden, allow them a few minutes to be quiet before God.

After this time, pray: **Dear God, sometimes we've done or said things that aren't pleasing to you. We know you don't like them, so we hide them from you. We would like to take this time now to tell you what these things are.**

Wait a few seconds and say: **Take this time to consider things you've been hiding from God and would like to tell God about. When you've finished your confession, come out from your hiding place and remain silent.** Allow a few moments of silence while the kids confess their sins and come out of hiding.

When kids have all left their hiding places, read Proverbs 28:13-14. Say: **We find mercy from the Lord when we confess our sins. Because we've just confessed, we can now live openly in God's presence as forgiven people.**

PROVERBS 31:10-31

THEME:
Qualities of an excellent mate

SUMMARY:
In this MUSIC IDEA, kids define the qualities of excellent mates through a musical interview.

PREPARATION: Make four photocopies of the "In Search of the Proverbs 31 Woman/Man" handout (p. 278). To address the qualities of both genders, the script has been written so you can choose one gender or the other; for example, woman/man, her/him, and she/he. On two of the scripts, circle all the female words, and on the other two scripts, circle the male words. You'll also need four tape recorders (with adequate microphones for recording voices) and four Bibles.

(Note: Use this activity as a special event for a Friday evening or as a change of pace for a weekly youth meeting.)

Form four groups. Give each group a photocopy of the handout and a Bible. Have groups read

Proverbs 31:10-31 and then complete the interview. Tell groups to answer the questions posed in the interview with recorded musical responses, most likely a line of a song, to appropriately answer the question. For example, an appropriate answer to the question "What does she do for a living?" could be the lyrics "She works hard for her money." Emphasize that answers must be in line with the Proverbs passage.

Designate two groups to do the female version and two groups to do the male version. Have groups doing the male version answer the interview questions with qualities that are similar to the qualities describing the excellent wife of Proverbs 31:10-31.

Tell groups that once they've determined answers to the questions, each group must choose a narrator to read the script, tape the narration, and insert the appropriate songs to answer the questions. If the group has an appropriate song but does not have access to a recording of it, it can still use the song by having the group sing the words into the tape recorder. Give the groups two hours to complete their tapes and then gather back in the meeting room to play the interviews.

IN SEARCH OF THE PROVERBS 31 WOMAN/MAN

They say a good woman/man is hard to find. We're interviewing people on the street, asking them what the qualities are of an excellent woman/man. Here's a passerby now.

Excuse me... I'm interviewing people about excellent women/men. Could you tell me where I can find an excellent woman/man?

_____ What does she/he do for a living? _____
(Insert musical answer here.)   *(Insert musi-*

_____ Please, could you tell me how she/he cares for her/his
cal answer here.)

family? _____ What is she/he worth? _____
           (Insert musical answer here.)   *(Insert musical*

_____ What about her/his spending habits? _____
answer here.)   *(Insert musical answer*

_____ How do you know an excellent woman/man loves you? _____
here.)   *(Insert*

_____ What do others think about her/him? _____
musical answer here.)   *(Insert musical*

_____ What does the special woman/man in her/his life say
answer here.)

about her/him? _____
                    (Insert musical answer here.)

Thank you for taking the time to answer my questions. One last question: How will I know her/him when I find her/him? _____
                                                                          (Insert musical

_____ Once again, thanks for your answers.
answer here.)

ECCLESIASTES

*"If people please God, God will give them
wisdom, knowledge, and joy."*

Ecclesiastes 2:26a

ECCLESIASTES 2

THEME:

God draws us close to him.

SUMMARY:
Kids will participate in a RETREAT where they must use a compass to locate clues to specific objectives.

PREPARATION: You'll need enough compasses for each team of five to eight kids. Ahead of time, choose specific activities that require teams to follow their compasses to a location or goal. Make sure to walk the various courses with a compass to ensure that your directions and instructions are sound. You might want to write these instructions on paper and photocopy them for kids to follow.

You might also want to provide small prizes for teams that successfully follow their compasses to the location or goal. You'll also need Bibles for discussion times and new Bibles to present to all retreat attendees.

Create a retreat in which cooperation, carefulness, and a watchful eye on their compasses will lead teenagers to specific locations or activities. Form teams of five to eight kids who will attempt to follow the compass clues. (With a little cleverness, you can create an exciting camp that will help reinforce the need to carefully heed God's instruction.) Here is a sample instruction for locating a password for dinner:

"Start at the entrance to the meeting room. Go northwest until you come to a red trash can. Go south until you come to a large oak tree. Turn west and proceed straight until you come to a sign in the grass that gives you the password to enter the dining hall."

Compass quests can help kids locate clues, find passwords that will allow them to eat meals, or find objects to collect points toward a prize.

During the retreat, focus the discussion times on Ecclesiastes 2. You might ask questions like the following:

■ **Based on what you read in Ecclesiastes 2, how would you describe the goal of the author of Ecclesiastes?**

■ **How did the author try to reach his goal?**

■ **What are the goals that people today pursue? How do these goals compare to the goal of the author of Ecclesiastes?**

■ **How do people today try to reach their goals?**

■ **What happens when people pursue unfulfilling goals like the writer of Ecclesiastes did?**

■ **How can we make God our goal?**

■ **How is the Bible like a compass that directs us to God?**

■ **What's one thing you can do this week to help make God your goal? to help you use God's "compass"—the Bible?**

End the retreat by awarding new Bibles to everyone.

ECCLESIASTES 4:9-12

THEME:
Teamwork and friendship

SUMMARY:
In this SKIT, two hikers illustrate the importance of teamwork.

TWO IS BETTER THAN ONE

SCENE: Two hikers try to make it on their own, and they come up short.

PROPS: Two backpacks, a sack lunch, a small box, a cooler with ice water, an orange, and sunscreen. You'll also need Bibles for the discussion after the skit.

CHARACTERS:
Hiker 1
Hiker 2

SCRIPT

Hiker 1: *(Plops down on floor.)* Man, I'm starved! I'm glad my mom packed such a great lunch! *(Pulls sack out of backpack and unpacks lunch.)* Barbecued-beef sandwich, Oreos, a banana, potato chips, and... Wait a minute. Where's my drink? She's got to be kidding! She sends me on a desert hike without a drink? *(Shakes head, begins to eat slowly.)*

Hiker 2: *(Plops down on floor.)* Man, I'm starved! Wish I'd remembered to pack a lunch. All I've got is this cooler of ice water and an orange. This is going to be a long hike on one little orange!

Hiker 1: I'm thirsty, and my feet are killing me. Why didn't I wear that extra pair of socks? Maybe I can stuff my lunch bag in my shoe to keep these blisters from getting any worse... Ouch! *(Tries to stuff lunch bag into shoes.)*

Hiker 2: *(Rummaging through backpack.)* Maybe, just maybe, my brother left something in here the last time he went camping... *(Pulls out a box.)* Yes! Please, be cookies, a sandwich, dog food... any kind of food! *(Opens box, frowns.)* Great, a first-aid kit. Just what I needed. I wonder what Band-Aids taste like?

Hiker 1: A lot of fun this turned out to be. Between my blistered feet and my dry mouth, I'm miserable and too tired to move. At least I brought sunscreen so that I don't fry while I sit here and wait for the buzzards to get me. *(Starts putting sunscreen on his face.)*

Hiker 2: This is stupid. I went on this hike to have a good time, and here I am starving and getting the sunburn of my life. I'm going home!

(Hiker 2 gets up and walks past Hiker 1. The two look at each other, checking out what the other has. Both look as if they're going to say something but hesitate. They drop heads and freeze.)

If you use this skit as a discussion starter, here are possible questions:

■ How did the two hikers need each other?

■ How successful were they on their own?

■ What might have happened if they had worked together?

■ Read Ecclesiastes 4:9-12. How do we need others in our lives?

■ What keeps us from going to others for help?

ECCLESIASTES 8:9-15

THEME:
The good and bad in life

SUMMARY:
In this PROJECT/ MUSIC IDEA, kids will

write and perform a musical that illustrates a theme from Ecclesiastes 8:9-15.

PREPARATION: You'll need pencils, paper, hymnals, songbooks, Bibles, and whatever supplies and props are necessary for the musical. You'll also need pizzas and soft drinks for a pizza celebration afterward.

Use this idea with a church drama group or a group of kids interested in theater. At a meeting with these kids, ask a volunteer to read Ecclesiastes 8:9-15. Then form pairs and have partners discuss the following questions. Ask:

■ What does this passage tell you about God?

■ What does this passage tell you about people who seem to get away with living in rebellion against God?

■ How would you summarize the theme of Ecclesiastes 8:9-15?

Say: Using this passage and the theme of Ecclesiastes 8:9-15, let's create a 30-minute youth musical for our group to perform.

Tell kids they should plan on spending three to six months to pull this project off. Then over the next few months, have them work together to accomplish the following tasks:

• Set a production schedule to keep the cast and crew on track as they create the musical and make preparations to perform the show.

• Create a budget for the production (including planning any fund-raisers).

• Select five to eight songs to use during the musical.

• Write a script that periodically incorporates the songs into the story.

• Make arrangements for a place to hold the performance.

• Gather or make the necessary props and settings.

• Publicize the show.

Give kids the freedom to select songs that they think best reflect the theme of Ecclesiastes 8:9-15 and to write a script around those songs. Encourage kids to quote Ecclesiastes 8:9-15 at least once during the musical. Make hymnals and songbooks available for kids to use as references. Kids might also benefit from books about drama, such as *Youth Ministry Drama and Comedy* by Chuck Bolte and Paul McCusker (available from Group Publishing).

When the group is ready, stage the production. Afterward, hold a pizza celebration to congratulate kids on their efforts. Sometime during the pizza celebration, have kids share with a partner one thing they learned about Ecclesiastes 8:9-15 as a result of their work on this project.

ECCLESIASTES 10:1

THEME:
Avoiding foolish actions

SUMMARY:
In this PROJECT, kids will create skits to demonstrate the annoyance that foolish actions can cause in people's lives.

PREPARATION: You'll need 3×5 cards, flypaper, pencils, paper, and Bibles. Write a word on each 3×5 card, such as "money," "relationships," "romance," "education," "time," "talent," "friends," and "family." Have enough cards so that each group of three to five kids will have one.

Have a volunteer read Ecclesiastes 10:1. Ask:
∎ **How would you feel if you squeezed out a strip of toothpaste onto your toothbrush and** found a fly had gotten mixed in with the toothpaste?
∎ **What do you think the writer of Ecclesiastes was getting at with this example of "flies in the perfume"?**
∎ **What do you think the Bible means when it talks about foolishness?**
∎ **How does foolishness give a person's life a foul smell?**

Form groups of three to five. Give each group a card with a situation word. Say: **You're to create a skit or pantomime showing how a person could act, think, or talk foolishly in your situation. Keep in mind that foolishness is not lunacy but rather actions that are contrary to God's will and desire.**

Pass out pencils and paper to each group (in case kids want to take notes as they compose their skits). After 20 minutes, have each group perform its skit for the entire group. Have teenagers discuss the foolish behavior that was demonstrated in each skit and suggest a wise alternative.

Hang a strip of flypaper from the ceiling and invite teenagers to prayerfully consider a behavior or attitude they have that is like a "fly in the ointment of their lives." Ask each teenager to write that action or thought on a slip of paper and, after closing in prayer, stick that slip of paper on the flypaper.

ECCLESIASTES 12:1-7

THEME:
Appreciating youthfulness

SUMMARY:
Teenagers will visit a nursing or retirement home in this ADVENTURE to get a better appreciation of their youth.

PREPARATION: Arrange to visit a nursing or retirement home. Have kids prepare and present gifts to the residents at the home. Arrange transportation to and from the home and a meeting place afterward to debrief.

Before you leave for the nursing or retirement home, have a volunteer read Ecclesiastes 12:1-7. Say: **Today we'll be visiting some people who fit the description we've just read. Keep in mind that most of you will be in their place someday.**

Explain to the kids that they will be visiting a nursing or retirement home. Have them prepare the gifts they'll be delivering to the elderly residents (choose items such as flowers, room decorations, or plaques with Scripture passages). Encourage teenagers to talk with the residents as they deliver their gifts.

Afterward, meet to discuss the following questions:

■ **What was it like to visit the elderly residents?**

■ **What was the most mean-**ingful thing you saw or did today?

■ **What are some of the limitations of old age?**

■ **What new appreciation do you have about your youth?**

■ **How can you follow Christ while you're young?**

Close in a time of prayer for the elderly people who were visited and give thanks for the group members' youth, health, and energy.

ECCLESIASTES 12:9-14

THEME:
The purpose of life

SUMMARY:
Teenagers will discuss the purpose and meaning of life in this OBJECT LESSON.

PREPARATION: Collect a number of small items, such as a can opener, a pencil, a sponge, a flea collar, a belt buckle, a coaster, and a picture of a person to symbolize life (label it "life" on the back). Place these items in a bag or box. You'll also need candy snacks and Bibles.

Form groups of no more than five. Say: **In the bag (or box), I have a number of items, each of which has a unique purpose. Your job is to guess the object and its purpose. These are common objects, and you can determine what they are by asking enough "yes" or "no" questions.**

Choose an object from the bag

(without letting kids see it). One by one, allow kids to ask "yes" or "no" questions about the item until someone correctly guesses the object you chose. Award that person a candy snack then choose a new object and repeat the process.

Play this game as long as you like, but save the picture until last. Then say: **I'll show you this next object, and you must guess what its purpose is.**

Pull the picture labeled "life" from the bag. Have kids share their thoughts about what the purpose of life is. Then have a volunteer read aloud Ecclesiastes 12:9-14. Wrap up the experience by asking:

■ **What does this passage say about the purpose of life?**

■ **How is the purpose in this passage like the purpose people claim they live for? How is it unlike the purpose?**

■ **In what way does a person "fear" God?**

Have group members memorize verse 13 as a constant reminder of their purpose in life.

SONG OF SOLOMON

*"He brought me to the banquet room, and
his banner over me is love."*

Song of Solomon 2:4

SONG OF SOLOMON 1–4

THEME:
God created and approves of romance.

SUMMARY:
Teenagers will do a modern CREATIVE READING of selected romantic passages from Song of Solomon.

PREPARATION: Provide pencils, paper, and Bibles so kids can rewrite the lines in the songs. Play syrupy romance music while kids are working on their rewrites. Decorate the room with hearts and flowers.

Welcome teenagers as they enter the romantically decorated room. Say: **Today we're going to look at something most of you probably never thought was in the Bible—a true romance story. It's a story of a young king and his new bride.**

Assign each teenager a verse (or verses) of Song of Solomon 1–4 to rewrite using modern terms. For example, in verse 2:9, instead of "My lover is like a gazelle," a teenager could write "My lover is like an aerobics instructor." Keep in mind that this reading will be full of humor since it's difficult to say these lines with a straight face. Invite kids to ham it up and have fun reworking the verses.

Assign the following verses for girls to read: 1:2-4, 12, 13, 14, 16;

2:1, 3-6, 16-17. Assign these verses for the guys to read: 1:9-11, 15, 2:2, 14; 4:1-3.

Play romantic music when the reading begins and dim the lights. When the kids are done reading, ask:

∎ **How do you feel about these kinds of verses being in the Bible?**

∎ **What does this tell you about how God views love and romance?**

∎ **What are the "conditions" that God says must accompany intimacy?**

SONG OF SOLOMON 4:1-4

THEME:
Describing love

SUMMARY:
In this OBJECT LESSON teenagers will draw pictures, in which they illustrate the literal translation of the passage, and learn how difficult it is to describe love.

PREPARATION: You'll need paper, colored markers, and Bibles.

Give teenagers each a sheet of paper and colored markers. Say: **As I read the following description of a woman, draw a picture of her just the way she's literally described. For exam-**

ple, for verse 1, you should draw a woman's head with doves for eyes.

Read aloud Song of Solomon 4:1-4. Read the passage slowly, verse by verse (or read it over several times), to give kids enough time to draw their pictures. When kids are finished drawing, have them hold up their finished pictures. Ask:

■ Why did Solomon choose these words to describe his beloved?

■ What words do we use to describe others that shouldn't be taken literally?

■ Why do people use descriptions like these for love?

■ Why is love difficult to express?

■ What can we learn from this passage about love?

SONG OF SOLOMON 4:1-5

THEME:
Inner beauty

SUMMARY:
In this SKIT, two guys discuss their opinions about beauty.

THE GIRL NEXT DOOR

SCENE: Patrick and Marc have a lunchtime discussion about girls.

PROPS: A table, two chairs, and two sack lunches. You'll also need Bibles for the discussion after the skit.

CHARACTERS:
Patrick
Marc

SCRIPT
(Patrick and Marc are sitting at a table eating lunch.)

Patrick: So, what do you have today?

Marc: It looks like tuna on wheat, an apple, leftover birthday cake, and a Coke. Not bad for a Monday. You?

Patrick: A burrito, chips, banana, one of mom's caramel-fudge brownies, and milk. I definitely win!

Marc: Yeah, yeah, I guess so. Hey, I'm taking Kaitlin to see the new Schwarzenegger movie on Friday. You want to take Marissa and make it a double?

Patrick: *(Rolls eyes.)* Marc, you know I'm not interested in Marissa.

Marc: You're so weird, Pat. Any guy in this school would kill and die for a date with her! She's gorgeous!

Patrick: I know... She's definitely good looking. But it's just that I've been spending time with Stephanie Kramer, and I think I'd like to ask her out.

Marc: Stephanie Kramer? Are you kidding? You could have a date with Marissa Martinelli, and you want to go out with Stephanie Kramer?

Patrick: Yeah, what's wrong with that?

Marc: Patrick, my man! Marissa is a model. She's from Italy. She's beautiful! Stephanie is... well... not.

Patrick: You don't even know her, Marc. She's so cool. She makes me laugh all the time, and she is really smart. When I'm around her, I just feel... I don't know... good, I guess.

Marc: *(Sarcastically)* So you're saying she's got a great personality, right?

Patrick: It's more than personality. Marc, you look at her and you see the girl next door. But when I look at her, I see all these other things. Like how she takes care of her baby sister. Or hearing her get excited about learning something new. Or when she's sharing something at Bible study. Those are all beautiful.

Marc: Wow. Sounds like you're really serious.

Patrick: I'm not serious or anything. It's just that I'm seeing a different side of her. And it's really opened my eyes to who she really is.

Marc: Well, does she like Schwarzenegger?

Patrick: Huh?

Marc: Why don't you ask her out for this Friday night? Maybe Kaitlin and I can get to see this other side of her, too.

Patrick: Thanks, man. You won't regret it.

Marc: OK. Now how about half of your mom's caramel-fudge brownie?

(Guys laugh and lights go out.)

If you use this skit as a discussion starter, here are possible questions:

■ **Why do you think Patrick wanted to ask out Stephanie Kramer after spending time with her?**

■ **Why wasn't Patrick impressed by the physical beauty of Marissa?**

■ **Read Song of Solomon 4:1-5. How does the description of beauty in this passage compare with descriptions of beauty today?**

■ **How would you describe inner beauty?**

■ **How important to you is physical beauty in someone you date? How important is inner beauty? Explain your answers.**

SONG OF SOLOMON 8:6-7

THEME:

Real love means commitment.

SUMMARY:

In this PROJECT, teenagers will write questions about love for a panel of experts to answer.

PREPARATION: Select a panel of men and women who regularly counsel people involved in relationship struggles (such as pastors and Christian counselors). Ask them to be prepared to answer written and verbal questions about love and relationships. You'll also need 3×5 cards, pencils, and Bibles.

Have a volunteer read Song of Solomon 8:6-7. Ask:

■ **What does this passage say about the nature of real love?**

■ **If real love is like this passage, why do so many relationships fail?**

Distribute pencils and 3×5 cards to the teenagers. Introduce the panel and say: **Today you'll have a chance to hear what experts in human relationships think about love, romance, and commitment. For the next few minutes, write any questions you'd like to ask these experts. Don't sign your name so all the questions will remain anonymous.**

You may wish to fill out several cards yourself to help get things started. Sample questions might include: Do you believe in love at first sight? Can a person fall in love with someone he or she isn't really romantically attracted to? Does romance go away with age? How do the commitments that a young person might feel toward a friend compare to the commitment of real love?

Collect the cards and have the experts answer them to the best of their ability, using Scripture as a basis for their answers whenever possible. Encourage teenagers to ask other questions that come to mind, too.

ISAIAH

"A child has been born to us; God has given a son to us. He will be responsible for leading the people. His name will be Wonderful Counselor, Powerful God, Father Who Lives Forever, Prince of Peace."

Isaiah 9:6

ISAIAH
1:2-20

THEME:
God's perspective

SUMMARY:
In this OBJECT LESSON, kids experience a change of perspective and discuss Isaiah 1:2-20.

PREPARATION: Choose a large outdoor space on the church grounds, such as a basketball court or courtyard. With help from adult volunteers, move all the furniture out of the youth room and arrange it in the outdoor space. Make sure you place everything just as it was in the youth room. Leave a clue to the location of the new youth area on the door of the old room. You'll also need Bibles.

When everyone has gathered for the meeting, ask kids to respond to questions such as these:

■ **What's it like for you to participate in this youth meeting in a different location than normal?**

■ **How does changing the surroundings affect your attitude or actions in this meeting?**

■ **What kinds of forces shape the way we see the world?**

■ **Can we change the way we see the world? Why or why not?**

Say: Isaiah 1:2-20 describes a difference in perspective between God and the people of Israel. They thought that going through all the "religious" motions of sacrifices of feasts was all they need-ed to do to please God. In your groups, read Isaiah 1:2-20 to see what God's perspective was on their actions.

Ask groups to wrap up this experience by discussing these questions:

■ **Based on what you read in Isaiah 1:2-20, how would you summarize God's perspective in one sentence?**

■ **Why do you think God had such a different perspective from the Israelites?**

■ **Why is it difficult at times to see things from God's perspective?**

■ **How can we consistently have God's perspective as we go through life this week?**

After the discussion, continue the meeting as normal.

ISAIAH
2:2-4

THEME:
War and peace

SUMMARY:
In this OBJECT LESSON, kids will look for symbols of fighting and war and turn them into symbols of love and compassion.

PREPARATION: Have kids search their houses for symbols of war or fighting. These could include toy guns, swords, and weapons; or any type of war toys, such as military equipment, vehicles, or action figures. Have kids bring these to the meeting. (If you decide to display the new, nonviolent symbols, you'll need to provide the necessary supplies to make a display.) You'll also need Bibles.

At the meeting, have kids presented the items they found and describe how they're symbols of war or fighting. Then have kids form groups of no more than four. Have a volunteer read aloud Isaiah 2:2-4. Ask:

■ **How will it feel to live in a land without fighting or wars?**

Have groups each choose two or three of the fighting symbols and brainstorm productive, compassionate ways (rather than warring ways) to use the items. Encourage kids to be creative as they "turn their swords into plows." For example, a toy sword could be used to cut firewood, or an action figure could trade its weapons for food to give to the needy. Once groups have finished brainstorming new uses for the symbols of war and fighting, have them present their ideas to the rest of the kids.

After the presentations, if possible, have kids create a display showing the new, nonviolent uses for the weapons, quoting Isaiah 2:4. Place the display in the church foyer for members of the congregation to see. To close the meeting, have volunteers lead a prayer, asking God to teach us how to live peacefully in his kingdom today.

ISAIAH
6:8-10

THEME:
Following God

SUMMARY:
In this LEARNING GAME, kids will send each other on strange assignments and learn what it means to follow God.

PREPARATION: You'll need Bibles.

Form groups of no more than four. Say: **Choose one person in your group to be the "prophet." The rest of the people in your group will be sending this prophet out on strange assignments for the next few minutes.**

Have groups choose unusual things for their prophets to do, such as sing "Happy Birthday" to a chair in the room, make a cup of mud, dust a church pew, dance with a broom, read a Scripture verse backward, and so on. If you feel it's necessary, caution kids not to ask their prophets to do anything inappropriate or unkind (such as kissing another group member or putting down someone else in the group).

After about three minutes, have groups each choose a new prophet and repeat the activity with new assignments. Continue until each person has been a prophet.

To wrap up the activity, form a circle. Have the group read in unison Isaiah 6:8-10 and discuss these questions:

■ **How is the way you were sent on assignments like the way Isaiah was sent?**

■ **How did it feel to go on missions that didn't make sense to you?**

■ **How is that like how Isaiah might've felt?**

■ **Why did Isaiah follow even though he was given a difficult assignment?**

■ **How can we follow God when we're given unusual or tough assignments?**

ISAIAH
6:9-10

THEME:
Understanding God

SUMMARY:
In this OBJECT LESSON, teenagers will compare mirror images to their mental images of God.

PREPARATION: You'll need handheld mirrors (one for each group of three), paper, pencils, and Bibles.

Form groups of no more than three. Give each group a handheld mirror, paper, and a pencil. (If you don't have enough mirrors for each group to have one, have groups take turns.) Have one person in each group sit at a table with paper and a pencil. Have the other two people in each group hold the mirror over the seated person's head, with the reflecting side facing downward.

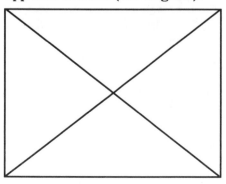

On "go," have the seated people look up into their mirrors and draw a large rectangle on their papers. (No peeking at the drawing at any time!) Then have them each draw an X in their rectangles with the end points of each diagonal line in opposite corners (see diagram).

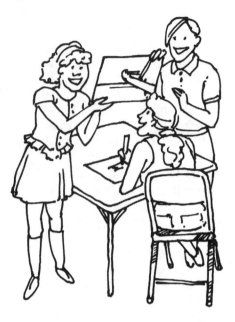

Have seated people switch off with standing people until everyone in the group has had a turn to draw. Then have kids in each group take turns doing the following:

•Have someone in each group draw a design on a sheet of paper. Then have the standing group members hold the mirror in front of the seated person with the design behind the person so it reflects in the mirror. Have the seated person re-create the design on a sheet of paper while looking at its reflection in the mirror.

•Have someone hold the mirror over the seated person's head and have the seated person look into the mirror and write, in cursive, the full name of the person holding the mirror.

(**Note:** Because the mirror distorts the images, it'll be difficult for kids to clearly reproduce mirrored images.) After the activity, ask:

■ **What thoughts went through your mind during this activity?**

Have kids read Isaiah 6:9-10 and discuss how the Holy Spirit uses Scripture to give them genuine understanding of God. Ask kids to talk about how their own opinions and speculations, apart from prayer and Scripture, may give them a distorted understanding of God. To emphasize the theme of understanding God, you can also use passages such as Matthew 13:10-17; 1 Corinthians 2:11-16; and 1 Corinthians 13:9-12.

ISAIAH
9:6-7

THEME:
Jesus, the Messiah

SUMMARY:
In this DEVOTION, teenagers will have a chance to learn about their names and the names of Jesus.

PREPARATION: At your local library, get a book that explains the meanings of names. You'll also need pencils, one slip of paper for each teenager, a container for the paper slips, Bibles, a recording of Handel's *Messiah* that includes the chorus "For Unto Us a Child Is Born," and a compact disc or cassette player.

EXPERIENCE
As the group arrives, have each person write his or her name on a slip of paper. Collect the papers in a container. Pull names out at random and look up their meanings in the name book. Share the meanings with the group.

RESPONSE
Form groups of no more than three and have trios discuss the following questions. Have the oldest person in each trio report his or her group's answers to the first question, the second oldest report answers to the second question, and so on. Ask:

■ **What did you think when you heard the meanings of the names of people in our group?**

■ Do the meanings reflect the personalities of the people who have those names? Why or why not?

■ If you could choose a new name for yourself, what would it be? Explain.

Have the person with the most vowels in his or her name read Isaiah 9:6-7. Explain that this passage lists some of the names that God used to describe his Son, Jesus, and announce his coming birth. Ask:

■ What descriptive names for the Messiah do you find in these verses?

■ How do these names reflect the personality of Jesus?

■ If you were to announce the birth of Christ, what names would you use to describe the coming Savior?

CLOSING

Tell the group that more than 200 years ago, a man named George Frederick Handel put Isaiah 9:6 to music. Close the devotion by playing the recording of "For Unto Us a Child Is Born" from Handel's *Messiah*. Ask kids to be in an attitude of worship as they listen.

ISAIAH 10:1-4

THEME:
Justice

SUMMARY:
In this LEARNING GAME, kids will treat each other unjustly and explore how their experiences are similar to the message of Isaiah 10:1-4.

PREPARATION: You'll need various recreational supplies and equipment for a day of games and sports. You'll also need Bibles.

Have kids choose games or sports to enjoy during a time of fun. When they've chosen what they'd like to do, designate one person for each game or sport to be the "rule maker." Take the rule makers aside and tell them to make rules that aren't fair for all players. Encourage rule makers to alienate everyone at some point during the game or sport. Tell the kids that the rule makers' rules must be followed. Then have kids play their games.

After a little time has passed, designate new rule makers to take over the task of making up new rules. Give these rule makers the same instructions. Continue to designate new rule makers until each person has had a chance to be a rule maker (if possible).

(**Note:** Depending on the size of your group, you may want to have several games going at one time, or you might want to have kids play only one game at a time.)

When kids are finished with their games, call them together and ask:

■ **How did you feel when you were unjustly treated by the rule makers?**

■ **How does God feel about justice?**

Have kids read Isaiah 10:1-4 and discuss how this passage applies to the experience they just had. Ask:

■ **What are the injustices we have in our world?**

■ **What injustices do you face at school? at home?**

■ **What can Christians do to fight injustice?**

End the experience by having kids play a game or sport, following all the rules and treating each other fairly. Encourage kids to fight injustice at school, home, and in other areas of their lives.

ISAIAH 10:24-25

THEME:
Overcoming obstacles with God's help

SUMMARY:
In this LEARNING GAME, kids will discover what it's like to be outnumbered.

PREPARATION: You'll need enough foam balls or beach balls for everyone to have one and enough plastic or foam bats for half the group. You'll also need masking tape and Bibles.

Form two teams of unequal size. For example, if you have 10 people in your group, form one team of three and another of seven people. Give each person a foam ball or a beach ball. Give half the people on each team a plastic or foam bat.

Using masking tape, set up a play area by marking two parallel lines down the middle of your room. The lines should be about four or five feet apart. The area between the lines will be called the "no-entry zone." Have teams gather on opposite sides of the no-entry zone.

Say: **The object of this game is to "knock out" all the other team's members. A person is knocked out of the game when he or she is hit below the knees with a foam ball or beach ball. When you're knocked out of the game, you must leave your team and sit along the wall to watch the rest of the game.**

You may use the bats or balls to block the other team's throws, but you may not use your hands to block. You may not enter the no-entry zone at any time.

When kids are ready, start the game. Allow kids on the smaller team to complain about the unfairness of team size, but play anyway. Play the game more than once, forming different teams each time (but always having one be about twice the size of the other).

During one game, step into the fray and declare the smaller team the winner (even if they've lost more members).

After the game, form groups of no more than four. Read aloud Isaiah 10:24-25, then have groups discuss the following questions:

■ **How did you feel when you were outnumbered in this game?**

■ **How is that like the way the Israelites might've felt about the Assyrians?**

■ **How is the way I stepped into the game and declared a winner like the way God steps into our lives and makes us winners?**

■ **How does God help us overcome obstacles?**

■ **What are ways we can help each other when faced with fears or troubles?**

ISAIAH
11:1-16

THEME:
  The promise of peace

SUMMARY:
  In this PROJECT, kids will create a display, illustrating the promise of peace in this passage.

PREPARATION: You'll need a large piece of plasterboard (drywall) and art supplies, such as paints, paintbrushes, markers, pens, and pencils. You'll also need Bibles.

Have kids read Isaiah 11:1-16 and discuss the images in the passage. Ask:

■ **Which of the pictures in**

verses 6-9 means the most to you? Explain.

■ **How is this promise of peace still a part of Christianity today?**

Form groups of no more than five and assign each group a section of the Scripture. Place the plasterboard on the floor. Then provide groups with art supplies and have them each spend the next 30 minutes or more illustrating the section of Scripture they were assigned. Encourage groups to be creative in their depictions of the verses, using symbols, creative writing styles, or other artistic expressions.

When the picture is completed, have someone with good handwriting title the picture *The Picture of Peace* and list the Scripture reference Isaiah 11:1-16.

Display the sturdy mural on the front lawn of the church or in the youth room. To turn this activity into a fund-raiser, auction off the masterpiece after church. Donate the money to an organization whose cause is to further world peace.

ISAIAH
12:1-6

THEME:
  Praise

SUMMARY:
  Kids will go on a praise ADVENTURE.

PREPARATION: Have kids bring plain T-shirts (that they can write on) and portable cassette or compact disc players to the meeting. You'll need colored fabric markers, cassettes or CDs of upbeat praise music, and Bibles.

When kids arrive, have them read aloud Isaiah 12:1-6, then form groups of no more than five. Using fabric markers, have groups each write on their T-shirts the words from one of the phrases in the Scripture. For example, a group might write, "The Lord gives me strength and makes me sing" or "Shout and sing for joy." Encourage kids to be creative in how they write the phrase. For example, one group might write a different word on each person's T-shirt, and in order to read the phrase, the entire group must stand together. Another group might write the whole phrase on each T-shirt and draw a picture to enhance the meaning of the phrase.

When the T-shirts are completed, send groups out into the church grounds with their portable cassette players. Have kids play the praise music and encourage them to praise God together during this time. Ask kids to be open to people who stop them and want to talk. After a specified amount of time, have groups report back to the meeting room and discuss how they felt praising God in the open. Have kids brainstorm practical ways to praise God in everyday circumstances.

ISAIAH
13–23

THEME:
God's judgment

SUMMARY:
Kids will act out God's judgments against the sinful nations in this OBJECT LESSON.

PREPARATION: You'll need Bibles.

Form teams of no more than four. Say: **Isaiah 13–23 illustrates the judgment God proclaims on many sinful nations. We're going to play a game to see how well you can illustrate these judgments.**
Tell teams to skim through Isaiah 13–23 and choose one of the judgments to depict for the rest of the group. When teams have each chosen a passage, have them create frozen human sculptures that depict something unique in their passages. Teams will have to skim the whole 11 chapters to determine if the choices of action they'll depict are unique.

Then have teams take turns presenting their sculptures for the rest of the kids. Have other teams quickly try to find the judgment they're depicting. The first team to correctly guess the judgment gets 1 point (teams may only get two guesses).

When all the teams have presented their sculptures, discuss the following questions:
■ **How did it feel to depict God's judgment?**

■ **What do these passages tell us about God? about God's justice? about the Israelites? about the various nations?**

■ **What implications do these chapters of Isaiah have for us today?**

ISAIAH
24:1-23; 25:1-5

THEME:
God's power

SUMMARY:
In this PARTY, kids will create sweet treats to enjoy and then watch as they are destroyed.

PREPARATION: You'll need access to the church kitchen; supplies for kids to make their own desserts, such as cookies, cupcakes, and brownies; beverages; plastic tablecloths; and Bibles.

As kids arrive, warn them to expect the unexpected during this party. Then have them form three groups (one for each dessert) and assign them cooking responsibilities. Allow plenty of time for kids to create their desserts.

When the desserts are done, have kids seat themselves around the tables and prepare to eat. (The tables should be protected with tablecloths.) Then go around the tables and, one at a time, dump the desserts into the middle of each table in a big mess. (Do not dump

drinks.) Allow kids to complain, but don't explain your actions.

When all the food has been dumped, have volunteers read aloud Isaiah 24:1-23. Ask kids to find a table partner (someone sitting next to them) and discuss the following questions:

■ **How did you feel when I destroyed your desserts?**

■ **How is this experience like the description in the Isaiah passage? How is it unlike the description?**

■ **Why is God angry in this passage?**

■ **Why did God want to punish the world?**

■ **How are the results of my destroying your desserts like the results of God's punishments? How are they unlike God's punishments?**

Have kids tell how this passage makes them feel. Then have them read aloud Isaiah 25:1-5 and compare the tone of this passage with that in Isaiah 24:1-23. Have kids piece together their snacks from the parts strewn across the table and enjoy their edible reminders of God's power and justice. As a great contrast, use the next activity based on Isaiah 25:1-12 immediately following this one. Or plan to use the next activity the following week.

ISAIAH
25:1-12

THEME:
God's triumph

SUMMARY:
Kids will enjoy a banquet-type PARTY and celebrate God's love for his servants.

PREPARATION: Plan a nice meal for the kids and, if possible, arrange to have the party outdoors on a hill or mountain. You'll need transportation to and from the location and Bibles.

As kids arrive at the party, treat them as banquet guests and try to give them especially good service throughout the entire meal. (You might want to enlist the help of other adult volunteers and dress up in nice clothes or waiter/waitress outfits for the event.) During the meal, have kids take turns completing the following sentence: "Thank you, God, for protecting us from *(blank)*."

Sometime during the party, have volunteers read aloud Isaiah 25:1-12. Have kids briefly explain how this passage makes them feel. Then ask:

■ **How is this banquet like the way God says he'll care for his people in Isaiah?**

■ **How does God care for us today?**

■ **How does God help us defeat our enemies?**

At the close of the party, lead kids in a time of thankful prayer.

ISAIAH
26:1-19

THEME:
Praise

SUMMARY:
In this PROJECT, kids will prepare a praise service for the whole congregation.

PREPARATION: Talk with your pastor and get permission for the kids to lead a morning or evening worship service. You'll need paper, pencils, markers, songbooks or hymnals, and Bibles. You'll also need various decorating supplies, depending on what verses kids select to illustrate the passage.

Form groups to help prepare a praise and worship service centered around Isaiah 26:1-19. One group could organize the music (getting accompanists, choosing songs, choosing a song leader), another group could prepare a program or bulletin for the service, another group could plan the nonmusical portions of the service, and another group could decorate the sanctuary based on the images in Isaiah 26:1-19.

As kids prepare their service, have them study Isaiah 26:1-19 and determine the ways people praised God in Old Testament times. Have kids choose phrases from the passage as focal points for the praise and worship service. For example, the decorating group might choose to decorate the sanctuary with bricks or rocks to symbolize

God's protection (as in Isaiah 26:1). Or they might create a pathway in the sanctuary (as described in Isaiah 26:7).

Give kids concordances and help them look up other Old Testament passages that praise God. Have kids include some of these passages as Scripture readings during the service.

ISAIAH
35:1-10

THEME:
God's comfort

SUMMARY:
In this DEVOTION, teenagers will comfort each other and explore the breadth of God's comfort.

PREPARATION: You'll need Bibles. (**Note:** Since this is a high-risk activity, plan to do this only if the kids are comfortable sharing deeply with each other.)

EXPERIENCE

Form groups of no more than four and give kids the following assignment: **Beginning with the person who's been in the group the longest, share with your group members the one thing that's been the most painful for you in the past year. This could be a relationship that didn't work, something that didn't go right at school, the death of a loved one, and so on. Speak honestly and from your heart and listen care-fully with respect as others talk.**

Allow two or three minutes per group member for this discussion. Kids may become emotional as they discuss their pain. That's OK. Encourage fellow group members to comfort the people who are telling about their pain.

RESPONSE

After kids have each told about a painful experience, encourage groups to comfort their members with words or actions (such as pats on the back or hugs). Then have groups discuss the following questions and share their insights with the whole group:

■ **How did you feel telling about a painful time?**

■ **What was it like to be comforted by a friend?**

■ **Read Isaiah 35:1-10. How does God comfort his people?**

■ **How can the message in this passage help comfort us in our times of need?**

CLOSING

Have groups each think of one thing they can do to comfort someone outside of their group who's going through a tough time. This could be a relative, friend, or someone they barely know. Then have groups commit to comfort that person in the coming week. Have volunteers in each group close in prayer, thanking God for comfort and asking God to make them comforters of others.

ISAIAH
40:3

THEME:

Preparing the way for the Lord

SUMMARY:

In this OBJECT LESSON, kids will untangle Christmas lights and compare that to the work it takes to prepare for Christ's birthday.

PREPARATION: Gather several same-sized boxes of Christmas decorations (enough for each group to have a box). Tangled light cords are a must—even if you have to tangle some yourself. The messier the boxes, the better. You'll also need candy canes and Bibles.

Say: **Only** (the correct number of days until Christmas) **preparation days left until Christmas. Not just shopping days, but "preparation" days.**

Have the group read in unison Isaiah 40:3. Next, form several groups and give each group a box of Christmas decorations.

Say: **We're going to prepare for Christmas by getting our decorations ready. Each group has four minutes to untangle the light cords, unwrap the decorations, and lay everything out on the floor in the shape of a Christmas tree. Go!**

Call time after four minutes and inspect each group's tree decorations. Award candy canes to all group members for a job well done. Then ask:

■ **How did you feel during this game?**

■ **What was frustrating? fun?**

■ **Who emerged as group leader? Who held back?**

■ **How were these preparations like preparing the way for Christ this Christmas? How were they unlike preparing the way?**

Have another person reread the passage aloud. Ask:

■ **As you prepare for Christmas, what rough places in your spiritual life need to be smoothed out?**

■ **In what ways does your life get tangled like the light cords?**

■ **How can you "unpack" your life so it can become a beautiful decoration for the coming King?**

Close with a directed silent prayer. Pray: **Coming King, help us use these weeks before Christmas to prepare for you. Smooth out the rough places in our lives, especially** (pause for kids to silently finish the sentence). **Untangle the confusion and problems within, especially** (pause for kids to silently finish the sentence). **Come, Lord Jesus, into our lives this Christmas season. Make us ready to receive you. Amen.**

ISAIAH
40:28-31

THEME:
God gives us
strength.

SUMMARY:
Kids will help each other suc-
ceed at a difficult task in this
LEARNING GAME.

PREPARATION: You'll need a supply of heavy objects such as blocks,
books, or bricks. You can create
heavy objects by placing a bunch of
hymnals or other books in cardboard boxes. You'll also need masking tape and Bibles.

Before kids arrive, use masking
tape to mark off two separate 4-foot
diameter circles on the floor, at
least 20 feet apart (one can be in
another room). Place all the heavy
items in one of the circles.

W hen kids arrive, designate
three or four people to be the
"carriers" for this activity. Then give
the carriers the task of moving all the
heavy items from one circle to the
other. Before saying "go," tell the carriers they may not use their hands to
move the objects—they must slide
them using their feet or backs. Tell
other kids they may only watch and
cheer on the carriers. Caution kids to
be careful not to hurt themselves as
they move the heavy objects.

After the heavy items have been
moved, ask the carriers:

■ **What was it like to move all
these objects?**

■ **How did you feel at the end
of the activity?**

Have someone read aloud Isaiah
40:28-31. Then say: **Let's perform
this activity again. But this time
the rest of the class may help the
carriers move the items back to
the original circle, and people
who aren't carriers may use their
hands to help.**

After this part of the activity, ask:

■ **Why was moving the objects
the second time easier than the
first?**

■ **How is helping the carriers
like the way God promises to
help in Isaiah 40:28-31?**

Have kids each tell about a time
when they felt like God gave them
renewed energy or helped them
overcome tiredness. Then close by
having kids each call out one thing
they're thankful for that involved
God's help.

ISAIAH
42:6-7

THEME:
Being a light to
the world

SUMMARY:
Use this SKIT to help teenagers understand some of the
ways that Christians are God's
light to the world.

SHOW ME THE LIGHT

SCENE: Two people are trying to
find their way in the dark.

PROPS: Two flashlights, a bright-
colored T-shirt for Christian 3 to
wear, and Bibles for the discussion
after the skit.

CHARACTERS:
Carly and Dustin (lost and frustrated)
Christians 1, 2, and 3 (unsympathetic)
Christian 4 (warm and friendly)

SCRIPT

(Carly and Dustin are standing in the dark. Note: The darker the room, the more effective the skit will be.)

Carly: Wow! Now this is dark.

Dustin: Yeah, I know. It's impossible to see where you're going.

Carly: Seems like we've been running around in this pitch blackness for ages! I'm ready to give up. We never get anywhere! *(Sits on floor.)*

Dustin: *(Sighs.)* I'm with you on that one. *(Sits on floor.)*

Christian 1: *(Enters, trips over Carly and Dustin, and falls on floor.)* Hey, ouch! Let me up! You must be sinners. They're always sitting around in the dark. Well, here's a tract that tells you about God...

Dustin: But it's dark! We can't read in the dark!

Christian 1: ...and gives directions to my church. See ya 'round *(Stands and exits.)*

Carly: Big help he was. We don't need those things! We need a light!

Dustin: I know, I know. Let's at least stand up so we don't get walked on again.

Christian 2: *(Enters, stays on far side of stage. Speaks loudly.)* Sit down, you sinners!

Carly: Huh?

Christian 2: Yes, I mean you. You, wallowing in the depths of darkness! You, trying to pull faithful, godly people out of the light! Repent! Get down on your knees and beg for God's forgiveness.

Dustin: Uh, sir... We just need a light.

Christian 2: Repent, I tell you! Now let us pray... "Our Father, who art in heaven, hallowed be thy name..." *(Fades and exits.)*

Dustin: Another great help.

Carly: Wow! I'd rather be in the dark if he's in the light!

Dustin: No kidding. Hey, do you see that? It's a light! I know I saw it! Look, over there! Hey, you! You with the light!

Christian 3: *(Enters, with flashlight on, but under his shirt.)* Who...me? I-I-I don't have a light! You must be thinking of someone else.

Carly: We can see it right there! Please, you've got to help us!

Christian 3: N-no, um, I can't. It just looks like I have a light; it's really a...uh... It's a neon-colored T-shirt. Yeah, that's it! Look, I gotta go. I'm going to a big party, so, uh, you won't say anything about my li—I mean my neon-colored T-shirt—will you?

Dustin: What? We just need you to help us out of here!

Christian 3: Sorry, gotta go. *(Exits.)*

Carly: *(Sighs.)* He could've helped us! We were so close, Dustin.

Dustin: I know. I just don't understand people like that.

Christian 4: *(Enters with flashlight.)* Did I hear someone in here?

Carly: *(Excitedly)* Yeah, over here!

Christian 4: *(Walks over to them.)* Wow. Two of you in here! Did you get lost?

Dustin: We've been lost for... well... for a long, long time.

Christian 4: Then let's not waste a moment getting you out of here! Just hold onto my hand, and I'll lead the way. By the way, my name's Michael. What's yours?

Dustin: I'm Dustin, and this is Carly...

(Three exit, talking.)

Permission to use this skit from *Youth Worker's Encyclopedia: OT* granted for local church use. Copyright © Group Publishing, Inc., Box 481, Loveland, CO 80539.

If you use this skit as a discussion starter, here are possible questions:

■ **Which character in this skit do you relate to most? Why?**

■ **Why do you think Isaiah 42:6-7 describes God's followers as "light"?**

■ **How are Christians light in today's world?**

ISAIAH
49:13

THEME:
Compassion

SUMMARY:
In this PROJECT, kids will show compassion for needy people in their community.

PREPARATION: Arrange with local social service agencies for kids to help needy people in whatever way possible. This could include serving food at a soup kitchen, collecting and bringing clothes to homeless people, or winterizing homes for the elderly. Arrange the necessary transportation and have volunteers donate needed supplies. You'll also need Bibles.

Plan only service projects that can be completed in the amount of time you have available for your meeting and don't tell kids ahead of time what they'll be doing at this meeting.

When kids arrive, divide them into several groups and open the meeting by reading aloud Isaiah 49:13. Then ask kids to be silent as they head out on a compassion project. Tell kids not to speak to each other on the way to their destination or on the way back. Send different groups of kids to different service opportunities. Be sure kids spend at least an hour in their compassion activities.

Meet back at the church at a predetermined time. Then have members of different groups form new groups consisting of one person from each of the other groups. Have kids tell their new group members about their compassion projects. Then have groups discuss the following questions:

■ **What impacted you the most about your experience?**

■ **What was it like to show compassion to others?**

■ **How is the way you showed compassion like the way God shows us compassion? How is it unlike the way God shows us compassion?**

■ **Why is showing compassion a joyful activity?**

■ **What are practical ways to show compassion to those around us?**

ISAIAH
53:1-12

THEME:
The suffering servant

SUMMARY:
In this LEARNING GAME, kids will go on a scavenger hunt to find something that represents a king or royalty and learn the difference between earthly kings and the King of kings.

PREPARATION: You'll need five rose stems (or some other thorny branches) and Bibles.

Form teams of no more than five. Say: **The object of this scavenger hunt is to bring back items that represent a king or royalty. You may be as creative as you wish, but each team must bring back 10 representative items. I'll award points for each item that meets my test of royalty, and the winning team gets a prize.**

Allow 20 to 30 minutes for teams to go into the community and search for kingly items. Kids will probably choose things that symbolize kings as they've come to know them through history or popular media.

When teams return, have them each display their items. Discount all items that represent earthly kings (such as things with crowns, royal names, and so on). Award points only for items that might represent Jesus, "the suffering servant," as depicted in Isaiah 53:1-12 (such as thorns, lambs, whips, and torn cloths). Then award the thorny stems or branches to the winning team members. If no team gets a point, display the prizes anyway before moving on.

When kids begin to complain, have someone read aloud Isaiah 53:1-12. Then ask:

■ **How is the way you felt when I discounted your scavenger hunt items like the way the Israelites might've felt when their king was described as a suffering servant, rather than a powerful ruler?**

■ **Why was it important for Jesus to suffer and die?**

■ **What implications does Jesus' type of "kingliness" have on how we should live our lives?**

■ **Is it easy to live as a suffering servant? Why or why not?**

ISAIAH
55:1-2

THEME:
Run for the money.

SUMMARY:
In this LEARNING GAME, kids will compare riches of the world to the riches of God.

PREPARATION: Before the meeting, decorate the meeting room with play money. Tape the money under chairs; behind pictures; and on the ceiling, floor, and walls. The money should cover the room. Buy or bake a cake with a happy face on the top. You'll also need Bibles.

After the kids arrive, point out the money scattered around the room and the cake. Say: **The goal of this game is to collect as much money as possible in two minutes. Whoever collects the most can buy this cake with his or her money. You can steal money from others, but torn bills will not be counted. Go.**

After two minutes, shout "stop" and have kids sit down to count their money. Declare a winner, take his or her money, and hand over the cake. Form a circle and ask the winner:

■ **How did you feel when you won?**

■ **Did it make you happy? Why or why not?**

Ask everyone:

■ **How did you feel when you were scrambling to horde the money?**

■ **How did you feel when someone took your money?**

■ **Were you disappointed that you didn't win? Why or why not?**

■ **How is this game similar to our society? How is it different?**

Read aloud Isaiah 55:1-2. Ask:

■ **What rewards do the rich enjoy? What rewards do the poor enjoy?**

■ **What are some "riches" that money can't buy?**

■ **How are God's riches different from the world's riches?**

■ **How can we gain God's riches this week?**

ISAIAH
55:1-13

THEME:
God's goodness

SUMMARY:
Kids will perform a CREATIVE READING based on Isaiah 55:1-13.

PREPARATION: You'll need Bibles and enough photocopies of the "Creative Reading for Isaiah 55:1-13" handout (p. 309) for everyone.

Have guys and girls take turns reading their lines in the following adaptation of Isaiah 55:1-13. You might want to use this reading in a church service that focuses on God's goodness. For added emphasis, have kids with musical talent perform a quiet accompaniment while kids read their parts.

ISAIAH
60:1-22

THEME:
The glory of the kingdom

SUMMARY:
Kids will prepare a PARTY for the whole church that illustrates God's promise to Jerusalem.

CREATIVE READING FOR ISAIAH 55:1-13

Guys: When we're thirsty...

Girls: God offers us drink. If we have no money...

Guys: God gives us food.

Girls: When we listen to God...

Guys: We can be filled with the richness of God's spirit.

Girls: If we listen to God...

Guys: God will bless us.

Girls: We must look to God...

Guys: Before it's too late. We must call upon God...

Girls: When God is near.

Guys: We must stop doing wrong...

Girls: And return to God. For God's ways aren't like our ways...

Guys: God's thoughts are higher than ours.

Girls: Just as rain and snow return to water the ground...

Guys: So God's words return only after doing God's will.

Girls: So we must be joyful...

Guys: And sing praises to God...

All: And remember God's promise of peace. Amen.

PREPARATION: Have kids publicize this party in advance so the whole congregation can come. You'll need enough food (including dessert) and beverages for all attendees, party supplies (paper products), and Bibles.

Form committees to plan and coordinate a party for the whole church, illustrating the glory of God's future kingdom. Have kids focus their plans on the picture Isaiah paints of the new Jerusalem in Isaiah 60:1-22. For example, kids could use a camel theme to decorate the walls or bring stuffed sheep as centerpieces for the tables.

Have one committee prepare a reading or devotion based on Isaiah 60:1-22 for the party. Have another committee prepare a skit depicting one section of the passage. And have another committee choose and prepare to lead everyone in songs proclaiming the glory of God's kingdom.

Sometime during the party (perhaps during the meal), ask attendees to discuss how heaven's riches will compare to the descriptions of Jerusalem in Isaiah 60:1-22. After the meal, have each committee present its prepared portion of the party.

Close the event by serving rich desserts, such as chocolate cake or cheesecake.

ISAIAH
65:17-25

THEME:
Heaven

SUMMARY:
Kids will attend a RETREAT as if they're already in heaven.

PREPARATION: Involve kids in the preparation for this event as much as possible. Their feedback up front is an important part of this retreat. You'll also need Bibles.

Work with kids to create a schedule of activities for a retreat based on the theme of heaven. Have kids help you choose activities, meals, and devotions that they might associate with the picture they have of heaven. For example, if kids believe there will be lots of music in heaven, have them plan plenty of singing times.

Have kids choose the foods they find most "heavenly" for their retreat meals. Have them play games that celebrate each other's gifts, rather than games that single people out as winners and losers.

Use Isaiah 65:17-25 as the focal point of this retreat. When kids leave for the retreat center, tell them they're to act as if this experience is a glimpse of what heaven will really be like. Encourage kids to act accordingly toward each other.

After the retreat, have kids explain what parts were most heavenly and what parts were least heavenly. Encourage kids to find ways to experience God's future kingdom today—in their relationships with others and their daily living.

ISAIAH
66:15-16

THEME:
God's judgment

SUMMARY:
In this OBJECT LESSON, kids will watch as paper "people" are destroyed.

PREPARATION: You'll need paper, tape, markers, a fire-resistant trash can, and matches. You'll also need Bibles.

Place paper, tape, and markers on tables and have kids use the supplies to create paper people. Encourage kids to base these people on friends at school (without actually naming them or telling anyone who the people represent).

When kids have finished making their paper people, have them describe one or more character traits these people have in real life. For example, someone might say that their person is "outgoing" or "a good friend."

After each paper person has been introduced, randomly collect 60 to 70 percent of the people and place them in a fire-resistant trash can, then set them on fire.

Have someone read aloud Isaiah 66:15-16. Ask:

■ **How did you feel when I burned your paper people?**

■ **How is this activity an illustration of the Bible passage?**

■ **How does this passage apply to our relationships with friends like those represented by the paper people?**

■ **How can we reach out to our non-Christian friends and encourage them to avoid God's judgment by trusting in Jesus?**

Close with a time of silent prayer, asking God to open non-Christian friends' eyes and ears to Christ's message of love and salvation.

JEREMIAH

" 'I say this because I know what I am planning for you,' says the Lord. 'I have good plans for you, not plans to hurt you. I will give you hope and a good future.' "

Jeremiah 29:11

JEREMIAH
1:6-9

THEME:
Proclaiming God's message

SUMMARY:
This CREATIVE PRAYER will empower teenagers to work in God's kingdom in spite of their feelings of inadequacy.

PREPARATION: You'll need Bibles.

Ask kids to think of something that frightens them about the Christian life or something they feel they can't do because they're too young or inexperienced (such as teach Sunday school, tell others about their faith, or read Scripture in worship services). Share an experience or feeling of your own to get things rolling.

When kids have had a few minutes to consider this, have them open their Bibles to Jeremiah 1:6-9. Read the passage aloud as kids read along. Then form pairs to discuss the following questions:

■ **How does Jeremiah respond to God's request to tell others about his message?**

■ **Has God ever asked you to do something that made you feel like Jeremiah did? If so, what did you do?**

Form a circle and have teenagers pray together about aspects of serving God that frighten them. End the prayer time by praying: **God, sometimes the things you ask us to do are difficult for us.** We don't feel worthy to bring your message of love and grace to others. It's overwhelming to be your messengers. Sometimes people don't want to listen. Sometimes we can't find the right words or actions. Give us strength to do your will and tell others of your love.

After each teenager prays about a fear or trial (specific or general), have the group repeat in unison God's words from Jeremiah 1:7-8: "Don't say, 'I am only a boy.' You must go everywhere I send you, and you must say everything I tell you to say. Don't be afraid of anyone, because I am with you to protect you."

JEREMIAH
5:1

THEME:
Honesty

SUMMARY:
Use this SKIT to show kids that true honesty is a rare thing.

ASK ME NO QUESTIONS

SCENE: A roving reporter searches for an honest person.

PROPS: A baseball cap decorated with foil to serve as a "lie detector," a microphone (real or fake), and a buzzer of some sort—this could be a youth group member who can make an obnoxious buzzing sound. You'll also need Bibles for the discussion after the skit.

CHARACTERS:
Sally
Jean
Marv

SCRIPT

Sally: *(Speaking into the microphone)* Good evening. Sally Smooth from News 7 here with an unusual experiment. *(Holds up cap with foil attached.)* We have obtained this portable lie detector from the experts at State University, and I'm going to use it to attempt to find an honest man... er, woman... er, person! Now, let's see, let me check this out. *(She slips the cap on.)* My name is Louise. *(A buzzer is heard. She looks pleased.)* As you can see, I can only say that my name is Sally. *(Waits for buzz. There is none.)* I am a reporter. *(Silence.)* I am married. *(Buzz.)* I'm engaged to be married. *(Buzz.)* I am going steady. *(Buzz. She looks annoyed.)* I am dating a nice gentleman off and on. *(Buzz. She speaks somewhat haughtily.)* I am currently enjoying a single lifestyle. *(Silence. She is relieved.)* Oh, good, here comes someone now. *(Sally removes the cap as Jean enters.)*

Sally: Excuse me, miss. We're looking for an honest person. Do you consider yourself honest?

Jean: Why, of course!

Sally: Would you mind wearing our lie detector and answering a few simple questions?

Jean: No, not at all.
(Sally puts the cap on Jean.)

Jean: What are the questions?

Sally: What is your name?

Jean: Jean.

Sally: What is your occupation?

Jean: I'm an electrical engineer.

Sally: Do you ever lie?

Jean: No. *(Buzz.)* Well, not knowingly. *(Buzz.)* I mean, not that ever hurts anyone! *(Buzz. She tears off the cap and hands it back to Sally.)* Get this thing away from me! *(She walks hurriedly off, angry.)*

Sally: *(To viewing audience)* Hmm... Well, let's try again, shall we? *(Marv enters.)*

Sally: Excuse me, sir. Sally Smooth, News 7. Could I ask you a few questions?

Marv: I s'pose.

Sally: Would you put on this cap? It's a lie detector for an experiment we're conducting.

Marv: I s'pose. *(He puts on cap.)*

Sally: OK, what is your name?

Marv: Marv.

Sally: And your job?

Marv: I'm a baker.

Sally: Do you make a sizable income?

Marv: Sure. The benefits aren't much, but I make lots of dough! *(Buzz.)* What was that? I was just trying to get a "rise" out of you by using a little bakery humor! *(Buzz.)*

Sally: Very little, it seems.

Marv: *(Takes off cap.)* I don't have to put up with insults. I'm gonna get my buns out of here! *(He exits.)*

Sally: Well, so far it looks like I'm not having any luck. *(To audience)* Would any of you like to try? *(She freezes.)*

If you use this skit as a discussion starter, here are possible questions:

■ How would you feel about wearing the lie detector cap? Why?

■ Why do you think honesty is such a rare quality?

■ Read Jeremiah 5:1. What if your life depended upon your honesty? How would that change the way you are now?

■ How does honesty affect our relationships with others? with God?

JEREMIAH 8:18–9:1

THEME:
Speaking boldly against wrong behavior

SUMMARY:
Through this SKIT, kids will experience the discomfort of bringing warnings to others as Jeremiah was called to do.

TO SPEAK OR NOT TO SPEAK

SCENE: Two high school students are leaving a schoolyard.

PROPS: You'll need a few school books and Bibles for the discussion after the skit.

CHARACTERS:
Matt
Jay

SCRIPT
(Matt and Jay are talking as they leave school. Both are carrying books.)

Matt: Hey, a bunch of us are going out tonight to soap the windows and slash the tires on my math teacher's car. Wanna come?

Jay: Why would you wanna do that?

Matt: He said he was going to flunk me if I acted up in class anymore. So I got a bunch of the guys to go with me to do his car. He'll get the message not to mess with me.

Jay: Do you really think that's a good solution? Why not just act human in class?

Matt: Whose side are you on anyway?

Jay: I'm not taking sides. I'm just asking you to think. There might be an easier way to get what you want.

Matt: What I want is to see this guy scared.

Jay: I thought you were brighter than that. You won't pass the class this way, and you probably won't even scare him. You'll just make him more upset than he already is.

Matt: Well, maybe I want to do it anyway.

Jay: Did you ever stop and think that maybe acting like that was just wrong?

Matt: No, but I'm sure you're gonna tell me.

Jay: Just listen for a minute. What you want to do hurts other people, and that's wrong in God's eyes. How would you like it if someone soaped your car?

Matt: And who are you to decide what's right or wrong?

Jay: It's not my job; it's God's. I'm just conveying the message. Think about it next time you pray.

Matt: What makes you so sure I ever pray or that I need God for anything?

Jay: Tell me you didn't pray over that math test, or when your mom was sick last month, or when you busted up your last car and broke your leg. Just remember, relationships go two ways. God is there all the time, not just when it's convenient. *(Freeze.)*

If you use this skit as a discussion starter, here are possible questions:

■ **How does it feel to be in a position where you need to say difficult things to another person?**

■ **Have you ever been put in that position? If so, what happened?**

Explain that Jeremiah was in the position of telling God's people that punishment was coming because they'd been unfaithful to God. Then have someone read Jeremiah 8:18–9:1. Ask:

■ **How is Jeremiah's situation like those in our skit?**

■ **How is Jeremiah's situation like the real-life experience you have when telling others a difficult message?**

JEREMIAH 15:10-21

THEME:
Serving God in tough times

SUMMARY:
In this MUSIC IDEA, kids will write and perform an original blues song or take passages from Jeremiah and set them to music.

PREPARATION: You'll need Bibles, pens, paper, and some source of music (recorded music, a piano, or a guitar) for kids to perform their songs.

Say: **We've all discovered by now that serving God is not always easy or fun. This was also true centuries ago for prophets like Jeremiah. Jeremiah spent a lot of time "singing the blues" about the way God's people would not be faithful.**

Ask kids to read Jeremiah 15:10-21. Other passages which might be helpful include Jeremiah 4:19-26; 18:19-23; and 20:7-12. Let teenagers know that these passages are printed as poetry rather than prose. Like the poetic lyrics of songs today, these may have been sung originally.

Form groups of no more than five. Have them paraphrase Jeremiah's lament and put it to music or write their own blues songs about the things that trouble them personally. Then have the groups perform their blues songs for everyone.

JEREMIAH
18:1-6

THEME:
Being molded by
God

SUMMARY:
In this ADVENTURE, kids will visit a potter, watch clay being molded, and draw parallels to Christian life.

PREPARATION: Make arrangements with a local Christian potter, or an artist who works with clay, to bring in your group to observe him or her. Explain your purpose in bringing the group and request that the artist be prepared to give short explanations of the various steps in creating something with clay. Have the potter read the Jeremiah passage and ask him or her to "remold" the piece, as Jeremiah describes, for the kids to see. (Or you can read the passage while the potter molds.) You'll need Bibles and transportation to and from the potter's studio.

Before visiting the potter, have the group read Jeremiah 18:1-6 together. Car pool to the potter's studio and, when the group arrives, give a brief introduction about the day's activity. Encourage teenagers to observe and listen while the clay is molded.

When the potter is finished, allow time for questions then ask kids to identify things about molding clay that remind them of life as a Christian. Here are a few comparisons to get things rolling if kids get stuck:

• The process of molding involves action that can seem almost violent at times. The artist must exert some force upon the clay if it is to become what he or she envisions it to be.

• Tension between clay's cohesion to itself and the centrifugal force of the potter's wheel is like the cohesion of the Christian community and the need to go outward (pulled by God) to share the message with the rest of the world.

• God can choose to mold us into something different than we had expected, as the potter remolds the clay into something new.

• The pottery becomes stronger when it is heated in a kiln, as we become stronger after times when the "heat is turned up" on us.

If possible, give kids a chance to mold some clay before you leave. Have a closing prayer together around the pottery wheel.

JEREMIAH
18:1-6

THEME:
Being molded by
God

SUMMARY:
In this OBJECT LESSON, kids will compare wet, moldable clay and old, dry clay to people who are or aren't moldable by God.

PREPARATION: You'll need Bibles

and two samples of clay, one wet and pliable and the other dry and hard. You'll also need a handful of good clay for each person.

Form a circle. Pass around two samples of clay—one that's soft and pliable and one that's hard and crusty. Say: **Like this hard clay, we often resist God's will because of our pride, willfulness, and fears. We're hardheaded and hardhearted, like cement. We don't trust God. We won't let go of our egos. We need to be ourselves and to define our individuality. Yet, the Creator wants us to surrender to his guidance—to be flexible, to stretch and grow like the soft clay. Through the living water of Christ, we stay moist and pliable. We need to remember that God is the potter, and we are the clay.**

Give each teenager a handful of clay. Have kids mold a symbol of how they see themselves in relationship with God. For example, someone might shape a ball and say that he or she tries to roll easily in the direction God points. While the kids are shaping their clay, read aloud Jeremiah 18:1-6.

Have each person explain his or her clay creation. Then place the clay symbols in the center of your circle. Say: **We individually have a relationship with God, and we, as a group, have a relationship with God. Let's commit to listen and trust God to mold us in his image and guide us through life.**

Close by praying that God will mold your group like a potter molds clay.

JEREMIAH
19:1-11; 27:1-7, 12; 31:7-14

THEME:
Communicating with one another

SUMMARY:
Kids will communicate with poetic language in this DEVOTION.

PREPARATION: You'll need Bibles.

EXPERIENCE
Form pairs. Tell teenagers that for the next 10 minutes they must communicate with their partners using only poetic, descriptive language. This will be difficult at first, but they'll get the hang of it. Have pairs discuss the events of the past week. You might suggest examples like "When he came to pick me up, he was smiling like a Cheshire cat" or "I felt like a BMW racing down the highway when, all of a sudden, this Ford pickup truck sideswiped me." Some of the kids' phrases will sound corny or melodramatic and produce grins and laughter, and others may be very meaningful or serious.

RESPONSE
Ask pairs to discuss the following questions:
■ **What are different ways people communicate?**
■ **What are different ways God communicates with us?**
Kids might suggest that God communicates through the words

of the prophets and other people, dreams, object lessons, miracles, and the Bible. After discussing their answers, ask:

■ **How did it feel to communicate through poetic language?**

Say: **God's words are recorded in many different forms, including poetry. There is a great deal of poetry and allegory in the book of Jeremiah.**

Assign pairs one of the following passages to read as an example of the poetic language in Jeremiah 19:1-11; 27:1-7, 12; 31:7-14. When they're finished reading, ask:

■ **What's the most unique way someone has ever tried to communicate with you?**

■ **What's the most unique way God has ever communicated with you?**

■ **How did you react to these different ways of communicating?**

■ **Have you ever seen the gospel communicated in a unique way? If so, what was it and what was your reaction?**

CLOSING

Pray the following prayer together: **God, there are many ways in which you speak to us and many ways other people speak your love and grace to us, with and without words. Help us to listen carefully and be receptive so we can learn from other people and from you.**

JEREMIAH 29:1, 4-11

THEME:
Seeking peace

SUMMARY:
Kids will write letters of encouragement in this AFFIRMATION.

PREPARATION: You'll need pens, paper, envelopes, and Bibles.

Read Jeremiah 29:1, 4-11 together. Ask teenagers to describe Jeremiah's circumstances in this passage. For further background information, have them read Jeremiah 52:12-16 or check a Bible dictionary or commentary.

Say: **Sometimes life brings difficult times and situations that make us miserable. We need to encourage one another through those times and help each other find new strength through our common faith.**

Ask kids to think of something in their lives right now that's uncomfortable and makes it difficult for them to feel peace, such as moving to a new town, being dragged to a formal dinner with parents, taking a difficult class, or trying out for a sports team.

Have each teenager describe his or her situation for the whole group. (Some kids may want to be vague about their situations due to abusive problems or personal issues. That's OK. Encourage them to say as much as they wish and no more. Remind everyone that God's peace is always available to us and that no outside circumstances can pull us away from God.)

After each teenager speaks, assign another teenager to write a brief letter of encouragement to the teenager who shared his or her situation. When everyone has finished speaking and all responses are written, have teenagers deliver their encouraging letters. Ask kids to pray for the people needing encouragement throughout the coming week or month.

If you have more time, ask kids to write letters to their future selves. Say: **Pretend you can look into your future and see difficult times ahead. Write yourself a letter of encouragement to help you get through those times and look toward better days.**

JEREMIAH 29:13

THEME:
God's presence

SUMMARY:
Kids will realize that God is always present in this LEARNING GAME.

PREPARATION: You'll need a dozen sewing needles (plus enough for each person to have one), paper, pencils, Bibles, and a small magnifying glass as a prize.

Before the meeting begins, hide a dozen sewing needles in the room. Make it tough by hiding the needles in cracks in the wall, in a chalkboard eraser with only the tip showing, or in acoustical-tile ceiling. Be creative in your hiding places.

When kids arrive, have them search the room for the needles. When they find the needles, have them make mental notes of the hiding places but not tell other kids. After about 10 minutes, bring the kids together and reveal the hiding places. Present a magnifying glass to the person who found the most needles.

Have group members think about what they were feeling as they searched for the needles. Ask:

■ **How is this experience like the times you seek God?**

■ **How is the presence of the difficult-to-see needles like God's presence?**

Read Jeremiah 29:13 and ask:

■ **How many of you have had an experience of seeking and finding God? What was that experience like?**

■ **What do you think will happen to you if you seek God?**

■ **How do you seek God?**

Give each person a sheet of paper, a pencil, and a needle. Ask kids to stick the needles into their papers then write, "Search, and you will find" (Luke 11:9). Have kids take their papers home as a reminder of God's presence every moment, every day, in each one of their lives.

JEREMIAH
31:10-13

THEME:
God blesses us.

SUMMARY:
In this PROJECT, kids will rejoice in God's goodness by planning a worship service.

PREPARATIONS: Arrange with your pastor to set aside a day for kids to participate in, and perhaps conduct, most of the worship service. In churches following a three-year liturgical cycle, the first Sunday after Christmas in year C contains Jeremiah 31:10-13.

As a group, read together Jeremiah 31:10-13. Ask kids what worship activities this passage brings to mind. They'll likely picture dancing, singing, playing instruments, and similar activities. Remind them that God wants us to worship with joy and that the Jews (including Jesus) were a people who sang, danced, and celebrated their identity as God's people with great joy and pride.

Discuss with the teenagers what talents they can offer in worship. Perhaps someone reads well, another person has a beautiful singing voice, while another is an accomplished dancer. Work together to create a worship service of readings (including the text from Jeremiah), music, and dance, if possible. You may wish to leave the preaching to your pastor, unless you have someone who is willing and able to take on that

responsibility. After the worship experience, ask:

■ **How did it feel to use God's blessings—our special gifts and talents—to serve him?**

■ **In what other ways could you use those blessings to help others? to praise God?**

■ **How did it feel to lead others in worship?**

■ **How was this experience like your usual worship? How was it unlike your usual worship?**

■ **Did you feel different about yourself, the Christian community, or God during this worship experience? Explain.**

JEREMIAH
31:31-34

THEME:
God's covenant

SUMMARY:
In this AFFIRMATION, kids will understand how God's covenant is already written on their hearts.

PREPARATION: You'll need inspirational stickers that will remind kids of their relationship with God (such as ones that read "Our God Is Awesome") and Bibles.

Read Jeremiah 31:31-34 together. Ask for teenagers' initial impressions of what it means to have God's covenant written on their hearts. Read the following scenario to them and ask them what they believe would be the right thing to do. Ask for teenagers' immediate gut reactions, keeping God's grace in mind.

Say: **A new student joins your English class. During class, some of the other students are making fun of her clothing. After class, she bumps into you on her way out the door and drops her books. You . . .**

After kids have given different answers, say: **There are two kinds of agreements. In the first one, each person honors the agreement because, if it isn't honored, there are legal consequences. In the second, the agreement is honored because the people care for one another and do not want to cause the other any pain.**

Ask kids to relate stories of times in their lives when they chose to "do the right thing" just because they knew it was right. As they tell their stories, give each a sticker. Explain that these stickers will remind them that they're special people who have God's covenant written on their hearts.

Then point out the marriage imagery in this passage and ask kids to compare our relationship with God to a marriage. Then ask:

■ **Which kind of relationship did God want to have with Israel and with us?**

■ **Which kind do you feel you have with God?**

Read Jeremiah 31:31-34 again. Close with a prayer for God to write his will upon our hearts and to keep us in relationships with him—and with one another—that are based on love.

JEREMIAH 42:19–43:7

THEME:
Deciphering God's will

SUMMARY:
Through this DEVOTION, kids will learn how to decide who's really telling them about God's will.

PREPARATION: You'll need to prepare four slips of paper with instructions on how to deal with a fictional strained friendship. The slips should read:

• Run to the nearest person and make up gossip about your friend.

• Sit in a corner and pout because your friend is being so unreasonable.

• Jump up and down screaming, "Things never work the way I want them to."

• Find the person you're fighting with (in this activity), hug him or her, and say, "I'm sorry we had a misunderstanding. Let's talk it over."

You'll also need chalk and a chalkboard or a marker and a large piece of drawing paper to write down the questions that will be discussed in the closing. Prepare the questions before the meeting. Don't forget Bibles.

EXPERIENCE
Read Jeremiah 42:19–43:7 together. Go around the room and have kids quickly answer the following questions:

■ **How do you decide what God's will is for you?**

■ **Who do you trust to help you know God's will?**

Distribute the four slips of paper to four volunteers and tell them to spread out around the room. Those without a slip of paper are to go around to those with paper slips and ask what God's will is concerning a fictional strained friendship. For example, kids might ask a teenager with a paper slip, "What am I supposed to do? My friend and I just aren't getting along." Have each teenager holding a paper slip suggest the advice on his or her slip. Encourage kids to go around and ask all four people with paper slips what they should do about their fictional friendships.

RESPONSE

When everyone has finished, ask kids to be seated. Form trios and have them discuss the following questions:

■ **Which of the messages would actually be helpful in solving the problem?**

■ **Which of the messages really seemed to be from God?**

■ **How did you decide which was really God's will?**

■ **Looking back at the Jeremiah passage, why do you think the people did not listen to Jeremiah?**

■ **How could they know that a prophet speaks for God?**

CLOSING

Say: **Many voices try to tell us what God's will is. We hear them on television, on the street, in church, or any num-**ber of places. Some truly come from God, and others don't. To decide which voice is which, we can ask a few questions (these should be written on the chalkboard or drawing paper):

■ **Does this instruction involve a great personal gain for the speaker (in terms of money, power, and so on)?**

■ **Does this message make the cross of Christ unnecessary? That is, does "salvation" come through some other means?**

■ **Is this good news for (are God's arms open to) everyone or just a select few?**

■ **Is this something that builds up or destroys people and relationships?**

Pray together for God to help us discern his will and recognize "false prophets."

JEREMIAH
52:1-30

THEME:
Facing consequences

SUMMARY:

In this LEARNING GAME, kids will experience consequences for simple things they've said or done in the past then talk about consequences in their relationships with God.

PREPARATION: You'll need masking tape, silly hats, costume make-up, snacks (cookies or doughnuts—enough for each person to have one), and Bibles.

Place the hats, makeup, and snacks on a table that is visible and convenient for kids to reach. Mark off exactly enough seats for everyone in the class with a masking tape X. If possible, make some of the marks on chairs, couches, the floor, or other unusual places.

When kids arrive, ask them to each take a seat on one of the X markings. Explain that you'll be asking a series of questions and, in answer to each, kids must obey the commands that follow each question.

• If you brushed your teeth this morning, move one seat to the right. If it's taken, sit on that person's lap.

• If you've read a book, cover to cover, in the past month, get a snack and return to the place you were sitting.

• If you didn't wear shoes with laces today, put on a funny hat.

• If you ate breakfast today, move one seat to the right.

• If you prayed before bed last night, get a snack (if you don't have one) and move one seat to the right (no matter how many people are sitting there).

• If you read your Bible this morning, get a snack (if you don't have one) and move two seats to the left.

• If you told a family member that you love them in the past 24 hours, use the makeup to draw a mustache on the person to your left.

• If you told someone in the past week that you're a Christian,

move one seat to the right.

• If you've done something nice for someone in the past 24 hours, get a snack—but hop on one foot to get it and get back.

• If you've written to a family member (aunt, uncle, grandparent, and so on) in the past month, move one seat to the left.

• If you said no to something you knew was wrong in the past week, trade seats with the person to your right.

• If you haven't gotten a snack yet, get one and move two seats to the left (no matter how many people are sitting there).

When you're finished giving these instructions, have kids take their original seats and find a partner. Have partners read Jeremiah 52 together. Then ask:

■ God repeatedly warned the people of Israel not to worship idols. Many people did these things anyway. What were the consequences of their actions?

■ Imagine what it must have been like to have lived in Jerusalem at the time when it fell. What sorts of things would you feel?

■ Have you ever felt like you did something that God couldn't forgive? Explain. (Assure teenagers that nothing is beyond God's grace.)

■ Knowing that you're indeed forgiven for anything you've ever asked God's forgiveness for, how do you feel?

Assure kids that God later brought the people of Jerusalem back to their homeland and gave them another chance to be faithful. Then say: Though there are consequences for the things we do, our God is loving and forgiving. As Christians, we can be sure that through Jesus' death and resurrection, God opens the door for us to ask forgiveness for anything we've done, and it will be granted in Jesus' name.

Close with a prayer of thanksgiving for God's grace. Psalm 100 or Psalm 103 would be appropriate for this.

LAMENTATIONS

"But I have hope when I think of this:
The Lord's love never ends; his mercies
never stop."

Lamentations 3:21-22

LAMENTATIONS
1:1-11

THEME:

The consequences of sin

SUMMARY:
In this LEARNING GAME, kids will discover the negative consequences of sin when they're punished for telling a lie.

PREPARATION: You'll need paper, pencils, and Bibles.

Ask for three or four contestants to participate in a new game show called *Lies or Consequences.* Say: **The object of *Lies or Consequences* is for the contestants to fool you, our studio audience, by telling two stories: one that's true and one that's false. The audience must guess which story is false. If the contestant can't fool the audience, he or she must** (pause, then loudly) **FACE THE CONSEQUENCES!** Take the contestants out of the room. Tell them to each think of a personal story that's completely true—something that actually happened to them but is hard to believe. They should also make up a second story that's completely false but sounds like it's possible. Give them about five minutes. Then bring them back in and have them sit in chairs in front of the group. Introduce each contestant and welcome them to the game.

Then, one by one, have contestants tell both stories. After each contestant is finished, have the audience (your group members) vote on which story is false—the majority wins. If the audience is right, the contestant must "face the consequences." Give the audience one minute to decide what those consequences will be and to then carry out what they decide. Do the same for all the contestants.

After the game, say: **In a game like this, the consequences for doing something wrong are clear-cut and swift. But is that the way it is in real life?**

Have someone read aloud Lamentations 1:1-11. Then ask:

■ **Do you think God's punishment for Jerusalem's sins was fair? Why or why not?**

■ **Is it important for the consequences of sin to be fair? Why or why not?**

■ **Is it possible to sin and never face negative consequences? Why or why not?**

Have kids form groups of three, then give each group paper and a pencil. Have them first brainstorm a list of sins they see people committing around them every day and then list what consequences, if any, they've seen. After five or 10 minutes, have groups each pick a spokesperson to tell about their lists. Then ask:

■ **Why is it that some people can sin and seem to get away with it, but others have to pay for their sins?**

■ **What consequences of sin have you experienced?**

■ **How did you feel as a result of those consequences?**

■ **How did you respond to those consequences?**

■ **What do you know about God's character and personality based on what we read in Lamentations?**

Form a circle to close in prayer. Ask kids to each say, "And so do I" after you pray this prayer if they believe it applies to them, too. Pray: **Lord, please forgive me for the ways I sin against you— I know that I sometimes choose against what you want me to do.**

After kids finish responding, say: **Thank you, Lord, for your cleansing forgiveness.**

LAMENTATIONS 2:1-10

THEME:
When we sin, God feels angry.

SUMMARY:
By consciously breaking the rules of a game in this DEVOTION, kids will learn how God feels about sin.

PREPARATION: You'll need whatever sports equipment you can gather, paper, markers, newsprint, any old games you might have at home, and Bibles.

EXPERIENCE

Ask for three or four volunteers to help create a new game for your group. Take them out of the room and tell them they have 15 minutes to devise a new game for the rest of the group to play. They can use any, all, or none of the materials you've provided for them. Help guide kids in developing the game by asking them to complete the following sentences:

•The object of the game is...
•The rules of the game are...
•The penalty for breaking a rule is...

While your volunteers are creating their new game, say to the rest of the kids: **You're about to play a new game invented by our volunteers. They'll tell you what the rules are, but just between you and me, you don't have to follow those rules. Just do whatever you want. But make sure the game leaders don't realize you're breaking the rules on purpose. Let's see who can be the sneakiest rule breaker!**

Have the volunteers come in and explain their game. Have your kids play the game for about 15 minutes. Then have everyone sit down.

RESPONSE

Ask:

■ **Game makers, how did you feel when some group members ignored the rules? Explain.**

■ **How did the rule breakers affect the game?**

■ **If we had followed the rules, would you have enjoyed the game more? Why or why not?**

Have someone read aloud Lamentations 2:1-10. Then ask:

■ **What made God angry? Why?**

■ **Have you ever felt like God was angry with you? What was that like?**

■ **What's the best way to respond to God after we've sinned?**

CLOSING

Give kids a few minutes of quiet to think about God's reaction to sin and to confess their sins privately to God.

LAMENTATIONS
3:14-26

THEME:
God's mercy

SUMMARY:
At this PARTY, kids will be treated like outlaws, and they'll remind one another that God is merciful toward those who love and seek him.

PREPARATION: You'll need to make enough photocopies of the "Wanted Poster" handout (p. 330) for each person to have one. You'll also need an instant-print camera and enough film to take a picture of each person. And you'll need glue, red markers, paper, pencils, bottles of root beer, cups, and Bibles. Tell kids you're going to have a "Wild West night" and that they should dress up as outlaws or bandits.

As kids arrive, take an instant-print picture of each one. Ask for three volunteers to be part of the "sheriff's posse" for the night. Then have kids play Wild West games, such as "quick-draw" Pictionary, using western words such as "sheriff," "gun," "cowboy," "horse," "tumbleweed," or "bandit." You could also hold Wild West contests for best outlaw impersonation, best outlaw costume, or fastest root beer chugging. (For more Wild West game ideas, get a copy of the October/November 1993 issue of JR. HIGH MINISTRY Magazine, available from Group Publishing, Inc., Box 481, Loveland, CO 80539.)

While the kids are playing Wild West games, gather the members of your sheriff's posse and take them to a separate room. Have them glue the instant-print pictures onto the "Wanted Posters" and make up crazy outlaw names for each person, such as Slow-Draw Jeremy.

When your posse finishes, have them rush into the game room, hand out the "Wanted Posters," arrest everyone, and take them to jail (a nearby room that's much smaller than your meeting room).

Have one of your posse members read aloud Lamentations 3:14-26. Then ask:

■ **How does it feel to be in jail for your "sins"?**

■ **How would you feel if this really were a jail and you really had to pay for all the wrong things you've done?**

■ **How are those feelings like the feelings the writer of Lamentations was experiencing?**

■ **What does it mean to have mercy on someone?**

■ **Do you have as much hope for God's mercy as the writer of Lamentations? Why or why not?**

Have kids form pairs and give each pair a red marker (make sure they each have their own posters). One at a time, have partners read aloud Lamentations 3:21-25 to each

(continued on p. 331)

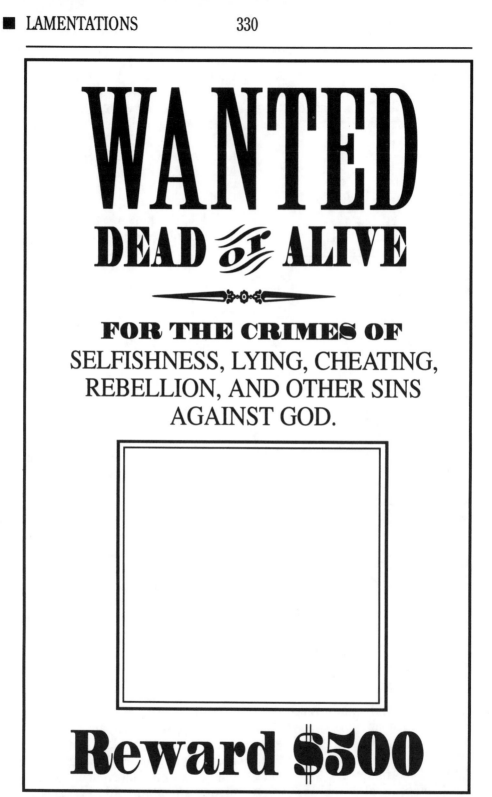

other, then use the red marker to write over the sins on the poster these words: "Pardoned by God's mercy."

Close by singing a song about God's mercy, such as "Great is Thy Faithfulness" or "Change My Heart, Oh God."

LAMENTATIONS 3:55-58

THEME:

God answers those who ask for help.

SUMMARY:
In this PROJECT, kids will keep a prayer journal for one month to track how God answers their prayers.

PREPARATION: You'll need a three-ring binder filled with paper that can be used to record your group members' prayer requests for at least one month. Label the binder "Our Prayer Journal." Make five columns on each page and title them "Name," "Date," "Request," "Answer," and "Date Answered." You'll also need Bibles and pencils.

Read aloud Lamentations 3:55-58. Then say: **Today we'll begin an exciting new prayer project. At the next three meetings, we'll spend about 15 minutes sharing our prayer requests and praying for one another. At the fourth meeting, we'll spend 30 minutes talking about the answers to our prayers.**

Show kids the prayer journal and ask for a volunteer recorder (at each of the first three meetings, ask for a different recorder). Ask kids to think about what's going on in their lives, or in the world around them, and then call out prayer requests. Have the recorder write each one in the journal. Tell kids who are uncomfortable calling out prayer requests to write their requests in the journal after your meeting.

After 10 minutes, have kids form small groups by joining with those who voiced prayer requests. Each person who called out a request should be in a group. Then have groups take five minutes to pray for their group members' requests.

Throughout the month, tell kids they can add prayer requests to the journal and record answers to those prayers in the appropriate column.

Each week, ask kids if God has answered any of the previous week's prayers. Remind kids that God's answers may not always coincide with our answers. At the fourth meeting, have a volunteer read aloud the prayer requests and answers. Then ask:

■ **Were you surprised by the answers to prayer? Why or why not?**

■ **How did God answer our prayers?**

■ **How has your perspective about prayer changed because of this project?**

■ **How are you different because of this project?**

Close by thanking God for his goodness in answering our prayers.

LAMENTATIONS 5:15-21

THEME:
Repentance

SUMMARY:
In this DEVOTION, kids will experience repentance as they turn from their own way and commit to following God.

PREPARATION: You'll need a 3×5 card and a pencil for each person, a rope or a few old sheets tied together, two cardboard signs titled "God's Way" and "My Way," a roll of masking tape, and Bibles.

EXPERIENCE

Form two equal teams for a Tug of War competition. Tape the "God's Way" sign to the wall on one side of the room and the "My Way" sign to the wall on the other side. Have one team line up single file underneath one sign and the other team line up underneath the other sign. Place a strip of masking tape down the center of the room between the two teams.

Begin the Tug of War competition. After one team pulls all the other team members across the line, declare it the winner. Then have teams switch sides of the room and play again.

Then say: **Sometimes in our Christian lives we struggle between choosing God's way and choosing our own way. Sometimes "God's Way" wins and sometimes "My Way" wins.**

Read aloud Lamentations 5:15-21 and say: **The people of Israel were miserable because they lived their lives their own way instead of God's way. Often, we experience the same thing.**

RESPONSE

Give kids each a 3×5 card and a pencil. Have them title the front "My Way" and the back "God's Way." Then have the kids write on the "My Way" side at least three ways they choose to live their own way instead of God's way. Then have them write on the "God's Way" side one action they can do to "tug" against each of the three things they listed on the front.

CLOSING

After kids complete their cards, have everyone meet where there's plenty of room to walk in a straight line for about 50 feet (a parking lot would probably work well for this). Then have kids walk in a straight line, one after the other, softly confessing to God what they wrote on the front of their cards. Then turn your kids around and have them walk back to where they started, softly saying what they'll do to follow God's ways more closely.

In closing, ask:
■ **What does it mean to repent?**
■ **How is repentance like this activity?**
■ **Why is it sometimes hard to repent?**
■ **What would make repentance easier?**

EZEKIEL

" 'I will give them a desire to respect me completely, and I will put inside them a new way of thinking. I will take out the stubborn heart of stone from their bodies, and I will give them an obedient heart of flesh.' "

Ezekiel 11:19

EZEKIEL
2:1-7

THEME:
God's purpose for our lives

SUMMARY:
During this LEARNING GAME, kids will find assurance that God has a plan and purpose for their lives.

PREPARATION: You'll need a chair, a hat, a bag of hard candy for prizes, pencils, and Bibles. You'll also need to cut one paper strip for each person.

Say: **Today we'll play "What's My Line?" Take a slip of paper and write on it your dream occupation. Don't show anyone else what you've written. As I pass the hat around, place your folded slip of paper inside.**
Once you collect all the paper slips, have kids sit in a circle around a chair. Then say: **One by one, come forward and draw one occupation from the hat. Then sit in this special chair. The rest of us will take turns asking you questions until someone thinks he or she knows your occupation. You can make a guess only when it's your turn. If your guess is incorrect, you lose one turn.** (Reward correct guesses with a piece of candy.) **When you're in the middle, you may answer questions only with the words "could be" or "couldn't be."**

After everyone has had a turn in the chair, ask a volunteer to read aloud Ezekiel 2:1-7. Then ask:
■ **God had a plan and purpose for Ezekiel. Do you think he has a plan and purpose for you? Why or why not?**
■ **How does your dream occupation compare to God's "occupation" for Ezekiel?**
■ **How might you have responded to God's choice if you were Ezekiel?**
■ **Are some occupations better than others? Why or why not?**
■ **How can you know what God's plan is for your future?**

EZEKIEL
7:1-4

THEME:
Pleasing God with our actions

SUMMARY:
In this DEVOTION, kids will nominate people for a "God-Pleasers Award" and learn what it takes to please God.

PREPARATION: You'll need magazines, newspapers, and Bibles. And you'll need paper, pencils, and one blue ribbon for each person (you may purchase these or make them yourself).

EXPERIENCE
Form teams of no more than three people. Give each team mag-

azines, newspapers, paper, and pencils.

Say: **Today we're going to choose the recipient of** (insert the name of your youth group)**'s God-Pleasers Award. Each team is a nominating committee that will choose three candidates for this award. Look for articles or pictures of people whose actions would be pleasing to God. Choose the top three to submit as your nominees. Be ready to explain why you think your nominees deserve the award.**

Give kids 20 minutes to make their selections. Ask a representative from each group to present the nominations to the group and explain what the nominees did to qualify for the award.

Once all nominations have been made, have kids vote to determine the overall winner.

RESPONSE

Ask a volunteer to read aloud Ezekiel 7:1-4. Then ask:

■ **How were the people nominated for our award today different from the people profiled in this Scripture passage?**

■ **Why was God angry with the people in this Scripture passage?**

■ **How could the people of Ezekiel's day have avoided punishment?**

■ **What does it take to please God?**

■ **What's one thing you do that pleases God?**

■ **What's one thing you do that probably doesn't please God? What can you do about it?**

CLOSING

Say: **If you love God and try to live your life to please him, you qualify for the God-Pleasers Award.** Hand out one ribbon to each person. **Take this award home and keep it as a reminder to be a God pleaser in all that you do!**

EZEKIEL
11:18-20

THEME:
Respect for God

SUMMARY:
During this PROJECT, kids will show their respect for God and for his people by planning a church "work day."

PREPARATION: Ask kids to each choose which of three committees they'll join to help plan a church work day: a planning committee, an advertising committee, or a resource committee. Everyone should volunteer for one of the committees. You'll need Bibles for this activity.

Have a volunteer read aloud Ezekiel 11:18-20. Then ask:

■ **What makes someone worthy of respect?**

■ **In what way does God deserve our respect?**

■ **What are ways we can show our respect for God?**

Ask each committee to begin working on plans for a work day at your church.

The planning committee should do the following:

• consult your pastor, church board, and facilities manager and compile a list of all projects that need to be completed;

• obtain the pastor's approval of the final list;

• choose a date when most of the adults in the church would be available;

• determine the need for child care and what options can be offered to parents of small children; and

• make arrangements for lunch. (Kids might either ask everyone to provide their own sack lunches or plan a potluck. If you have the money, you may choose to provide lunch for your workers.)

The advertising committee should do the following:

• make posters announcing the event to the congregation, posting them at strategic locations within the church, and

• write and place an announcement in the church bulletin or newsletter. Consider creating and performing a skit to announce the event to your congregation several weeks before the scheduled date.

The resource committee should do the following:

• make a list of all needed supplies and equipment;

• collect or purchase all the items on the list well in advance of the date the event is to take place;

• organize the materials for easy dispensing;

• recruit volunteers for each project; and

• place one person in charge of each task that's to be completed on the work day. Try to match jobs to people who have the appropriate skills. (For example, roofing would require someone who has experience in this field.)

After the event, have your group members gather to talk about how they feel about the outcome. Ask:

■ **What was good about our work day?**

■ **What could we have done better?**

■ **How was our work project an expression of our respect for God?**

■ **What's something we can do daily to express our respect for God?**

EZEKIEL
12:21-28

THEME:
The truth of God's Word

SUMMARY:

In this OBJECT LESSON, kids must be patient as they prepare bread dough for baking, and they'll learn that it takes patience to see that God keeps his word.

PREPARATION: You'll need to choose a meeting place that has an oven. Just prior to your meeting time, set out ingredients for the yeast rolls recipe (p. 337). You'll need to make a separate pile of ingredients for each of four groups. In half of those piles, place regular yeast. In the other half, place rapid-rise yeast. (Rapid-rise yeast works the same way regular yeast does—just in half the time!) To keep this a secret, pour the yeast into a small bowl so no one sees the packaging. Also set out the following: mixing bowls, mixing spoons, measuring cups and spoons, and baking sheets. Have kids bring lunch meats, cheese, lettuce, tomatoes, and condiments to make sandwiches. You'll need Bibles for this activity.

Have kids form four groups (a group can be one person), then give each group its ingredients for the yeast rolls and a photocopy of the recipe. Have kids work together in their groups to prepare the dough. Give assistance as needed. When everyone is ready, have groups place their dough in a warm place to rise. Each group should watch its dough and bring it to the kitchen for baking when it's ready.

Some groups may feel anxious when their dough doesn't rise as fast as the others. That's OK—simply assure them that they did nothing wrong.

While you're waiting for the bread to rise, ask your kids to prepare the lunch meats and other toppings for sandwiches.

Once the dough is in the oven baking, ask:

■ **Those of you who had to wait longer for your dough to rise, how did you feel when you saw others already baking their bread?**

■ **Is it hard for you to wait when others seem to be moving ahead? Why or why not?**

Ask a volunteer to read aloud Ezekiel 12:21-28. Then ask:

YEAST ROLLS

1 cup hot milk
½ cup warm water
¼ cup margarine (half a stick)
3 tablespoons sugar
1 teaspoon salt
2 packages yeast
4 cups flour

Mix milk and water. Put margarine in liquid and stir until it melts. Then add sugar and salt, then yeast. Stir until yeast is dissolved. Then mix liquid into flour. Stir until mixed, then turn onto counter and lightly knead, adding extra flour until smooth. Shape into rolls and place on greased baking sheet. Cover with a cloth and let rise half an hour. Bake at 350 degrees for 15 to 20 minutes or until tops of rolls are brown.

■ **Why did people in Ezekiel's day doubt that God would fulfill his Word?**

■ **Is it hard or easy for you to believe God will fulfill what he promises? Explain.**

■ **As you waited for your bread to rise, did you doubt it would happen? Why or why not?**

Say: **Some of you used yeast that rose slower, just as God responds to requests with different timing.** Ask:

■ **What have you learned through this experience that will help you trust God in the future?**

Close by enjoying sandwiches made with freshly baked rolls!

EZEKIEL 14:1-8

THEME:
Banishing idols

SUMMARY:
In this DEVOTION, kids define "idol" and learn how idolatry could influence their lives.

PREPARATION: You'll need enough clay for half of your group members to have a small lump. You'll also need a large sheet of newsprint, tape, markers, and Bibles.

EXPERIENCE
Form two groups. Have group 1's members use clay to form replicas of things they'd describe as idols. For example, kids might make a model of a mythological god, a sportscar, or money. Each group member should craft an idol. Tape a large sheet of newsprint to the wall and ask group 2's members to use markers to draw pictures of modern idols. Give groups 10 to 15 minutes to complete their tasks.

Ask group 1's members to hold up their idols for everyone to see. Then ask group 2's members to explain the pictures they've drawn. Ask:

■ **What's an idol?**

■ **How are the idols from Bible days different from the idols of today? How are they alike?**

■ **Can you think of any other modern idols that we don't have pictured here?**

RESPONSE
Ask a volunteer to read aloud Ezekiel 14:1-8.

■ **How does this Scripture pertain to Christians today?**

■ **If God made a list of idols in our society, what would be at the top of that list?**

■ **Can something be an idol to one person and not to another? Why or why not?**

■ **How can we determine what's an idol and what's not?**

CLOSING
To close, ask group 1's members to destroy their clay idols. Ask group 2's members to tear down the pictures of modern idols. Then form a circle and sing your favorite praise song to God.

EZEKIEL 16:60

THEME:
God keeps his promises.

SUMMARY:
In this LEARNING GAME, teenagers will discover it's sometimes hard for them to keep promises, but it's not hard for God to keep his promises.

PREPARATION: You'll need pencils, slips of paper, and Bibles.

Form a circle and give kids each a pencil and a slip of paper. Have them each write on the paper one promise they can fulfill for someone in the group right now; for example, "I promise I will give you a back rub." Collect all the slips and mix them together in the center of the circle. On "go," have kids each pick one slip from the pile that's not their own. Then, one by one, have them read aloud their promises. The person who wrote the promise then has 10 seconds to fulfill it. Have the rest of the kids count down from 10 while the promiser goes into action.

After everyone has read a promise, ask:

■ **What was hard about keeping your promise?**

■ **What was easy about keeping your promise?**

■ **Do you always keep all your promises? Why or why not?**

Ask a volunteer to read aloud Ezekiel 16:60. Then ask:

■ **Is it really true that God keeps all his promises? Why or why not?**

■ **Has God always kept his promises to you? Explain.**

■ **What's one promise you'd like God to keep in your life?**

■ **What's one promise you're working hard to fulfill?**

Close by asking kids to form pairs and pray for patience as they wait on God to fulfill his promises in their lives.

EZEKIEL 20:40-41

THEME:
Reflecting God's holiness

SUMMARY:
In this OBJECT LESSON, kids will experiment with mirrors to create light.

PREPARATION: Gather mirrors, aluminum foil, and other reflective items. You'll also need at least one lamp or lantern, a small candle for each person, and Bibles.

Darken your meeting room as much as possible. Turn on the lamp or lantern and place it in the center of the room. Turn off all other lights. Ask kids to work together using the materials you provide to bring as much light into your room as possible. (The key is to use the mirrors and other reflective surfaces to reflect off of one another to produce more light.) Give kids 30 minutes to experiment.

Afterward, form a circle and read aloud Ezekiel 20:40-41. Then turn off the lamp and ask:

■ **Were you surprised at how bright you could make this room using just one lamp and some mirrors? Why or why not?**

■ **What was the key ingredient in this experiment? Explain.**

■ **How is the lamp like God?**

■ **How are we like mirrors?**

■ **How does God show his holiness to everyone through Christians?**

■ **How do you reflect God's holiness?**

Close by giving kids each a small candle to take home. Say: **This is your reminder that you are reflections of God's holiness to the world around you.**

EZEKIEL
33:1-10

THEME:
The consequences of sin

SUMMARY:
In this ADVENTURE, kids will videotape warning signs and learn the importance of warning others of impending danger.

PREPARATION: You'll need four video cameras, a VCR, a television, and Bibles. (If you don't have access to video cameras, instant-print cameras and tape recorders will work.)

Form four teams and give each team a video camera. Ask each team to find and videotape as many warning signs as possible. They can use the video cameras to record signs or sounds that warn us of danger. Ask an adult to drive or walk with each group, but give them specific boundaries that will be acceptable to all, such as the city limits. Allow 45 minutes for the groups to complete this task.

After 45 minutes, gather back together and show each group's videotape. Have team members explain what they've videotaped. Then ask:

■ **What would happen to us if there were no warning signs like those we just watched?**

■ **What happens when people fail to heed the signs we've just witnessed?**

Ask a volunteer to read aloud Ezekiel 33:1-10. Ask:

■ **What does it mean to be a watchman like Ezekiel?**

■ **How are a Christian's responsibilities like a watchman's?**

EZEKIEL
37:1-14

THEME:
Hope for the hopeless

SUMMARY:
Kids will echo one another in this CREATIVE READING as they read a portion of Scripture.

PREPARATION: Recruit four people to read the parts of Voices 1, 2, 3, and 4. Make a photocopy of the "Creative Reading for Ezekiel 37:1-14" handout (p. 342) for each person and allow the readers time to look over the reading before performing it.

EZEKIEL
47:21-23

THEME:
Our inheritance

SUMMARY:
In this AFFIRMATION, kids will affirm others' good qualities by willing things to one another.

PREPARATION: Get copies of sample wills from your library. If you can, bring a copy of a school annual that contains a class will. You'll also need paper, pencils, and Bibles.

As kids arrive, ask them to read the various wills you've brought. Then ask:

■ **In the wills you've been looking at, what was the most valuable item willed? Explain.**

■ **What nonmaterial things do parents will to their children?**

■ **What have your parents already willed to you in the way they've raised you?**

Form pairs and give each person paper and a pencil. Then say: **Think of a good personality trait your partner possesses that you wish you had. Write it on your paper. Now exchange papers. Then write a will that makes your partner the beneficiary for the quality he or she listed; for example, "I, David, being of sound mind and body, will to you the gift of compassion you see in me. My prayer for you is that God would nurture and develop that gift in you, all the days of your life."**

Give pairs 10 minutes to exchange wills. Then ask:

■ **What feelings did you experience as you wrote your will?**

■ **Were you surprised by what others value in you? Explain.**

Ask a volunteer to read aloud Ezekiel 47:21-23.

Say: **Sometimes we forget that God's children have an inheritance that will never pass away.**

Ask kids to take their wills home and hang them up as a reminder of how special they are to each other and to God!

CREATIVE READING FOR EZEKIEL 37:1-14

Voice 1: God's Spirit was upon me. He put me down in the middle of a valley—a valley full of bones.

All others: *(Sitting)* Bones, bones, full of bones.

Voice 1: He led me around among the bones. There were many, many bones... And they were dry!

All others: Dry, dry... the bones were dry.

Voice 1: God asked me, "Do you think these bones can live?"

All others: Live, live... can these dry bones live?

Voice 1: I answered him, "Only you know, Lord!"

All others: You alone, Lord, only you!

Voice 2: Prophesy to all these bones.

Voice 1: And so I did. Listen, bones, to the Word of the Lord.

All others: We're listening, Lord, we're listening.

Voice 2: I'll give you muscles. I'll give you flesh. I'll give you skin, and I'll give you breath. You'll come to life. Then you'll know that I am the Lord.

Voice 1: And so I spoke. And I heard a loud noise—those old bones began to shake.

All others: We all came together—we really did.

Voice 1: I watched as the bones were connected and covered with flesh.

All others: He covered us with skin—he covered our bones.

Voice 1: God told me to say to the wind, "Wind, blow on them and give them breath." And so it did!

All others: These dry, dead bones, they came to life. He gave us life; he gave us breath. *(All stand.)*

Voice 1: It's an army.

Voice 2: It's my army.

All others: *(Shouting)* We're God's army!

Voice 3: Once we were dead.

Voice 4: But now we live.

All: Thanks be to God.

DANIEL

"But even if God does not save us, we want you, O King, to know this: We will not serve your gods or worship the gold statue you have set up."

Daniel 3:18

DANIEL
1:1-21

THEME:
Being faithful to
God

SUMMARY:
In this LEARNING GAME, kids
will pantomime four different
faithful characters and learn
why it's important to be faithful.

PREPARATION: You'll need one
3×5 card for each person. Number
these cards 1 through 4. Write on
card 1, "a loyal pet"; on card 2 write,
"a dependable friend"; on card 3
write, "our faithful God"; and on
card 4 write, "an obedient child."
Ask an adult volunteer to be the
judge for your contest. You'll also
need Bibles.

Form teams of four. Give each
team a set of four numbered
cards and have kids each pick one.
Tell kids not to show their cards to
anyone.

Then say: **One by one, each of
you will pantomime the character listed on your card. Your goal
as a team is to quickly guess
what your teammate is pan-
tomiming and then send one
person to the front of the room
where our judge is sitting. If
you're the first team to reach the
judge with a correct answer,
your team wins that round. We'll
continue with cards 2, 3, and 4.
The team that wins the most
rounds wins the game! The only
rule to this game is that the pan-
tomiming person cannot speak
or make any noise.** (For groups
of fewer than eight, have kids form
teams of two and have each team
member act out two of the characters.)

When you've played the game
and declared a winner, ask:

■ **What do each of these characters have in common?**

■ **Do you respect that quality
in others? Why or why not?**

■ **How does it feel when someone is faithful to you?**

■ **How do you feel when you're
faithful to another person?**

Read aloud Daniel 1:1-21 and
then ask:

■ **How can we follow Daniel's
example of faithfulness in our relationship with God?**

■ **When were you challenged
to be faithful? How did it turn
out?**

Say: **Choosing to be faithful is
usually a difficult decision, but
God favors faithful decisions
and faithful people.**

DANIEL
1; 3; 6

THEME:
Positive rebellion

SUMMARY:
In this DEVOTION, teenagers
will learn that sometimes rebellion can be positive.

PREPARATION: You'll need two
large sheets of newsprint, tape, a
marker, paper, pencils, and Bibles.

EXPERIENCE

Tape two large sheets of newsprint on two opposing walls. On one draw a "+" symbol; on the other draw a "—" symbol. Tell kids to stand near the symbol that best expresses how they feel about rebellion. Then ask:

■ **Why did you choose that symbol?**

■ **What are examples of negative rebellion? positive rebellion?**

Form groups of three and give them each a piece of paper and a pencil. Ask groups to each brainstorm and list the names of people who accomplished something positive through rebellion. The goal is to list as many people as possible and to be prepared to defend the actions of those listed.

After five minutes, have groups present their lists. Tell kids they can challenge the "positive actions" of any person listed on any group's list. The group should vote on any contested name. When all groups have presented their lists, declare a winner.

Then say: **People in the Bible also rebelled. The book of Daniel is full of examples of people who rebelled positively.**

Assign groups each one of these Scripture passages: Daniel 1; Daniel 3; or Daniel 6. Have groups each create a short rap that tells the story of their Scripture passages.

Have groups each perform their raps.

RESPONSE

Ask:

■ **From our Bible study raps and the list of famous rebels,** **how can we define positive rebellion?**

Write kids' definitions on newsprint. Then ask:

■ **How can we rebel without hurting others?**

■ **What might be the consequences of positive rebellion?**

■ **When can positive rebellion turn negative?**

■ **What guidelines should we follow to rebel positively?**

CLOSING

Challenge groups to each come up with one way they can positively rebel in the next week. Have them keep their ideas a secret until next week, when they'll be expected to report on the outcome of their rebellion.

DANIEL
2:2-28

THEME:
    All things are possible with God.

SUMMARY:
    In this OBJECT LESSON, kids will try to bore a hole in a piece of wood using only a drill bit, then learn how God can make impossible situations possible.

PREPARATION: You'll need a few pieces of wood (2×4s work well). You'll also need a drill bit (or nail) for each person, an electric drill (or hammer if you're using nails), an extension cord, and Bibles.

Set up the 2×4s, one on top of another, so that the drill bits won't go into the floor. Give kids each a drill bit. Then give one of the kids the electric drill and the extension cord. Tell them that the person who can bore a hole through the piece of wood fastest is the winner. Obviously, the person with the electric drill should win! (Caution the electric drill-holder to handle the tool carefully to avoid possible injury.)

After the lucky person finishes boring a hole in the wood, have kids form pairs and read Daniel 2:2-28 together. Then ask one person to summarize the story for the whole group. Ask:

■ **How was our contest and this story in Daniel similar?**

■ **How is God like or unlike the drill? the extension cord? the electricity to run the drill?**

■ **When in real life have you felt like you were trying to bore a hole through a piece of wood without a drill?**

■ **What's one thing about the Christian life that seems impossible for you to do?**

■ **What have you learned from Daniel about facing impossible situations?**

Say: **Sometimes it feels like it's impossible to live the Christian life, but if we seek God's presence in our lives, God makes the impossible possible.**

DANIEL
3:1-18

THEME:
Never compromising the truth

SUMMARY:
In this ADVENTURE, teenagers will ask others about their values and discover how committed others (and they) are to those values.

PREPARATION: For each person, make a photocopy of the "Values Research" handout (p. 347). You'll also need a pencil and Bible for each person. Plan to go to a local shopping center, park, restaurant, or any place that has lots of people (if necessary, get permission from management before doing this).

Go to a shopping center (or some other public place) and give kids each a "Values Research" handout and a pencil. Send the kids out in pairs or trios for safety and have them interview at least three people each (have them choose people of various ages). Give kids 30 minutes to complete their interviews and meet back at a designated location. Have kids discuss their survey results. Ask:

■ **Were most people willing to compromise the thing they valued most for money? for their lives?**

■ **Do you think the people who answered "no" to questions 2 and 3 were being honest? Why or why not?**

(continued on p. 348)

VALUES RESEARCH

Say: **Hello my name is** _____, **and I'm doing a research project. May I ask you three quick questions?**

(If people ask, you can tell them it's for your youth group.)

Put a check mark next to each answer for each person you interview.

1. What do you value most?

Family	Friends	Self
House/car	Health	Money
Job	Religion	Other

2. Would you give up whatever you value most for one year (for example, not seeing or speaking to your family at all for one year) for $1 million in cash?

Yes

No

3. Would you give up what you value most if someone threatened to kill you if you didn't?

Yes

No

Have kids each take the survey themselves and then get back into their groups of two or three to discuss their answers. Then have a volunteer read aloud Daniel 3:1-18.

Say: **Daniel valued his relationship with God so much that he would not compromise. In fact, Daniel and his friends all risked their lives because they valued their relationships with God so much.**

Close by having kids make a list on the back of their surveys of things they value but sometimes compromise. For example, they might value spending time with their families, but they compromise this value by hanging out at the mall instead. Ask kids to each choose one area of compromise they'll commit to upholding for the next month.

DANIEL
5:17-31

THEME:

Causing trouble brings more trouble.

SUMMARY:
Use this SKIT to help kids understand that what goes around comes around.

CUSTOMER SERVICE

SCENE: A teenager who works for a pizza restaurant finds that his attitude gets him in trouble.

PROPS: Pizza boxes, aprons, a phone, an order pad, a pencil, a table to serve as a counter, a paperback book, and a newspaper. You'll also need Bibles for the discussion afterward.

CHARACTERS:
Zeno
Chi-Chi
Waylon

SCRIPT

Zeno: *(Talking on the phone and writing on an order pad)* So let's see, that's three medium pizzas, one with extra cheese and pepperoni, one with bacon and pineapple on one half and mushrooms and anchovies on the other half, and one Big Blubby with everything, hold the anchovies. Do you want any soft drinks with that? *(Pauses to listen.)* We've got Kooky Kola, Diet Kooky Kola, Caffeine-Free Diet Kooky Kola, Caffeine-Free Diet Kooky Kola Klassic, Caffeine-Free Diet Cherry Kooky Kola Klassic, Caffeine-Free... *(Pauses, as if cut off. Looks frustrated.)* Nothing to drink. I see. Why didn't you tell me that before I went through that whole long list? You weren't sure? *(Sarcastically)* Well, maybe you're more sure of this: How about some dessert, or could I come and make you a glass of warm milk before bed? I could tuck you in, maybe, or bring you your teddy bear. *(Pauses, then looks at phone.)* Another crank call hanging up on me. What a pain!

Chi-Chi: *(Enters with two pizza boxes.)* Hey, Zeno, here are your two Big Blubbies with extra cheese. Did you get another order? I heard the phone.

Zeno: *(Picking up a paperback book and starting to read)* Nah— wrong number. *(He reads his book while he talks.)* Say, when's the boss coming in?

Chi-Chi: Are you kidding? He was in already. He looked around, made up the schedule for next week, and went home. Didn't he even say hi to you?

Zeno: No, but that's fine with me. *(He starts to read his book as Waylon enters. Chi-Chi steps off-stage, presumably to go cook pizza.)*

Waylon: Howdy!

Zeno: *(Looking up from his book)* "Howdy"? *(Rolls his eyes, then pretends to saunter up to the counter.)* Can I, uh, he'p ya, pardner?

Waylon: Whoo-eee, I shore hope so. *(He holds up a folded newspaper.)* See, I seen in the paper that yore lookin' fer someone to take orders. Well sir, I'm fresh out of the service, and I'm used to takin' orders.

Zeno: Well, pilgrim, you done mis-read that there paper. We-uns don't need any help at this time. Why don't you amble by after the next hog-calling contest and check?

Waylon: Well, shoot, I'm sorry I bothered ya'. You folks have yer-selfs a nice evenin'. *(He saunters out, leaving the paper on the counter.)*

Zeno: I suppose I better check next week's schedule. *(Calling out)* Hey, Chi-Chi, will you watch the front while I go check next week's schedule?

Chi-Chi: *(From offstage)* Sure! *(She enters, he exits. She begins to* leaf through the paper until she comes across something circled in the help-wanted section. She reads interestedly.)* Hey, Zeno, this is interesting. There's a help-wanted ad for our restaurant. It says, "Wanted to start immediately. One cheerful, hard-working person to answer phone and take orders." I didn't know we were going to take on another person to take orders.

Zeno: What was that? I wasn't pay-ing attention. I was looking at the schedule. Did you know that the boss only has me scheduled for four hours next week? What's the deal? *(Characters freeze.)*

If you use this skit as a discussion starter, here are possible questions:

■ **How does an attitude like Zeno's affect others?**

■ **How could Zeno change his attitude for the better? How might that change improve his relationships?**

■ **Read Daniel 5:17-31. What was Belshazzar's attitude problem? How did it eventually come back to him?**

■ **Why did Belshazzar's heart anger God?**

DANIEL 6:1-23

THEME:
Taking risks for
your faith

SUMMARY:
On this OVERNIGHTER, kids
will play risky games, watch a
risky movie, and learn about
spiritual risk taking.

PREPARATION: Promote the overnighter as a "thrill-seekers night."
You'll need a television, a VCR, supplies as needed for games, and
Bibles. You'll also need to rent a
public performance video that features thrill seekers, such as Warren Miller's snow skiing film *Steep
& Deep.* And for each person, you'll
need paper, an envelope, a stamp,
and a pencil.

Begin the evening by playing a
few "risky" games, such as
• **Sardines**—A game played
inside a home or church with several rooms. One person hides, and
the rest of the group tries to find
him or her. Once someone finds
the person who's hidden, he or she
must join the hidden person. The
game continues until everyone is
hidden together and only one person is looking. Send the kids out in
intervals of about 30 seconds. This
game works best if it's very dark!
• **Survival**—The goal of this
game is to make it from the drop-
off area to "safety" without getting
tagged. Drop off kids at a local
store or school in a residential area.
In pairs or trios, they must travel on

foot through the neighborhood
back to safety (the church, someone's house, or another specific
meeting place a few blocks away)
without being tagged.

The "taggers" (usually the
youth leader and a few other
adults) drive around in a car or
cars searching for the kids. When
they spot one, they must get out of
the car and tag them. Once kids
get tagged, they get in the car and
help tag others.

Set clear boundaries, such as no
trespassing on private property,
staying off streets that are out of
bounds, and keeping within a time
limit of 30 minutes. It's a good idea
to give kids a photocopied street
map of the area in a sealed envelope in case they get lost—but if
it's opened, they're disqualified!
Those who make it back without
getting tagged have survived!
• **Flashlight Tag**—Give kids
five minutes to hide, then have one
or more people search for them
with flashlights. When a group
member is spotted with the flashlight, the spotter must say that person's name, and that person is then
out of the game. Those who
remain hidden for 15 minutes (or
however long your time limit is)
win the game. You may want them
to hide in pairs or trios for safety.
Give kids clear boundaries, including a time limit and a designated
meeting place after time is up.

After two hours of "risky" game
playing, meet back for a thrill-seekers movie. (Warren Miller's *Steep
& Deep,* a snow skiing movie, is a
great one. Or choose any movie
with rock climbing, stunts, skydiv-
ing, or white-water rafting.)

Use Daniel 6:1-23 as the basis for a study on spiritual risks. Read aloud the Scripture passage, then form groups of no more than four to discuss the following questions:

■ **How did it feel to spend a night taking risks?**

■ **What's the difference between participating in healthy risk taking (the games we played) and watching others take risks (the movie we watched)?**

■ **What's the difference between healthy risk taking and unhealthy risk taking?**

■ **Would you have done what Daniel did? Why or why not?**

■ **What could you do this week to take a risk for God.**

Close by having kids each find a partner to talk about a risk they can take for God in the coming week. Give kids each paper and a pencil. Have them each write the risk they plan to take, then sign it at the bottom. Have partners sign each other's papers as witnesses. Collect the papers and mail them back to the kids in a week.

DANIEL
9:4-19

THEME:

The importance of praying for others

SUMMARY:
Teenagers will ask forgiveness for each other in this CREATIVE PRAYER.

PREPARATION: You'll need paper and a pencil for each person and Bibles.

Read aloud Daniel 9:4-19. Then ask:

■ **Who is Daniel praying for?**

■ **Why is he praying for these people?**

■ **What is he praying for?**

■ **What kinds of sins did the people commit?**

Give kids each a piece of paper and a pencil. Have them each think of a sin they've committed that they need forgiveness for and then write a prayer of confession and a plea for forgiveness for that sin. Tell them someone else will read their confessions and to beware of writing anything too personal.

Then say: **Trade your paper with another person, then take a few minutes to pray the prayer they've written.**

After a few minutes, ask:

■ **How often do you pray for God to forgive someone else?**

■ **How did it feel to pray for someone else's forgiveness?**

■ **How does it feel knowing that someone else is praying for you?**

■ **Would you feel comfortable praying for others like this on a regular basis? Why or why not?**

Close in prayer, asking forgiveness for the entire group and thanking God for his compassion.

HOSEA

"Come, let's go back to the Lord."

Hosea 6:1a

HOSEA
1:2-3; 3:1-5

THEME:
God loves every-one.

SUMMARY:
In this DEVOTION, kids will compare and contrast the qualities we look for in a marriage partner with the qualities Hosea got when he married Gomer.

PREPARATION: You'll need several pages of personal ads from your newspaper's classified section. (You want the ads that advertise people looking for relationships; for example, "Tall Hispanic female looking for tall white or Hispanic male with good personality, nice build, and large income to share conversation and friendship.") You'll also need paper, pens, and Bibles.

EXPERIENCE
Form groups of three or four and give each group a page or section of personal ads, a piece of paper, and a pen. Have each group read through several ads and come up with a list of the five most-desirable qualities in a relationship.

Next, have groups each read Hosea 2:14-23 then write a list of qualities that describe Gomer, the woman God chose for Hosea. When they finish, ask them to compare and contrast the lists.

RESPONSE
Ask:
■ **Which list looks more like**
what you'd look for in a rela-tionship?
■ **How do you think Hosea felt about marrying Gomer? Explain.**
■ **How would you feel if God chose a person like Gomer for you? Explain.**
■ **Why did God choose Gomer for Hosea?**
■ **What can you learn about God's character from this story?**

CLOSING
Ask kids to close in prayer, thanking God for choosing us even though we're unworthy.

HOSEA
1-3

THEME:
Costly love

SUMMARY:
In this DEVOTION, kids will be challenged to buy back a cloth-ing item that's being held for ransom.

PREPARATION: You'll need a pho-tocopy of the "Ransom Letter" handout (p. 354) for each person, a large box, and Bibles.

EXPERIENCE
As kids arrive, tell them they'll be playing a game that will require them to put something they're wearing into a large box; for exam-ple, a shoe, a watch, an earring, or a belt. Have everyone put their items in the box, then sit in a circle. Next, pass out photocopies of the

"Ransom Letter" handout.

After everyone has read the letter, allow time for questions or protests. No matter what, remain firm in the demands of the ransom letter. If some kids decide to pay, take their money and give them back their items. When things calm down, summarize the story told in Hosea 1–3, reading aloud key verses such as Hosea 1:2-3; 2:14-20; and 3:1-3.

RESPONSE
Ask:
■ **How do you think Hosea felt when he had to buy Gomer, even though she was already his wife?**
■ **How did you feel when you were told that your belongings were being held until you paid for them?**
■ **Why do you think God had Hosea buy Gomer back?**
■ **How is this game and Hosea's situation like what God has done for us?**

CLOSING
Return all kids' items and any ransom money you collected. Then ask:

■ **What price would you have paid to get your item back?**
■ **Think about the price God paid for us. What does that tell you about God? about yourself?**

HOSEA
6–7

THEME:
Softening a hardened heart

SUMMARY:
In this OBJECT LESSON, kids will form hearts out of clay to learn how to "soften" their own hearts toward God.

PREPARATION: Gather two large lumps of clay. The day before this activity, put one of them in the sun until it's hard and unpliable. Save the other one in a container so it stays soft. You'll also need Bibles.

RANSOM LETTER

The personal item you placed in my box is now being held for ransom. It will cost you $1 to redeem your item—no questions asked. If you do not pay, there's no guarantee you'll get your item back.

Give half of your kids a lump of hardened clay and the other half a lump of soft clay. Say: **You have 30 seconds to turn your lump of clay into a heart shape. Ready? Go!** After 30 seconds, have kids each hold up their clay hearts. Then ask:

■ **What made working with the dry clay difficult?**

■ **What made working with the soft clay easy?**

Read aloud or paraphrase Hosea 6–7. Then form pairs and ask partners to discuss the following questions:

■ **What are ways people harden their hearts?**

■ **What's one way I can soften my heart toward God this week?**

Close by asking partners to pray for "softened hearts" for one another.

HOSEA
11:1-11

THEME:
God's grace and compassion

SUMMARY:
In this SKIT, kids learn about God's compassion for those who repent.

EVEN THOUGH YOU DON'T DESERVE IT

PROPS: Audience cue cards that say, "Don't do it!" "Busted!" "That's what you think!" "Watch out!" "Oh no!" and "Uh oh!" You'll also need four chairs for scene 2 and Bibles for the discussion after the skit.

CHARACTERS:
Mom
Dad
Tim (son)
Kay (daughter)
All (the audience)
Ron (friend of Tim's)
Susan (friend of Kay's)

SCRIPT

(At home, Mom and Dad are saying goodbye to their kids as they leave for a little vacation.)

Mom: Are you sure you'll be all right, kids?

Tim: Mom, will you stop worrying already? We'll be fine. We're not children anymore.

Dad: Honey, they'll be fine. Have we forgotten anything?

Mom: I don't think so. I've left $40 for emergency expenses, numbers for the neighbors, police station, fire department...

Kay: *(Interrupting, in a sarcastic tone)* And I hope the National Guard. You just never know!

Mom: All right, I get the picture. Goodbye. We'll see you on Sunday night.
(Mom and Dad hug kids and exit.)

Tim: Boy! They treat us like infants.

Kay: I know! *(Noticing something)* Hey look!

Tim: What?

Kay: There's something they forgot.

Tim: I'll try to catch them. *(Starts to run after them.)*

Kay: No! Don't you see? They left the keys to the BMW.

All: *(Reading cue card)* Oh no!

Tim: Wow! We could have some serious fun with that.

Kay: Serious fun! Let's call Susan and Ron.

Tim: Yeah!

All: *(Reading cue card)* Don't do it! *(End of scene.)*

SCENE 2

(Place four chairs in two rows, one behind the other to simulate a car. Tim and Kay are standing, looking at the car. Ron and Susan enter, and all four of them stare at the car.)

Ron: What was so urgent?

Tim: Look at this. *(Points to the car.)*

Ron: So what? Your parents have had that car for over a year now.

Tim: Yeah, but I've never driven it.

Susan: What? You're going to drive your parents' BMW?

Kay: No, we all are!

Ron: Cool! *(He jumps in the front passenger chair.)*

All: *(Reading cue card)* Busted!

Tim: Yeah, get in. *(Sits in the front driver chair.)*

Kay: C'mon, Sue! *(Sits in the back.)*

Susan: I guess it wouldn't hurt anything. *(Sits in the back.)*

All: *(Reading cue card)* That's what you think.

(They all pretend like they're driving.)

Tim: This is so great!

Ron: You are just too hot, man! *(Suddenly another car swerves and hits them.)*

All: *(Reading cue card)* Watch out!

Kay: Look ouuut!

(The four of them simulate a crash by bouncing around wildly in their chairs for a moment then coming to a sudden stop.)

All: *(Reading cue card)* Oh no! *(Scene ends.)*

SCENE 3

(Two days later, Tim and Kay are back at home, waiting for their parents to show up.)

Kay: Mom and Dad will be home any minute . . . What're we gonna do?

Tim: I don't know. I feel so bad. Not just because we dented their car, but because they trusted us to act like responsible adults.

Kay: But we acted like little kids. I feel awful, too. *(She begins to pray.)* God, Tim and I are really sorry that we took something that wasn't ours and that we broke our parents' trust. Please forgive us.

Tim: I think God is more forgiving than Dad, unfortunately.

All: *(Reading cue card)* Uh oh! *(Mom and Dad walk in.)*

Dad: Hi, kids. We're home!

Kay: Oh, Dad. We've done something awful. Please forgive us. *(She runs up to her father.)*

Dad: What'sa matter, Kay?

Mom: What are you talking about?

Tim: You're gonna disown us!

Mom: Don't you know how much we love you? We'd never disown you, no matter what you've done.

Kay: Tim and I took the BMW out for a ride, and we hit a car. There's a dent in your fender now. We're really, really sorry.

Dad: You're right, that's serious . . . but not unforgivable. We'll work something out so you can get it fixed. The important thing is that you're not hurt.

Mom: And we forgive you. This is disappointing, but it's not disastrous—especially because you've been honest with us.

Tim: Thanks! I think I learned a lesson.

Kay: Me, too. *(Hugs Mom.)* Thanks for forgiving us.

Dad: OK. Now, let's go look at that car.

(The family exits.)

If you use this skit as a discussion starter, here are possible questions:

■ Do you agree with how the kids were "punished"? Explain.

■ Was the parents' reaction realistic? Why or why not?

■ How would most parents have reacted to this situation?

■ Is God more like the parents in this skit or the examples of parents we just talked about?

Have a volunteer read aloud Hosea 11:1-11, then ask:

■ What punishment did the people deserve in this passage?

■ Why did God give them something different instead?

■ In what ways has God shown you grace or forgiveness?

HOSEA
14:1-2

THEME:
Returning to God

SUMMARY:
Use this SKIT to help kids see that they can return to the Lord for forgiveness.

THE RETURN OF TRAVIS MCREADY

SCENE: A teenager calls home to see if he will be welcomed after staying out past curfew.

PROPS: Two chairs and two phones (chairs should be placed on opposite sides of the stage with a phone setting on each chair), the sound of a phone ringing, a bag of potato chips, and a magazine. You'll also need Bibles for the discussion after the skit.

CHARACTERS:
Travis
Brian
Mom

SCRIPT
(Travis is dialing one of the phones, trying to call home. Brian is standing near him, eating some chips. As Travis finishes dialing the number, a phone rings eight times with about a four-second pause between each ring. Travis and Brian start talking after the third ring.)

Travis: Hmm... Maybe they're not home.

Brian: Could be. I still say you're calling too soon. It was only last night that you stayed out past curfew. If it were me, I'd make 'em sweat a little longer. You know, make 'em think you're really not interested in coming home.

Travis: But I AM!

Brian: Well, sure, but it doesn't do any good for them to know that. They'll be expecting an apology and stuff.

(Travis should hang up after the

eighth ring or now, whichever comes first.)

Travis: Well, I've been thinking... Maybe they deserve an apology. I mean, I WAS out too late, and I HAD had a couple of beers. Maybe they were right to lock me out of the house.

Brian: Man, when are you going to learn? No question MY old man doesn't want you hanging out here. He says it's bad enough feeding one moose on a regular basis, he doesn't want to feed two. Even so, the last thing I want you to do is go groveling back to your parents. How uncool.

Travis: I don't even care if I'm uncool at this point, Brian. Among other things, I'll miss my mom's cooking if I stay here. I've heard that you eat Lucky Charms for every meal!

Brian: Hey, look. My old man works weird hours, and I have to cook my own meals. You get used to it.

Travis: Yeah, well you might try cooking something you have to heat up for a change. Even I can make grilled cheese.

Brian: *(Disgusted)* Why don't you try calling home again, Chef Boy-Are-We Picky?

(Brian picks up a magazine and starts to read, pretty much ignoring Travis. Travis sighs and tries calling home again. The phone rings three times, then Mom enters on the other side of the stage and answers the second phone.)

Mom: Hello?

(Travis is nervous—he wipes his hand over his face.)

Mom: Hello?

Travis: Hi... Mom?

(Freeze.)

Permission to photocopy this skit from *Youth Worker's Encyclopedia: OT* granted for local church use. Copyright © Group Publishing, Inc., Box 481, Loveland, CO 80539.

If you use this skit as a discussion starter, here are possible questions:

■ **What would you say next if you were Travis?**

■ **Which would be worse: living with Brian or living up to your responsibility? Why?**

■ **Read Hosea 14:1-2. Which is harder: returning to God or living your life without him? Explain.**

■ **How does your relationship with God change when you ask for forgiveness?**

JOEL

"After this, I will pour out my Spirit on all kinds of people..."

Joel 2:28a

JOEL
2:1-27

THEME:
God's forgiveness

SUMMARY:
Kids will witness an example of God's forgiveness and the purifying influence it has in their lives during this OBJECT LESSON.

PREPARATION: You'll need a water purifier (the canister type that can be obtained from any camping or outdoor-recreation store), a half-full pitcher of water, an empty pitcher, small paper cups, a two-liter bottle of cola, and Bibles.

Place a half-full pitcher of water in front of the kids. Ask for volunteers to pass out a small paper cup to each person. Then pass around a two-liter bottle of cola and have kids each pour a small amount into their cups.

Ask a volunteer to read aloud Joel 2:1-11, pausing after each sentence or verse. Tell kids that at each pause, someone should come quickly to the front and empty his or her cup into the pitcher. Have them take turns doing this until the reader finishes verse 11.

Then say: **This darkness in the water represents the guilt, sin, and regrets of the Israelites. The future looked terrible and grim for them because they ignored God's love and direction and went their own way instead.**

Ask another volunteer to read aloud Joel 2:12-27. Meanwhile,

slowly pour the darkened water through the water purifier and into the empty pitcher. Try to time your pouring with the length of the reading. Then ask:

■ **How is this water purifier like God's forgiveness?**

■ **Why would God choose to forgive the Israelites?**

■ **Why does God choose to forgive us?**

■ **What's one area of your life that seems dark to you now, something that needs God's purifying forgiveness?**

Then say: **Now close your eyes and offer up to God whatever you're thinking about now.**

JOEL
2:12-14

THEME:
Sincerely turning from sin

SUMMARY:
Use this SKIT to help kids see that it's important to have their actions match their words.

TAKING SIDES

SCENE: The left and right sides of a teenager's brain are talking to each other.

PROPS: Signs for each of the performers—one says "Left Brain," the other says "Right Brain"—and a clipboard for Left Brain. You'll also need Bibles for the discussion after the skit.

CHARACTERS:
Right Brain (RB)
Left Brain (LB)

SCRIPT

(Right Brain is standing with arms crossed looking down and pouting. As Left Brain enters, Right Brain turns away.)

LB: *(Claps hands together, rubs them, and looks around.)* So, what's going on in your neck of the head today?

(RB turns even farther away.)

LB: What's that? Are you ... pouting? You are; you're pouting! Now what?

RB: If you cared anything at all about me you'd know what I was pouting about.

LB: Now come on. That's not logical. What am I supposed to do, read your mind? *(To audience)* Would that mean I'd be reading my mind? *(To RB)* You have to help me out a little here.

RB: I don't have to do anything. Especially not anything logical. That's your department.

LB: *(Smiling)* That's true. But I really would like to know what's wrong. *(Picks up clipboard.)* Let's see, are we breathing? Yes. Eyes appear to be functioning normally. I woke us up right at the normal time this morning. *(Smacks forehead.)* I know! I'll bet it was my turn to monitor the bladder, huh? Did we have a little accident?

RB: *(Mortified)* Heavens no!!

LB: Well, I can't imagine what you must be sulking about... Oh, I know. You're still upset about my taking over that English essay we were writing!

RB: Well... If you must have me

tell you right out, yes! I was doing fine on my own, and then you came along and said it needed fixing—you took all the creativity out of it.

LB: It DID need fixing! The most creative part of it was the spelling. I mean, how many times have you seen "joyful" spelled with a "w"? Not to mention what you did to "glorious."

RB: I didn't need your help, I didn't ask for your help, and I didn't WANT your help!

LB: I'm sorry already.

RB: You are not sorry.

LB: Yes, I am. I said I was.

RB: Oh, yeah, like I'm convinced.

LB: Oh, come on. You, of all brains, should know I don't say anything I don't mean.

RB: I'm NOT convinced. *(Thinks.)* Show me you're sorry.

LB: Show you? By doing what?

RB: Be sad.

LB: *(Gives a "you must be kidding" look. Frowns a big, melodramatic frown.)* I'm sad.

RB: Sadder.

LB: Don't push it.

RB: *(Enjoying the sight of LB groveling for her/him)* Well, cry a little.

LB: Cry a lit...? *(Big sigh.)* OK. *(Sniffles a little bit and wipes away fake tears.)*

RB: Go without meals.

LB: *(At the end of his/her rope)* That's it! I'm sorry, OK?! I didn't mean to hurt your feelings! I'm sorry, I'm sorry, I'm sorry! *(Gets on knees.)* Please forgive me!

RB: *(Smiling a little)* Aww...all right. You're forgiven.

(They shake hands and start to walk off.)

LB: Great! Now, about the spelling of the word "glorious."

RB: *(Suddenly mad)* Oh, no you don't! *(Stomps off in opposite direction.)*

LB: *(Smacks forehead.)* Not again! *(Freeze.)*

If you use this skit as a discussion starter, here are possible questions:

■ **How can you tell when someone is truly sorry?**

■ **How does it make you feel when they aren't?**

■ **How do you show that you are truly sorry?**

■ **Read Joel 2:12-14. What does God mean when he says, "Even now, come back to me with all your heart... Tearing your clothes is not enough to show you are sad"?**

■ **How do we show God that our hearts have truly turned from sin?**

JOEL
2:28-29

THEME:
The Holy Spirit

SUMMARY:
Use this SKIT to help kids see that when God pours out his Holy Spirit, things really happen.

THE CLASS

SCENE: Two teenagers try to control some preschoolers.

PROPS: Bibles for the discussion after the skit.

CHARACTERS:
Kelsey
Max

SCRIPT
(Kelsey and Max stand in front of the audience. They're looking from the audience to each other with worried expressions on their faces.)

Kelsey: *(Imitating what Max must sound like)* "Let's help with vacation Bible school—it'll be fun!" I should clobber you!

Max: Oh, come on, where's your sense of adventure, your sense of fun?

Kelsey: Where's your COMMON sense? This isn't a preschool class; it's the monkey house at the zoo! Just look at them!
(They look out over the audience, gesturing to specific audience members as they speak. Kelsey is worried; Max sees humor in the situation.)

Kelsey: Over in the corner, Josh has Drew by the earlobes; Taylor over there is trying to stick his pinkie in the electric pencil sharpener; and, don't look now, but Ashley is coloring on the wall.

Max: *(Laughing)* Well, at least it's crayon—that's erasable. It could be permanent ink.

Kelsey: I'm serious, Max. How on earth are we going to teach anything to these kids? They're going WILD!

Max: Just wait and see. I've got a secret weapon! Watch this. *(He addresses the class.)* Kids... Kids... *(He cups his hands around his mouth and yells.)* KIDS! Let's sit in a circle on the floor! *(He notices something in the back of the audience.)* No, Cyndi... Cyndi, I didn't say, "Open the door!" I said, "SIT ON THE FLOOR!" *(He notices something else.)* No, I didn't say, "Let's play war."

(Kelsey is watching this all with amusement now.)

Max: I said, "floor..." Floor... Floor! *(To Kelsey)* I guess it's time for the secret weapon.

Kelsey: *(Disbelieving)* I can't wait.

Max: *(Shouting)* Kids... If you get quiet and sit in a circle on the floor, I'll tell you about today's SNACK!

(They both freeze. Silence for a few seconds.)

Kelsey: I don't believe it. They're quiet... and...

Both: They're sitting in a circle!

Max: With snacks, anything is possible!

If you use this skit as a discussion starter, here are possible questions:

■ **Share a time when you felt hopeless or out of control. What did you do?**

■ **Was there any "secret weapon" that you used or could have used?**

■ **Read Joel 2:28-29. How does the Holy Spirit work in your life?**

■ **How is the Holy Spirit like a secret weapon?**

■ **What might it be a secret weapon against?**

JOEL 3:1-16

THEME:
God's judgment

SUMMARY:
In this PROJECT, kids will create and perform videotaped skits to illustrate the consequences of disobedience.

PREPARATION: You'll need photocopies of the "Skit Starters" handout (p. 364) (one for each group of three or more), a video camera, a videotape, a television, and a videocassette recorder. Set up a video-viewing area, with a VCR and a television ready to go. Pop popcorn to serve during the video-viewing time. You'll also need Bibles.

Form groups of three or more and give each group one of the ideas from the "Skit Starters" handout.

Tell groups they'll each have 10 minutes to come up with a 60- to 90-second skit based on their assigned skit starter. When groups are ready, videotape each skit in one "take." Then gather everyone together in your video-viewing area. Serve popcorn and watch the skits. Pause after each one to ask the following questions:

■ **On a scale of 1 to 10, with**

10 being "terrible" and 1 being "not so bad," how would you rate the disobedient act in this skit? Explain.

■ Did the punishment fit the crime? Why or why not?

■ If you'd done the same thing, how would your parents react?

After you've viewed all the skits, read aloud Joel 3:1-16. Then ask:

■ On a scale of 1 to 10, with 10 being "terrible" and 1 being "not so bad," how would you rate the disobedient acts in this Scripture passage?

■ Do you feel like the punishment fit the crime? Why or why not?

■ How can we be sure that God will always be just?

■ How is God's judgment different from your parents'? How is it similar?

Say: If God's judgments are fair and just, we can seek forgiveness with confidence.

Close by giving kids two or three minutes of total silence to think about what they learned through the skits.

SKIT STARTERS

Directions: Photocopy and cut apart this handout for use in the Joel 3:1-16 project.

Skit Starter 1

Kay goes to an all-night party at her boyfriend's house but tells her parents she's spending the night at Andrea's house. Her mom finds out about the lie when she calls Andrea's house to ask Kay a question. She tells Kay, "Wait 'til your father gets home!"

Skit Starter 2

Michael's mom has been secretly saving money in her closet for some time. Once Michael secretly counted the money and found out there was more than $500. A few weeks later, Michael got involved in a "harmless" poker game with friends. But by the end of the night, he owed Derrick $80. He took the money from his mom's secret stash, thinking she wouldn't miss it until he could return the money. Unfortunately, his mom found out one afternoon, confronted Michael, and shouted, "Wait 'til your father gets home!"

Skit Starter 3

Paul and Jill had been dating for more than three months, and Jill's parents really liked Paul. But they were very strict about Jill's curfew—she had to be home by 11 p.m. One night Paul and Jill were out together, and they lost track of time. It was 1:30 a.m. when Paul pulled his car into Jill's driveway. They thought her parents would understand. But when she got home, her mother met her at the door (Jill's father worked night shift) and said, "Wait 'til your father gets home!"

AMOS

"The kingdom of David is like a fallen tent, but in that day I will set it up again and mind its broken places. I will rebuild its ruins as it was before."

Amos 9:11

AMOS
4:1-5

THEME:
Reaching out to those in need

SUMMARY:
In this PROJECT, kids will give help and encouragement to needy people as part of an all-day "helping-hands holiday."

PREPARATION: You'll need to plan three or four service/outreach projects—all in the same day—with organizations in your community. You'll also need transportation to and from the various locations. Don't forget Bibles.

Take the group on an all-day "helping-hands holiday." The goal is to spend the entire day meeting others' needs in your community. For fun, make T-shirts or buttons that feature a logo of a cow in a circle with a slash through it—"no cows"—that means you're determined not to be like the people Amos called cows in Amos 4:1.

Your day might go something like this:

In the morning, car pool to an unwed mothers' shelter, bringing baby gifts and supplies to the moms. If there's work to be done around the shelter, have kids offer to do it. After lunch, have the group stop by a local convalescent hospital to bring new magazines, books, hard candies, fresh fruit, games, and other simple pleasures to the elderly residents. Plan to spend time with the residents playing games or singing songs. Wrap up the day by having kids serve a meal at a local homeless shelter or rescue mission.

Return to the church or a group member's house for debriefing. Read aloud Amos 4:1-5, then ask:

■ **How did it feel to help those in need today?**

■ **Which place had the greatest impact on you? Why?**

■ **Why did Amos call the Israelites cows?**

■ **How were you a "cow-buster" today?**

■ **What have you learned that will impact your everyday life?**

Close by asking kids to pray for the people they helped today.

AMOS
6:1-7

THEME:
Taking God for granted

SUMMARY:
Kids will learn to express their gratitude to God in this MUSICAL IDEA.

PREPARATION: You'll need several songbooks or hymnals, paper, pencils, and Bibles. You'll also need a large table to place at the front of your room.

Form groups of three or four. Have each group read Amos 6:1-7 and answer the following questions:

■ How did the people described in this passage take God for granted?

■ How do we sometimes take God—and his provisions for us—for granted?

Say: **It's sometimes easy for us to take for granted all that God has given us. But God has called us to recognize his grace and give thanks. And one of the best ways we can express our gratitude is through music.**

Give each group a piece of paper, a pencil, and a hymnal or songbook. Ask each group to select a song with a grateful or thankful theme.

Then say: **Your group has 10 minutes to search this building for things that represent your song's message. For example, if you picked "Great Is Thy Faithfulness," you might search for items that represent the line "all I have needed thy hand hath provided," such as clothing, a piece of food, or even a friend. Any questions? Ready? Go!**

After 10 minutes, gather groups together again. Set up a large table at the front of your room and tell groups to place their items on it. Have groups come forward one at a time, perform their songs, and tell why they chose the items they did. Next, form a circle and thank God together in song. Suggested songs: "Give Thanks (With a Grateful Heart)," "Count Your Blessings," "You Are So Good to Me," "Great Is Thy Faithfulness," and "God Is So Good."

Ask kids to close by saying one-sentence prayers of thanksgiving.

AMOS
8:1-14

THEME:
Reaping what you sow

SUMMARY:
Kids will play a LEARNING GAME that challenges them to match produce, herbs, or flowers with their original seeds to see how we reap what we sow.

PREPARATION: You'll need to purchase eight packages of seeds—fruits, vegetables, herbs, or flowers. You'll also need to photocopy the front of each seed package four times. Make a kit for each team of four that includes a plastic bag with all eight types of seeds and a photocopy of each seed package. (Leave at least one seed in each package so you can keep track of which seeds are which.) You'll also need Bibles.

Form four teams and give each team a seed kit. Say: **When I say "go," you'll have 60 seconds to match the correct seed with its package. The team that has the most correct matches wins! Ready? Go!**

After one minute, check kids' matches and declare a winning team. Then ask:

■ **What was difficult about this game?**

■ **How did you determine which seeds would go with which packages?**

■ **Could there have been more than one right answer? Why or why not?**

Have a volunteer read aloud Amos 8:1-14. Then ask:

■ **What did the people in these verses "sow"?**

■ **What did the people in these verses "reap"?**

■ **Do we always reap what we sow? Why or why not?**

■ **What kinds of things do people in our society sow today?**

■ **What are we reaping from what's been sown by others in the past?**

■ **What can we do to sow good seeds?**

AMOS 9:11-15

THEME:
Being recharged by God

SUMMARY:
In this OBJECT LESSON, kids will learn how batteries can be recharged by a recharger, just as a Christian's life can be recharged by the Holy Spirit.

PREPARATION: You'll need a battery recharger, two (or more) dead batteries, a battery-operated flashlight or toy to demonstrate the batteries' power, and Bibles.

Hold the dead batteries up to the group and ask:

■ **Who can tell whether these batteries are dead or brand-new?**

Give the batteries to kids and ask them to study the batteries and decide whether they're dead or new. After a couple of minutes, have kids vote on an answer. Then ask:

■ **What's the only real way to determine whether these batteries are dead or new?**

Say: **Let's see how effective they are at powering this flashlight.** (Put the batteries into the flashlight and turn it on.) **Obviously these batteries are dead, because they're ineffective in powering this flashlight.**

Next, put the batteries in the recharger and ask a volunteer to read aloud Amos 9:11-15 while the batteries recharge. (It usually takes five to seven minutes to get a sufficient charge to power the flashlight for a brief time.) As the batteries are recharging, ask:

■ **How did the Israelites feel before God promised to "recharge" them? When have you felt like that?**

■ **What made the Israelites ready to be recharged?**

■ **What makes you ready for God to recharge you?**

■ **In what ways do you need God to recharge you?**

Put the recharged batteries in the flashlight and turn on. Say: **Now these batteries are effective because they've been recharged. In Amos 9:11-15, God promised the people of Israel he'd recharge them.** Then ask:

■ **If God has recharged us, how will others know?**

Form a circle and have kids hold hands. To end the object lesson, give kids a minute or two to pray silently for God to recharge them this week.

OBADIAH

"Your pride has fooled you..."

Obadiah 3a

OBADIAH
1-15

THEME:
Results of our actions

SUMMARY:
In this AFFIRMATION, teenagers will perform acts of kindness for one another.

PREPARATION: You'll need a hat, slips of paper with each person's name (also include your own name), and Bibles. You'll kick off the activity by performing a sample act of kindness for one of the kids.

Have kids choose names randomly from a hat. Explain that you'll begin the activity by doing something nice for the person whose name you picked from the hat. After that person has experienced your act of kindness, he or she is to do something good for the person whose name he or she chose from the hat. Have teenagers choose affirmation actions that are inspired by whatever was done for them, but they shouldn't do exactly the same thing.

Encourage kids to be as creative as possible. For example, they might write an uplifting note, solicit the whole group to give a hug, or go into another room and shout out a compliment so all can hear.

After everyone has participated in the activity, read Obadiah 1-15 together. Form pairs and have partners take turns answering the following questions. Then have volunteers share their partners' insight with the whole group. Ask:

■ **What were the end results of your acts of kindness to each other?**

■ **What was the end result of the people's actions described in this passage?**

■ **Have you ever gloated over the misfortune of someone you didn't like? Explain.**

■ **When have you stood up for someone who was picked on?**

■ **What good or bad things happened to you as a result of your treatment of someone else?**

■ **How did it feel for someone from this group to do something nice for you?**

■ **How did it feel for you to do something nice for someone else?**

Close with a prayer similar to this one: **Dear God, help us to see the needs of others and respond as we would like them to respond to our own needs. Give us patience and fill us with your love so that we can love other people as you do.**

OBADIAH
12-15

THEME:
Being advocates for others

SUMMARY:
In this PROJECT, teenagers will write a letter to encourage people who are treated unjustly.

PREPARATION: Write to Amnesty International (322 Eighth Ave., New York, NY 10001) and ask for information about its Freedom Writers Network. Freedom Writers provides the names of people for whom you can be an advocate. The organization provides addresses of heads of governments and proper authorities to contact concerning murders, disappearances, and people who are currently being unjustly jailed or tortured. It also provides sample letters to guide you.

In addition to the Amnesty International information, you'll need Bibles, paper, pens, envelopes, and stamps for this activity. (If letters are going overseas, inquire about airmail postage costs.)

Read Obadiah 12-15. Ask:

■ **What does this text say about how we treat others?**

■ **Has someone ever spoken up for you when you couldn't defend yourself? If so, how did it feel?**

■ **When have you spoken up for a person who was in trouble and couldn't defend him- or herself?**

■ **How is Jesus our advocate? Explain.**

After the discussion, pass out a sample letter from the Freedom Writers Network. Say: **Many people in the world don't have a voice within their system of government to speak against injustice. We are lucky enough to live in a country that gives us a voice to speak not only for ourselves, but on behalf of others.**

Tell kids they may use the sample letter or write letters in their own words to encourage one or more of the people described in the Freedom Writers' information. Encourage teenagers to not only send the letters but to pray for these victims of injustice in the coming weeks.

Another group that can provide kids with direct involvement in advocacy is Habitat for Humanity. This organization helps people build homes. The address is 121 Habitat St., Americus, GA 31709-3498.

JONAH

"I [Jonah] knew that you are a God who is kind and shows mercy. You don't become angry quickly, and you have great love. I knew you would choose not to cause harm."

Jonah 4:26

JONAH
1-4

THEME:
Jonah and the big fish

SUMMARY:
Kids will participate in a simple SKIT to learn about Jonah's story.

JONAH AND THE BIG FISH

SCENE: Jonah tries to run away from God and is swallowed by a big fish.

PROPS: A chair and two microphones (place one center stage and one stage left). You'll also need Bibles for the discussion after the skit.

CHARACTERS:
Narrator
Jonah
Bunch o' Kids (to play God, Whale, Ninevites, and Plant)
Two Sailors

SCRIPT
(Narrator enters stage left and goes to the microphone.)
Narrator: Welcome! This story is about a prophet of the Lord named Jonah.
Jonah: *(Pops in proudly from stage right. Struts to center stage microphone.)* That's me!
Narrator: *(Chastising)* A reluctant prophet of the Lord...
(Jonah shrinks back a bit and sits on the floor.)
Narrator: One day God spoke to Jonah. God said...
God: *(Kids enter stage left and stand in straight line center stage, speaking in unison.)* Get up! Go to the great city of Nineveh and preach against it, because I see the evil things they do.
Narrator: Jonah got up...
(Jonah gets up proudly, maybe even flexes his muscles.)
Narrator: ... and ran away.
Jonah: *(Disbelieving)* What?
Narrator: *(Shooing him off)* Jonah ran away! He hopped a ride on a ship going the opposite direction, *(rolling eyes)* figuring the Lord wouldn't think to look for him there.
(Jonah runs around the line of Kids and stands center stage. Two Sailors enter from stage left with thumbs hooked in armpits doing a cocky side-to-side step and whistling the Popeye theme. They stand on either side of Jonah, who looks at them and joins in.)
Narrator: To get Jonah's attention, God sent a great wind.
(Kids blow slightly. Jonah and Sailors keep dancing.)
Narrator: I said a GREAT WIND!
(Kids take a huge breath and blow noisily. Jonah and Sailors put their arms up in front of their faces and grimace as though facing a gale.)
Jonah: *(To Sailors)* Later, guys. I'm going below to ride this one out! *(Sits between them.)*
Narrator: The Sailors didn't know what to do. They cried out to their gods to ask for mercy.
(Sailors pray with upraised arms, looking up beseechingly.)
Narrator: But the wind continued.
(Kids have become bored and are doing things such as whispering to each other and buffing their nails.)

Narrator: THE...WIND...CONTINUED!

(Kids hop to it, blowing with vigor. Sailors resume gale position.)

Narrator: The Sailors even tried throwing all nonessentials overboard.

(Sailors look around for something to pretend to pitch overboard. Seeing the Narrator, they approach him menacingly, making fists and pretending to roll up their sleeves.)

Narrator: *(Quickly)* But then they thought of something!

(Sailors stop and think.)

Narrator: Whew!

(Sailors walk over to Jonah.)

Sailor 1: Hey! Why aren't you up here praying with the rest of us? Maybe your god will listen!

Sailor 2: We didn't have this kind of trouble 'til you joined us! What kind of troublemaker are you?

Sailor 1: *(Angrily)* Yeah!

Jonah: *(Fearfully)* I'm a prophet of the God of Israel, who made everything, and I'm running away from him.

Narrator: The Sailors were a little upset.

(Sailors bristle at this.)

Sailors: *(Glaring at Narrator)* A little upset?

Narrator: Actually, they were really ticked off!

Sailors: *(Nod heads.)* That's better.

Sailor 2: *(To Jonah)* Now, what are we going to do about this situation?

Jonah: *(Gulps loudly.)* Pick me up and throw me into the sea, and then it will calm.

(Kids resume strong, noisy blowing. Sailors resume gale position.)

Narrator: The Sailors didn't want to do that.

(Sailors put hands on hips and look at Narrator incredulously, mouths agape.)

Narrator: But after some thought, they decided it probably was the best course of action.

(Sailors take Jonah's arms and "pitch" him overboard. Jonah pretends to swim. Kids stop noisy blowing immediately.)

Narrator: As promised, the waters calmed immediately. Jonah figured he was doomed, but God made a big fish swallow Jonah.

Jonah: *(Still swimming)* I thought it was a whale.

Narrator: Whale, fish, whatever. You were swallowed.

(Kids make a circle around Jonah.)

Narrator: Time passed.

Jonah: *(Praying)* Lord, I've been in here for three days. I thought I'd die when those Sailors threw me into the water, but you had mercy on me and allowed me to live on in the belly of this fish...which, other than the smell, isn't too bad. Thank you, Lord.

Narrator: God heard Jonah's prayers of thanksgiving and had the fish throw Jonah up on dry land.

Kids: *(Throw-up sound)* Blah!

(Jonah pops out from the middle of the circle and falls on the ground, wiping off his body. Kids line up and speak as God.)

God: Get up! Go to the great city of Nineveh and preach to it what I tell you to say!

Jonah: OK, OK. I get the picture.

Narrator: So Jonah went to Nineveh.

(Kids act like Ninevites—mime rolling dice, drunkenness, and fighting.)

Narrator: And after looking around a bit, he preached there.

(Jonah stands on a chair to preach. Kids continue their rowdiness.)

Jonah: *(Pointing finger in air)* After 40 days, Nineveh will be destroyed!

(Kids freeze.)

Kid 1: *(Shakes cupped hands as though preparing to roll dice.)* What'd he say?

(Kids are still frozen.)

Kid 2: I think it was "After 40 days, Nineveh will be destroyed!"

Kid 1: Whoops.

(Kids drop their sinful poses.)

Narrator: All the Ninevites, from the lowliest beggars to the highest royalty, saw the error in their ways and became most humble. They even stopped eating!

(Kids bow low to the ground.)

Jonah: *(Obviously pleased)* Now prepare to experience the wrath of my mighty God!

Narrator: God, however, saw their humility and had mercy on them.

Jonah: Oh, great! I knew this would happen! That's why I ran away in the first place! *(Jumps off the chair, sits, and sulks.)*

Narrator: After pitching a fit, Jonah rested in the desert outside the city. But God had mercy on him and made a plant grow quickly beside him to provide him with shade.

(Two Kids pretend to be a plant growing beside Jonah.)

Jonah: *(Staring admiringly at Plant)*

I love my plant.

Narrator: Then God sent a destructive insect and hot dry winds, and the plant died!

(Plant dies dramatically.)

Jonah: *(Standing up, looking up)* That's it. No more. Just strike me dead! You took away the only thing I have, so go ahead and take me, too!

God: *(Kids in line)* Jonah, are you angry?

Jonah: Read my lips!

God: You care so much for your plant, which lived only a day. Don't you see that a whole city is so much more worth being concerned about? I'm their God, too!

Narrator: So Jonah finally understood.

(Jonah nods grudgingly.)

Narrator: He had learned that...

Jonah: *(To audience)* You can run, but you can't hide.

Narrator: *(Leading him on, voice rising in pitch)* And...

All: The Lord is a loving God, with mercy for all.

(All characters bow.)

If you use this skit as a discussion starter, here are possible questions:

■ **Why do you think this story about Jonah is included in the Bible?**

■ **In what ways are you and Jonah similar? In what ways are you different?**

■ **What's one thing you can learn from the story of Jonah to help you this week?**

JONAH
1–4

> ### THEME:
>
> Reluctant servants
>
> ### SUMMARY:
> In this CREATIVE READING/PROJECT, kids will perform a drama based on the book of Jonah to gain a greater appreciation of this story.

PREPARATION: Depending on how elaborate this project will be, you may want to have scripts, or simply Bibles, from which kids may read. Props are optional.

Have kids create a dramatic reading based on Jonah's story and have them play the parts of God, Jonah, sailors, and the people of Nineveh. Allow kids to choose whether they want to perform a very simple or very elaborate drama. They may also wish to adapt the story into something more contemporary. Photocopy a few of the Creative Readings in this book (see index on pg. 404) for kids to use as sample references as they create their own readings.

If kids enjoy acting, they may wish to perform their skit for the congregation or a group of younger children. (If kids want to perform for others, make the necessary arrangements.)

After kids have prepared and practiced their reading, ask:

■ **How does it feel to play your part? What emotions do you experience when playing the part?**

■ **Why do you think Jonah ran from God's work?**

■ **Have you ever run from doing something you knew God wanted you to do?**

■ **What are ways God encourages us when we are reluctant to serve him?**

After kids perform their reading, close with a prayer asking for guidance to know and do God's will.

JONAH
1

> ### THEME:
>
> God's will
>
> ### SUMMARY:
> Kids will visit elderly or disabled members of the congregation in this ADVENTURE.

PREPARATION: Get names from your pastor of church members who are elderly or shut-ins.

Assign kids, in pairs, to visit members of your congregation or community who are elderly or shut-ins. Suggest that the visit last a minimum of 30 and a maximum of 90 minutes. Encourage kids to offer help with household chores, which these people may be having trouble with, and to spend time simply talking with them.

When the group meets after this adventure, ask:

■ **What did you learn about the person you visited?**

■ **What did you learn about yourself and your relationship with God?**

Read Jonah 1 together. Ask:

■ **Why do you think Jonah responded as he did to God's command?**

■ **Have you ever run away from something you felt God wanted you to do? If so, what happened?**

■ **How did you feel about the assignment to visit the person you visited?**

■ **In what ways did you feel you were serving God through this encounter?**

■ **What are other ways God calls us to serve?**

JONAH 1:1-3

THEME:
  Running away from God

SUMMARY:
  In this LEARNING GAME, kids will see how fast they can run away from some of the unpleasant tasks God gives us.

PREPARATION: Prepare two 3×5 cards by writing on each of them an unpleasant church task, such as sweeping the meeting room or volunteering to help with cleanup after a worship service on Sunday. (Every congregation has its unique, tedious tasks that no one wants to do.) Place a large, rolled-up piece of duct tape (sticky side out) on each card. Arrange to meet in a large area with space to run (outdoors is ideal). You'll need Bibles and a timer.

Give 3×5 cards to two teenagers and tell them they must perform the tasks listed unless they can stick the cards on someone else. The other teenagers are allowed to run to get away, but they cannot use their hands to prevent someone from sticking a card on them. Kids may take the cards off after they've been "caught" and attempt to stick them on someone else. Explain that whoever has the cards when the timer goes off in five minutes must do the chores.

After the game, ask:

■ **What are the tasks you hate most, relating to the Christian faith?**

■ **What is something you've felt particularly called to do but didn't want to?**

Have someone read aloud Jonah 1:1-3, then ask:

■ **How is Jonah's response to God like the response we sometimes give?**

■ **How can we work on improving our response to God's calls?**

JONAH 2

THEME:
  Calling on God for help

SUMMARY:
  In this CREATIVE PRAYER, kids will rewrite the second chapter of Jonah in their own words to personalize the call for God's help.

PREPARATION: You'll need Bibles, paper, and pens. A thesaurus and a dictionary might also be helpful.

Read Jonah 2 together. (It may be helpful to read the entire book of Jonah. This will give kids a more complete picture.) When you finish, say: **Think of a time you've asked God for help when things seemed almost hopeless. What are things that seem to "swallow people up" today? Rewrite the words of Jonah to be the people's cry for help in today's world.**

Kids who need more inspiration or an example of how to write a prayer request may want to look at Psalm 86:1-7.

When kids finish rewriting Jonah 2, have volunteers share what they wrote. Encourage kids to save their newly composed prayers for a time when they feel overcome and need God's help. Be sure to note that in verse 10, God rescued Jonah. Say: **When we cry for help, we don't always get the answer we want, but we know God always hears us.**

Have kids close in prayer for friends and family who need God's special help for a specific need. End the prayer time by saying: **Thank you for hearing our cries, Lord. Help us, heal us, empower us, and give us strength to meet each day's challenges. Remind us each morning that we are your children and that you love us through good times and bad. We pray in Jesus' name. Amen.**

JONAH
3:1–4:11

THEME:
God's grace

SUMMARY:
In this OBJECT LESSON, kids will tear pieces off a paper cross to illustrate that God's love is for all people.

PREPARATION: Make a large cross out of heavy paper. You'll also need a black marker, glue or tape, and Bibles.

Read Jonah 3:1–4:11 together. (You may wish to read through the entire four chapters.) When you finish, ask teenagers to think about people or groups of people who they once thought (or may still think) didn't deserve God's grace. Go around the room and ask each teenager to walk over the cross and tear a piece off.

When all teenagers are holding a piece of the paper cross, have them write the names of the people they had in mind on the paper. Then ask:

■ **Why do you or did you once think these people or groups didn't deserve God's grace?**

■ **How did it affect the way you treated them?**

■ **What (if anything) changed your mind?**

■ **When have you thought that you didn't deserve God's grace after a specific thing you'd done?**

Remind kids that God will forgive them for their sins if they only ask. Then have volunteers look up and read the following passages: Psalm 103:8-13; Matthew 7:1-2; Matthew 18:21-22; Matthew 20; Mark 12:28-34; and John 8:1-11.

Then have kids look again at Jonah 3:10–4:4. Ask kids to answer God's question to Jonah, "Do you think it is right for you to be angry?" in light of the verses they just read. Every time kids answer "no," ask them to re-attach their pieces to the cross.

Say: **Even people we don't especially like—the worst sinners—can all have God's forgiveness if they ask for it. We must treat all people as brothers and sisters who Christ died to save. The cross is for us all.**

JONAH
4

THEME:
What really matters

SUMMARY:
Use this SKIT to help kids see that sometimes we get things that aren't very important mixed up with things that are.

SUCH A BARGAIN!

SCENE: A teen and his father go car shopping.

PROPS: Two chairs pushed together (facing audience) and a folded-up newspaper. You'll also need Bibles for the discussion after the skit.

CHARACTERS:
Larry
Dad

SCRIPT
(Larry and Dad enter, pretend to open car doors, and sit on chairs, with Larry in the driver's seat. Throughout the skit Larry is driving. Dad has a folded-up newspaper.)

Dad: Well, that one was no good. It's beyond me how they can advertise a heap like that in the paper as a "classic."

Larry: Yeah, did you see the holes in the passenger-side floor? It looked like someone had taken a blowtorch to it just to make a little extra leg room.

Dad: Um-hmm. But that was nothing compared to the rust I saw on the engine. *(Looks at the paper.)* Let's see what you've circled next. Hmmm... "1981 Gallop, sunroof, AM/FM stereo cassette, chrome mags, *(acting surprised)* 133,000 miles. Must see." Must see? I don't have to see! Larry, how could you think that would even be worth looking at?

Larry: Dad, that's a great car! You ought to see the lines on that year's style. And I want to get a look at those hubcaps.

Dad: That car has so many miles on it, it might not make it to the wrecking yard. Larry, hubcaps don't make the car run any better.

Larry: But they don't make it run any worse. Plus, it'll look really hot!

Dad: As hot as a car can look when it's standing still all the time. *(Looks in the paper.)* Now here's something...a great car! "1989

Roadcraft Pony, lime green, 4-speed, original factory AM radio, 60,000 miles." Now that's a good car!

Larry: Dad... a station wagon? I wouldn't be caught dead in a station wagon!

Dad: No, but you might be, in the other one we just talked about. *(Freeze.)*

If you use this skit as a discussion starter, here are possible questions:

■ **Whose priorities were more important: Dad's or Larry's? Why?**

■ **What are some things that really matter in your life? Are those important to everyone? Why or why not?**

■ **Read Jonah 4. What did God want Jonah to understand? Why is that an important lesson?**

■ **How might this passage influence your attitudes and actions this week?**

MICAH

"The Lord has told you, human, what is good; he has told you what he wants from you: to do what is right to other people, love being kind to others, and live humbly, obeying your God."

Micah 6:8

MICAH
1:1-9

THEME:
Idols

SUMMARY:
In this OBJECT LESSON, kids will see how we must strip away the idols that separate us from God.

PREPARATION: You'll need marking pens; old, ragged (but clean) clothing—enough to piece together an entire outfit; and Bibles.

Read Micah 1:1-9. Ask kids what things they'd consider as idols in today's society. When they begin to name idols, pass out the old, ragged clothing and have them write the names of idols on each piece. When each piece of clothing has the name of an idol on it, dress a volunteer in the clothes.

Then have teenagers name ways we can avoid these idols; for example, praying, encouraging one another, and studying God's Word. When a teenager comes up with a way to get rid of a particular idol, he or she may rip the rags that list that idol off the volunteer. Remind kids to be careful not to rip the person's regular clothes.

When all the ragged clothing has been ripped away, have kids discuss the ways we can keep idols out of our lives. Close with the following prayer (or one of your own): **God, help us to worship only you in every part of our lives. Tear away any idols we sometimes clutter our hearts with and help us to focus on you each day.**

MICAH
4:1-5

THEME:
No more war.

SUMMARY:
In this PROJECT, kids will teach younger children non-competitive games.

PREPARATION: Make arrangements with a younger Sunday school class, the local YMCA, or a local preschool to have your group spend an hour with young children, teaching them non-competitive games. You'll find ideas for these games in the *Cooperative Sports & Games Book: Challenge Without Competition,* by Terry Orlick (Pantheon) and other game books. Arrange to have the necessary game supplies available.

Teenagers may wish to choose games from books or create their own games by converting familiar competitive games into cooperative ones. After teenagers have spent time teaching the younger children the games and playing with them, ask:
■ **How did it feel to teach young people to play cooperatively rather than competitively?**
■ **What are your experiences with competitive games?**
■ **What are the pros and cons of competitive games?**
Read Micah 4:1-5 together.
■ **What comes to mind when you hear these words?**
■ **How does this fit with the way God calls us to live as**

Christians?
- How do people "learn war"?
- Who teaches about war?
- How might learning war in small ways lead to aggressive behavior in larger ways?
- How might it help us to "not learn war" by learning to play cooperatively as small children?

Read in unison Micah 4:3 as a closing.

MICAH
6:1-8

THEME:

Do justice and love kindness.

SUMMARY:
In this ADVENTURE, kids will go to a nursing home, a homeless shelter, or a soup kitchen and help in various aspects of running the facility.

PREPARATION: Make arrangements for your group to help out for an afternoon at a nursing home, a homeless shelter, or a soup kitchen (any facility that assists the needy would be appropriate for this activity). Find out what would be most helpful for your group to do then make plans with teenagers to perform those tasks. Plan to stay between two and three hours, depending on the specific circumstances. You'll need transportation to and from the location. Don't forget Bibles.

Car pool to the facility you've chosen and then have kids spend two or three hours performing various tasks, such as food preparation, entertainment, visiting or worshiping with residents, reading to people or writing letters for them, and feeding those who need help.

When you return from the adventure, read Micah 6:1-8. Pay special attention to verse 8. Then form groups of no more than four and have kids take turns answering the following questions in their group. Ask:
- In the work we just completed, how did you see these words in action?
- What were specific ways you experienced justice, kindness, or humility?
- How did the people we served today experience these things?
- What things would you wish for someone to do for you if you were in the situation of the people we met today?
- Why is it important to treat people with dignity?
- How are you just and kind in your actions?

NAHUM

"The Lord is good, giving protection in times of trouble. He knows who trusts in him."

Nahum 1:7

NAHUM
1:7

THEME:
God protects us.

SUMMARY:
Teenagers will play a LEARN-
ING GAME with two sets of rules.

PREPARATION: You'll need a small
throw rug, three empty wastebas-
kets, a sponge ball, and Bibles. Place
one wastebasket at each end of the
room and one on a rug in the center.

Form two teams. Take one team
to one side of the room and say:
**Your strategy for the game is to
get the ball into the center basket
as quickly as you can. You can
throw the ball to another player or
run to the basket if an opponent
isn't in the way. If the opposing
team has the ball, you can form a
circle around the player. If the
player throws the ball, you can
catch it and get it to the center
goal.**

Take the second team to the
other side of the room and say:
**Your strategy is to get the ball into
a basket. If you use the baskets at
either end of the room, you can
throw the ball from any distance.
If you use the basket in the middle of the room, you must have at
least one foot on the rug. Each
time your team has the ball, you
have to pass it to at least two players before making a basket.
When the other team has posses-
sion, only one person may
"guard" the person with the ball.**

Bring the teams back together
and play the game for five to 10
minutes. Expect some complaining
as each team uses its own strategies. When kids begin to get frustrated, but while the game is still
fun, call time and bring the group
back together.

Form pairs consisting of one
member from each team. Have
partners discuss the following
questions:
■ **How did you feel when the
other team was making baskets?**
■ **What was so frustrating
about this game?**
■ **How did you feel when your
team was winning?**
Have a volunteer read Nahum
1:7. Then ask:
■ **How is Nahum 1:7 like the
game we just played?**
Say: **Sometimes those around
us don't follow the same rules
Christians observe. Like one
team in this game, it may seem
like they have an advantage. But
God protects us in all circumstances. We can be confident in
that protection because God
promises it.**

With the whole group together,
decide which rules kids would like
to follow to play the game again.
Spend several minutes playing by
these rules. Whenever a disagree-
ment occurs, decide proper action
based on the group's chosen rules,
reminding them that they decided
to play by those rules.

NAHUM
1:15

THEME:
Encouragement in difficult times

SUMMARY:
In this AFFIRMATION, teenagers will learn about encouragement and create affirmations for each other.

PREPARATION: You'll need enough stacks of 20 colored index cards for half the people in the group. You'll also need pens and Bibles.

Assign each person a partner. Give one person from each pair 20 index cards. Say: **Everyone with index cards is to give them, one at a time, to his or her partner. The receiving partner should then use the cards to build as high a tower as he or she can. The partner handing out the cards may not do any building or talking. If the cards fall down, both people can pick them up. Then the builder must start over.**

After a few minutes of building, say: **Now we're going to change the directions a little. The person handing the cards may talk with his or her partner—but only by using encouraging words. For example, if the stack falls, the** encourager can say things like "That's OK—I'll help you start again" or "We'll get this done if we keep at it."

Allow a few more minutes for this activity then have kids collect their index cards and gather as a group. Ask:

■ **Builders, how did you feel when your cards fell and your partners said nothing?**

■ **Silent partners, how did you feel when you couldn't say anything?**

■ **What changes, if any, did you notice when you could encourage your partners?**

Ask a volunteer to read Nahum 1:15. Then ask:

■ **How do you think the people felt when Nahum pointed out the messenger bringing good news?**

Say: **God sends us encouragement in difficult times in the words of a friend, in a song, or in something we read in Scripture. God wants us to get through the difficult times and gives us hope.**

Have each person write his or her name on an index card. Then pass the cards around the group and have group members write a few words of affirmation and encouragement about the person named on each card.

Allow a moment for teenagers to read their affirmations. Then collect the cards. Make a photocopy of each group member's card and, at a later date, mail him or her a copy.

HABAKKUK

"The Lord God is my strength. He makes me like a deer that does not stumble..."

Habakkuk 3:19a

HABAKKUK
2:2-4

> **THEME:**
> Faithfulness
>
> **SUMMARY:**
> In this ADVENTURE, kids will collect stories of faithfulness from members of the congregation or community.

PREPARATION: Arrange to visit three or four adult members of the congregation or community who can share stories about trusting God or waiting on God. You'll need paper, pencils or pens, envelopes, Bibles, and transportation to and from the homes of the people you visit.

Before leaving for the first visit, give each person a sheet of paper, a pen or pencil, and an envelope. Have teenagers describe three things they feel while waiting for answers to their prayers. They can either write about their feelings or draw pictures that symbolize them. Examples might include peace after praying, anxiety that their prayers haven't been heard, and curiosity or wonder in how God will answer their prayers.

When teenagers have finished describing their feelings, have them seal their papers in the envelopes. Collect the envelopes and put them in a Bible. Leave the Bible in the meeting room while you're gone.

On the way to each visit, have kids think of questions they can ask the interviewee about a time when he or she waited for God to answer prayers. Sample questions might include the following:
• How did you feel while you were waiting for God to answer your prayer?
• What did you do until the answer came?
• In what ways did your faith change because of the wait?
• What verses in the Bible have special meaning to you now?

Encourage each group member to ask one question of the interviewee.

If the group has more than eight people, form several smaller groups. Have each group collect one or two faith stories and bring them back to the larger group. When you return, ask:

■ **What surprised you about the stories people told concerning faithfulness and waiting?**

■ **How did you feel before the first visit?**

■ **How did you feel after the last visit?**

Distribute the sealed envelopes. On the outside of their envelopes, have teenagers write three words that describe the person(s) they visited. Then have a volunteer read Habakkuk 2:2-4. Ask:

■ **What would you tell a friend who was waiting for an answer to prayer?**

Have group members open their sealed envelopes and read the feelings they experience while waiting for answers to prayer. Then ask each person to share the three words written on the outside of his or her envelope. Say: **Like the people we visited and the people God encouraged through Habakkuk,** we often feel anxious while we wait for answers to our prayers. But God wants us to hang in there and be faithful. We'll see our prayers answered, and we'll also see confidence in our lives.

Have kids put their papers back in the envelopes and write Habakkuk 2:2-4 on the envelopes. Suggest that they use the envelopes as bookmarks in their Bibles.

HABAKKUK
3:17-19

THEME:
Joy

SUMMARY:
Kids will participate in a RETREAT to identify and experience joy.

PREPARATION: Use the following ideas to create a fun retreat based on the theme of joy. You'll need supplies for the various activities and Bibles.

BALLOON GAME
You'll need lots of balloons, paper, pencils, string or tape (to hang the balloons after the game), and Bibles.

Form teams of four or five. Give each team 12 to 15 balloons, paper, and pencils. Ask team members to draw small pictures of each other and several friends. Next, have them roll up the pictures, put them into separate balloons, blow up the balloons, and tie them. Then have each team form a circle and hit a

balloon back and forth, keeping it in the air at all times. Add a couple of balloons at a time, until all the balloons are in the air.

After a couple of minutes, have teams put the balloons in the center of their circles. Ask:
■ **What was it like to keep all the balloons in the air?**

Give each team 90 seconds to suggest a way to keep the balloons in the air without having to hit them. Share the ideas. Then have a volunteer read Habakkuk 3:17-19. Ask:
■ **How would you compare our solutions for keeping the balloons in the air to the joy Habakkuk talks about?**

Hang the balloons around the meeting area for the rest of the retreat.

FACE PAINTING
You'll need water-based face paint, brushes or cotton swabs, water, mirrors, and Bibles.

Form pairs and give them face paint, water, and brushes or swabs. Have one partner describe to the other 10 things that give him or her joy. Then have the listening partner paint a symbol of one of those things on the speaking partner's face. After a few minutes, have kids change roles.

When kids are finished painting their faces, have them take turns asking their partners a few "yes" or "no" questions about the symbols on their faces and guessing what their partners have painted. Pass around mirrors and let kids look at the symbols on their faces. Then ask:
■ **How did you feel when try-**

ing to guess what your partner had painted?

Have a volunteer read Habakkuk 3:18. Say: **There's one thing we can count on—knowing God gives us joy. Wear the face symbols throughout the retreat as a reminder of the joy we find in God.**

MUSIC ACTIVITY

You'll need upbeat music and a cassette or compact disc player.

Throughout the event, play the upbeat music. At some point, gather the group and ask:

■ **How does this music make you feel?**

■ **How do you show that happiness?**

Say: **Knowing God makes us happy. It's only natural to show that happiness and joy. Music is one way we express it.**

PLANE JOY

For each group of five or six, you'll need a bottle of soap-bubble liquid, bendable wire to make bubble wands, tape, and several sheets of stiff paper.

Form groups of five or six. Give each group a bottle of bubbles, wire, and a couple sheets of stiff paper. Have each group design two or three paper airplanes, then form an equal number of small bubble wands out of the wire. Tell kids to bend the handles of the bubble wands and tape them to the airplanes, making sure the wands face the front of the airplanes. Then have them dip the wands into the bubble liquid and fly the airplanes. See which airplanes make the most bubbles or fly the farthest.

After flying the bubble planes, ask:

■ **How is your bubble plane an expression of joy?**

■ **How can working together on a project such as this be a joyful experience?**

Encourage kids to have fun "fine tuning" their airplanes and bubble wands.

ZEPHANIAH

"The Lord your God is with you; the mighty One will save you."

Zephaniah 3:17a

ZEPHANIAH 3:1-5

THEME:
God never abandons us.

SUMMARY:
In this CREATIVE READING, teenagers will produce a "news show" where two eyewitnesses always point to God.

PREPARATION: Write each line of Zephaniah 3:1-5 on separate index cards. Number each card so the verses are read in order. You'll also need at least two old hats (with the word "press" written on a piece of paper and taped to each hat), a video camera, a videocassette recorder, a television, and Bibles.

Assign three groups to play the following parts:

• Reporters (at least two, who wear "press" hats and interview People on the Street and Eyewitnesses)

• People on the Street (several, who read verses 1-4)

• Eyewitnesses (at least two, who read verse 5)

Give kids their parts (written on index cards) and tell them they're to say their lines using their own words. Set up the video camera to record the "on-the-street" interviews and encourage kids to ham it up as they participate in this interview reading.

During the reading, have Reporters ask People on the Street and Eyewitnesses, "Why do you think the city is in so much trouble today?" Have people on the street take turns reading the Scriptures on their cards as "responses" to the interview questions. Have Reporters ask clarifying questions if appropriate, then move on, one by one, to the next person until everyone has read his or her Scripture and been interviewed. When the interviews are finished, stop the videotape and ask:

■ **How do you feel when bad things are happening all around?**

■ **How is the Scripture that made up our script like one of today's news reports?**

■ **What message does Zephaniah have for people today?**

Play the videotape and compare it to today's newscasts. Have kids close in prayer, thanking God that he doesn't abandon us in difficult times.

ZEPHANIAH 3:17

THEME:
Reaching the goal of Christian living.

SUMMARY:
Teenagers will move toward a goal using CREATIVE PRAYERS.

PREPARATION: You'll need a chalkboard and chalk (or newsprint and markers), masking tape, two chairs, a sponge football, and Bibles. Use masking tape to mark the room into "10-yard" sections similar to a football field (scale down to smaller sections, perhaps 3 or 4 feet wide, to fit your room). Set up two chairs 6 feet apart at one end of the room for goal posts. Prepare slips of paper with the numbers 1 to 10 written on them.

Form two teams and have them gather in a huddle. Instruct each team to write on the chalkboard (or newsprint) five one-sentence prayers about each of the following subjects:

• Patience with friends and family.

• Forgiveness when someone hurts you.

• Better understanding of the Bible.

• Ability to show God's love at home and in school.

Have teams line up single file, side by side, at one end of the "field." Beginning with the team who has the most colorful shoes, have the first person in line pick up the football and hand it back to the person behind him or her. Draw one of the numbered slips of paper then have the first person in line move that many "yards" toward the goal (the other end of the field). The person holding the football will then pray one of his or her team's prayers (by referring to the chalkboard or newsprint) and toss the football to the person downfield. If the receiver catches the ball, the whole team moves up to that line. Then the person who

caught the ball moves to the end of his or her team's line. Replace the numbered slips each time you draw one so any number may be drawn.

Alternating between teams (one team playing at a time), repeat this activity until both teams have reached the opposite goal line. Teams may need to come up with more prayers if they don't reach the goal within five plays.

After the game, ask:

■ **What was it like to get closer to the goal with your passes and prayers?**

■ **When you reach a goal in sports, how do you feel?**

■ **How do you feel when your prayers are answered?**

■ **How would you describe the "goal" of Christian living?**

Have a volunteer read Zephaniah 3:17. Ask:

■ **How is our football prayer activity like this Scripture?**

■ **How could Zephaniah 3:17 encourage you as you pursue the goal of Christian living this week?**

Say: **God is happy to give us the power to do the right thing. As we pray, we move closer to the goal of Christian living—to reflect God's love to those around us.**

Have the whole group huddle in a circle. Invite kids to offer a sentence prayer as you toss them the football. End with a team "amen."

HAGGAI

"This is what the Lord All-Powerful says:
'Think about what you have done.' "

Haggai 1:5

HAGGAI
1:1-15

THEME:
Growing closer to
God

SUMMARY:
In this DEVOTION, teenagers
will move closer to or farther
away from a goal in response to
things they've done.

PREPARATION: Place a Bible in the
middle of the room.

EXPERIENCE

Have kids form a large circle by
holding hands and moving back
three or four steps. Then have
them drop hands. Say: **As I read
each of the following statements, I'll tell you whether you
can move one step closer to the
center or whether you must
take one step back (away from
the center).**

Use the following statements or
add your own:

• **Move one step closer if
you've ever prayed for a friend.**

• **Move one step closer if
you've ever prayed for a parent.**

• **Move one step back if
you've ever broken one of the
Ten Commandments.**

• **Move one step closer if
you've ever told someone about
God's love.**

• **Move one step back if
you've ever slept in on Sunday
and missed worship.**

• **Move one step closer if
you've ever fed or helped a
stranger.**

• **Move one step closer if
you've ever believed in someone when nobody else would.**

• **Move one step back if
you've ever pretended not to
see someone in need.**

• **Move one step closer if
you've ever been honest when
it would have been easier to
tell a lie.**

Continue with instructions until
someone reaches the middle
where the Bible is.

RESPONSE

Form pairs and have them discuss the following questions:

∎ **How did you feel as you
moved closer to the center of
the circle?**

∎ **What did you notice about
the group as the activity went
on?**

Have a volunteer pick up the
Bible from the center of the circle
and read Haggai 1:1-15. Ask:

∎ **How is the way the people
in this passage were acting like
the way we responded in our
activity?**

∎ **What value is there in
doing the right things if we
don't do them to honor God?**

CLOSING

Have teenagers form a close circle with their arms over each other's shoulders. Encourage kids to
ask for God to help them grow
closer to him by honoring him in
the things they do and say.

HAGGAI
1:1-15

THEME:
Putting God first

SUMMARY:
In this PROJECT, kids create a "temple," and help feed the hungry.

PREPARATION: You'll need a grocery bag for each person in the group. Then contact a local food pantry to get a list of their most needed food items. You'll also need Bibles and transportation to and from the food pantry.

Say: **Today we're going to focus on putting God first and showing our gratitude for the blessings we've been given.**

Form groups of two or three and give each person a grocery bag. Have groups go out into the community to collect items for the food pantry. Let kids know that any dona-tions are welcome but also explain what items are most needed.

When groups return to the church, have them use the foods they collected to build a "temple" for God by stacking boxes and cans in the appropriate shape. Then ask the following questions:

■ **What does it feel like to ask people to donate food?**

Have a volunteer read Haggai 1:1-15. Ask:

■ **How does Haggai's mes-sage—of putting God first—apply to us today?**

■ **How is building a temple of food like the temple Haggai told the people God wanted them to build?**

Gather the group around the food temple and pray this prayer: **God, you've blessed us more than we deserve. Please accept our worship of service and bless others through our effort. Help us to put you first in all we do. Amen.**

Have the group take the food to the food pantry and learn about the hungry in your community.

ZECHARIAH

" 'Return to me, and I will return to you,'
says the Lord All-Powerful."

Zechariah 1:3b

ZECHARIAH
1:2-6

THEME:
Second chances

SUMMARY:
In this DEVOTION, teenagers will role play parental responses to situations and consider their own response to God's invitation of friendship.

PREPARATION: You'll need parent costumes, such as a hat and a tie or an apron and potholders. You'll also need Bibles.

EXPERIENCE
Form four groups. Be sure each group includes both guys and girls. Ask:

■ **What would happen if you had to discipline your parents?**

■ **Would you handle the situation differently than the way they discipline you?**

Assign each group one of the following scenarios to act out for the whole class:

• Your parent's boss calls and tells you that your dad or mom has consistently been one to two hours late for work. Create a skit where you sit down to talk with your parent about this situation.

• Your parent forgets to complete an important household chore. Create a skit where you talk with your parent about being responsible.

• Your parent is always on the phone, gabbing with friends. Create a skit where you talk with your parent about being considerate of others.

• Your parent smashes the family car in a mall parking lot because of carelessness. Create a skit where you talk with your parent about taking care of property.

Allow a few minutes for groups to decide what they'll say, then have them perform the skits for the whole group.

RESPONSE
After the skits, have groups discuss the following questions and report insights to the whole group. Ask:

■ **How did you determine the best way to correct your parent in your skit?**

■ **What was easy about correcting your parent? What was difficult?**

■ **What would it take for you to give your parent in the skit a second chance?**

■ **How do you feel when a parent corrects you in real life?**

Have a volunteer read Zechariah 1:2-6. Ask:

■ **How do you think God felt dealing with the people in this passage?**

■ **How is this Scripture like our skits?**

■ **Think about your friendship with God. When have you needed to ask for a second chance?**

Say: **Fortunately, God offers us a second chance—a fresh start, even when we don't deserve it. God is willing to forgive us and begin again when our past is full of mistakes.**

CLOSING
Close with prayer by having volunteers complete the following sentence prayers:

• "Lord, when we're selfish..."

• "God, when we're unwilling to listen to you. . ."

• "Lord, when we want to do our own thing. . ."

ZECHARIAH
7:8-10

THEME:
Caring for others

SUMMARY:
Teenagers will search for care opportunities and extend care to others in this PROJECT.

PREPARATION: You'll need computer labels, markers, self-stick notes, and Bibles. You'll also need ingredients to make cupcakes or cookies (as well as access to the church kitchen) and transportation to deliver the baked goods.

Form groups of three or four people. Give each group several computer labels and markers. Say: **Each group has five minutes to think of as many people needing care as it can. One group member will be the "care giver." The rest of the group will write the categories of people needing care on labels and stick them on the care giver in the appropriate spot. For example, on the hand you might put "preschool children" because they need someone to take their hands.**

If groups have trouble getting started, use a few of these categories as ideas: congregation members (place a label on the knees since they pray for us), people in the neighborhood (place a label on the feet since they're within walking distance), and kids in other youth groups (place a label on the shoulder, since they're friends).

(**Note:** If you think it's necessary, caution kids not to place labels on private parts of group members' bodies.)

After five minutes, have groups share their ideas. Then ask the labeled individuals to come to the front. Have a representative from each group explain the categories.

Give everyone two self-stick notes. Say: **Each person has two votes for a care-giving category that you'd like to help out with. Attach your sticky notes to the label (on the care giver) with the category you'd most like to see us care for.** Allow a couple of minutes for kids to vote.

After everyone has voted, start to throw away the two category labels with the most votes. Say: **We don't need to do anything now that we've figured out who we should help.** When kids protest, keep the labels and ask them why it's important to actually help others rather than just talk about helping.

Then have the whole group bake cookies or cupcakes to give to the people in the top-two care-giving categories. While kids are baking, read Zechariah 7:8-14. Ask:

∎ **How is this Scripture like the activity we just did?**

∎ **What do we miss out on when we don't care for those God wants us to help?**

Deliver the food at the end of your meeting.

ZECHARIAH 10:2

THEME:
Looking for answers

SUMMARY:
In this ADVENTURE, teenagers will participate in a scavenger hunt where the answers can be found in both the community and church, but the prize is found only in the church.

PREPARATION: Adapt the scavenger hunt categories suggested below for use in your church and neighborhood. Hide a prize at the foot of the cross (in the church) before the event. Create a "clue list" and photocopy it for everyone in your group. You'll also need an instant-print camera or video camera and viewing equipment for each team. Don't forget Bibles.

The following are sample scavenger hunt clues (and acceptable items to photograph) that you might want to use in your clue lists:

• "directs traffic" (In the community: a street sign, a traffic light, or a police officer. At church: an usher or sign.)

• "travel guide" (In the community: tourism information. At church: a Bible or a hymnal.)

• "feeding frenzy" (In the community: a restaurant. At church: the kitchen.)

• "where you'll find fun" (In the community: a popular recreational facility, such as a bowling alley, or the mall. At church: the youth room.)

Form teams of four or five. Have a volunteer read Zechariah 10:2. Say: **We're going to have a scavenger hunt. Your goal is to follow the clues I'll give you, find the items, and photograph them to prove you've found them. There are multiple answers for each clue, so think carefully about where you can find the items.**

Give each team the list of clues and a camera. Set a time for everyone to return to the church with answers to the clues. Remind teenagers that the first team back with all the answers (or the most correct answers at the end of the time) wins.

When teams return, have them show their pictures. Determine the winning team and give the winning team members this cryptic clue to direct them to the prize: Busiest intersection on the narrowest street in the church. (You may need to offer a few more clues.)

After the prize is found, have a volunteer read Zechariah 10:2. Then ask:

■ **How was our scavenger hunt like the Scripture we read?**

■ **Why was the final prize hidden at the foot of the cross?**

■ **What would you say to someone who's looking for answers outside of faith in Jesus Christ?**

Malachi

" 'From the east to the west I will be honored among the nations. Everywhere they will bring incense and clean offerings to me because I will be honored among the nations,' says the Lord All-Powerful."

Malachi 1:11

MALACHI
1:6-14

THEME:
Giving God our best

SUMMARY:
In this MUSIC IDEA, teenagers will play charades with popular love songs to discover what people do for those they love.

PREPARATION: Ask kids to bring cassettes or compact discs of their favorite love songs (but ask them not to tell other group members what songs they're bringing). You'll also need a cassette or CD player for each group of three or four, and Bibles.

Form groups of three or four. Give each group a cassette or CD player and send them to separate areas of the room to quietly listen to the songs they brought. Tell kids to listen closely to what the singers are claiming they will do to show love to others. Encourage groups to listen for themes that are appropriate to the youth group setting, such as putting another's welfare above your own, forgiving the other person, being devoted to another person, or showing self-control. Have groups choose a theme that they'll act out to help the other groups guess their songs.

Allow five minutes for listening to music and selecting themes, then call the groups together. Have them take turns acting out the themes while the other groups guess the song titles and artists. Afterward, have groups discuss the following questions:

■ **What are people willing to do for someone they really love?**

■ **How do you feel when someone gives his or her best to show love for you?**

Have a volunteer read Malachi 1:6-14. Ask:

■ **What kind of love do we show when we give God our second best?**

■ **In what ways do we give God less than our very best?**

■ **How can we make giving God our best a priority this week?**

Have kids choose one way they'll show God how much they love him by giving him their best this week. Then ask them to commit to following through with those loving actions in the coming week.

MALACHI
3:13-18

THEME:
God blesses those who serve him.

SUMMARY:
In this OBJECT LESSON, teenagers will attempt to win prizes by picking out a working battery from a bunch of non-working batteries.

PREPARATION: Collect four or five batteries that don't work. (If you don't have any dead batteries, make your own by leaving them in a turned-on flashlight.) You'll also need one working battery (be sure to secretly keep track of which battery is the working one during the activity), a battery-powered toy or flashlight, pencils or pens, a long table, and Bibles.

Prepare "prize" envelopes for all participants. Prize envelopes should contain coupons for fun things, such as a trip to the mall, an ice-cream cone, a standing ovation from the group, or a home-cooked meal from the pastor's family.

Give teenagers each a prize envelope and have them write their names on the outside. Tell them to leave the envelopes sealed. Spread the batteries across a long table.

Say: **Only one of these batteries works. In your envelopes you'll find a coupon for a great prize. But only those who pick the working battery, by placing their envelopes in front of it, will get the prize inside.**

Allow a minute or so for kids to make their choices. After everyone has selected a battery, ask:

■ **How does it feel to have put your prize on the line?**

Put one of the dead batteries in the toy or flashlight to show it doesn't work. Open the envelopes next to that battery and let kids know about the prizes they didn't win.

Allow remaining participants to change their choices now if they want. Then pick another dead battery and demonstrate that it doesn't work. Again, read the lost prizes.

Continue, allowing those still in the game to change their choices until only two batteries remain. This time, pick the working battery. Before demonstrating that it works, open the envelopes and identify the prizes inside (keep the prize coupons in the envelopes). Ask those whose prizes have just been read:

■ **How do you feel now that I've told you what your envelope contained?**

Have a volunteer read Malachi 3:13-18. Say: **You have each risked your prize on something you can't be sure will work. You won't know if you made the right choice until the end. How is this like the Scripture we just heard?**

Put the working battery in the toy or flashlight. Have kids who chose the working battery stand up. Demonstrate that their battery worked and give kids their prizes. Ask:

■ **What does the last verse of the Scripture mean to you?**

Say: **God blesses those who serve him.**

OLD TESTAMENT SCRIPTURE INDEX

OLD TESTAMENT THEME INDEX

A

B

OLD TESTAMENT TEACHING IDEAS INDEX

 ADVENTURES

AFFIRMATIONS

 ## CREATIVE PRAYERS

 ## CREATIVE READINGS

DEVOTIONS

LEARNING GAMES

MUSIC IDEAS

OBJECT LESSONS

OVERNIGHTERS/ RETREATS

PARTIES

PROJECTS

SKITS